Date Due

DEC - 4 1987			

Advances
in COMPUTERS
VOLUME 26

Contributors to This Volume

Anupam Bhide

A. Dollas

Amitava Dutta

Vijay Garg

J. B. Glickman

S. Sitharama Iyengar

S. C. Kothari

Abha Moitra

C. O'Toole

W. J. Poppelbaum

Atul Prakash

C. V. Ramamoorthy

H. K. Reghbati

Wing N. Toy

Lee J. White

Tsuneo Yamaura

Advances in
COMPUTERS

EDITED BY

MARSHALL C. YOVITS

Purdue School of Science
Indiana University—Purdue University at Indianapolis
Indianapolis, Indiana

VOLUME 26

ACADEMIC PRESS, INC.

Harcourt Brace Jovanovich, Publishers

Boston   Orlando   San Diego
New York   Austin   London   Sydney
Tokyo   Toronto

QA
76
.A3
V.26
1987

ACADEMIC PRESS, INC.
Orlando, Florida 32887

United Kingdom Edition published by
ACADEMIC PRESS INC. (LONDON) LTD.
24–28 Oval Road, London NW1 7DX

LIBRARY OF CONGRESS CATALOG CARD NUMBER: 59-15761

ISBN 0–12–012126–3

PRINTED IN THE UNITED STATES OF AMERICA

87 88 89 90   9 8 7 6 5 4 3 2 1

#1461174
6-22-87

Contents

Multistage Interconnection Networks for Multiprocessor Systems

S. C. Kothari

Fault-Tolerant Computing

Wing N. Toy

Techniques and Issues in Testing and Validation of VLSI Systems

H. K. Reghbati

Software Testing and Verification

Lee J. White

Issues in the Development of Large, Distributed, and Reliable Software

C. V. Ramamoorthy, Atul Prakash, Vijay Garg, Tsuneo Yamaura, and Anupam Bhide

Preface

The publication of Volume 26 of *Advances in Computers* continues the presentation in depth of subjects of both current and continuing interest to the computer and information science community. Contributions have been solicited from well-known experts in their fields who recognize the importance of writing substantial review and tutorial articles in their areas of expertise. *Advances in Computers* permits the publication of survey-type articles which have been written from a relatively leisurely perspective; authors are thus able to treat their subjects both in depth and in breadth. *Advances in Computers* is a series that began in 1960 and now continues in its 27th year with Volume 26. During this period, which witnessed great expansion and dynamic change in the computer and information fields, this series has played an important role in the development of computers and their applications. The continuation of the series over this lengthy period is a tribute to the quality of presentation and to the reputations and capabilities of the authors who have written articles for it.

Included in Volume 26 are chapters on decision support systems, unary processing, parallel algorithms, multiprocessor systems, fault tolerant computing, VLSI systems, software verification, and development of reliable software.

In the first chapter Professor Amitava Dutta points out that a major characteristic of decision support systems is the interaction and synergy between human and machine during the decision-making process. Accordingly, he focuses specifically on one resulting issue of theoretical and practical interest—that of supporting human reasoning activities. In particular, he explains, advances in artificial intelligence are providing powerful new computational tools that greatly expand the potential to support human reasoning activities in complex work environments.

Dr. Poppelbaum and his co-workers discuss unary processing, for which representation of the digits all have the same weight as opposed to the more conventional weighted binary representation. Although machines using this type of processing are obviously handicapped in terms of compactness, they compensate in a multitude of ways, which may include fault tolerance, simplicity in design, and low cost. He discusses in detail UNIFIELD, a computer using unary representation built at the University of Illinois. Included is a discussion of the advantages and disadvantages of this computer.

In their article, Professors Moitra and Iyengar point out that the design of parallel algorithms for various parallel computer architectures is motivated by factors such as speed and the need to solve complex problems of practical interest. With the continuing decrease in hardware cost, the objective is to trade the number of processors for a gain in computational speed. They illustrate and emphasize the systematic study of parallel algorithms and summarize current research in this field.

Dr. Kothari discusses multistage interconnection networks. The reason for using a multistage interconnection network is to connect several stages of smaller crossbar switches to provide required interconnections. He shows that the reduction in hardware achieved by using these interconnection networks can be significant. In his discussion he emphasizes underlying topological design principles.

In his article, Dr. Wing Toy reminds us that system reliability has been a major concern from the inception of electronic digital computers. There are two approaches to increased reliability: fault avoidance and fault tolerance. To obtain fault tolerance additional components are used—hardware, software, or both—to bypass the effects of failures. His chapter gives an overview of fault-tolerant computing design, including both hardware and software techniques.

Professor Reghbati defines a very large scale integrated (VLSI) circuit as a single chip that contains more than 100,000 devices. Generally, the metal-oxide-semiconductor technology is being used with a minimum feature size in the 1–2 micron range. The advent of VLSI systems, while making significant contributions to the cost effectiveness of many products, also presents challenges not previously faced by design and test engineers. His article concerns the techniques and tools that may help solve this VLSI design validation and testing crisis.

In Dr. Lee White's chapter we are reminded that computer-program testing is currently an active research field. Testing, he points out, is applied in virtually every software development project—yet the process is often not based upon a solid theoretical framework. His article surveys some of the basic concepts, approaches, and results in testing. He concludes that although many essential problems in program testing are undecidable, there has been notable progress with a number of testing approaches. This has been achieved by concentrating on certain classes of programs and also on the detection of certain types of errors.

In the final chapter, Professor Ramamoorthy and his colleagues point out that ad hoc programming techniques do not work for the development of large, distributed, and reliable software systems. There are important problems facing software engineers in the areas of requirement specification and design, resource and activity management, and reliability assessment. In their paper, the authors examine some of the issues that must be solved before applying software engineering techniques to practice.

I am pleased to thank the contributors to this volume. They have given extensively of their time and effort and have made this an important and timely contribution to their profession. Despite the many calls upon their time and their busy schedules, they recognize the necessity of writing substantial review and tutorial contributions in their areas of expertise. It has required considerable effort on their part, and their cooperation and assistance have been greatly appreciated. Because of their efforts this volume achieves a high level of excellence. It should be of great value and substantial interest for many years to come. It has been a pleasant and rewarding experience for me to edit this volume and to work with these authors.

MARSHALL C. YOVITS

The Explicit Support of Human Reasoning in Decision Support Systems

AMITAVA DUTTA

Information Systems Area
Management Sciences Department
College of Business
University of Iowa
Iowa City, Iowa 52242

1. Introduction

The term "decision support system" has been used rather nebulously to refer to computer-based systems that *aid human decision-making activities* in a variety of ways. Many systems, ranging from simple spreadsheets to complex programs that support battlefield decision making, have been labeled as such. The literature is replete with examples of DSS implementations. There has been, however, remarkably little consolidation of theoretical developments and issues. Since a major characteristic of DSS environments is interaction and synergy between human and machine during the decision-making process, this paper focuses specifically on one resulting issue of theoretical and practical interest—that of *supporting human reasoning activities*. In particular,

ADVANCES IN COMPUTERS, VOL. 26

advances in artificial intelligence (AI) are providing powerful new computational tools that greatly expand the potential to support human reasoning activities in complex work environments (e.g., monitoring, planning, fault management, problem solving). Some additional and related theoretical issues will be raised in passing, without much elaboration.

Human decision making in complex environments is at present not a well understood process. It is, however, precisely this ill-understood process that is supported by a DSS. In the absence of a comprehensive understanding of this process, our limited focus on reasoning activities is motivated by the following observations and views. It is our view that reasoning lies at the heart of any decision-making activity. Also, in the conclusion we will observe that, while reasoning issues have been implicitly recognized by researchers in DSS, there has been hardly any effort in the DSS literature to explicitly recognize and support this basic activity. The following presentation therefore seeks to raise reasoning and its explicit support as a fundamental research issue in DSS. It will summarize recent efforts to that end, together with additional developments in AI that can be the basis for further theoretical advancements in decision support. While the theoretical developments noted have applications in a wide variety of decision environments, our primary interest, for a variety of reasons that appear in the next section, is in managerial decision making. Recognizing this wider applicability, however, we have occasionally used the term "human decision-making processes" in the paper, although the intent, mainly, is to refer to managerial decision-making processes.

To the extent that reasoning is a core activity in human decision-making processes, a primary function of a decision support system is that of providing an *extension* of the *reasoning* capabilities of the human in such situations. The term "reasoning" is used here to mean the general methods (albeit ill-understood ones) by which a human processes a body of knowledge to reach a conclusion. Reasoning, together with ancillary activities, lies at the core of any decision-making task. A well-known model of decision making, proposed by Simon (1960), consists of three phases—intelligence, design, and choice. Intelligence involves searching the environment for conditions calling for decisions; data inputs are obtained, processed, and examined for clues that may identify problems or opportunities. Design consists of inventing, developing, and analyzing possible courses of action. Choice requires the selection of an alternative from among those available. Whether or not this model is comprehensive enough is not important for our purposes here. It does serve to indicate, however, the important role played by reasoning. Even a casual analysis of common decision environments will show that the ability to draw conclusions from bodies of knowledge is vital to all three phases.

Humans are knowledge processors. Computers have the potential to be such if one has some confidence in the hypothesis that, "Physical symbol manipulation systems have the necessary and sufficient means for general intelligent action" (Simon, 1982, page 28). (Investigations of the limits of computer intelligence are beyond the scope of the present discussion.) There are, however, clear differences in the nature and capabilities of human versus computerized knowledge processing. The term "extension" is used to mean a combination of the strengths of the machine with those of the human agent to yield better decisions than could be achieved by a human alone. The emphasis here, on computer-based support of reasoning activities, is a departure from traditional thinking in DSS, where reasoning activities are deliberately left to the human agent.

The traditional view of the technical capabilities of a DSS, epitomized in the structural model shown in Fig. 1 (Sprague and Carlson, 1982, page 29), is held by many (Thierauf, 1982, page 70; Zmud, 1983, pages 194, 196; Davis and Olson, 1985, page 45). See Bonczek et al., (1984) for a different view. Certain terms in Fig. 1 bear clarification. The DBMS, of course, is the data base management software, charged with the management of raw data in the system. The "model base" is a collection of programs that perform numerical transformations on data. An example is regression programs. The MBMS, the model base management software, is charged with the management of these models. This includes their instantiation, synthesis with other models, input preparation, etc. The DGMS is the dialogue generation and management software. Notice the emphasis, in Fig. 1, on flexible access to data and computational models. Reasoning activities associated with decision making have implicitly been relegated to the human in that model. There is no recognition of the explicit support of reasoning activities as a required technical capability of a DSS.

It is difficult to quantitatively estimate all the improvements that may be expected as a result of supporting human reasoning processes. Quantification and measurement of such improvements has proved to be most elusive, as several dimensions are quite intangible. Support of human reasoning activities can, potentially, result in enormous benefits, above and beyond those accruing from the support of data access and computational activity. Experiments in psychology have repeatedly established that humans exhibit limited or bounded rationality in different task environments (Simon 1947). Bounded rationality has many dimensions, one of which is a limit on the number of symbols the human agent can retain and manipulate during the course of a decision-making task. Any attempt by a DSS to support reasoning necessarily requires some formalization of the human reasoning process in a way amenable to machine representation and execution. The process of formalization will itself lead to a better understanding of reasoning processes. Furthermore, in theory, if an adequate formalization of human reasoning can be achieved (and we are a long way from doing so), the strengths of the

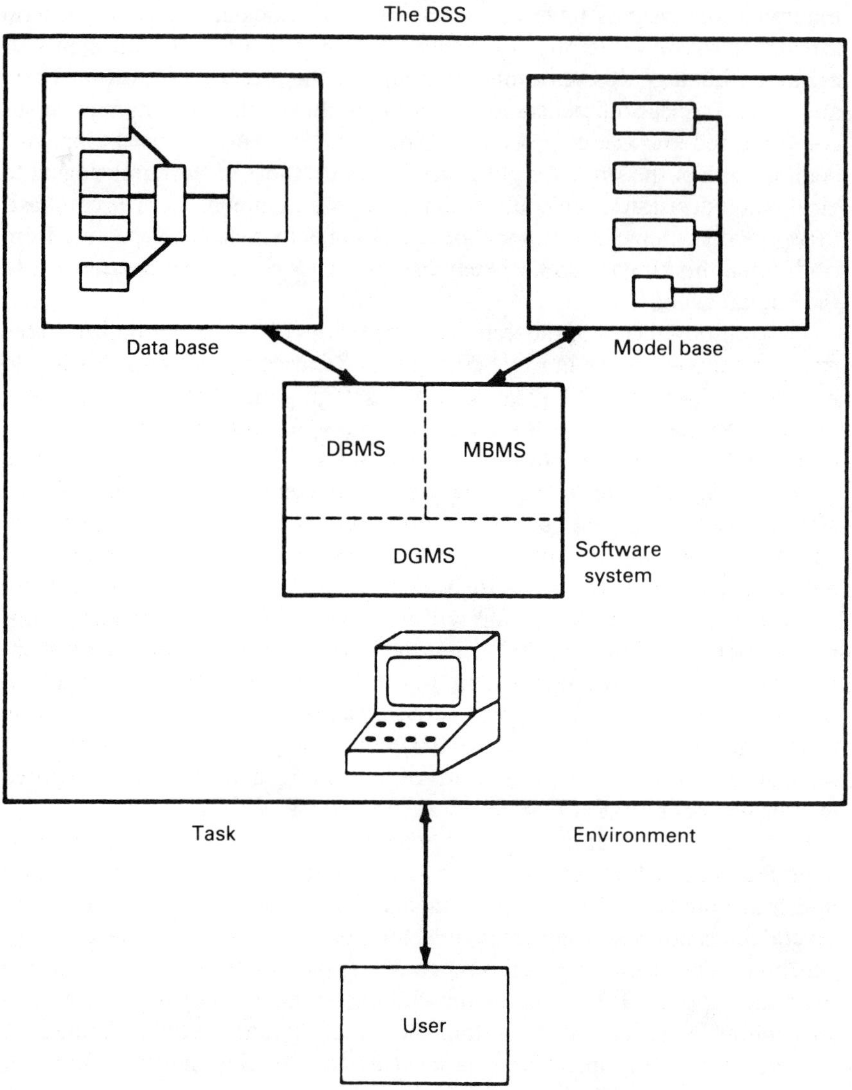

The DSS

FIG. 1. Components of a decision support system.

computer can be used to extend human capabilities for reasoning, since the computer is far less bounded than the human in its ability to manipulate symbols repetitively and quickly. More realistically, even a partial formalization of reasoning processes holds the promise of augmenting the decision-making capabilities of a human agent using a DSS.

To set the direction for the rest of the paper, we here summarize the views presented in this section: Reasoning is a major, if not the basic, activity that underlies managerial (and other) decision-making tasks. Computer-based support of reasoning should thus be of major theoretical interest in DSS research. This is a departure from traditional DSS thinking, where reasoning is left to the human agent. The potential benefits from supporting reasoning activity are enormous. While developments in AI present attractive computational means to attempt this rather difficult task, the need for further theoretical developments is acute.

2. Human Decision Processes

There are several reasons for the choice of managerial decision making as the type of human decision activity to be supported. First, it is a fundamental activity in any organization. Briefly, the activity is one of making decisions on the proper use of resources (broadly interpreted) to meet the objectives of the organization. Thus we are referring to economic decisions that managers have to make as part of their function. Often, a lot of deliberation is involved, which in turn means that the potential for understanding and supporting the underlying reasoning processes is much greater than in more informal environments. There is also a rich body of theory that has resulted in models (too numerous to cite individually), normative and positive, of managerial decision making in various situations. In fact, much of the work in economics, finance, accounting, and marketing and operations management is devoted to decision making. Such formal models often have to be complemented with more heuristic human decision processes in practical environments. Thus, managerial decision making is an activity that, by and large, is formal enough and has sufficient theoretical underpinnings to be a good candidate for computer-based support. Furthermore, the results of attempts to support reasoning in managerial decision environments would be applicable to many other domains as well. It is instructive to quickly review some chronological developments in computer-based support of managerial decision making, as it underscores the need for DSS to explicitly support reasoning activities.

2.1 Chronological Developments in Decision Support

One dimension along which decision making environments vary is that of structuredness. At one extreme there are structured problems, which are usually well understood and where the associated reasoning process can be easily externalized. Examples of such environments include order processing and billing. In the middle are semistructured environments where the reasoning activity is reasonably well understood, is readily applied to problem situations, but cannot easily be externalized. Take the air-traffic control function at a busy airport like O'Hare, for instance. ATCs constantly make decisions about how to sequence taxiing planes to their respective runways, sequence or resequence landings and takeoffs, etc.. The ATC's job gets even more hectic at peak hours or when there are disruptions such as bad weather conditions. There must be some well-understood reasoning procedures used by these decision makers, since human ATCs repeatedly apply them to the decision environment with success, practically all the time. It would be most difficult, however, to explicate a large part of that underlying reasoning process. Several managerial decision problems are of this type, including portfolio management or production planning and operation.

At the other extreme are environments where the reasoning processes required to make the decisions are themselves not well developed. Developing long-term plans to regain market share or to improve profitability, making decisions to open a new line of business, and deciding on large mergers and acquisitions are examples of this type of environment. The reasoning processes associated with such unstructured tasks are extremely difficult to explicate. Furthermore, they are perhaps ill understood at best, even by those who perform them. One indication is that no reasoning processes are applied successfully to such environments a large fraction of the time.

Decision support systems purport to aid semistructured decision-making tasks, i.e., environments that lie close to the middle of the spectrum just described. It is clear that one key ingredient in decision making is data, which has often been defined as "facts that can be used as the basis for reasoning." Data, often in large volumes, is necessary during the decision-making process. The early uses of computers to aid decision making were, not surprisingly, aimed at efficient storage and retrieval of data. Storage media such as tapes and disks provided the physical means (hardware) to store large volumes of data cheaply, compactly, and reliably. These media also provided much faster raw speed of access. Equally important, the development of file and data base management systems (software) provided the means to exploit the raw speed of hardware with mechanisms for efficient storage and access schemes. Various file organizations (Bradley, 1982; Wiederhold, 1977), including indexed sequential, hash, linked list, inverted files, and endless variations of these, were designed for this purpose. Hierarchical, relational, and network data base models (Date, 1986; Ullman, 1980; Atre, 1980) provided the theoretical basis for structuring collections of files and the primitive operators to manipulate these collections. Soon DBMSs were being sold with ad hoc query languages. The latter were simply languages that allowed casual users to state, in fairly simple terms, what data needed to be extracted from the data base. The "how," i.e., the exact sequence of operators needed to effect the retrieval, was generated by the query language processor itself. Thus the early use of computers to support human decision making took the form of *data management*.

Note that, while data represents "facts that can be used as the basis for reasoning," it is common to *transform data*, independent of how it has been accessed, in a variety of ways during the course of decision making. Common operations such as computing totals, averages, maximums, or minimums, all constitute data transformations. Data transformation is necessary for a variety of reasons. Often raw data is too voluminous, and meaningful summary figures such as means and standard deviations must be extracted. At other times, historical data has to be projected into the future, using various econometric models. Additionally, planners may use complex linear or integer programming models. In brief, data transformation techniques help to transform raw data into a form that is more usable for decision-making purposes. Data transformation procedures often go by the name of *models* in the DSS literature. Thus a chronological development in the use of computer-based aids for decision making focused on the management of such models. Just as data needed to be organized in a systematic manner, there is a need to store such models in an efficient manner, instantiate them whenever appropriate during a decision making process, make the necessary data available to such models, guide the selection and synthesis of multiple models, etc. Model management is a central concern of present-day DSS (Sprague and Carlson, 1982, chap. 9; Bonczek et al., 1981, 1984; Dutta and Basu, 1984; Dolk and Konsynski, 1984; Pan et al., 1984; Blanning 1985). Models provide the foundation for answering "what if" questions during decision making. Sometimes the model must be designed by the user, as with the ubiquitous spreadsheet or packages like IFPS (Execucom, 1982). The research efforts cited a little earlier are much more ambitious in scope. Many of them attempt to help and guide the model-building procedure, and in some cases even to automate it. To summarize, most present-day DSSs facilitate the transformation of data, in addition to the convenient data access provided by earlier developments in the area of DBMS. These developments account for two major components (DBMS and MBMS) in the schematic diagram of Fig. 1.

The third component, namely the dialogue component, has also been the subject of considerable research effort. Basically, this component makes the transformation between representations that are conducive to human decision-making processes and representations that are more suitable for expeditious internal processing. A sample structure of the dialogue management component is reproduced from Sprague and Carlson (1982, page 215) in Fig. 2. One of the issues of concern in this component is the relative efficacy of natural-language interfaces, graphical interfaces, command-language interfaces, etc.

AMITAVA DUTTA

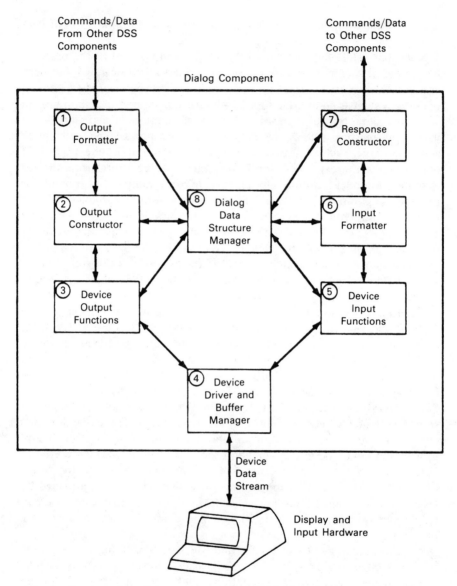

FIG. 2. Structure of the dialogue component of a DSS. (From Sprague and Carlson, 1982, page 215)

The foregoing summary of traditional DSS structure serves to highlight the need to explicitly support the reasoning processes associated with decision making. A little inspection reveals that data accesses and model executions are spawned from some underlying reasoning processes. It is this latter processes that maintains overall control of the decision making activity. In current DSS architectures, reasoning activities reside almost entirely with the human agent involved in the decision activity. [A notable exception is the generic DSS schema of Bonczek et al. (1984), which consists of a language subsystem, a problem processing subsystem, and a knowledge subsystem.] There is hardly any attempt to recognize reasoning as a basic underlying task in decision making, or to explicitly support this activity. Interestingly enough, reasoning activities in structured environments have indeed been supported, to the extent that they have been codified as applications programs written in some procedural language like COBOL. Examples include check processing, order entry, report generation, inventory control, and accounts receivable. An application program is, simply put, a codified form of the exact reasoning procedure to be followed in a particular decision-making environment. The logic of the applications program controls data accesses and data-trans-formation activity. In other words, reasoning activities are embodied in the logic of the applications program.

Algorithmic solution techniques tend to become less and less available or effective as one migrates towards unstructuredness in the decision-making environment. Heuristic techniques and reasoning capabilities assume increased importance instead. We proceed, shortly, to show how developments in artificial intelligence have now made it attractive to consider computer-based support of this fundamental activity underlying decision making, especially in less-structured environments.

3. Computer-Based Support of Reasoning

Epistemological studies in AI focus on what kinds of facts about the world are available to an observer with given opportunities to observe, how these facts can be represented in the memory of a computer, and what rules permit legitimate conclusions to be drawn from these facts. AI literature is rich with different knowledge-representation schemes (Barr and Fiegenbaum, 1982a, chap. 3) and different mechanisms to permit the manipulation of this knowledge for the purpose of reasoning. There is as yet, however, no computational model of human reasoning that is comprehensive in any sense. Most studies have, perhaps for reasons of tractability, concentrated on one or two facets of human reasoning at a time. Some studies, for instance, investigate reasoning by human experts operating in specialized domains. Others are interested in common-sense reasoning performed by practically all humans in everyday environments. Inexact reasoning is yet another area of interest. These areas of research often overlap, but the developments therein have yet to be crystallized into one comprehensive model of human reasoning. We have chosen to present results on three dimensions of human reasoning: imprecision, nonmonotonicity, and learning. While not a complete view, these dimensions are of particular importance to DSS for reasons that will be stated as each one is presented. The reader will notice a stronger emphasis on imprecision as compared to the other two. Study of reasoning under imprecision probably has a much longer history, dating back at least to Bayes's theorem. Within the context of decision support, some desirable capabilities of a representation and manipulation method to aid human reasoning would be the following:

(a) The method should synthesize fragmented and imprecise knowledge during the reasoning process, to generate useful solutions for different problem instances. Recall that domain knowledge tends to be rather fragmented for the types of problems that DSSs are used to solve.

(b) It should select and use different computational procedures where relevant, together with data inputs. These two functions, data access and data transformation, have already been recognized to be necessary for decision support. Any reasoning mechanism that is devised should therefore be capable of integrating these two functions into the reasoning process.

(c) The method should provide some measure of the "goodness" of alternate recommendations that follow from different lines of reasoning, to aid in their evaluation and final selection. This would aid in the choice phase of Simon's model of the decision process.

(d) The method must be able to explain the reasoning process in any specific problem instance. This is an important capability, but one that is extremely difficult to obtain. Explanation does not entail simply regurgitating the sequence of decision rules used to arrive at a conclusion, although that can help. Among other things, it entails the justification of choices of different rules, statements of alternate lines of reasoning for the same conclusion, and presentation of the explanation at different levels of aggregation. For instance, if a Department Chairman is asked to explain why person X was hired, he may say that X appears to be a good researcher and a good teacher. If pressed further, he may say that X has fifty published papers, and that his teaching evaluations were above average. Most current DSSs have little or no explanatory capability.

(e) The method should be able to acquire new knowledge and improve its reasoning ability over time as it aids in more and more decision-making instances. Recall our earlier statement that reasoning entails the drawing of conclusions from bodies of knowledge. Humans are able to improve decision-making performance over time as they have repeated interactions with the decision environment. This improvement can arise from the acquisition of better ways to reason, better domain knowledge, etc. Operationally, it is highly desirable that the DSS be able to acquire new knowledge of different forms during the course of its use.

(f) The method should be able to recognize situations where it has insufficient knowledge to continue with the reasoning process on its own. This is an important characteristic in humans. Good decision makers will recognize situations where they simply do not have enough knowledge to proceed. This realization usually triggers some knowledge acquisition activity.

Undoubtedly, there are additional desirable capabilities. As will become amply clear, however, even the limited agenda above presents a formidable challenge.

3.1 Imprecise Reasoning in Decision Making

Humans making decisions in practice face a less-than-ideal environment. They have to work with less-than-perfect information. One pervasive characteristic of real-world environments is the presence of imprecision. Data is often missing or unreliable, decision rules are not well tested or in some cases unknown, etc. The problem gets compounded in semi-structured or un-structured environments, where reasoning processes tend to be increasingly more heuristic and domain knowledge more fragmented, yet humans cope quite effectively with imprecision in their environment. Given the pervasive-ness of imprecision in decision-making environments, it would be appropriate, as a starting point, to develop methods for supporting reasoning activity in the presence of imprecision. Specifically, there is a need to develop a machine representation of imprecise knowledge, together with some mechanical means for its manipulation. The latter will facilitate the process of drawing conclusions from this body of knowledge.

3.2 Fuzziness and Uncertainty

There are two major sources of imprecision that are commonly encountered in the reasoning process in unstructured problems, namely *fuzziness* and *uncertainty*. It is only fair to point out that one school of thought holds the view that a measure of uncertainty is sufficient, and that either measures of fuzziness are unnecessary or anything that can be captured by a fuzziness measure can also be captured by a probability measure. On the other hand, at least one of the major proponents of fuzzy logic holds the opposite view, that fuzzy reasoning is conceptually different from probabilistic reasoning (L.A. Zadeh, personal communication), and one is not a substitute for the other. We have argued (Dutta, 1985) that fuzziness and uncertainty are quite different in nature and that they interact during the course of decision making. Separate measures for each can improve the quality of decisions or conclusions that can be reached in the process.

Fuzziness refers to the use of fuzzy or vague concepts and operators in representing unstructured knowledge. Some of the values used to represent attributes of objects, relationships, and computational procedures are characterized more appropriately by fuzzy sets (in which some or all of the elements have partial membership [Zadeh, 1965]), rather than by "crisp" sets. To see this, consider the following heuristic rule:

R1:   The balance on this transaction is collectible IF
(a) the customer has a *high* credit rating;
(b) the customer's record on *recent* transactions is *good*;
(c) *recent* contact with the customer about this transaction has been *positive*.

In this rule, several terms (*high, recent,* etc.) are fuzzy, since in their usual interpretation they do not represent sharply defined concepts. For instance, it is hard to define the term *recent* using a specific date as the cutoff date for an event to be considered *recent*; instead, there is a range of dates that are somewhere between *recent* and *not recent,* and thus a fuzzy-set-based representation is more suitable. In addition to fuzzy terms, the implicit AND operator connecting the three premises in **R1** is also typically a fuzzy one; useful conclusions about the collectibility of a transaction's debt may be obtained even when all the premises are not strictly satisfied.

On the other hand, uncertainty occurs when only partial knowledge is available about an entity or process, when future events are involved in the reasoning process, or when the underlying process is inherently stochastic (that is, some events may be well defined, yet their likelihood is less than certain). In rule **R1**, for instance, satisfaction of the three premises does not guarantee collectibility of the outstanding debt, even though it may be highly likely (also, satisfaction of the premises themselves may be difficult to determine with certainty). Since much of the reasoning necessary to solve unstructured problems is uncertain or fuzzy or both, support for such reasoning necessitates some method to represent and manipulate both fuzzy and uncertain knowledge. A review of some current approaches to imprecise reasoning follows.

Bayesian Methods.   The earliest and most traditional approach to imprecise reasoning is based on probability theory (Feller, 1971). This approach usually models the reasoning process on a hypothesis–test paradigm. Entities represented in the knowledge base and data are viewed as evidence that can be used to prove different hypotheses. Each item of evidence E_i (and each hypothesis H_j) is assigned a prior probability $P(E_i)[P(H_j)]$. In addition, the relationships between the different E_i and the hypotheses they support are characterized by conditional or joint probabilities, which may be estimated from statistical samples. During the problem-solving process in which these relationships are instantiated (where relevant) to infer specific hypotheses, the conditional probability of each inferred hypothesis is computed using a mechanism such as Bayes's rule. For instance, given a relationship of the form "If E then H," the application of Bayes's rule gives

$$P(H \mid E) = \frac{P(E \cdot H)}{P(E)} = \frac{P(E \mid H) \cdot P(H)}{P(E)}$$

There are several operational difficulties with using this model. It is easy to get into practical situations where an enormously large number of conditional probabilities have to be known, giving rise to estimation and computational difficulties. Furthermore, the use of subjective estimates of probabilities can give rise to inconsistencies [such as $P(H \mid E) \geq 1$].

In some existing systems the Bayesian approach has been modified by assuming conditional independence, so that

$$P(E_1, \ldots, E_n \mid H) = \prod_i P(E_i \mid H), \quad \text{and } P(E_1, \ldots, E_n \mid \bar{H}) = \prod_i P(E_i \mid \bar{H})$$

and by expressing uncertainty in terms of odds rather than probabilities, where

$$O(H) = \frac{P(H)}{P(\bar{H})} \quad \text{and } O(H \mid E) = \frac{P(H \mid E)}{P(\bar{H} \mid E)}$$

Then the conditional odds of the implicand in a relationship can be computed as

$$O(H \mid E) = \left[\prod_{i=1}^{n} \frac{P(E_i \mid H)}{P(E_i \mid \bar{H})} \right] \cdot O(H)$$

With this formulation the problems of normalization are avoided, so that subjective estimates of probabilities can be used, as in PROSPECTOR (Duda et al., 1979; 1976) and AL/X (Reiter, 1981). For more on the propagation of uncertainty in Bayesian networks, the reader is referred to Pearl (1982).

Certainty Factors. This approach has been applied in a number of expert systems and expert-system shells, such as MYCIN (Shortliffe, 1974), EMYCIN (van Melle, 1980), and SACON (Bennet et al., 1978). Each hypothesis is assigned a certainty factor (CF, $-1 \leq \text{CF} \leq 1$) derived from associated measures of belief (MB) and disbelief (MD). These latter measures are defined by:

1. $\text{MB}[h, e] = X$ means, "The measure of increased belief in the hypothesis h, based on the evidence e, is X."

$$\text{MB}[h, e] = \begin{cases} 1 & \text{if } P(h) = 1, \\ \dfrac{\max[P(h \mid e), P(h)] - P(h)}{\max[1, 0] - P(h)} & \text{otherwise} \end{cases}$$

2. $\text{MD}[h, e] = Y$ means, "The measure of increased disbelief in the hypothesis h, given the evidence e, is Y."

$$\text{MD}[h, e] = \begin{cases} 1 & \text{if } P(h) = 0, \\ \dfrac{\min[P(h \mid e), P(h)] - P(h)}{\min[1, 0] - P(h)} & \text{otherwise} \end{cases}$$

The certainty factor CF is then computed as

$$\text{CF}[h, e] = \text{MD}[h, e] - \text{MB}[h, e]$$

The measures MB and MD, and consequently CF, are revised during the diagnosis process by the incidence of each premise implying the hypothesis, so that the uncertainty in the hypothesis is always reflected in its CF. The combination of evidence in this approach is based on a set of rules, such as:

1. The CF of the implicand in a rule is the product of the rule's CF and the CF of the collective premise.
2. The CF of a conjunction of several propositions is the minimum of the CFs of each proposition.
3. If several rules implying the same hypothesis are instantiated, the CF of the hypothesis is taken as the maximum such CF obtained.

The major drawback of this approach is that it provides no mechanism for representing fuzzy knowledge, and at the same time loses some of the firm foundation provided by probability theory. Nevertheless, it has been used quite successfully in several existing systems and is quite popular with developers of expert systems (Hayes–Roth et al., 1983).

The Dempster–Shafer Theory of Evidence. This theory has attracted significant interest in recent years. The approach used here is to consider an uncertain proposition A_i in terms of its possible states. The state space for all the relevant propositions in a problem setting is called the *frame of discernment* θ, so that every proposition is characterized by a suitable subset of θ. Then a belief function $\text{Bel}:2^\theta \to [0, 1]$ is defined for every collection $A_i, \ldots, A_n$ of subsets of θ,

$$\text{Bel}(A_i \cup A_2 \cdots \cup A_n) \geq \sum_{I \subset \{1 \ldots n\}} (-1)^{|I|+1} \text{Bel}(\bigcap_{i \in I} A_i)$$

with $\text{Bel}(\phi) = 0$, and $\text{Bel}(\theta) = 1$. Also, the *doubt function* is defined as $\text{Dou}(A) = \text{Bel}(-A)$, and the function $P^*(A) = 1 - \text{Dou}(A)$ is called the *upper probability function*. This framework provides for evaluation of evidence supporting a proposition A by the pair $(\text{Bel}(A), P^*(A))$. Under suitable functions, it can be shown that this pair corresponds to the pair $(s(A), p(A))$, whose $s(A)$ is a lower bound for $P(A)$ (the probability of A), and $p(A)$ is a lower bound for $P(-A)$ [and thus an upper bound for $P(A)$]. The major attraction of this approach is that, instead of assuming that uncertainty can be measured precisely, each proposition A is represented by the interval estimate of uncertainty (s, p). As evidence is accumulated during the problem-solving process, these bounds are updated, using an "orthogonal sum" operation to combine evidence [Barnett, 1981]. By using a conservative approach of preserving valid bounds on the true probability value, this approach is able to conform to probability theory without making some of the restrictive assumptions of other approaches, and has thus been widely used (Garvey et al., 1981). A modified evidential approach has been developed for INFERNO (Quinlan, 1982). Quinlan also uses a pair (t, f) to bound the uncertainty of a proposition. Interestingly, his methods of propagation can detect inconsistencies of the type $(t + f > 1)$ and recover by making minimal modification to these bounds so as to restore consistency.

A variety of other methods for incorporating uncertain knowledge and reasoning have been suggested. These include the use of information theory and entropy, the use of meta-level probability evaluation in logic-based systems (Shapiro, 1981), and the approach of CASNET (Weiss et al., 1978). Although some of these have interesting theoretical bases, their applicability to a broad range of systems is as yet untested.

Methods for Fuzzy Reasoning. This category of research on imprecise reasoning, which focuses on fuzziness as a source of imprecision, is mostly based on the use of many-valued logics and especially Fuzzy logic (Zadeh, 1979). Fuzzy logic is radically different from traditional binary logic. Its basis is that many concepts in natural language and problem-domain knowledge are fuzzy, in that some of their elements may not have binary membership levels in the membership set of the concepts, but instead are characterized by a "possibility distribution" Π_X over the unit interval $[0, 1]$. Thus a fuzzy proposition $p \equiv \{X \text{ is } A\}$, where X is a variable defined over the universe U

and A is a fuzzy subset of U, can be represented by the possibility distribution

$$\prod_X = \mathrm{Poss}\{X = u \mid X \text{ is } A\} = \mu_A(u) \qquad \forall u \in U$$

where $\mu_A(x)$ is the membership function of A (i.e., $\mu_A(x)$ specifies the membership level of x in the fuzzy set A). Using a suitable language [such as PRUF (Zadeh, 1979)], fuzzy propositions can be stated and converted into equivalent possibility assignment equations by operators such as projection and particularization. During the problem-solving process, the compositional rule of inference (Zadeh, 1979) is used to draw fuzzy conclusions from these equations and the underlying possibility distributions.

In situations where both fuzziness and uncertainty are present, the uncertainty can be incorporated into the fuzzy framework in the following way. Given a probability space defined by (R^n, σ, P), where R^n is a Euclidean n space, Σ is the σ field of Borel sets in R^n, and P is a probability measure over R^n, the probability of a fuzzy event $A \in \Sigma$ is given by (Zadeh, 1968)

$$P(A) = \int_{R^n} \mu_A(x)p(x)\,dx = E(\mu_A)$$

where $p(x)$ is the probability distribution function of x over A.

Among the criticisms leveled at fuzzy logic (Haac 1977) is the failure of closure arising from linguistic approximation. In fuzzy logic, truth can have a structured countable set of values. Now, it is possible that at the end of a fuzzy reasoning process the concluded proposition can have a truth value that does not fall in this countable set. The process of approximating its actual truth

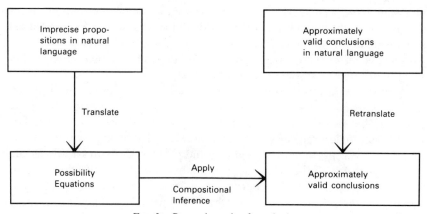

FIG. 3.   Reasoning using fuzzy logic.

value by one from this set is called "linguistic approximation." This process can cause problems of completeness, although proponents feel that the issue of completeness is much less critical in approximate reasoning. The fuzzy reasoning process is shown schematically in Fig. 3.

Many of the problems with fuzzy logic mentioned here do not hold for the use of fuzzy sets themselves. In fact, fuzzy-set theory, along with appropriate measures for uncertainty, has been used for several problem areas, such as medical diagnosis (Gupta and Sanchez, 1982), structural damage assessment (Ishizuka et al., 1981) and pattern recognition (Kandel, 1982).

4.   Reasoning with Fuzzy and Uncertain Knowledge

In this section we reproduce, in very condensed form, some representation techniques that support reasoning activities in DSS environments. The representation attempts to capture both fuzziness and uncertainty in the environment, and the manipulation methods propagate measures of imprecision, through a line of reasoning, to any conclusion that is drawn from a body of imprecise knowledge so represented. Technical details may be found in Basu and Dutta (1986) and Dutta and Basu (1986). The characteristics of these representation and manipulation methods will first be presented through an example. Some technical details associated with the methods will follow.

First-order logic (FOL) (Chang and Lee 1973) has special appeal as a language for such representation, in view of our interest in supporting managerial decision-making processes. FOL has been used as a basis for modeling and manipulating relational databases. Relational languages (Chamberlin et al., 1976; Kim, 1979) based on the relational calculus of Codd (1972) are of this type. There have also been several studies on deductive data bases (Gallaire and Minker, 1978). The ability to perform data accesses during the course of reasoning is especially important for decision support. FOL is also the basis for some programming languages, an example being PROLOG, developed by Alain Colmerauer and his associates. Proof techniques have also been used for query-answering purposes (Robinson, 1965; Green, 1969). As a bonus, the explanation of the reasoning behind a particular answer can also be generated. Several researchers have also shown how computational activities associated with data transformation can be initiated and sequenced during the course of such reasoning (Dutta and Basu, 1984; Pan et al., 1984). In short, FOL provides a foundation for the support of human reasoning processes in a manner that allows for the integration of data accesses and data transformation activity.

Recall that the environments in which DSSs are used often call for the use of fragmented knowledge. Operationally, our knowledge base consists of a collection of Horn clauses (Kowalski and vanEmden, 1976), appropriately augmented to capture imprecision. Each Horn clause is considered to be a fragment of knowledge to be used in combination with others in a specific instance. New rules can be added as learning occurs. Existing fragments of knowledge can easily be modified or deleted. This operationalization of the knowledge base facilitates the maintenance and use of fragmented knowledge for reasoning purposes in DSS environments. A typical modified Horn clause in the knowledge base has the form

$$w_1 A_1 \wedge^k w_2 A_2 \wedge^k \cdots \wedge^k w_n A_n \rightarrow^\gamma B$$

The premises A_i (predicates) will have imprecision measures associated with them. Whenever such a rule is used in a reasoning instance, the imprecision in the premises are combined and propagated to the consequent B, in a manner to be shown subsequently. These measures are in turn propagated to any fragment of knowledge in which B participates. Ultimately, the imprecision in a line of reasoning is reflected in the conclusions, in the form of appropriate measures. The weights w_i capture the relative importance of the premises; k is the degree of the conjunction and takes values in the range $[1, \infty)$; γ ranges over $(0, 1]$ and captures the strength of the implication, i.e., the extent to which the collection of premises affects the consequent. The knowledge base used for the example appears in Fig. 4.

Consider the following query, posed to a decision maker: "Should the collection of the balance on transaction 9 be pursued?" The reasoning associated with answering this query is represented as a tree in Fig. 5. More accurately, Fig. 5 shows one successful line of reasoning. Some details have been omitted so as not to crowd the figure, but they may be determined easily from Fig. 4. Each node in the tree, together with all its children, constitutes one fragment of knowledge that was used in the line of reasoning. The reasoning process consists of combining fragments of knowledge available in the knowledge base, so as to support the final conclusion (at the root) with an acceptable level of precision. Therefore, the fragment selected at the root is one that would enable us to make some decision on PURSUEing the payment. This happens to be the rule whose consequent is PURSUE, which is why it appears at the root. Of course, the premises of this rule have not yet been evaluated. If the final decision is to be made with a minimum acceptable level of precision, its premises must also meet some minimum acceptable levels. Therefore, reasoning about the final conclusion, together with estimation of its precision level, is postponed until we have evaluated the premises of the associated rule. Thus the reasoning process unfolds to draw conclusions about each of the premises that affects the root. We continue in this manner until the leaf nodes are reached, where evaluation can be performed directly, with the

$CONTACT_2(x, Recent, Positive)$ $\wedge^3$ $CREDIT - RATE_3(x, High)$
$\rightarrow^{\gamma=0.95}$ $CORRESPOND(x)$

$\mathbf{AVERAGE}_1(DUE, x, Y_1)$ $\wedge^\infty$ $\mathbf{AVERAGE}_1(DUE, x, > 30days, Y_2)$ $\wedge^\infty$
$\mathbf{DIFF}_1(Y_1, Y_2, Increasing)$ $\rightarrow^1$ $AVEAMTINC(x)$

$SALE(x, Recent)$ $\rightarrow^{\phi=S(.4,.6,1)}$ $ACTIVE(x)$

$SALE_1(t, x, a)$ $\wedge^\infty$ $\mathbf{SUM}_1(PAID, t, x, y)$ $\wedge^\infty$ $\mathbf{DIFF}_1(a, y, d)$
$\rightarrow^1$ $DUE(x, d)$

$MAXAGE_3(x, NotDelinquent)$ $\wedge^3$ $\mathbf{AVERAGE}_1(DUE, x, Small)$
$\rightarrow^{\gamma=0.9}$ $RECORD(x, Good)$

$\mathbf{MIN}(DUE, x, d)$ $\rightarrow^1$ $MAXAGE(x, d)$

$DUE_1(t, x, d, a)$ $\wedge^4$ $PAID - UP_3(x, t_1, d_1)$ $\wedge^4$ $GT(d_1, d)$
$\rightarrow^{\gamma=0.95}$ $NEWPAID(x, t)$

$SALE_1(t, x, d, a)$ $\wedge^\infty$ $\mathbf{SUM}_1(PAID, x, t, b)$ $\wedge^\infty$ $GE(b, a)$
$\rightarrow^1$ $PAID - UP(x, t, d)$

$\mathbf{SUM}_1(SALE, x, a)$ $\wedge^\infty$ $\mathbf{SUM}_1(PAID, x, b)$ $\wedge^\infty$ $\mathbf{DIFF}_1(a, b, d)$
$\rightarrow^1$ $BALANCE(x, d)$

$DUE_4(t, x, Overdue, a)$ $\wedge^5$ $ACTIVE_5(x)$ $\wedge^5$ $CONTACT_3(x, Positive)$
$\wedge^5$ $NEWPAID(x, t)$ $\rightarrow^{\gamma=0.9}$ $WRITE - OFF(x, t)$

$DUE_3(t, x, Overdue)$ $\wedge^5$ $NOTPAYEVER_2(x, t)$
$\wedge^5$ $LEGAP - OP_1(x, t, Negative)$ $\rightarrow^{\gamma=0.95}$ $WRITE - OFF(x, t)$

$DUE_5(t, x, Overdue, a)$ $\wedge^3$ $CORRESPOND_5(x, t)$ $\wedge^3$ $RECORD_3(x, Good)$
$\wedge^3$ $ACTIVE_1(x)$ $\rightarrow^{\gamma=0.9}$ $PURSUE(x, t)$

FIG. 4.   Knowledge base for imprecise reasoning example.

help of raw data. During the entire reasoning process, imprecision estimates at lower levels are continually propagated upward until they culminate in imprecision measures for the root. Humans are adept at focusing their reasoning process; i.e., somehow they are able to marshall the right knowledge that bears on the problem at hand without undue search through the enormous amount of knowledge available to them. Mechanized reasoning procedures generally are quite poor in this regard.

Returning to the example, the decision on whether or not to PURSUE a

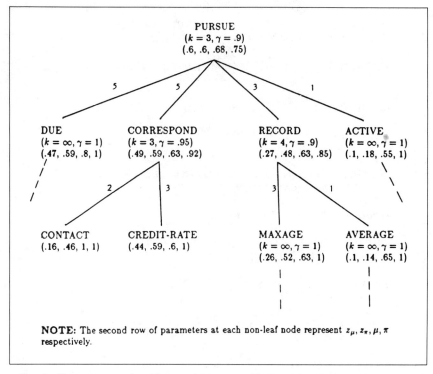

FIG. 5. Tree representation of reasoning process. The second row of parameters at each nonleaf node represents z_μ, z_π, μ, π, respectively.

payment is based on a combination of premises:

(a) DUE: Is the amount actually overdue, and if so, how overdue is it?
(b) CORRESPOND: Has the company been contacted, have they indicated an intent to pay, and what is their credit rating?
(c) RECORD: What is their past payment record? Have they been meeting most of their dues more or less on time?
(d) ACTIVE: Is the company still actively in business?

Basically, the payment should be pursued if the company has indicated some willingness to pay, is capable of paying, has had a good record of past payments, and is still a viable, ongoing organization. Notice, however, that all the premises are imprecise (i.e., have fuzziness and uncertainty associated with them). Thus it is vital to be able to capture imprecision in the environment and to reason with such imprecise knowledge. The propagation of measures of imprecision generated by a query like the one above are now presented informally.

There is a minimum acceptable level of precision associated with the query; i.e., pursuing the payment will be recommended by the reasoning process if some minimum level of uncertainty and of fuzziness is met. These levels may be determined via default values or may be specified by the user; in Fig. 5 they are the first two numbers in the second line below each node. For example, the minimum acceptable levels at the root are 0.6 for fuzziness (called the z_μ value) and 0.6 for uncertainty (called the z_π value) (in that order). Of course, we cannot know the actual precision levels for PURSUE until those of its children (premises) are known. Thus we work backward and compute the required minimum acceptable levels of precision in each of the premises that would cause PURSUE to meet its minimum acceptable levels. The expressions for the propagation of these z values are shown more formally in subsequent sections. This propagation process unfolds until we reach leaf nodes at which the imprecision levels are actually known. Thus the imprecision levels evaluated at the root node reflect, albeit in fairly aggregated form, the imprecision of the entire reasoning process used to support the root. After all, conclusions should reflect the imprecision in the body of knowledge from which they have been drawn. This informal description of the reasoning process will set the stage for a more formal presentation of the methods. The example will be revisited thereafter, to highlight additional characteristics.

4.1   Representing Fuzziness

Predicates in the knowledge base serve two purposes. First, they are used to specify some or all attributes of single object. In addition, however, they are also used to represent predicative relationships among different objects [e.g., FATHER(John, Peter)]. One way that fuzziness measures can be obtained for predicates is from their terms.

The imprecision level of an atomic formula (predicate) is defined by the μ values of its terms, using the following rule (notationally, the fuzziness of x is denoted by μ_x):

$$\mu_{\text{PREDICATE(term}_1 \cdots \text{term}_n)} = \min_i \{\mu_{\text{term}_i}\}$$

Example. Consider an explicit tuple $C_1 = \text{STUDENT}(John,\ 170,\ Blond)$ in the knowledge base, with

John $\in$ Name, with $\mu_{\text{Name}}(\text{John}) = 1$
170 $\in$ Height, with $\mu_{\text{Height}}(170) = 1$
Blond $\in$ Color, with $\mu_{\text{Color}}(\text{Blond}) = 0.7$

so that $\mu_{\text{STUDENT(Name, Height, Hair)}}(\text{John},\ 170,\ \text{Blond}) = \min\{1, 1, 0.7\} = 0.7$

Predicates will participate in different relationships that are expressed using various connectives. We start by examining the conjunction and disjunction operators. Consider the binary expressions $w_X X \wedge^k w_Y Y$ and $w_X X \wedge^k w_Y Y$. The fuzziness measure for an imprecise conjunction or disjunction is obtained by a simple generalization of the following expressions:

$$\mu_{w_x} X \wedge^k w_y Y(u, v) = 1 - \left[\frac{w_x^k(1 - \mu_X(u))^k + w_y^k(1 - \mu_Y(v))^k}{w_x^k + w_y^k} \right]^{\frac{1}{k}} \quad (4.1)$$

$$\mu_{w_x} X \vee^k w_y Y(u, v) = \left[\frac{(w_x^k \mu_X(u))^k + (w_y^k \mu_Y(v))^k}{w_x^k + w_y^k} \right]^{\frac{1}{k}} \quad (4.2)$$

where w_x and w_y are the relative weights of the concepts X and Y in the relationship; $\mu_X(u)$ and $\mu_Y(v)$ are the values of the membership functions of X and Y for the elements u and v respectively; and the proximity of the logical operator to the corresponding precise (boolean) operator is defined by k.

The weights are useful because they enable the formulation of fuzzy relationships in which several factors (represented by suitable literals) are relevant, but are not all equally important. For example, the quality of a financial investment such as a stock might be determined by both the level of sales growth of the firm and its return on assets (ROA), but the two factors may have different levels of significance (e.g., the ROA may be predominant). Such a relationship would be extremely difficult to represent in a boolean system, but can be represented effectively using Eq. (4.1). The effect of changing k is to alter the impact of the relative weights w_i of the different literals. For low k values the weights are relatively unimportant; as k increases and the relationship becomes better defined, the weights become more significant. The k value is thus a measure of how well the collection of premises is defined, particularly with reference to the weights w_i. Formulation of a rule with a high k value in the premise indicates that the form of the premise (i.e., the relevant premise predicates and their relative weights) is well known to the person formulating the rule. Additional interesting properties of the μ function, which ease computational burden, can be found in Basu and Dutta (1986). For instance, it can be shown that the computation of the μ function is invariant to application of DeMorgan's laws. Certain associativity properties can also be shown. The task of selecting the k value from the range $[1, \infty)$ can be quite daunting. However, the norm function in Eq. (4.1) varies significantly with k only for low values of k, in the range one to ten. For practical purposes it is adequate to choose k values from this reduced range, and even from a discrete set of values in this range (e.g., 1, 3, 5, 9, ∞, with ∞ as the special extreme case of a precise conjunction).

Once the fuzziness measure for a conjunction has been obtained as above, it is next necessary to obtain that of its consequent. To compute μ_B, a suitable characterization of the relationship between A and B is required. This is likely to be difficult to obtain in practice, however, (for instance, A and B may have different metrics, dimensions, etc.). A reasonable simplification is to characterize the implication in terms of the relevant μ values, rather than A and B themselves. This is achieved by using a function $\phi(x)$: $\mu_A \to \mu_B$ (i.e., $\phi(x)$: $[0, 1] \to [0, 1]$). Then, given μ_A, the value of μ_B is computed as $\phi(\mu_A)$.

Work on the use of fuzzy membership functions (Zadeh, 1979) has shown that a few functional forms should be adequate for specifying ϕ, These include the S form and the K form (see Fig. 6). The major difference between these two forms is that in the S form the transition in μ values is smoother and it is possible to define the lower end of the range where μ is significant. For instance, an implication that is nearly categorical can be represented by an S-form function with $(c - a) \ll 1$. On the other hand, the K form is simpler. In constructing a knowledge base, an expert (or a user) can characterize most

The S-FORM Fuzzy Membership Function

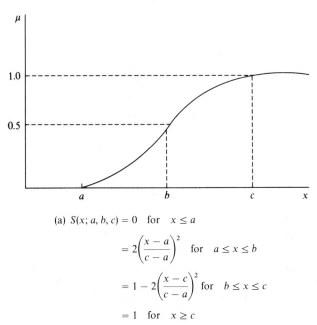

(a) $S(x; a, b, c) = 0$ for $x \leq a$

$$= 2\left(\frac{x - a}{c - a}\right)^2 \quad \text{for} \quad a \leq x \leq b$$

$$= 1 - 2\left(\frac{x - c}{c - a}\right)^2 \quad \text{for} \quad b \leq x \leq c$$

$$= 1 \quad \text{for} \quad x \geq c$$

Fig. 6.   Alternate forms for propagating fuzziness measures across an implication: (a) $S =$ form fuzzy membership function; (b) $K =$ form fuzzy membership function.

The *K*-FORM Fuzzy Membership Function

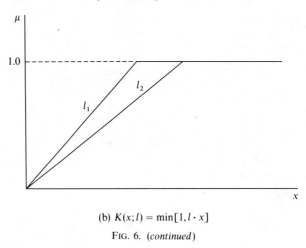

(b) $K(x;l) = \min[1, l \cdot x]$

FIG. 6. (*continued*)

fuzzy implications using suitable functions $\phi(x)$ from these forms, thus significantly reducing the complexity of both storage and computation. From the form of our Horn clauses, it is clear that the *K* form is used in the knowledge base. The implication can be interpreted as a sufficient but not strictly necessary condition.

Thus far, we have shown how to represent imprecise knowledge and how to obtain imprecision measures for a fragment of knowledge represented as a modified Horn clause in the knowledge base. Several fragments of knowledge, however, will typically be combined in any reasoning instance. It is therefore necessary to develop methods to combine and propagate fuzziness measures across multiple fragments of knowledge during reasoning.

4.2   Reasoning with Fuzziness

Recall that in our method reasoning develops "backward" from the root. [In principle it is also possible to reason "forward" from the entire body of knowledge available in the DSS. There are situations where one is more efficient than the other (Nilsson, 1980).] Since the development of a proof is backward from the root, which has a minimum acceptable level of imprecision called the z bound, this value can be used to set the z values of all the premises of the rule used to match with the root. (Actually, the z bound has two components, one for fuzziness, the other for uncertainty. We will ignore the latter until the next section.) To illustrate how this can be done, consider the use of a rule such as the one shown below, at the root:

$$w_1 x_1 \wedge^k w_2 x_2 \cdots \wedge^k w_n x_n \rightarrow y_i$$

In the proof tree, $x_1, \ldots, x_n$ form the children nodes of y_i, with arc weights $w_1, \ldots, w_n$ respectively. Now consider x_1. Even if $x_2, \ldots, x_n$ are all precise terms, so that $\mu_2 = \mu_3 = \cdots = \mu_n = 1$, the lowest value of μ_1 that will still yield $\mu_i \geq z_i$ is given by μ_1^*, where

$$\mu_1^* = 1 - \frac{[1 - z_i]}{w_1^*}$$

with

$$w_1^* = \frac{w_1}{[w_1^k + \cdots + w_n^k]^{\frac{1}{k}}}$$

Proof: At the very least, we need

$$\mu_i = z_i$$

$$= 1 - \left[\frac{w_1^k(1 - \mu_1)^k + \cdots + w_n^k(1 - \mu_n)^k}{w_1^k + \cdots + w_n^k} \right]^{\frac{1}{k}}$$

$$= 1 - \frac{w_1(1 - \mu_1)}{[w_1^k + \cdots + w_n^k]^{\frac{1}{k}}}$$

$$= 1 - w_1^*(1 - \mu_1)$$

and the result follows.

Thus the value of μ_1^* provides a lower bound for μ_1 to be acceptable and can be used as z_1. Values of z_i thus computed for each child node of a literal that has been matched with a rule also have the desirable property that they take the weights w_i of the different premises of the axiom into account. Thus, if $w_i > w_j$, then $z_i > z_j$ (the relative magnitudes of z_i, z_j depend upon the k value of the axiom, in addition to the w_i's). This is an important and useful property. Different chunks of knowledge used in imprecise reasoning may be imprecise to different degrees. In using imprecise information, however, it is desirable to be able to specify how imprecise any specific chunk may be without jeopardizing the quality of solutions obtained. In practice, the tolerance for imprecision is typically a function of the role played by the specific item. That is, if the item is very important, the decision maker would like to obtain it with a high degree of precision; on the other hand, one can be fairly tolerant of low levels of precision in relatively unimportant items. The z-bound computation scheme described above directly supports this idea, and in the process also helps reduce the complexity of the heuristic search process, due to the resulting pruning.

Although the z bounds generated thus are useful and intuitively appealing, they are still quite conservative. This is due to the assumption made when computing the z bound for a specific node i, that all its siblings are nonfuzzy (i.e., have $\mu = 1$). This assumption is quite adequate for the z bound of the first sibling x_1 of a set $x_1, x_2, \ldots, x_n$ (where $x_1, \ldots, x_n$ together form the premises of a rule), since at that point all the available information is taken into account. However, once one or more of the x_i have been evaluated successfully, the z bounds for the remaining siblings could take the additional information available about the computed μ-values into account. This is not done in the above method. As a result, the effect of the z bounds becomes progressively weaker with each x_i evaluated, especially if some of the x_i have $\mu_i \ll 1$.

A more efficient bound-generation method is thus possible, and it is described next. In this procedure the z bound at each node is determined not just by the form of the rule and the z bound of the parent node, but also by the μ values of all sibling ndoes that have already been evaluated. Thus, once x_1 is evaluated, the value of z_2 is computed as

$$z_2 = 1 - \frac{1}{w_2^*} [(1 - z_0)^k - (w_1^*)^k (1 - \mu_1^*)^k]^{\frac{1}{k}}$$

with w_1^*, w_2^* defined as before and z_0 as the z bound of the parent node of x_1 and x_2.

Proof: As in the earlier proof, the smallest μ_2 allowed if $\mu_j = 1 \ \forall \ j > 2$ is such that

$$z_0 = 1 - [(w_1^*)^k (1 - \mu_1)^k + \cdots + (w_n^*)^k (1 - \mu_n^*)^k]^{\frac{1}{k}}$$

$$= 1 - [(w_1^*)^k (1 - \mu_1)^k + (w_2^*)^k (1 - \mu_2^*)^k]^{\frac{1}{k}}$$

so that $(w_2^*)^k (1 - \mu_2)^k = (1 - z_0)^k - (w_1^*)^k (1 - \mu_1^*)^k$, and the result follows.

Furthermore, as each leaf node l is evaluated, its tuples' μ values can be used to update the z bounds of its siblings. In general, if there are n siblings $x_1, \ldots, x_n$, and if these are evaluated in order, the z bound z_l of the lth sibling

x_l is given by

$$z_l = 1 - \frac{1}{w_l^*} \left[(1 - z_0)^k - \sum_{i=1}^{l-1} (w_i^*)^k (1 - \mu_i)^k \right]^{\frac{1}{k}}$$

This method of dynamically updating the z bounds obviously requires more computation than that for the static bound shown earlier, but it significantly improves the effectiveness of the bounding process. For instance, if $i < j$ and $w_i \gg w_j$, the static bound would yield $z_i \gg z_j$. Now assume that x_i is evaluated with a μ value that is only marginally acceptable (i.e., $\mu_i \simeq z_i$). Use of the static bound computation for z_j in this situation would likely result in a local solution for x_j that would be rejected once the parent node of i and j is evaluated. On the other hand, use of the dynamic bound formula would result in $z_j \simeq 1$, that is, a much tighter constraint on μ_j, even though it has a low weight w_j. Therefore much more efficient pruning of the search process for a solution for x_j would be achieved at the cost of some additional computational overhead. Some time earlier, we mentioned that humans have an ability to focus their reasoning and use knowledge that looks promising, without having to perform undue searches. The pruning that occurs above is an attempt to retain only promising lines of reasoning. Of course, there are additional facets of focused search that are ignored here.

4.3   Representing Uncertainty

The representation will now be extended to capture uncertainty in the environment. Recall that the decision rules in the knowledge base are modified Horn clauses, which allow unequally weighted premises and different levels of conjunction. The impact of these factors on the evaluation of uncertainty must be considered. First, if one premise is more significant than another in implying a conclusion, it would seem intuitively sound that the uncertainty in the conclusion should be more closely related to that in the more important premise. To see this, consider the following abstract rule (notationally, the uncertainty in a proposition x is denoted by π_x):

$$0.9 \ A_1 \ \wedge^\infty 0.1 A_2 \rightarrow^1 B$$

with $\pi_{A_1} = 1$ and $\pi_{A_2} = 0.4$. Then, assuming that A_1 and A_2 are independent and ignoring the weights, we would get $\pi_B = 0.4$. Given that A_1 is certain, and the predominant determinant of B, however, this seems an unreasonable estimate for π_B. Thus some method that allows unequally weighted terms in a conjunction should be used. In addition, the level of conjunction k also has to be considered, since this parameter defines the form of the conjunction in the premise of a rule.

Based on these considerations, the computation of the certainty level of a weighted conjunction of premises is performed as follows. If $\pi_1, \pi_2, \ldots, \pi_n$ are the levels of certainty in the individual premises, then the π value of the composite premise is given by

$$\pi_{(w_1 A_1 \wedge^k w_2 A_2 \cdots \wedge^k w_n A_n)} = \left[\prod_{r=1}^{n} \pi_r^{w_r} \right]^{[1/\Sigma_i w_i^k]^{\frac{1}{k}}}$$

which can also be expressed as

$$\pi_{(w_1 A_1 \wedge^k w_2 A_2 \cdots \wedge^k w_n A_n)} = \prod_{r=1}^{n} \pi_r^{w_r^*}$$

where $w_r^* = w_r/[\Sigma_i[w_i^k]]^{\frac{1}{k}} \, \forall r$ is the k-normalized weight of A_r in the relationship.

The π function just shown has some interesting properties. First, it is easy to see that the π value of a collection of premises is determined more by those A_i that have high *relative* weights. Since $0 \leq \pi$, $w_i^* \leq 1$, $\pi_i^{w_i^*} \geq \pi_i$, and as w_i^* decreases, $\pi_i^{w_i^*}$ approaches 1 for any π_i, thus progressively decreasing the impact of π_i on the certainty level for the conjunction. In the limit, when $w_i^* = 0$, then $\pi_i^{w_i^*} = 1$, causing the ith term to become totally inconsequential. On the other hand, if a particular term A_j has $w_j^* = 1$ and all other $w_i^* = 0$, then the uncertainty level of the conjunction becomes π_j, which again conforms to intuition.

It is also desirable that as k, the level of conjunction, varies, so should the uncertainty level in the relationship. To see this, consider the following conjunction:

$$R = (10)A \wedge^k (1)B$$

If $k = \infty$, then the conjunction is strict, suggesting that the uncertainty function should resemble the product form of a probabilistic conjunction as far as possible. As k decreases, however, the conjunction becomes progressively weaker, indicating that its certainty value should be correspondingly higher (in an extreme case, if the operator were a disjunction, then the certainty value would be the highest). It is easy to prove that the expression for computing the uncertainty of a conjunction is a monotonically nonincreasing function of k, $\forall k \geq 1$.

Once the certainty level of a conjunction of premises can be determined, that of the consequent literal in a decision rule has to be obtained from the implication and its associated strength. If an implication is a precise and certain one, then the certainty level of the consequent should be the same as that of the premise. The reason for this is that confidence in the implicand in a rule is limited by the confidence in its premises. In cases where the implication is itself uncertain, it is commonly characterized by a factor (we call this γ, with $0 \le \gamma \le 1$). The certainty level of the implicand inferred by a rule such as $A \to B$ is then given by $\pi_B = \gamma \cdot \pi_A$. We desire a more general propagation that takes into account the interaction we feel exists between fuzziness and uncertainty. As an example, consider the rule "If sales growth is high, then stock price is volatile," which can be represented as

$$\text{SALESGROWTH}(x, \text{high}) \to^\gamma \text{STOCK}(x, \text{volatile})$$

This rule may hold with different certainty levels for different ranges of μ values of the premise. For instance, when the sales growth is clearly high, the certainty of the stock price being volatile is greater than when the sales growth is only marginally high. Thus, $\mu_{\text{SALESGROWTH}(x, \text{high})}$ affects both $\mu_{\text{STOCK}(x, \text{volatile})}$ and $\pi_{\text{STOCK}(x, \text{volatile})}$.

Computation of the π value of a consequent should thus use a function that takes the interaction of fuzziness and uncertainty into account. A generalized form of such a function, which modifies the uncertainty in the consequent if the antecedent of an axiom is fuzzy, can be expressed as follows, for a rule of the form $A \to B$:

$$\pi_B = f(\pi_A, \mu_A, \gamma)$$

where γ is a normalized factor characterizing the uncertainty in the implication when no fuzziness is present. That is, when $\mu_A = 1$, then π_B is computed as $\pi_B = \gamma \cdot \pi_A$. The definition of a suitable form for $f(\pi_A, \mu_A, \gamma)$ is based on the consideration of several desirable characteristics:

(a) *When π and μ are related, π should be a monotonically nondecreasing function of μ.* This results from the usual interpretation of an implication as a positive statement; that is, the greater the extent to which a premise holds, the greater should be the certainty of the implicand being true. Violation of this property would suggest an inverse form of relationship between the premise and implicand, which is contradictory to the interpretation of implication.

(b) *The function f should allow situations where $\pi \ge \mu$.* Such situations can occur, since fuzziness and uncertainty have different sources, and although they interact, each can occur independent of the other. For instance, a statement may be very fuzzy (i.e., $\mu \ll 1$), even though it is certain ($\pi \simeq 1$).

(c) *The function f should allow situations where π and μ are not related.* That is, it should permit representation of relationships in which the certainty level of the implicand is not affected by any fuzziness in the premise. Such a situation would occur when the implication itself is certain, so that the only source of uncertainty is the premise.

Based on these desirable characteristics, we use the following formulation for propagating uncertainty through an imprecise implication:

$$\pi_B = [\gamma]^{\frac{1}{\mu_A}} \cdot \pi_A$$

In other words, $\pi_B = \gamma_{\text{eff}} \cdot \pi_A$, where $\gamma_{\text{eff}} = \gamma^{\frac{1}{\mu_A}}$ represents the imprecision in the implication itself. The choice of this function is based on several factors. First, it possesses all the above characteristics. Characteristic (a) follows from the nonnegativity of γ and μ and their range $(0, 1]$ of possible values. For (b), when $\mu_A = 1$ the above expression yields $\pi_B = \gamma \cdot \pi_A$, which is commonly used in AI systems. On the other hand, when $\mu < 1$, $\pi_B \leq \gamma \cdot \pi_A$, though, π_B may be greater than μ_B. Also, in situations where (c) is relevant, the independence of π and μ is achieved by setting $\gamma = 1$. In this instance, the uncertainty or fuzziness in the consequent is determined *solely* by that of its premises.

4.4   Reasoning with Uncertainty

The propagation is similar to that for fuzziness. Assume that, at some point in the reasoning process, literal B is substituted by a set of literals $A_1, A_2, \ldots., A_n$, using a rule of the form

$$A_1 \wedge^k A_2 \wedge^k \cdots \wedge^k A_n \rightarrow^\gamma B$$

i.e., a node B in the search tree is expanded to its children $A_1, A_2, \ldots, A_n$. The minimum acceptable level of uncertainty for each new node A_i can be computed using

$$\pi_{A_i}^0 = \left[\frac{\pi_B^0}{\gamma} \right]^{\frac{1}{w_i^*}}$$

where π_B^0 is the minimum acceptable uncertainty level of node B. The term on the right side of the expression is essentially the lowest value of π_{A_i} that would yield $\pi_B \geq \pi_B^0$, in the most optimistic situation (i.e., $\mu_{(A_1 \wedge^k \cdots \wedge^k A_n)} = 1 \ \forall j \neq i$). Note that the above is essentially a static method of propagation, though it is possible to have a more dynamic computation of such bounds. As each node A_i is evaluated, the boundary values for all its siblings can be updated as follows:

$$\pi_{A_j(\text{new})}^0 = \frac{\pi_{A_j}^0}{\pi_{A_i}^{w_i^*}}$$

Proof:

$$\pi_B = \gamma \, \frac{1}{\mu_{(w_1 A_1 \wedge^k \cdots \wedge^k w_n A_n)}} \cdot \pi_{A_1}^{w_1^*} \cdot \pi_{A_2}^{w_2^*} \cdots \pi_{A_n}^{w_j^*}$$

Assuming that $\mu_{(w_1 A_1 \wedge^k \cdots \wedge^k w_n A_n)} = 1$ and $\pi_{A_k} = 1 \; \forall k \neq i, j$,

$$\pi_B = \gamma \cdot \pi_{A_i}^{w_i^*} \cdot \pi_{A_j}^{w_j^*}$$

thus

$$\pi_{A_j(\text{new})}^0 = \left[\frac{\pi_B^0}{\gamma \cdot \pi_{A_i}^{w_i^*}} \right]^{\frac{1}{w_j^*}}$$

$$= \left[\frac{\pi_B^0}{\gamma} \right]^{\frac{1}{w_j^*}} \cdot \frac{1}{\pi_{A_i}^{\frac{w_i^*}{w_j^*}}}$$

and the result follows.

Even this more dynamic bound estimate is still conservative. The reason is that in computing them we have assumed that $\mu_{(w_1 A_1 \wedge^k \cdots \wedge^k w_n A_n)} = 1$. Since the propagation of fuzziness and uncertainty is done *in step*, however, as each node is evaluated the bound update procedure for its siblings can use both its π value and its μ value. Thus a modified bound-updating procedure, which generates tighter bounds, is as follows:

$$\pi_{A_j(\text{new})}^0 = \left[\frac{\pi_B^0}{\bar{\gamma}} \right]^{\frac{1}{w_j^*}} \cdot \frac{1}{\pi_{A_i}^{\frac{w_i^*}{w_j^*}}}$$

where

$$\bar{\gamma} = \gamma \, \frac{1}{1 - [\Sigma_{1 \leq i}(w_1^*)^k (1 - \mu_1)^k]^{\frac{1}{k}}}$$

In other words, γ is modified by considering the highest possible value that $\mu_{(w_1 A_1 \wedge^k \cdots \wedge^k w_n A_n)}$ can have, with the values of $\mu_{A_1}, \ldots, \mu_{A_i}$ that are already known (we are assuming, for simplicity and without loss of generality, that the siblings are evaluated in order). Using this method, once all the siblings are evaluated successfully, the parent literal B is ensured a certainty level $\pi_B \geq \pi_B^0$. Of course, dynamic bounds, while resulting in better pruning, also require more computational resources.

4.5   Reasoning Example Revisited

At this point we revisit the example to emphasize some of the characteristics of our methods. Each node had associated with it parameters (z_μ, z_π, μ, π) and (k, γ). The parameters z_μ and z_π are respectively, the minimum acceptable levels of fuzziness and uncertainty, obtained either from the user (or using default values, if necessary) or by propagation by any of the bound-propagation expressions derived earlier. The parameters μ and π are the actual values of the imprecision measures returned after evaluation during the reasoning process. Obviously, for a successful line of reasoning $\mu \geq z_\mu$ and $\pi \geq z_\pi$ at every node. The pair (k, γ) represents the level of conjunction and strength of implication in the decision rule that has the node as a consequent.

Several interesting observations can be made. First, the values generated for the z bounds of different premises are influenced by their relative weights. For instance, the bounds for CORRESPOND, with $w = 5$, are (0.49, 0.59), while those for ACTIVE, with $w = 1$, are (0.1, 0.18). Thus we are able to tolerate less precision in ACTIVE than in CORRESPOND, in accordance with the former's lower relative importance. The more important premises must be met with a higher level of precision than less important ones. A second characteristic is the effect of imprecise instances of evaluated nodes upon the z bounds of its remaining siblings. This is illustrated in the bounds of RECORD, which are (0.27, 0.48). If the preceding siblings DUE and CORRESPOND had precise solutions, the z bounds for RECORD would be (0.13, 0.42). In other words, if the initial premises are met with acceptable but not very high levels of precision, the remaining premises must be met with progressively higher levels of precision. In fact, these updated bounds can become ≥ 1, in which case the current search is fathomed. For instance, if CORRESPOND were evaluated with measures (0.5, 0.6), the nodes RECORD and ACTIVE would be immediately fathomed, since their minimum acceptable levels of precision become ≥ 1. On the other hand, if important premises are evaluated fairly precisely, the less-important premises become even less significant.

The example also demonstrates the interaction of μ and π at several points during reasoning. For instance, RECORD is inferred from two premises, MAXAGE and AVERAGE, which are both certain but fuzzy. As a result, the implicand RECORD is also fuzzy. This fuzziness also causes the π value of the implicand to be lowered to 0.85 from 0.9, which would be the case if μ_{RECORD} were 1 rather than 0.63. A similar effect is found in inferring CORRESPOND from its premises CONTACT and CREDIT-RATE. The certainty of the final conclusion, PURSUE, is also modified by the fuzziness in all the knowledge and data used.

Earlier on we stated that data accesses and data-transformation activity could be spawned from the reasoning process. The example clearly shows that such activity can be accommodated within the reasoning mechanism. For instance, many of the leaf nodes involve both types of activity. The evaluation of CREDIT-RATE requires access to data, as well as transformation into an aggregate measure of credit-worthiness. The same can be said of MAXAGE and AVERAGE. This ability is specially important in DSS environments.

The concepts and methods presented have been implemented in a prototype built around a theorem prover called HORNE (Allen et al., 1984). Further details of the prototype may be found in Basu and Dutta (1986) and Dutta and Basu (1986). In summary, sections 3 and 4 have presented some current approaches to reasoning with imprecision. The methods shown in section 4 have been developed specifically with the DSS environment in mind. The demands of this environment had significant effects on the choice of representation and manipulation techniques.

5. Further Issues in Reasoning

In view of the observation that reasoning constitutes a basic activity in decision making, we have devoted much of the past two sections to the development of representation and manipulation methods that would aid human reasoning activities in decision-making environments. In particular, the emphasis has been on capturing imprecision, characterized by fuzziness and uncertainty, in the reasoning environment. As noted earlier, the reason for this initial concern is that imprecision is pervasive in most human decision-making environments. Thus it is clear that any reasoning mechanism would do well to capture this facet of the environment. To aid humans in decision making, however, the reasoning facility of a DSS must be capable of capturing more than just imprecision in the environment. The remainder of this paper is devoted to exposing two additional theoretical issues in the support of human reasoning activities: the nonmonotonicity of human reasoning and humans' ability to learn from repeated interaction with the decision environment. Nonmonotonicity is especially important for the type of environment in which DSSs are used. The learning issue, apart from being of great theoretical interest, must be addressed, however crudely or simplistically, for practical reasons.

5.1   Nonmonotonic Reasoning

Consider the following instances of reasoning:

(a) Suppose that a person filing his taxes reports his year's wages as $30,000, and interest income of $400. What is his total taxable income for the year? The auditor concludes that it is $30,400. Subsequently, a check reveals that the person also had $4000 in dividend payments. The auditor then concludes that his taxable income for the year is $34,400, that he has understated his income by a substantial amount, and is thus a potential candidate for an audit.

(b) A department head has received an allocation from the dean, from which he allocates $25,000 for the salary of Prof. Getmoney. He proceeds, on this basis, to make allocations for the salaries of other faculty, staff, and various ancillary activities. A few weeks later, Prof. Getmoney is notified that his NSF proposal, submitted six months ago, has been funded. The amount covers part of his salary and includes overhead. The department head then alters the allocations in view of this extra source of funds.

(c) A production schedule is drawn up at a plant, assuming the availability of certain amounts of various resources (such as energy, labor, machines, raw materials) to meet production plans. During the course of execution of the schedule, unanticipated changes in resource conditions occur; say a machine goes down, or some raw material does not arrive on time. The schedule is modified so as to maintain feasibility and minimize the disruptions caused by such deviations from plan.

(d) At the end of the day, a person begins to drive along his usual route back home. Along the way he notices that the road is blocked off, due to an accident. He then chooses an alternate route for the remaining distance and returns home.

The reasoning in the preceeding examples, chosen to range from the instinctive (d) to consciously deliberation (c and b), have one thing in common. The conclusions drawn, decisions made, etc., are all possibly altered as a result of new evidence or events. This phenomenon is common, since we often do not have complete information (or it would be too much to process in any case), or there are events that are simply beyond our control. It is common to make assumptions in the absence of complete information. Reasoning then proceeds under certain assumptions; if and when these assumptions need to be modified, the conclusions are suitably modified too.

Take the simple case in (a). The first conclusion, that the total income is $30,400, is a plausible one. It is good, but not necessarily correct, since alternate income sources may have been left out. Subsequent evidence does indeed cause this plausible inference to be revised. As it happens, there is no way to get such a plausible inference out of classical proof procedures. In other words, if the formal system first concludes that total income is $30,400, that conclusion is undoable, even with the addition of a new fact such as "Dividend income is $4000." With this additional fact it is possible to arrive at either conclusion: "Income is $30,400," or "Income is $34,400," which is not entirely helpful.

A logic in which a conclusion stands, no matter what new axioms are added, is called *monotonic*. Classical formal systems, for example resolution theorem-proving (Robinson, 1965), are all monotonic. The word "resolution" has come to be associated with general-purpose types of theorem provers that use very little domain-dependent information. It has also connoted the use of clauses and refutation proofs. There are nonresolution theorem-proving techniques also (Bledsoe, 1978) that are designed to develop proofs in a goal-directed manner that is easy for humans to understand. Unlike resolution methods, nonresolution methods use many proof rules and often include domain-specific information to speed up parts of the proof. Any proof that can be derived by such natural deduction can also be obtained by resolution, given enough time. The advantage of the former is that it produces proofs that are easier to understand.

Nonmonotonicity is of special relevance in semistructured environments. There, a substantial part of decision making consists of common-sense and heuristic reasoning, and the process often starts with very incomplete information. The need to make assumptions, at least initially, is acute in such environments. Also, the decision-making process usually spans a certain amount of time, within which additional information often becomes available. This may cause some initial assumptions to be confirmed and others to modified or discarded. There just does not seem to be any way to avoid nonmonotonicity in such environments. Thus mechanized reasoning methods should admit such nonmonotonic behavior. As a general issue in reasoning, nonmonotonicity has attracted the attention of some researchers. We briefly review two proposed techniques, reasoning by default and reasoning by circumscription.

5.1.1 Reasoning by Default

Defaults are commonly used by humans to express generalities, to which exceptions may be acknowledged without catastrophe. In a job shop, for instance, a set of jobs may be scheduled on the assumption that two out of three turret lathes will always be operative at any time. Later on, if two lathes go down, changes can be made to the schedule. A person on trial is "innocent until proven guilty." A travel agent may book the cheapest flight until restrictions placed by the customer cause that to change. Defaults arise commonly in many AI techniques.

A well-known representation scheme for knowledge uses *frames* (Minsky, 1975; Roberts and Goldstein, 1977, Bobrow and Winograd, 1977; Fahlman, 1979). A frame may be considered to be a stereotype in a particular domain. It consists of slots which, among other things, can hold default values. A frame used to reason about motor vehicles may have a default value of four in the slot "number of wheels." Of course, this may change if it is later found that we are talking about a motor home. Defaults also arise in planning systems such as STRIPS (Fikes and Nilsson, 1971), where the only changes to the state of the world after the application of an operator are those listed explicitly in the operator. An example of such an operator in the real world could be that of turning up the thermostat in a room. The resulting state change could be stated to be an increase in room temperature. We do not usually find it necessary to add that the furniture in the room will remain in the same place, that the color of the walls will not change, and so on. In other words, if an alteration is not mentioned among the effects of an operator, we assume that change does not occur. Of course, that assumption may not be altogether accurate. For instance, we may notice that an additional effect of turning up the thermostat is to substantially reduce room humidity.

Defaults also implicitly enter into many knowledge representation systems through the *closed world assumption* (CWA). The CWA is that all relationships not stated to hold do not hold. This assumption is often made in inheriting properties across frames, for instance. The same assumption has also been made in a deductive data base for query evaluation (Reiter, 1978). Specifically, if no proof of a positive ground literal exists, then the negation of the literal is assumed true. Two major types of detailed formalization of defaults have been proposed. They are Reiter's logic of defaults (Reiter, 1980) and McDermott and Doyle's (1980) nonmonotonic logics. The interpretation of Default A in both logics is roughly: "A is provable unless and until A can be disproved." The theoretical problem addressed by these nonmonotonic logics is that of providing good semantics for defaults, that allow a single set of axioms and defaults to have several coherent interpretations.

In his logic of defaults, Reiter formalizes defaults by adding *default inference rules* to an ordinary logic of statements and inference rules. Such a rule is of the form "If P, and it is consistent to assume Q, then infer R," written $P:Q/R$. P, Q and R are ordinary formulas. Given condition P, a default allows the inference of R, providing that Q is not disprovable. Therefore the simplest default, "Assume A if it cannot be disproved," is written as A/A: that is, P is empty and $Q = R = A$. McDermott and Doyle state defaults as modal formulas, using the modal operator "not disprovable." The default inference rule above could be stated as $P \wedge$ not disprovable $Q \rightarrow R$. Each of these approaches has concentrated on individual inference steps, or on the set of beliefs immediately preceding and following an inference step. There has been relatively less work devoted to studying the evolution of such reasoning processes in the large. Fruitful formulations of nondeductive reasoning techniques have yet to be developed. Some beginnings have been made in Doyle (1980) and Weyrausch (1980).

5.1.2 Circumscription

McCarthy (1980) states that "circumscription is a rule of conjecture that can be used by a person or program for 'jumping to conclusions.' Namely, the objects that can be shown to have a certain property P by reasoning from certain facts A are all the objects that satisfy P." Circumscription is a form of nonmonotonic reasoning augmenting ordinary first-order logic. To circumscribe a set of axioms A with respect to a predicate P that appears in them, one constructs a sentence schema stating that the only objects satisfying P are those whose doing so follows from A. All statements following from that sentence schema via ordinary deductive rules of inference are said to be reached by circumscriptive inference with respect to P and the original axioms A. It is, of course, possible to circumscribe several predicates jointly. The most direct way of using circumscription in AI is in a heuristic reasoning program that represents much of what it believes by sentences of logic. When it wants to perform an action that might be prevented by something, it circumscribes the preventing predicate in a sentence A representing the information being taken into account. Domain-dependent heuristics are needed to make good circumscriptions and to later withdraw them. A simple example of circumscription follows.

Suppose the only Japanese sports car that I know of is a Datsun 300ZX. If someone tells me that John bought a new Japanese sports car, I might, by circumscription, conclude that it is a 300ZX. Of course, when I learn that Toyota has recently produced a sports car called the MR2, I can no longer make that conclusion. More formally, the collection of initial facts A is the axiom JSports (300ZX). Circumscription of the predicate JSports in the set of axioms (the initial collection could contain more axioms that contain the same predicate) results in the axiom schema

$$\phi(300ZX) \wedge \forall x (\phi(x) \rightarrow JSports(x)) \rightarrow \forall x (JSports(x) \rightarrow \phi(x))$$

If we now substitute $x = 300ZX$ into this schema, we get

$$300ZX = 300ZX \wedge \forall x (x = 300ZX \rightarrow JSports(x)) \rightarrow \forall x$$
$$\times (JSports(x) \rightarrow x = 300ZX)$$

which can be simplified to $.\forall x (JSports(x) \rightarrow x = 300ZX)$. This formula can be matched with any Japanese sports car to yield 300ZX as the answer. If we add the additional axiom JSports(MR2), however, we can only reach the less specific conclusion

$$\forall x (JSports(x) \rightarrow x = 300ZX \vee x = MR2),$$

showing the nonmonotonic nature of circumscription.

We conclude this topic by repeating the observation that reasoning mechanisms designed to support human decision-making activities should admit nonmonotonicity. While the study of individual proof steps provides good foundations, considerable study remains to be done on more complex ways of performing nondeductive inferencing, and on how humans maintain their belief systems in light of such nonmonotonicity.

5.2   Learning

Learning is a very general term used to denote the way in which people and computers increase their knowledge and skills. Understanding the learning process has been of interest to AI researchers and philosophers for a very long time. One of the reasons for this interest, of course, is to understand the process itself. The other reason is that it may provide us with mechanisms to help computers learn. Our interest in learning is somewhat more limited in scope. Any DSS that purports to aid the reasoning activities of the decision-makers can benefit from learning. It is clear, even from casual observation, that managers make considerable use of domain-specific knowledge in their decision making. There is a considerable learning phenomenon, both formal and informal, associated with acquiring and using such knolwedge. Recall an earlier remark that decision making in semistructured or unstructured environments often involves the use of fragmented knowledge. Such frag-mented knowledge was represented in our knowledge base as a collection of Horn clauses. The generation of this knowledge base to be used for reasoning is itself a formidable problem. Currently, there is no provision in our prototype for any kind of learning other than explicitly entering new knowledge in the form of additional rules. Ideally, the knowledge base would have some mechanism to learn from the many decision problems it is used to solve. It may improve its performance by applying new reasoning methods, by acquiring new rules on its own, or by improving existing methods and knowledge to make them faster, more accurate, or more robust. Thus the ability to learn will play an important role over the life cycle of a DSS. We will now review some of the conceptual modes of learning that have been identified. Attempts at operationalizing some of them will be mentioned in passing.

5.2.1   Modes of Learning

A learning element, after all, learns through interaction with its environ-ment. Repeated interaction with the environment should lead to greater and greater insights into performance of the related tasks, if any learning has occurred; at least, that is one of the marks of intelligent human behaivor. The level and quality of information provided by the environment is an important factor in the learning process. High-level information is usually more domain-independent, thus being applicable to a wider range of problems, but details have to be filled out during their use. Low-level information is more domain-specific, and is more directly useful in solving a particular problem. The system must be capable, however, of abstracting out inconsequential details if it is to learn something from this instance that will also be applicable in additional situations. "The task of learning can be viewed as the task of bridging the gap between the level at which information is provided by the environment and the level at which the performance element can use it to carry out its function" (Cohen and Fiegenbaum, 1982, page 328). In a trial-and-error process, the system forms hypotheses about how to bridge the gap and revises these hypotheses according to feedback received from the environment. Three major learning modes will be discussed below.

Learning by Rote. Here the environment provides information more or less at the level the learning element needs to perform its tasks. The element must simply remember the information for future use. The knowledge representation scheme we have presented in section 5 may be considered to learn by rote. Rules in the knowledge base must be explicitly altered, deleted, or added by some external agent. Some would not consider this mode to be learning at all. Nevertheless, it is a widespread mode of "learning" among many AI programs. Several expert systems such as MYCIN (Shortliffe, 1974), DENDRAL (Lindsay et al., 1980), or PROSPECTOR (Duda et al., 1978) must have their knowledge explicitly inserted by an external agent (knowledge-acquisition programs have been written for some of them; see following sections), and thus may be considered to learn by rote. An early program for playing checkers (Samuel, 1959, 1967) was able to improve its preformance by memorizing every board position that it evaluated, using minmax search with limited lookahead. These memorized positions were used to improve the speed and depth of search during subsequent games. The program was trained and tested rather extensively, by playing both against itself and against humans. It became capable of playing a good opening game and end game, but midgame performance did not greatly improve with rote learning.

Overall, these experiments indicated that significant and measurable learning can occur from rote learning alone. The obvious limitations are in terms of space and retrieval times. Samuel estimated that his program would have to store about one million positions to approximate a masters level of play. In general, the primary gain from rote learning is in speed. Memorized knowledge can be used to avoid wasting resources on something that had been computed before. Instead, these stored results can be used to further sharpen reasoning or problem-solving abilities. Humans exhibit this pattern continually. We do not derive every result from first principles. Partial results are often memorized after they have been proved once. Thereafter, they are used without proof. It is simply more expedient to do so in terms of speed. Im most practical decision-making environments that we would be interested in, the space requirements could very easily become prohibitive for rote learning to be too effective, yet it should not be discarded as a way of imparting already-distilled knowledge to the learning element, which can then use it for further processing.

Learning from General Advice. This mode of learning attempts to get from the general to the specific. Advice is received in rather general form from the environment and must then be made more specific before it can be put to actual use. The steps in advice-taking have been described by Hayes–Roth, Klahr, and Mostow (Cohen and Fiegenbaum, 1982, page 345) as:

  (a) request — request advice from expert
  (b) interpret — assimilate into internal representation
  (c) integrate — integrate into knowledge base
  (d) evaluate — evaluate resulting actions of performing agent

Many researchers, specially those in the area of knowledge-based expert systems, have opted for a semiautomated approach to advice taking, where human experts form an essential part of the learning process. Tools have been built to help the human expert in carrying out these five steps. Example systems include EMYCIN and TERESIAS (Davies and Lenat, 1982). We will briefly describe the functioning of TERESIAS (T henceforth) to impart some flavor of the nature of this kind of advice taking.

T may be viewed as an advice-taking front end for MYCIN, although its applicability ranges beyond MYCIN. It is important to remember that T does not attempt to derive new knowledge on its own. Instead, it helps the human expert to modify the knowledge base. The expert runs the target program and invokes T when he notices an error. An error may simply be a response that the expert would not have made, or a line of reasoning that looks inappropriate. Transfer of expertise begins when T is called in. T assists in finding the source of error by *explaining* the target program's line of reasoning. The latter simply consists of tracing back the reasoning steps until the faulty rule is isolated or a rule is found to be missing. T is automatically able to generate "rule models," i.e., models of the nature of different classes of rules in the target program. These "templates" help in adding rules or modifying existing rules when the causes of errors have been found by the human. While programs such as T can be said to be learning programs, it is clear that we are very far away from producing programs that actually self-learn from experience.

Learning from Examples or Generalization. Here the environment provides very detailed advice, and the performing program has to generalize suitably to be able to fruitfully use that knowledge. This is one of the better-understood modes of learning. Humans have used this mode quite effectively, and it goes by the name "learning from experience." More specifically, the process of learning from examples has been described as that of judiciously selecting some training examples from a space of possible examples, so as to guide a search for general rules (Simon and Lea, 1974). Again, a brief description of a representative system will be now be given.

META-DENDRAL (MD henceforth) (Mitchell, 1978; Lindsay et al., 1980) addressed the problem of automatically inferring the rules of mass spectrometry from examples of molecular structures that had been properly analyzed by humans. While the previous mode was dominated by an interactive knowledge transfer, MD works in a more automated mode. A chemical analyst can infer the molecular structure of a chemical sample from the mass spectrum. (The molecules are bombarded by electrons, which in turn cause the molecule to break into many charged fragments. A histogram of the number of fragments plotted against their charge-to-mass ratio is the mass spectrum.) The input to MD consists of the structure of each of a set of related molecules, their spectral data points, and some theory (domain-specific) that will constrain the generation of rules. As a first step, MD attempts to explain each peak in its spectrum by finding one or more fragmentation processes that would account for the peak. The number of such fragmentation rules so generated is limited by the above-mentioned theory. At the second step, MD generates rules that are more general than the ones obtained from the previous step. It starts with rules that are overly general and then gradually places more and more constraints on them. The above process is not perfect, and it is necessary as a last step to "clean up" the output from phase two. Redundant rules are eliminated, rules may be altered slightly to handle exceptions, etc. MD has been successful at duplicating known fragmentation rules for two classes of molecules, and it discovered new rules for some others.

While these modes of learning are by no means the only ones, they at least provide a basis for operationalizing the process. While AI may have as one of its goals the complete emulation of human learning, the more immediate need in the area of Decision support is to provide DSSs with the ability to improve performance through some form of learning, even though it may not equal human capabilities. This is a more modest and perhaps more realistic goal.

6. Concluding Remarks

This paper has sought to raise the issue of reasoning as central to decision-making by humans. As such, it implies that the support of human reasoning activities should be a central research issue in decision support. It would perhaps be inaccurate to say that reasoning issues have been ignored altogether in the DSS literature. Most reasoning issues appear to have been disguised as problems of control. The basis for that remark follows. The activities performed by a decision support system are, conceptually, computational in nature. In other words, when a human agent engages the help of a DSS, the DSS is essentially performing a series of computations. The control problem in any computational activity is that of deciding which computation should be done next. For instance, in an application program written in COBOL, the control is embodied in the various branching, looping, and other control statements of the language. Reverting to the schematic of a DSS that was shown in Figure 1, the elementary operations that are performed therein consist of data access and data transformations. This naturally begs the question, "How do we know which data accesses or data transformations to perform next?" Put another way, how do we synthesize a sequence of elementary operations that will, in any particular instance, help the human make a decision for which he wants support? We contend that reasoning provides an answer to that question. Furthermore, human reasoning is complex enough to warrant its explicit support. Traditional DSS literature emphasizes that the DSS should facilitate *user control* of activities in the data and model components. A sample excerpt (Sprague and Carlson, 1982, pages 262, 263) follows: "The model base and its management system must be integrated with the dialog directly, to give the user direct control over the operation, manipulation, and use of models."

Sentiments like this reflect an opinion that direct human control of the solution process can make up for deficiencies in the algorithmic part being performed by the machine. Reasoning constitutes an inseparable and major part of "human control" and is clearly a nontrivial activity. In the past, it may have been prudent to delegate only algorithmic activity to a computer, because there were practically no computational models of human reasoning. In the absence of such computational models, it impossible to support reasoning activities in a mechanized way. While we definitely cannot say that a comprehensive computational model of human reasoning now exists, it is felt that adequate beginnings have been made toward that end to warrant considering the explicit support of reasoning as a fundamental capability of future decision support systems.

REFERENCES

Allen, J. F., Guilano, M., and Frisch, A. M. (1984). The Horne reasoning system. TR 126, Dept. of Computer Science, University of Rochester, Rochester, N.Y.

Atre, S. (1980). "Data Base: Structured Techniques for Design, Performance and Management." Wiley, New York.

Barnett, J. A. (1981). Computational methods for a mathematical theory of evidence. *7th Internat. Joint Conf. Artif. Intell.* 868–875.

Barr, A., and Fiegenbaum, E. A. (1982a). "The Handbook of Artificial Intelligence," Vol. 1. Kaufmann, Los Altos, California.

Barr, A., and Fiegenbaum, E. A. (1982b). "The Handbook of Artificial Intelligence," Vol. 2. Kaufmann, Los Altos, California.

Basu, A., and Dutta, A. (1986). Computer based support of reasoning activities for decision support in the presence of fuzzy knowledge. To appear in *Decis. Support Syst.*

Bennet, J. S., Creary, L. A., Englemore, R. M., and Melosh, R. E. (1978). SACON: A knowledge based consultant in structural analysis. Heuristic Programming Project Report No. HPP-78-23, Computer Science Department, Stanford University. Stanford, Calif.

Blanning, R. (1985). A relational framework for join implementation in model management systems. *Decis. Support Syst.* **1** (1), 69–82.

Bledsoe, W. W. (1978). Non-resolution theorem proving. *Artif. Intell.* **9** (1), 1–35.

Bobrow, D. G., and Winograd, T. (1977). An overview of KRL, a knowledge representation language. *Cognit. Sci.* **1** (1), 3–46.

Bonczek, R., Holsapple, C. W., and Whinston, A. (1981). A generalized decision support system using predicate calculus and network database management. *Oper. Res.* **29** (2), 263–281.

Bonczek, R., Holsapple, C. W., and Whinston, A. (1984). Developments in decision support systems. Advances in Computers **23**, Academic Press, Orlando, 141–175.

Bradley, J. (1982). "File and Database Techniques." Holt, Rinehart, New York.

Chang, C. L., and Lee, R. C. (1973). "Symbolic Logic and Mechanical Theorem Proving." Academic, New York.

Chamberlin, D. D., Gray, J. N., Griffiths, P. P., Traiger, I. L., and Wade, B. (1976). SEQUEL 2: A unified approach to data definition, manipulation and control, *IBM J. Res. Dev.*, Nov. 1976, 560–575.

Charniak, E., and McDermott, D. (1985). "Introduction to Artificial Intelligence." Addison–Wesley, Reading, Massachusetts.

Cloksin, W. F., and Mellish, C. S. (1981). "Programming in PROLOG." Springer Verlag, New York.

Codd, E. F. (1972). Relational completeness of database sublanguages. In "Database Systems," R. Rustin, ed.. Prentice–Hall, Englewood Cliffs, N.J., pages 65–98.

Cohen, P., Fiegenbaum, E. A. (1982). "The Handbook of Artificial Intelligence," Vol. 3. Kaufmann, Los Altos, California.

Davies, R., and Lenat, D. (1982). "Knowledge Based Systems in Artificial Intelligence." McGraw–Hill, New York.

Davis, Gordon B., and Olson, M. (1985). "Management Information systems: Conceptual Foundations, Structure and Development." McGraw–Hill, New York.

Date, C. J. (1986). "Introduction to Database systems," 4th ed., Vol. 1. Addison–Wesley, Reading, Massachusetts.

Dolk, D., Konsynski, B. (1984). Knowledge representation for model management systems. *IEEE Trans. Software Eng.* **SE-10** (6), 619–627.

Doyle, J. (1980). A truth maintainence system. *Artif. Intell.* **12**, 231–272.

Duda, R., Hart, P., and Nilsson, N. (1976). Subjective Bayesian methods for rule based inference systems. *Proc. Nat. Computer Conf.*, AFIPS, **45**, 1075–1082.

Duda, R. O., Gaschnig, J., Hart, P. E., Konolige, K., Reboh, R., Barrett, P., and Slocum, J. (1978). "Development of the PROSPECTOR consultation system for mineral exploration." Final Report, SRI Projects 5821 and 6415, SRI International, Menlo Park, California.

Duda, R., Gaschnig, J., and Hart, P. E. (1979). Model design in the prospector consultation system for mineral exploration. In "Expert Systems in the Microelectronics Age," D. Michie, ed. Edinburg University Press, pages 334–348.

Dutta, A. (1985). Reasoning with imprecise knowledge in expert systems. *Inf. Sci.* **37** (1), 3–24.

Dutta, A., and Basu, A. (1984). An artificial intelligence approach to model management in decision support systems. *IEEE Computer*, **17** (9), 88–97.

Dutta, A., and Basu, A. (1986). Computer based support of reasoning in the presence of fuzziness and uncertainty. To appear in *Decis. Support Syst.*

Execucom Corp. (1982). "IFPS User's Manual." Execucom, Austin, Texas.

Fahlman, S. E. (1979). "NETL: A System for Representing and Using Real-World Knowledge." MIT Press, Cambridge, Mass.

Feller, W. (1971). "An Introduction to Probability Theory and Its Applications." Wiley, New York.

Fikes, R. E., and Nilsson, N. J. (1971). STRIPS: A new approach to the application of theorem proving to problem solving. *Artif. Intell.* **2**, 189–208.

Gallaire, H., and Minker, J. (1978). "Logic and Databases." Plenum, New York.

Garvey, T. D., Garvey T. D, Lowrance J. D., and Fischler, M. A., (1981). An inference technique for integrating knowledge from disparate sources. *Proc. IJCAI 7*, 319–325.

Green, C. (1969). Theorem proving by resolution as a basis for question answering systems. In "Machine Intelligence," Vol. 4, B. Meltzer and D. Michie, eds. American Elsevier, New York, pages 183–208.

Gupta, M. M., and Sanchez, A., eds. (1982). "Approximate Reasoning in Decision Analysis." North–Holland, Amsterdam.

Haac, S. (1977). Do we need fuzzy logic. Tech. Report, Dept. of Philosophy, University of Warwick,

Hayes–Roth, F., Waterman, D. A., Lenat, D. B., eds., (1983). "Building Expert Systems." Addison–Wesley, Reading, Mass.

Ishizuka, M., Fu, K. S., and Yao, J. T. P. (1981). Inexact inference for rule based damage assessment of existing structures. *Proc. IJCAI 7*, 837–842.

Kandel, A. (1982). "Fuzzy Techniques in Pattern Recognition." Wiley, New York.

Kim, W. (1979). Relational database systems. *ACM Comput. Surv.* **11** (3), 185–212.

Kowalski, R. A., and van Emden, M. (1976). The semantics of predicate logic as a programming language. *J. ACM* **23**, 733–742.

Lindsay, R., Buchanan, B. G., Feigenbaum, E. A., and Lederberg, J. (1980). "DENDRAL." McGraw–Hill, New York.

McCarthy, J. (1980). Circumscription—A form of non-monotonic reasoning. *Artif. Intell.* **13**, 27–39.

McDermott, D., and Doyle, J. (1980). Non-monotonic logic I. *Artif. Intell.* **13**, 41–72.

Minsky, M. (1975). A framework for representing knowledge. In "The Psychology of Computer Vision," P. H. Winston, ed. McGraw–Hill, New York, pages 211–277.

Mitchell, T. M. (1978). Version spaces: An approach to concept learning. Rep. No. CS-78-711, Computer Science Department, Stanford University.

Newell, A., and Simon, H. A. (1972). "Human Problem Solving." Prentice–Hall, Englewood Cliffs, N.J.

Nilsson, N J. (1980). "Principles of Artificial Intelligence." Tioga, Palo Alto, Calif.

Pan, S. S., Pick, R., and Whinston, A. (1984). A formal approach to decision support. In "Management and Office Information Systems," S. K. Chang, ed Plenum, New York, pages 91–118.

Pearl, Judea (1982). Reverend Bayes on inference engines: A distributed hierarchical approach. *Proc. AAAI 2*, 133–136.

Quilan, J. R. (1982). INFERNO: A cautious approach to uncertain inference. Technical Note N-1898-RC, Rand Corp., Santa Monica, Calif.

Reiter, J. E. (1981). AL/X: An inference system for probabilistic reasoning. M. S. Thesis, Computer Science Department, University of Illinois, Urbana-Champaign.

Reiter, R. (1978). On closed world databases. In "Logic and Databases," H. Gallaire and J. Minker, eds. Plenum, New York, pages 55–76.

Reiter, R. (1980). A logic for default reasoning. *Artif. Intell.* **13**, 81–132.

Roberts, B. R., and Goldstein, Ira (1977). The FRL primer. Report AIM-408, Artificial Intelligence Laboratory, MIT, Cambridge, Mass.

Robinson, J. A. (1965). A machine-oriented logic based on the resolution principle. *J. ACM* **12**, 23–41.

Samuel, A. L. (1959). Some studies in machine learning using the game of checkers. *IBM J. Res. Dev.* **3,** 210–229.

Samuel, A. L. (1967). Some studies in machine learning using the game of checkers II — Recent progress. *IBM J. Res. Dev.* **11,** 601–617.

Shapiro, E. Y. (1981). Logic programs with uncertainties: A tool for implementing rule-based systems. *Proc. IJCAI,* 529–532.

Shortliffe, E. H. (1974). "MYCIN: Computer Based Medical Consultations." Elsevier, New York.

Simon, H. A. (1947). "Administrative Behaviour." Macmillan, New York.

Simon, H. A. (1960). "The New Science of Management Decision." Harper and Brothers, New York.

Simon, H. A., and Lea, G. (1974). Problem solving and rule induction: A unified view. In "Knowledge and Cognition," (L. Gregg, ed.) Erlbaum, Hillsdale N. J., pages 105–127.

Simon, H. A. (1982). "The Sciences of the Artificial." MIT Press, Cambridge, Massachesetts.

Sprague, R. H., and Carlson, E. D. (1982). "Building Effective Decision Support Systems." Prentice–Hall, Englewoods Cliffs, N. J.

Thierauf, R. J. (1982). "Decision Support Systems for Effective Planning and Control." Prentice–Hall, Englewood Cliffs, N. J.

Ullman, J. D. (1980). "Principles of Data Base Systems." Computer Science Press, Potomac, Maryland.

van Melle, W. (1980). *A domain independent system that aids in constructing consultation programs.* Rep. No. STAN-CS-80-820, Computer Science Dept, Stanford University. Stanford, Calif.

van Emden, M. H. (1977). Programming with resolution logic. In "Machine Intelligence," Vol. 8, D. Michie, ed. Wiley, New York, pages 266–299.

Weiss, S. M., Kulikowski, C. A., and Safir, A. (1978). A model based method for computer aided medical decision making. *Artif. Intell.* **11,** 145–172.

Weyrausch, R. (1980). Prolegomena to a mechanized formal theory of reasoning. *Artif. Intell.* **13,** 133–170.

Wiederhold, G. (1977), "Data Base Design." McGraw–Hall, New York.

Zadeh, L. A. (1965). Fuzzy sets. *Inf. Control* **8,** 338–353.

Zadeh, L. A. (1968). Probability measures of fuzzy events. *J. Math. Analy. Appl.* **23,** 421–427.

Zadeh, L. A. (1979). A theory of approximate reasoning. In "Machine Intelligence," Vol. 9, J. E. Hayes, D. Michie, and L. I. Mikulich, eds. Wiley, New York, 149–194.

Zmud, Robert W. (1983). "Information Systems in Organizations." Scott, Foresman and Company, Palo Alto, Calif.

Unary Processing

W. J. POPPELBAUM
A. DOLLAS
J. B. GLICKMAN
C. O'TOOLE

Information Engineering Laboratory
Department of Computer Science
University of Illinois
Urbana, Illinois

ADVANCES IN COMPUTERS, VOL. 26

1. Introduction

Weighted binary representation schemes have dominated the world of computers for a good reason: If bistable elements are used for computation and storage, the most economical representation is *weighted binary*. Over the years, there has been a substantial effort in the area of *unary* machines, which do not adhere to this representation. Although these machines are obviously handicapped in terms of compactness, they make up for it in a multitude of ways, which may include fault tolerance, simplicity in the design, and low cost. Unary machines can be probabilistic or deterministic, serial or parallel, averaging or nonaveraging, synchronous or asynchronous—each design has its pros and cons.

The outright dismissal of unary methods as "wasteful" can be challenged by the general argument of thermodynamical nature. Indeed, information processing, in a very qualitative way, obeys the laws of thermodynamics. The first law applies as follows: The overall system capacity is preserved and is in direct proportion to the number of components that are used. Architectural aspects of computer design are more related to the adaptability of a design to a certain class of problems rather than to making a design universally good or bad. The second law of thermodynamics is even more evident in information science: The results of a computation inevitably contain no more information (even though it is more useful information) than the original data; thus, the informational entropy of a system increases.

It is well known that every digital computer can be made out of NAND gates exclusively, each gate having the same cost and speed. Then, the ideal goal of the computer designer is to produce a machine in which all the gates are used all of the time in order to perform nonredundant calculations. Alas, one cannot even come close to such an ideal goal, and the real-life goals are reduced to getting good performance for the cost. This means that to quantify this rather ambiguous criterion, we must look to machines that can perform similar tasks. Therefore, computer architectures should be discussed within the scope of their intended applications. Of great significance is to know when a unary representation is desirable and why!

Thus far, unary processing has been discussed in an abstract way. In more concrete terms, *unary information representation is any representation in which all digits have the same weight.* Consider the following as a historical example of very early unary calculations: If we take each finger of the human hand with equal weight, we will have a radix 10 unary numbering scheme for every person. This very reason is the cause for the prevalence of the decimal system in our lives! There is a direct translation of such a coding scheme to digital computing. If binary elements are used for the coding of the information, then the binary value itself denotes a value, rather than a coefficient to a power of 2.

Such a scheme may exist in the time domain, or in the space domain. In the time domain, we may have one wire that has 0 and 1 pulses. Then, this pulse train may be used for processing, where an n-time-slot window represents $\frac{1}{n}$ information resolution (Poppelbaum *et al.*, 1967). In the space domain, we may have n wires, each with a binary value, for the same precision of calculation (i.e., n) in one time slot (Poppelbaum, 1968a, 1972, 1976). One can see that there is a linear tradeoff between time and space calculations (Poppelbaum, 1979). The aforementioned scheme does not preclude higher precision. Indeed, weighted unary may be used in the context of a pulsestream of n pulses of weight 1, followed by n pulses of weight n (overall resolution $\frac{1}{n^2}$). The position of the pulses in the pulse train may also convey useful information. The two most obvious schemes are a uniform distribution of 0 and 1 values or a sequence of one value (say, 1) followed by a sequence of the other value.

This general discussion of unary representation itself reveals to the reader the different ways of processing the information, as well as how both deterministic and probabilistic processing can be performed (Mars and Poppelbaum, 1981). One aspect that we shall not discuss here is how multivalued logic can be used for unary processing. Even though there is a direct correspondence of the number of states to the number of time slots, or the number of wires, the processing itself is different. Space limitations do not allow us to extend the scope to such forms of processing.

2. Counters, Calculators, Computers: Description of Historical Unary Methods

2.1 Ancient Times through the Middle Ages

As we mentioned in the introduction, finger counting is the most ancient unary processing method. Since that time, there has been an enormous evolution in counting, number representation, and arithmetic (Gittleman, 1975; Zepf, 1906). Finger counting led to the first arithmetic methods, in the form of the production of notches of equal weight. The example in Fig. 1 shows the representation of numbers in ancient Egypt, with the number 659

Fig. 1.   Representation of 659 in ancient Egypt.

as an example. The available symbols represented the different orders of magnitude, whereas the *number* of units of a certain weight denoted the value, so it was a unary representation scheme with radix 10. Arithmetic then was simple, because 10 units of one order were replaced by one unit of the next order. Already by the time of the Babylonians there was more practical number representation, in this case of radix 60. This led to higher sophistication in notation and arithmetic, which not only went past unary to other forms of representation but eventually yielded fairly complex forms of scientific notation, with Archimedes inventing a form of scientific notation.

The abacus is a simple unary calculator (Gittleman, 1975). This remarkably simple, yet elegant and powerful device has been used in the Orient as well as the Occident since ancient times, and is still in use in many parts of the world. In its simplest form, the abacus has two sections, each with a number (depending on the desired precision) of columns with beads that can slide. One section is used as a register with the dividing point of the beads giving the sum in unary form, and the other section can be used to store carry digits. The most widely used abacus, the Chinese abacus, actually uses a different arrangement, with one section of five beads of weight 1 and the other section of two beads of weight 5 for each order of magnitude. This more efficient arrangement allows for greater compactness plus the capability of holding carries for longer (due to the redundancy of the representation).

Time measurement has been a major task for engineers throughout the ages, with the first methods being analog (hour glass, rate of burning of candles, etc.). For the discrete measurement of time, all clocks are fundamentally unary counters tied to a device creating standardized time intervals. These intervals were first produced by an escapement tied to periodically self-emptying tumblers. Su-Sung constructed a periodically driven water clock in China in 1088 (Needham, 1959).

2.2 Middle Ages to the Twentieth Century

In the evolution of time measurement, a swinging string-plus-dumbell contraption called a *folliot* was used by Pierre Pipelot in Paris in around 1300. A steel ball rolling down an inclined plane was used by Christopher Margrave in Prague in 1595. Around 1656, Christian Huyghens advocated the pendulum as a timekeeper and the pendulum became standard for many years. The modern quartz clock uses a pendulum in the form of a vibrating quartz crystal. Thus, all clocks contain a time division mechanism in the form of unary gear trains or electronic unary counters or scalers.

This was a breakthrough not only for time counting but digital arithmetic as well because it was realized that gear methods could be used for calculators. Instead of a constant time period between successive teeth of the gears, the number of teeth to advance could easily correspond to a number. One complete revolution would generate a carry, and subtraction could be accomplished by rotation in the other direction. This is the description of the earliest mechanical calculators.

One of the earliest calculators was designed and built in 1623 by Wilhelm Schickard of Tubingen (Goldstine, 1972). Little is known of the original machine, due to the destruction of the only prototype in a fire and the death of its inventor shortly thereafter. Due to this historical misfortune, Blaise Pascal's calculator, Pascaline, is often credited as the first digital mechanical calculator. The Pascaline worked very much in the fashion that was described in the previous paragraph and could also perform addition and subtraction. In 1673, Gottfried Leibniz developed his own version known as Leibniz's Wheel. It had a section for addition and subtraction similar to Pascaline, and another section that enabled repeated addition for multiplication or repeated subtraction for division.

No one has refined the concept of computing by toothed gearwheels more than Charles Babbage (Morrison and Morrison, 1961). What Pascal and Leibniz did in a modest way he expanded to its greatest form of refinement and intricacy. In his effort to automate calculation of functions for tables, he designed a machine that performed these calculations with the method of finite differences. He worked on this "difference engine" from 1822 to 1833, and, even though his machine was never completed, the portion that performed the arithmetic operations was complete even at the early stages. By 1834, he launched a more ambitious project—to build a machine that would calculate general functions, perform conditional operations depending on the data, and store and print intermediate results. This machine, the "analytical engine", was never completed, mostly due to the fact that it required more advanced technology than was available at the time. The analytical engine deserves special mention in this historical overview because it not only had practically every architectural feature of the traditional von Neumann architecture (I/O, ALUs, primary and secondary memory, and programmability), but it operated without the use of a binary representation scheme. Indeed, at that time, digital computing was not associated in any form with binary computing. The question whether such machines are unary or decimal is of a philosophical nature and can be argued either way. Here, it will suffice for us to consider as unary any type of machine that involves processing of digits with the same weight (at least within one digit position).

2.3   Unary Processing in the Twentieth Century

The most influential abstraction of a computer is undoubtably the Turing machine (Turing, 1936; also, Hopcroft and Ullman, 1979; Jones, 1973; Loeckx, 1972). Whereas a Turing machine may have an alphabet of any finite number of symbols, only two symbols are truly needed: a blank symbol, which we will call 0 and a nonblank symbol which we will call 1. The blank on the Turing machine corresponds to our 0, and a succession of n 1 symbols corresponds to the nth letter of the generalized alphabet. Two successive 0 values can be used as character separators. This type of Turing machine, which is equivalent to the more general machine of the original definition, is in itself unary, as successions of unweighted 1 values are used for the processing. This is probably the simplest and most elegant construction proof that the deterministic unary and weighted binary (or any other representation for that matter) are equivalent from a computability point of view!

The study of human intelligence and function has been one of the earliest goals of philosophers and scientists; explanations as well as models have been made throughout the ages with analogues to the scientific and technological trends of each era. It was only natural that these intellectual curiosities were extended to computer science, even at the time of its infancy. In the 1956 volume *Automata Studies* (Shannon and McCarthy, 1956) several such attempts are made, from a variety of perspectives. The wealth of information and stimulating ideas of that volume makes it of extreme importance not only to the scientist who is interested in unary processing, but to the scientist who is interested in computers and computing in general. In this volume, we find the influential treatise, "Probabilistic Logics and the Synthesis of Reliable Organisms from Unreliable Components" by John von Neumann. In this treatise, which stems from an attempt to treat error in an informationally thermodynamical way, the author suggests "organs" that simulate nerves and functions and then proceeds to the study of the properties and interconnections of such organs. The universality of the Sheffer stroke organ, which corresponds to the NAND function, is proved; and threshold logic on organs is used to construct automata and study error properties of different configurations. The inputs to all of these are series of 0 and 1 values, generally weighted equally. Threshold logic, which later fell into disfavor due to technological trends rather than intrinsic shortcomings, is then the simplest form of unary processing.

During the sixties, there were a number of attempts to use "stochastic" elements (a term used by von Neumann in his 1956 treatise) not only to simulate nerve systems but also to perform general purpose calculations. The first actual machines were developed at the same time by Poppelbaum (Poppelbaum *et al.*, 1967) and Gaines (1967a). Both investigators relied on random sequences of pulses, and the operations on these sequences were often digital equivalents of analog methods. Later computers involved pseudorandom pulse sequences, as well as deterministic unary (burst) representations (Poppelbaum, 1979). These efforts, and especially a number of machines that were constructed at the University of Illinois not only proved that unary is a feasible form of information processing, but that it is often desirable, depending on the application. The latest addition to these machines is an abstraction of calculation by toothed gears, in which shift registers are used for storage as well as operations on words. Thus, there has been a five-century cycle of evolution of unary machines, with the latest machine remarkably similar conceptually to the first!

3. Premise for Proving Binary Superiority

The assertion may be made that weighted binary provides better representational efficiency than a unary representation. Claims have been made that what is lost in efficiency by using a unary representation scheme may be compensated by simpler hardware. In this section, we shall determine the radix with the highest theoretical efficiency and compare it to the efficiency of weighted binary.

Assuming a weighted scheme of precision m digits of radix r, then $M = r^m$ different numbers can be represented. Further, assume r need not be an integral value, and that *the cost to represent each digit is proportional to r*. An estimate of the cost S of representing m digits of radix r is

$$S = k_1 mr \qquad (3.1)$$

where k_1 is a constant. Now we find r that minimizes the above cost (subject to M being fixed):

$$\ln(M) = m \ln(r) \qquad (3.2)$$

and, therefore,

$$m = \frac{\ln(M)}{\ln(r)} \qquad (3.3)$$

Substituting Eq. 3.3 into Eq. 3.1:

$$S = \frac{k_2 r}{\ln(r)} \qquad (3.4)$$

where k_2 is an appropriate constant. Thus,

$$k_2 = k_1 \ln(M) \qquad (3.5)$$

Since k_2 is a constant,

$$\frac{dS}{dr} = \frac{k_2[\ln(r) - 1]}{\ln(r)^2} \qquad (3.6)$$

For S to be minimum, $\dfrac{dS}{dr} = 0$, thus $\ln(r) = 1$. This occurs at $r = e = 2.71828\dots$. If we assume that we must have integral values of r, S is minimized at $r = 3$, and is just slightly larger for $r = 2$ (Stifler, 1950).

Using Eq. 3.4, if $r = e$, then $S \approx 2.72k_2$. If $r = 2$, then $S \approx 2.89k_2$. Finally, for $r = 10$, $S \approx 4.34k_2$. The efficiencies of $r = 2$, and $r = 10$ normalized to $r = e$, are approximately 94.2% and 66.4%.

4. Probabilistic Unary Methods

4.1 Fundamental Concepts

The simplest forms of probabilistic (stochastic) number representation are shown in Fig. 2a; namely, a pulsestream of 0 and 1 values, which when averaged over time will yield a probability value; i.e., a number in the range $0 \leq x \leq 1$. The only difference between these schemes is that the first is *asynchronous* (i.e., the transition from one value to the other may occur at any time) whereas the other is *synchronous* (i.e., during a time slot that is determined by a central clock the value is preserved). It turns out that if purely digital methods are used for the processing, synchronous representation is preferable because the data remains stable during each quantum of time. For obvious reasons, the first scheme is called Random Pulse Sequence (RPS), and the second is called Synchronous Random Pulse Sequence (SRPS). Here, we will assume that our computations are made using SRPS pulsestreams (Afuso, 1968; Gaines, 1967a, 1967b). The generation of such pulsestreams is shown in Fig. 2b in which a noise diode is used to generate white noise. A reference generating circuit allows spikes above a certain threshold to go through; this threshold directly defines the probability to be represented. Wave-shaping circuits allow for generation of RPS or SRPS.

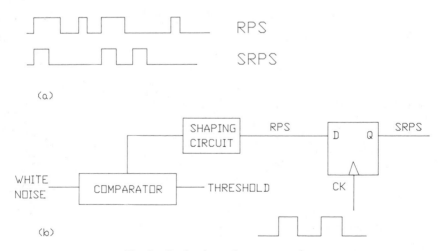

FIG. 2. Stochastic number representation.

The white noise does not have to be from a totally random source. Indeed, a shift register with appropriate feedback can be used to generate "quasi-noise". This approach not only is less sensitive to calibration, but bounds the variation of the values, and at the same time has very low autocorrelation, except for windows of exactly one period of the pseudorandom pulsestream. Figure 3 shows the connection of a shift register and an example of its output. It should be noted that the period of the quasi-noise sequence should be much higher than the averaging time, so that there is no bias in the results due to autocorrelation.

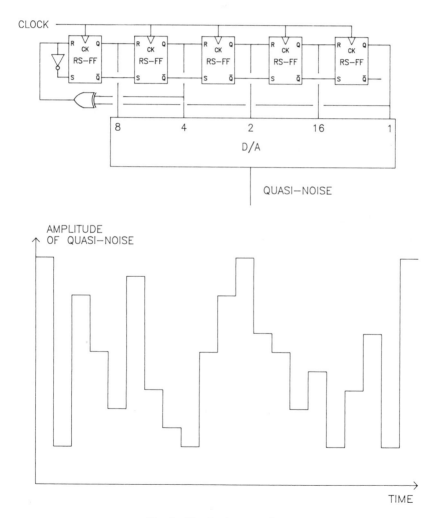

Fig. 3   Quasi-noise generation.

Arithmetic operations are very easy. OR corresponds to addition, whereas AND corresponds to multiplication. Figures 4a and 4b show examples of addition and multiplication. The careful reader will notice that in the case of addition we have cheated because the pulses are nonoverlapping. If they were overlapping, the OR gate would have counted two pulses as one! This is not a surprise because with $0 \leq a, b \leq 1$, it follows that $0 \leq a + b \leq 2$, even though we cannot have probabilities (and thus representation) greater than 1. In reality, the result of our simplified adder is $a + b - a \times b$. A more appropriate addition scheme would be a normalized addition, i.e., $\frac{a+b}{2}$; an example of this is shown in Fig. 4c. The implementation is rather easy—on the odd phases of the clock a goes through, whereas on the even phases b goes through. The ORed addition is preceded by a multiplication of a, b by $\frac{1}{2}$ in such a way that the results are mutually exclusive.

We have not yet discussed the significance of randomness in number representation (Gaines, 1974). This is illustrated in Fig. 5, where 0.4 and 0.5 representation is shown in both random and correlated fashions; if there should be any correlation between the pulses, the results will be totally meaningless. The same figure also demonstrates that short sequences are inherently unreliable. If we want a $\frac{1}{n}$ information resolution, the *least* number of pulses that we need is n. If we use random pulses of uniform distribution as we have assumed, the window, or average, of n samples will give us a confidence level of 68.3% (Poppelbaum, 1974a), a window of $2n$ samples yields

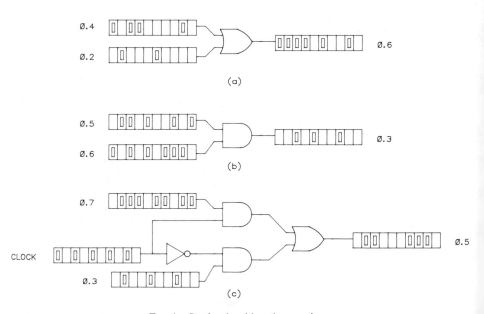

FIG. 4.   Stochastic arithmetic operations.

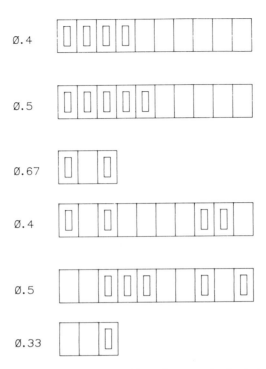

FIG. 5.   The significance of randomness and long-time averaging in stochastic processing.

a confidence level of 95.4%, and a window of $3n$ samples yields a confidence level of 99.7%. The result, however, will start converging from the beginning of the averaging, giving a rough approximation of the correct value; this is important in many applications, such as control.

4.2   More Stochastic Operations: Representation of Negative Numbers

Having discussed the fundamental stochastic operations, we can now proceed to such operations such as subtraction and division. These operations are less trivial to perform than multiplication and addition but, nonetheless, require a lot less hardware than their weighted binary counterparts. Stochastic subtraction requires that we know which of the two numbers is greater; then, a weighted binary counter can be used to keep track of the borrows; i.e., it is incremented by 1 for every pulse of the minuend and decremented by 1 for every pulse of the subtrahend: The output is a pulse if the contents are positive, and for every pulse of the output, the contents are decremented by 1. The size of the counter is dependent on the standard deviation and the precision of the number representation.

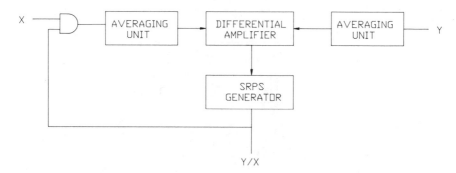

FIG. 6.   Stochastic divider.

A stochastic divider is shown in Fig. 6; the method of the division is simple and actually represents a digital counterpart of analog dividers. A resulting random pulsestream is formed by the divider circuit and is then multiplied by the divisor and compared to the dividend. Depending on the comparison, the result is incremented or decremented: This is much the same process as a servo-tracking mechanism, but the reader should notice that the result is a SRPS. The circuit that forms the result is a true SRPS generating circuit, and not a voltage controlled oscillator of any kind!

The method of linear remapping can be used in order to have both positive and negative number representation. If $a' = \frac{1-a}{2}$ with $-1 \leq a \leq 1$, then a' is in the range $0 \leq a' \leq 1$. This linear remapping does not buy us more precision but merely gives the capability of having both positive and negative numbers and still perform arithmetic in a similar fashion.

4.3   Applications of Stochastic Processing

During the evolution of stochastic processing, there have been many machines constructed, which prove not only the feasibility of this kind of approach, but its practicality as well. Such machines were built in England (Gaines, 1967a; Brown and Mars, 1978) and the United States of America (Poppelbaum 1968b). Due to the enormous size of the bibliography, we will not attempt an in-depth coverage here but rather show how the methods described thus far can be applied to real-life problems. For the interested reader, in addition to the references cited in this section, we have provided an extensive bibliography.

4.3.1   Stochastic Calculators and Computers

One of the earliest computing elements for stochastic calculations was the ADDIE, a stochastic/analog circuit that performed exponential averaging on the input. A machine called Stochastic Computer (Gaines, 1967a) used ADDIEs in order to perform operations such as adaptive control and adaptive filtering.

The POSTCOMP (POrtable STOchastic COMPuter) machine (Esch, 1969a) was a four-function calculator with two arguments and a result. The operations were performed very similarly to the descriptions given in the previous section. The two arguments A and B and the result were displayed in analog form, with the meters themselves performing some of the averaging operations on the pulsestreams.

Another machine, RASCEL (Regular Array of Stochastic Computing ELements), had a representation that included negative numbers and a tree structure of stochastic elements that could perform the four operations (Esch, 1969b). Algebraic operations could be performed from the leaves (inputs) to the root (result). In addition to demonstrating that stochastic elements could be used in succession, a variety of schemes (such as random duplication) were used in order to avoid round-off errors between successive stages.

A general purpose computer, DISCO, (Brown and Mars, 1978) could be automatically programmed from a visual display unit through a PDP-8 front-end computer and had several general purpose registers, as well as an automated interconnection scheme. This computer was used to investigate such applications of stochastic as matrix operations, linear programming, and process simulation.

4.3.2 Bundle and Ergodic Processing

So far we have discussed time stochastic processing (TSP); however, we may use n parallel wires, representing n time slots. Though the processing is exactly the same as in TSP, the time to convergence is shorter, due to the parallelism, and the cost is higher, due to the multiplicity of circuits. This scheme, shown in Fig. 7, does not only have the advantage of faster computations, but also the advantage of failsafe behavior (one wire more or less does not matter); the redundancy is built into the system. The BUndle Machine, BUM, (Ring, 1969) used this scheme, and its successor, the SAfe BUndle MAchine, SABUMA, (Coombes, 1970) used ternary threshold logic (with values $0, +1, -1$) in order to correct transmission errors on-line; furthermore, values depending on the neighboring wires were assigned to broken wires, which resulted in a failsoft behavior (Tse, 1974).

An advantage of averaging in the time domain and the space domain is that if the number that is represented in the space domain (i.e., in the n wires) is the same as the number on each wire in the time domain, then the space and the time averages *should* be equal. This behavior, known from physics as the ergodic property, can be used in computing in order to verify the correct

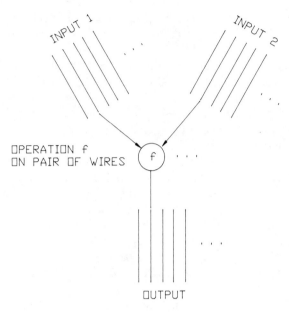

OPERATION f
ON PAIR OF WIRES

OUTPUT

FIG. 7.   Fundamentals of bundle processing.

operation on-line. ERGODIC was such a machine and demonstrated both the failsoft/failsafe attributes of bundle processing as well as the on-line verification of operation due to the encoding (Cutler, 1974).

4.3.3   Special Applications

One of the most interesting and powerful applications in stochastics was TRANSFORMATRIX (Poppelbaum, 1968a; Marvel, 1970; Ryan, 1971). This processor could perform real-time general linear transforms on a 32 × 32 image. These transforms included autocorrelation, convolution, rotations, scaling, and even Fourier transforms. The approach was that a general transform of a point of the 32 × 32 matrix necessitates a 32 × 32 coefficient matrix: TRANSFORMATRIX had 1024 processors that, in parallel, performed this operation for one point. Different points of the matrix were processed serially, but at a high enough rate to allow refresh rates of 30 frames/second; i.e., real-time!

The APE machine used autonomous processing elements in order to have a distributed system with self-checking and failsoft behavior. The load of computations could be distributed among the working elements, which is a very desirable feature in hostile environments (Wo, 1973).

5.   Deterministic Averaging Methods

5.1   Comparison of Characteristics of Information Processing Methods

As we have seen, there are two major ways of processing information in a computer: deterministically and probabilistically. Each form of processing has it own set of advantages and disadvantages. Deterministic processing has the following characteristics:

1. compact representation
2. rapid calculation (space domain)
3. complex circuitry
4. low noise immunity.

Stochastic processing has these characteristics:

1. sparse representation
2. slower calculation (time domain)
3. simple circuitry
4. high noise immunity.

BURST processing is a hybrid information processing technique that has characteristics common to both deterministic and stochastic processing and represents a compromise between the two techniques (Poppelbaum, 1974b, 1978). BURST truly is a deterministic method but borrows the concepts of averaging and serial pulse train methods from stochastics. This compromise allows the BURST method to utilize low precision arithmetic hardware to yield higher precision results, but over time. BURST has the following characteristics:

1. medium complexity circuitry
2. medium computational speed (time and space domain)
3. medium compactness of information representation
4. medium noise immunity.

Perhaps the main disadvantage of pure stochastic processing is the rate of computation; unfortunately, the convergence is quite slow. BURST, although more complex in terms of circuitry than a purely stochastic machine, converges in a time-linear manner. Because the pulse trains are correlated (as opposed to uncorrelated in the purely stochastic environment), the concept of confidence levels, which is an issue with pure stochastic machines, is not applicable to the burst method. This means that a number of desired precision can be computed with complete confidence as long as one is willing to wait for the result. BURST processing, like stochastic processing, is capable of providing a continuous result from the very start of the averaging process. In the stochastic case, the confidence interval will be very low at first. In BURST, an accurate result of the anticipated precision, will not truly be available until the leading edge of the burst stream is clocked entirely through the averager.

5.2   BURST—Fundamental Representation Concepts

The BURST method is based upon the concept that sequences of low-precision numbers may be used to represent higher precision numbers. Figure 8a shows 10 single digit numbers being transmitted (Poppelbaum, 1979). BURST interprets these 10 serial digits in the time domain during transmission, but in the space domain during averaging.

Through this process, we can represent numbers from 0.0 to 9.9 (Fig. 8a). By sending 10 numbers (a number is called a block for reasons that will be apparent soon), we have increased the precision by a factor of 10. A superblock consists of 10 blocks, which again takes 10 times as long to transmit but introduces a second decimal of precision. Likewise, the hyperblock may be used for a third digit of precision. Although there is in fact a loss of bandwidth by representing the information in this manner, there is a corresponding savings in hardware complexity.

5.2.1   Hardware Realization

To represent a digit, for instance the digit 7 from Fig. 8(a), a block of 10 bits is used in which a "burst" of 7 of the 10 bits are 1 (Fig. 8b). This is a unary pulse code modulated (PCM) format. To maintain correlated information, the representation takes on a compacted format, where the bits of the burst

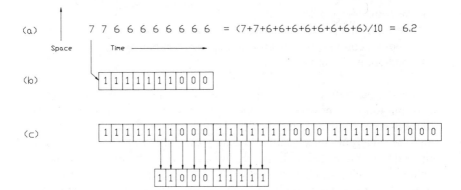

FIG. 8.   BURST number representation.

representation must be adjacent in the 10-bit block, and the burst must start in the first bit position of the block. Up until now, 10-bit blocks have been discussed, and any further reference to blocks in this paper assume length 10. One can easily show, however, that this represtation scheme functions well for other block sizes as well. Block lengths between 4 and 16 bits have been implemented (Poppelbaum, 1974c; Tietz, 1977).

5.2.2 The Windowing Property

An important property of BURST processing is the "window" concept. Suppose 10 blocks have been transmitted where each block contains a burst, each burst representing the number 7. We have 100 bits in a row, 7 on, 3 off, repeated 10 times. Now, as in Fig. 8c, slide a window of length 10 anywhere, not necessarily aligned with the start of a block. No matter where the window is placed, 7 bits will be on, although not necessarily in a compacted representation. Therefore, the averaging of a compacted burst stream does not need to be synchronized to the beginning of the incoming blocks. One only has to know the length of the blocks.

A special circuit, called a block-sum register (BSR) uses the window property to generate an analog voltage proportional to the number of bits set in the window.

5.3   Simple Arithmetic

Figure 9a shows a conceptual adder for adding two compacted BURST streams. Assume there are two input streams; one has the value 2.3, the other 4.5. By using the observation that the average of a sum is the same as the sum of the averages, it is possible to transform two compacted BURST streams into one by shifting the addition from the values to the elements that compose the value.

An easy way to implement such an adder is the selector adder (Poppelbaum, 1974c; Bracha, 1975). In this method, the output burst stream is generated by alternately copying a bit from each PCM input stream (given input streams A and B, the output stream is $\frac{A}{2} + \frac{B}{2}$. In the event of an odd number of bits from one or both input streams, the selector switches phases at the end of each block. This prevents unintentional biasing. The output of the simple selector adder is a normalized uncompacted burst that can be easily recompacted if required.

Another adder, called the "perverted adder" (PA), (Poppelbaum, 1974c; Taylor, 1975), is a modified serial full adder that given two compacted BURST input streams outputs a BURST stream that is normalized and uncompacted (given input streams A and B, the output stream is $\frac{A+B}{2}$) (Fig. 9b).

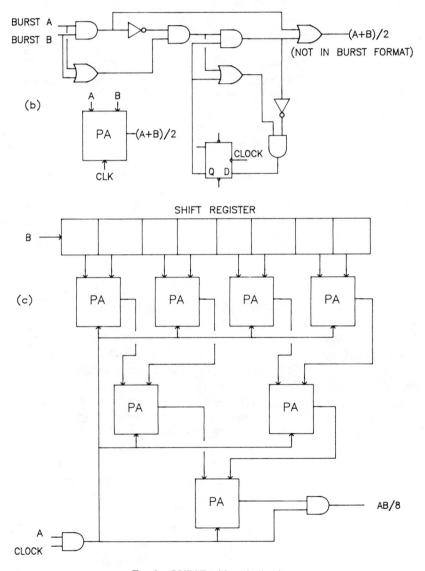

FIG. 9.   BURST arithmetic circuits.

What is particularly attractive about the PA is that it may be cascaded to form a multiplier (Fig. 9c). If, for, example a block length of eight is used, a tree of seven PAs and two AND gates is all that is needed to create a multiplying device. It is easy, although slightly less efficient, to create a PA multiplier tree for a 10-bit block length.

5.4   Examples of Applied BURST Technology

Finite impulse response filters (FIRs) are an excellent application of BURST processing (Fig. 10) (Poppelbaum, 1974c, 1975; Wells, 1977). In these filters, the input signal is delayed by varying amounts to form new signals, each of which is then multiplied by a corresponding constant, and then all are summed together. Since a BURST stream is a PCM stream, the delay elements need only be simple shift registers. Methods of multiplication and addition have already been discussed; however, the transformation of an analog signal, such as an audio signal, into a compacted BURST stream has not yet been discussed. This can be accomplished very easily with a circuit called a ramp-

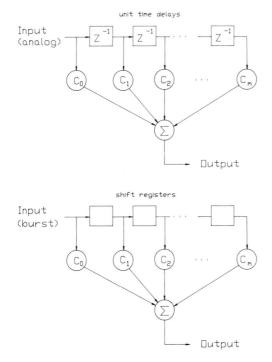

FIG. 10.   FIR and BURST FIR circuits.

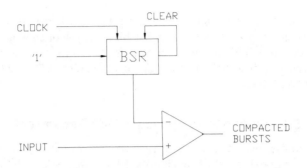

FIG. 11.   Ramp-encoder circuit.

encoder (Fig. 11) (Poppelbaum, 1974c, 1975; Taylor, 1975; Wolff, 1977). Comparing an analog input signal against a ramp with the same number of steps as the desired block length generates a compacted BURST stream.

Many interesting machines have been built that capitalize upon the FIR capabilities of BURST. The digital AM receiver (Poppelbaum 1974c, Mohan *et al.*, 1975) project created a completely digital AM receiver using BURST and FIR concepts.

Mohan continued on with the more complex digital FM receiver (Poppelbaum, 1974c, 1975; Mohan, 1976). Robinson followed with a BURST implementation of a phase-locked loop that was used to create BURSTLOCK (Poppelbaum, 1975, Robinson, 1977), an improved all-digital FM receiver.

BURFT (Poppelbaum, 1974c, 1976; Xydes, 1977) is a unit that provides real-time frequency analysis of speech by utilizing BURST to do on-line Fourier transforms.

WALSHSTORE (Poppelbaum, 1975; Bracha, 1977) uses BURST and two-dimensional Walsh transforms to transform an image into an electronic hologram for storage. In this storage format, the destruction of large portions of memory correspond to a loss of resolution in the image after an inverse transformation.

PREDICTORBURST (Poppelbaum, 1974c, Pitt, 1978a) is another application that uses BURST to calculate predictor coefficients on-line for bandwidth compression of speech (the coefficients are transmitted).

6.   Pulse Gear and Table Look-Up Methods

6.1   Pulse Gear Methods

The toothed gear methods that were used in Pascaline and Babbage's machines have been discussed in the introduction and the historical overview. Here we will present a direct electronic counterpart to these methods and show

how this simple processing method yields an elegant scheme for the storage of numbers as well as addition and subtraction. The radix 10 will be used throughout this discussion for simplicity reasons. Different values for the radix can be chosen without any loss of generality.

If we use a shift register to store a unary number, then, by having one serial input tied to 1 and the other tied to 0, a shift in one direction corresponds to addition of one unit, and a shift in the other direction corresponds to subtraction of one unit. This simple scheme allows storage, addition, and subtraction to be performed in the same hardware. In Fig. 12 we see the representation of the number 4. We shall call this construct a "tenstring" and the hardware to store it (plus the control that is needed for overflow and underflow detection) a "bar register" (Poppelbaum, 1983).

6.1.1   A Tutorial Example

The simple case of an addition is shown in Fig. 13. The contents of the addend are shifted r times (10 times in this case) with wraparound (i.e., nondestructive read) with the top bit being connected to the serial input of the augend. Thus, one bit at a time is ANDed with the clock of the augend, and as many 1's as the addend has will be added to the augend. The example that is shown does not have overflow, but overflow and underflow can be handled very easily. Unlike stochastic processing, the use of a compacted representation is essential here. If the ninth (r-1th bit for radix r) bit is 1 and we request

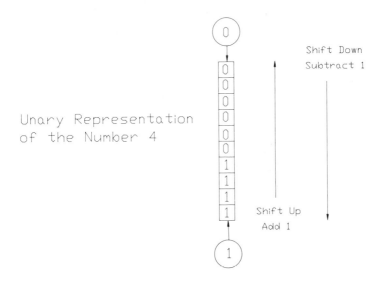

FIG. 12.   Representation for pulse gear methods.

W. J. POPPELBAUM *et al.*

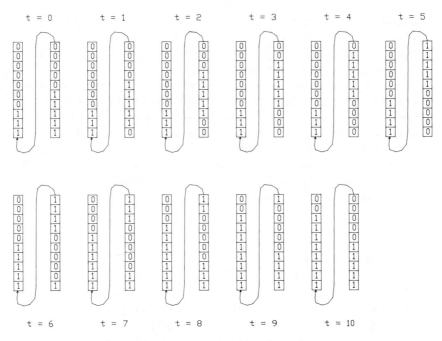

FIG. 13.   Example of addition of tenstrings.

an addition, then a carry should be generated, whereas if we have the first bit to be 0 and a subtraction is requested, a borrow should be generated. This simple scheme allows for ripple-type cascading of different orders of magnitude with minimal control complexity!

The implementation of this arithmetic scheme is straightforward. The clock that is used for the augend is a centralized clock (say, from the control unit) ANDed with the bit of the addend that is placed on the bus. Thus, for the 0 bits of the addend we have no resulting operation on the augend. This guarantees that the resulting number is *always* compacted; i.e., it has at most one 1-to-0 transition. This is particularly useful because the overflow and underflow occur in the two ends of the bar register, hence the simplified logic (one gate for overflow, one for underflow). Also, for the same reason it does not matter whether the addend is rotated clockwise or counterclockwise, or which bit of the addend is connected to the augend.

6.1.2   Implementation of Shift Registers for Compacted Strings

The traditional shift registers, made from master-slave flip-flops, can obviously be used in the implementation of the bar register. Happily, it turns out that the property of only one 1-to-0 transition within a bar register can be

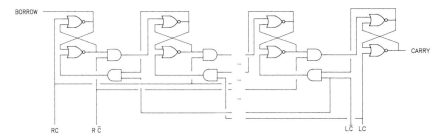

FIG. 14.   Raceless bidirectional shift register.

used in order to reduce the storage hardware to one-half and still have a static shift register! This configuration, named the raceless bidirectional shift register, was invented by Poppelbaum in 1983 and uses latches instead of master-slave flip-flops.

A raceless bidirectional shift register is shown in Fig. 14. During one transition of the clock, the odd latches will feed the even ones, whereas in the other transition, the even latches will feed the odd ones (the reader should notice that the problem of the two ends is solved by tying the input lines appropriately). Even though *five* latches are loaded at one time, the single 1-to-0 transition within the word *guarantees* that only one latch will have its output changed! A trivial note: if it is desired that the transitions occur at the same phase of the master clock, it can be divided by 2; also, if the control signals L and R are both 0, the register remains static.

6.2   Table Look-Up Techniques

In von Neumann architectures, table look-up multiplication techniques have been realized in the past decade (Stenzel, Kubitz, *et al.*, 1977). Such realizations have resulted in a compromise between the low speed sequences of add and shift instructions (Shaw, 1950) and the high complexity random-logic gate networks involved in array and parallel multipliers (Ghest, 1971).

As proposed by Poppelbaum *et al.* (1983), an electronic multiplication table can be constructed from an array of $r \times r$ AND gates (where r is the radix or positions in the bar cell) whose outputs are collected by as many as $r \times 2$ ORs. Only one row/column is selected at a time in the $r \times r$ array, resulting in one "high" AND gate whose output is connected to the appropriate OR output(s). Indication of the appropriate row/column can be done simply by connecting the output of the bar cells to be multiplied to a sequence of XOR gates (see Fig. 15). Conversion to a tenstring is trivial and will be discussed later.

Such a table format has the ability to be designed in different radix values with little hardware alteration. However, before discussing the different look-

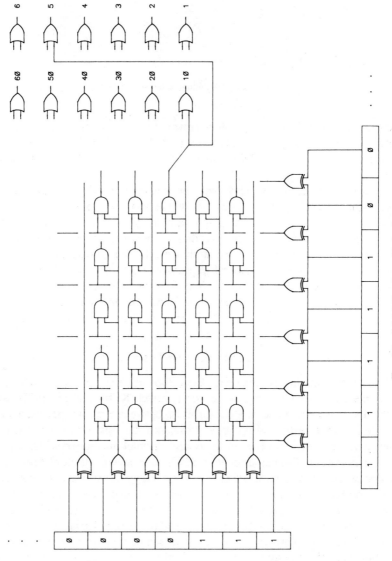

Fig. 15.   Multiplication table look-up array.

up techniques, it is appropriate to discuss algorithmic approaches for performing multiplication using pulse gear methods.

Machine multiplication can be performed much in the same way as one would perform multiplication on paper. As an example, consider multiplying two decimal numbers of precision 1 in 100 (see Fig. 16). The numbers are represented as AB and XY, where A and X represent the tens position and B and Y represent the ones position, respectively. As shown, it is necessary to have four accumulator registers to store the product. A total of four multiplications are necessary; namely, BY, AY, XB, and AX to form the product.The remaining task involves addition of the low order products (by, ay, bx, ax) and the high order products (BY, AY, BX, AX) into the appropriate sum registers.

In Fig. 17, Field I is loaded with A and B. Similarly, Field II is loaded with X and Y. Field III and Field IV will serve as product summation registers. Setup for multiplication takes r pulses, 10 in the case of decimal multiplication. Once the input registers are loaded, two cycles are necessary to perform the product, one for propagation delay, the other for latching the output. Upon completion of the multiplication, the product can be shifted into the appropriate output registers at the same time that the second multiplication is being loaded in. In step (a), the multiplier input registers are loaded with B and Y (setup). Two cycles later (after multiplication 1), step (b) occurs where upon product sum (PS) registers 1 and 2 are added with the contents of multiplier output registers containing by and BY, respectively. At the same time, the multiplier input registers are loaded with A and Y. Two cycles later (after multiplication 2), step (c) occurs where upon PS registers 2 and 3 are added with the contents of multiplier output registers containing ay and AY, respectively. At the same time, the multiplier input registers are loaded with B and X. Two cycles later (after multiplication 3), step (d) occurs where upon PS registers 2 and 3 are added with the contents of the multiplier output registers containing bx and

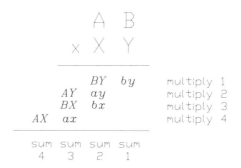

FIG. 16.   Basic multiplication.

72 W. J. POPPELBAUM *et al.*

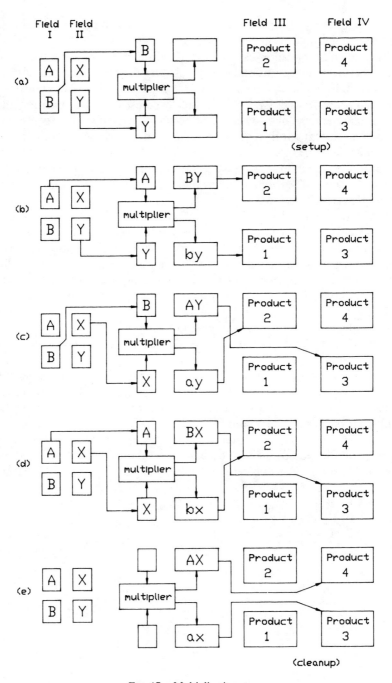

FIG. 17. Multiplication steps.

BX, respectively. At the same time, the multiplier input registers are loaded with *A* and *X*. Finally, two cycles later (after multiplication 4), step (e) occurs where upon PS register 3 and 4 are added with the contents of the multiplier output registers containing *ax* and *AX*, respectively.

As can be observed, the multiplication time is dependent upon radix *r* and the precision of the number. In general, the multiplication time, in cycles, for table look-up is:

$$\text{time} = n^2 + (r + 2)$$

where *n* equals the number of digits of precision and *r* equals the radix. For the case of two decimal digits of precision, the number of multiplication cycles is:

$$\text{cycles} = 2^2 \times (10 + 2) = 48 \text{ cycles}$$

The output from the multiplication table can be converted back into tenstring format via two methods. In the first method, a strict mapping can be performed by cascading OR gates connected between successive multiplier outputs. An OR output feeds one of 10 parallel inputs to the tenstring register and an input to the next lower position OR gate. The other method involves using a latch to detect when a 1 is shifted out of the top of the multiplier output register. Upon detection of a 1, the latch is set, allowing 1 values to be distributed to the appropriate destination register, which has been initialized at the start or the completion of the multiply instruction.

Each table look-up technique should be evaluated to determine cost/ performance. Among the various types of tables, we will consider ROMs, variations of ROMs, gate arrays, and variations in gate arrays.

Use of a single ROM for the look-up table is appropriate when the radix *r* is small (see Fig. 18a). The number of address bits necessary to perform a unary table look-up is:

$$\text{Addressbits} = 2^{2r} \times 2r$$

For the decimal radix case, the number of bits necessary for ROM table look-up is $2^{20} \times 20$ or 20,971,520 bits.

One approach to reduce the number of address bits has been developed by J. Glickman (1985). Using priority encoders to convert the bar cell representation into a weighted binary format, the number of address lines is reduced to 8 for radix values of 16 or less (see Fig. 18b). This approach brings the same ROM requirement for radix 4 representation, namely 2048 bits, at the cost of two priority encoders and two decoders. The cost of additional hardware remains somewhat constant between radix values of a power of two. This is largely due to priority encoder as well as decoder costs.

Gate arrays shall be considered as an $r \times r$ array of NAND gates. The AND to OR configuration previously discussed can be implemented with

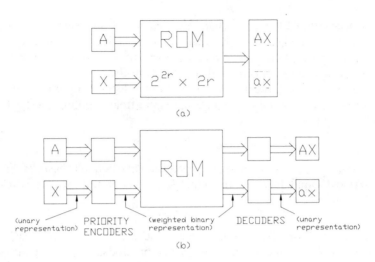

FIG. 18.   ROM look-up techniques.

NAND-NAND configurations via De Morgan's law. However, for clarity, we will still consider the components as AND-OR devices.

Two approaches can be considered to reduce the number of inputs into the OR gates. Both approaches take advantage of the symmetry of the table look-up multiplication table. To illustrate the importance of reduction, consider the straight AND to OR connections (Fig. 19a) of a decimal look-up table. The number of inputs to the OR gates is displayed in column 1 of Table I. By taking advantage of the symmetry of the table (requiring open collector output for TTL), connection of the AND gates about the center (Fig. 19b) results in OR connections displayed in column 2 of Table I. Further, connection of all the same output value (Fig. 19c) results in the OR connections of column 3.

Using the results of column 3 of Table I, for a decimal radix we would need 81 AND gates for the matrix table (omitting 0 as an input), two 6-input ORs, four 5-input ORs, three 4-input ORs, one 3-input OR, four 2-input ORs, and two 1-input ORs.

Further, gate reduction can also be observed if the matrix of ANDs can be condensed. Due to the tabular format of the input, a format (such as that in Fig. 20) can be constructed at a low hardware and complexity cost. With such a format, the number of gates (in this case n-MOSFETs) necessary to construct the matrix of the table is:

$$n\text{-MOSFETs} = (r + 1) \times r$$

The complexity of the ANDs (NANDs) is greatly decreased, while allowing for the OR (NAND) connections of column 3 of Table I.

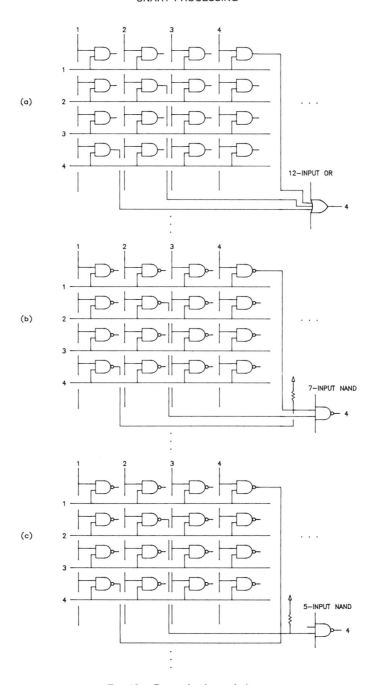

FIG. 19.   Gate reduction techniques.

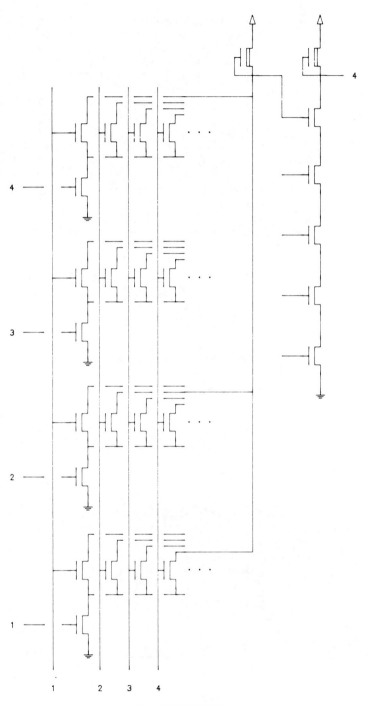

FIG. 20.   N-MOSFET layout.

TABLE I

GATE SAVINGS AS A RESULT OF VARIOUS OUTPUT COMBINATION SCHEMES

	Tens					Column 1	Column 2	Column 3
80	81					1	1	1
70	72					2	1	1
60	63	64				3	2	2
50	54	56				4	2	2
40	40	42	45	48	49	9	5	5
30	30	32	35	36		9	5	4
20	20	21	24	25	27	28	13	7	6
10	10	12	14	15	16	18	17	9	6

	Ones				Column 1	Column 2	Column 3
9	9	49				4	3	2
8	8	18	28	48		12	6	4
7	7	27				4	2	2
6	6	16	36	56		12	7	4
5	5	15	25	35	45	9	5	5
4	4	14	24	54	64	12	7	5
3	3	63				4	2	2
2	2	12	32	42	72	12	6	5
1	1	21	81			4	3	3

7. The UNIFIELD I: Architecture and Applications

A UNIFIELD computer is a SIMD machine in which information flow results in arithmetic operations, and the data movement is performed via a device that allows any number of predefined mappings to be used. The simplicity of the design allows for massive parallelism; thus, the machine is achieving high performance from the parallelism. The registers are two-dimensional (i.e., matrices). The UNIFIELD I computer is a radix-10 machine with 8×8 matrices. The precision of the machine is two decimal digits. The block diagram of the UNIFIELD I architecture is shown in Fig. 21, and it is recommended that the reader refers to this figure after the notation and functionality of the different components has been described (Dollas, 1985).

7.1 The UNIFIELD Concept

The length of each shift register, r, determines the radix of the computation. We will assume that $r = 10$, which is the case with UNIFIELD I. In general, any radix can be used, but for very low values the architecture loses the

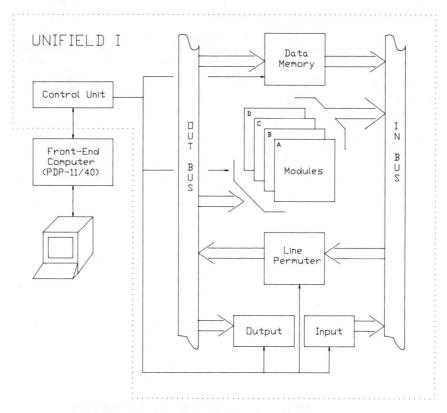

FIG. 21. The UNIFIELD I architecture.

advantage of the low control logic circuitry to overall component count, whereas for very high values (say, $r > 40$), the obvious tradeoff $O(r/lgr)$ of the storage expense and speed tradeoff become the dominating factors, making the architecture inefficient. Table II shows the storage inefficiency factor versus the radix value of the unary compared to a weighted binary representation. Since one can use $(r - 1)$ storage elements to store a radix r number, the storage inefficiency is an upper bound, with the formula $O[(r - 1)/lgr]$ being more appropriate. As r increases, the lower bound approaches asymptotically the upper bound, so either one can be used for our estimate. For an entire range of values of r, the storage overhead of compacted unary versus the weighted binary case is minimal, if any. The reason is that the coefficients of the straight line and the logarithmic curves are as important as the envelopes of the curves.

The communication between different parts of the computer (i.e., the routing of the pulsestreams) is done via a network, which we will call a "line

TABLE II

STORAGE INEFFICIENCY OF RADIX r
UNARY REPRESENTATION COMPARED TO
WEIGHTED BINARY REPRESENTATION

Radix (r)	Storage inefficiency (r/lgr)
2	2
4	2
8	2.667
10	3.010
12	3.347
16	4
20	4.627
24	5.234
28	5.824
32	6.400
64	10.667
128	18.286
256	32
512	56.889
1024	102.400

permuter." This, in its general form, is a crossbar network. Due to the physical limitations of implementing a full-fledged crossbar network of, for example, 64 inputs to 64 outputs (as is the case with UNIFIELD I), we resort to a less general device, one which can perform predefined permutations that are hardwired. Therefore, a menu of useful permutations (such as a matrix transpose, assortments of rotations and translations, etc.) can exist on-line. The advantage is tremendous; instead of having to change entire sections of the memory or swap the contents of many registers, the whole permutation is done simultaneously, in a time *independent* of the matrix size, and without any need for intermediate storage registers. The classical parallel architecture of the four neighbors of one position can be implemented on UNIFIELD, so that previously existing algorithms will run easily on UNIFIELD. Such formidable problems as a matrix transpose do not have to be solved with data movement among neighbors, resulting in simpler programming and faster operation. In cases where the matrix size is large, such limitations result in the inefficient use of resources in traditional SIMD architectures. Six examples of permutations of a 4 × 4 matrix are shown in Fig. 22.

The UNIFIELD computer will be formally defined by $U\langle n, r, p, m, l \rangle$, where the radix r determines the number representation scheme. The tradeoffs in the storage of compacted strings have been discussed in Section 6; therefore, we only need to assume that the radix value is not too high, so that the storage cost is still comparable to that of a weighted binary representation. The number n

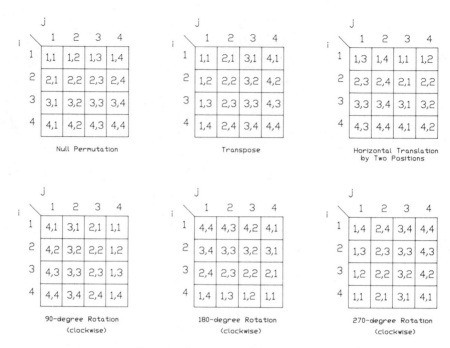

FIG. 22.   Six examples of permutations.

determines the size of the matrix in each dimension. The precision p is the maximum number of r-strings that can be used in order to represent a number. Since this is a parallel architecture of size $n \times n$, we have n^2 precision pr-strings that form a module. The total number of modules is m. Each module can be thought of as a two-dimensional register. Each position (i, j) of a module is connected to the respective input and output of the line permuter via two lines called "data in" and "data out." The line permuter, as the name suggests, is an interconnection scheme that allows data from position (i_p, j_q) to flow to position (i_m, j_n). For each permutation there is a distinct mapping from the input matrix to the output matrix. The total number of permutations is $l(l = 32$ in UNIFIELD I).

The elementary building block of the machine, an r-bit shift register, is a bar register, whereas the p bar registers of one position of a specific module form a bar cell. Then data transfer is trivial. Data is shifted out of the source module (serially in each position, but all positions operating in parallel) via the line permuter to the destination module. Figure 23 shows the architecture of the parallel part.

The pulse gear methods that were discussed in Section 6 are directly applicable to UNIFIELD; therefore, it is only a matter of expanding these

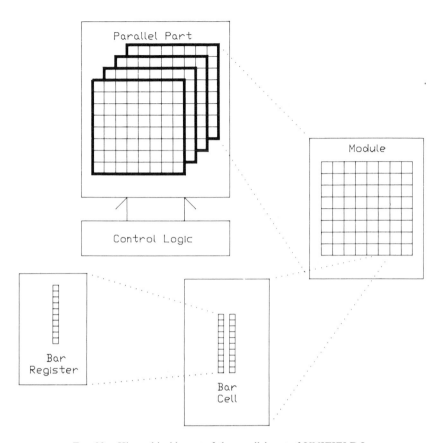

FIG. 23. Hierarchical layout of the parallel part of UNIFIELD I.

concepts to completely cover the new architecture. The bar register and bar cell notation denotes not merely a number of r-bit shift registers, but the appropriate control in order to interface them to one another (in our case overflow, underflow, and the capability of shifting a number with wraparound for nondestructive reads as well). Moreover, we will refer to the r entries of a bar register as bits because each has a binary value—this is also true in the hardware implementation, but the meaning of each of these bits is one unit of r^k, where k is the order ($0 \leq k \leq p - 1$). The interconnection of p bar registers forms a bar cell. This interconnection entails connection of the "carry out" and "borrow out" to the "carry in" and "borrow in" of the next higher order. Addition and subtraction are the fundamental operations in UNIFIELD I. We discussed the addition/subtraction operation prior to discussing data transfer for a good reason: Data transfer is trivial, being the addition of a number to a bar cell that has been initialized to zero!

7.2   Complexity of Operations

Generalizing on the complexity of operations, the UNIFIELD has a hardware complexity of $O(pr)$ for the data representation, and the control complexity is roughly cp where c is a small number of gates to detect overflow and underflow. We get addition and subtraction for the same cost, whereas the multiplication and the division can be implemented algorithmically or with table look-up methods. Contrasted with this, in the weighted binary case, if we assume a simple ripple-carry addition, we have $O(lgl)$ where $2^{l-1} = r^{p-1}$ complexity for the data representation and the same order of complexity for the adder circuitry. To this we should add the control complexity (which may be as high as 20–25% of the total chip count) to see that, inefficient as the radix r representation may be, for information resolution of 1 in 10^5 (close to 17 bits) the total number of gates is comparable, if not smaller (conservative upper bound). No one can argue that should the precision of, for example, 200 bits, be needed, weighted binary will certainly prove to be cheaper (in addition to faster). The same would be the case should the radix r be chosen to be very large, say, in excess of 100. It turns out that for $r = 10$ or $r = 16$ (and possibly higher values than that), the control structure to storage complexity ratio remains low (as desired), whereas the storage inefficiency $O(r/lgr)$ is not significant compared to the savings in overall circuitry. A significant reason for this is the raceless bidirectional shift register that was described in Section 6. The highly regular structure allows for much higher clock rates and is suitable for VLSI implementation.

Compared to binary machines, the UNIFIELD approach is significantly cheaper (comparable hardware can be used in order to get storage and arithmetic operations). As it always happens, we cannot get something free of charge—the specific UNIFIELD operations are slower than those of a weighted binary machine, exactly because of the space-to-time domain transformation. This is a small price to pay if we consider that we get several arithmetic operations nearly free of charge! This scheme is useful primarily in applications where integer arithmetic of only moderately high precision is needed. For example, consider that a state-of-the-art digitizer yields approximately 18 weighted binary bits. Depending on the application, it may be wasteful to use floating point format to process these data. This is an important assertion, and it has been applied to other parallel machines, like the MPP, that in addition to floating point have three integer modes (Batcher, 1980).

So far we have discussed operations without considering the line permuter. Any of the above operations can be performed with any predefined mapping of the data of one module, *without any penalty in time*. Thanks to the line permuter, the transpose of a matrix can be performed in $p \times r$ clock cycles.

The matrix size does not even matter! In the same time, one can have rotations, translations, scaling, and virtually any mapping that has been implemented as a line permuter function. This, however, does not mean that all of the power of the UNIFIELD comes from the line permuter. As the reader may have noticed, the flow of data and the processing thereof is the same thing. In a conventional architecture, the flow of data to the appropriate parts (registers or processors) of the computer is strictly overhead; pipelining may be used to avoid part of this overhead (Russel, 1978) at the cost of higher hardware complexity and, often, sensitive timing. An implicit assumption in pipelining is that the pipes are kept full after some initial overhead time to fill them up. It is very often the case that the pipes cannot be kept full more than an average of 20% of the time, a bottleneck that is highly dependent upon the algorithm and is not intrinsic to a pipelined machine. To the time-domain cost of pipelines (filling them up), one should add the hardware cost of the memory or register transfer control logic, multiport memories, and other hardware expenses that are needed in order to bridge the speed gap of different components. In the case of the UNIFIELD, all of the components are of matching speed, which results in minimal overhead. Most importantly, no latches are needed to keep the operands of the ALUs, pipes, etc. stable between clock phases.

The hardware of a UNIFIELD architecture can be enhanced to perform multiplication at a low hardware cost, as well as low hardware complexity (Fig. 24). The multiplier circuitry can be stand alone, interacting only with the output and input sides of the bar cells. Additional circuitry to perform parallel load to the multiplier input registers only provides a small speedup, due to the input registers ability to be loaded at the same time the output registers are unloaded. The data transfer to remove the product from the multiplier output registers can be routed into the appropriate sum register, resulting in the addition occurring at the same time of the data transfer. The latter is a unique attribute of the UNIFIELD architecture.

In order to give concrete examples, timing of different operations is provided here. The natural time unit for UNIFIELD is the clock cycle of the parallel part, which should not be assumed to be the same as one propagation delay. For a full-scale development UNIFIELD, this can easily be 100 MHz with nonsaturating bipolar logic (FAST TTL, ECL, etc) or, in excess of 40 MHz with 1 micron HCMOS logic. A speed improvement of approximately 30 over the nonsaturating bipolar silicon implementation can be achieved by utilizing state-of-the-art gallium–arsenide (GaAs) technology. The reference operations are on two-decimal arguments, (which is between 6 and 7 weighted binary bits). Time for addition or subtraction is 20 clock cycles, whereas time for multiplication is 400 clock cycles, as the multiplication is implemented by shifts and adds. These times should be divided by the number of elements in the matrix for a per operation time, with the entire

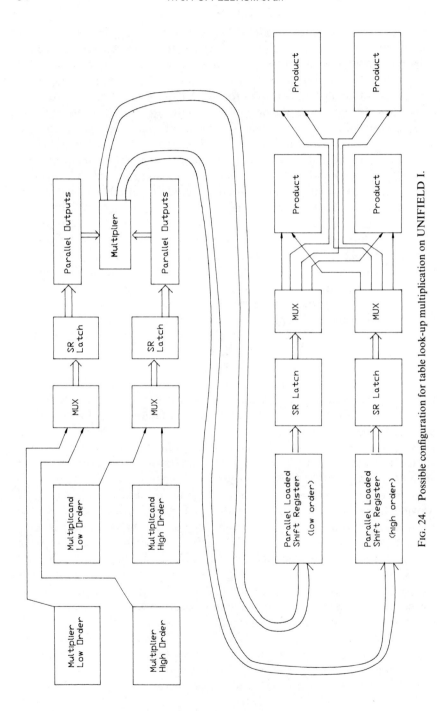

Fig. 24.   Possible configuration for table look-up multiplication on UNIFIELD I.

machine running (i.e., add time of $\frac{20}{64} = 0.31$ clock cycles and multiply time $400/64 = 6.25$ clock cycles). This would yield an effective rate of 130 MIPS if HCMOS is used, 320 MIPS if FAST TTL or ECL is used, and 9.6 GIPS if GaAs is used. These times are not impressive compared to the performance in the respective logic families of similar architectures (SIMD) if we use weighted binary representation; however, the latter would require adders and multipliers. Also, one should remember that there is no such thing as an ALU in UNIFIELD; all the operations are performed with data flowing from module to module. Thus, parallelism, and constant shuffling of data are the factors that affect the overall UNIFIELD speed.

An interesting comparison can be made to bit-slice architectures, of which no mention has been made yet. In a bit-slice architecture, the cost effectiveness comes from the use of relatively few weighted binary registers, with many operations available for two or three bits (e.g., XOR of two bits or addition with carry). This results in a very complicated control structure (which becomes even more complicated when partitioning of the registers is desirable in order to use more of the resources) coupled to a very efficient coding scheme (weighted binary). In this respect, bit-slice is the opposite of the UNIFIELD architecture. The preference of one type of architecture over another has a lot to do with the operations to be performed. For logical operations, bit-slice is undoubtedly superior. For number processing, such aspects as the clock rate or number of intermediate results (which have no overhead for UNIFIELD) are the dominant factor.

To conclude the comparisons to other architectures, the UNIFIELD is not a data flow machine (not in the conventional sense anyway) since there are neither processors to which the data has to be moved in order to perform arithmetic operations nor tags denoting the operations. Actually, UNIFIELD does not have any processors! All of the processing is done by shifting of data in and out of the registers to which they are stored!

7.3 The Line Permuter

The line permuter is an integral part of the UNIFIELD architecture, which deserves special merit. Generally, we could say that the line permuter is a crossbar network. If we wanted a generalized crossbar network for n^2 inputs to an equal number of outputs, the hardware complexity, which is of the order of n^4, would make the endeavor impossible for a high number of n. The implementation of such permutations, however, is exactly what is called for in the UNIFIELD architecture. To do so, one has to forgo the luxury of a general crossbar network and resort to the implementation of a given number of functions as needed; thus, the cost increases *linearly* with the number of functions, whereas the flexibility remains high (provided one knows in advance what kind of permutations are needed).

A predecessor of the line permuter was the FLIP network of the STARAN computer (Batcher, 1974). This was equivalent to a line permuter with shifts of powers of 2 modulo any power of 2. This has been benchmarked to substantially improve performance in FFT algorithms (the butterflies were formed by this network) as well as other applications (Rohrbacher and Potter, 1977). The need of permutation networks for image processing applications is well established (Siegel, 1979).

Comparing the line permuter as a bus scheme to traditional bus schemes of parallel architectures the reader should notice that UNIFIELD does not have the concept of "the neighbor." Generally, in parallel machines there are a few connections of a processor to others, usually to the north, south, west and east neighboring processors. In contrast, the specific permutation determines which position is connected to which other position, thus allowing a high degree of flexibility.

The use of this bus scheme allows us to think of operations applied to the data objects; thus, a rotation is really a rotation of the lines. Until now, all of the operations that were applied on two-dimensional objects (in traditional architectures) were by multiplication with matrices, or with neighbor-to-neighbor data movement till the operation had been completed. Whereas all of these schemes are functionally equivalent, there are direct advantages of the line permuter. A rotation in a traditional architecture may be implemented by multiplying every point in a picture by three matrices of sines and cosines (the general case of 3-D transformation), whereas it could be a mere pass through the line permuter, or (in order to save money) a number of different passes. The reader should notice that in Fig. 22 the 270-degree rotation can really be implemented in two passes, one of 90-degrees with the results passing through a 180-degree rotation!

An additional advantage of the line permuter is that the functions do not have to correspond to linear transformations but to mappings (a superset of linear transformations). Such mappings make certain types of data scrambling/descrambling trivial. Thus, the UNIFIELD machine can have applications even in cryptography. Applications of group theory can be made in real-time.

Solution of nonorthogonal lattices is also trivial. Even though the machine has $n \times n$ elements, which in general form a matrix with the appropriate permutation of lines, we can simulate any kind of lattice. An additional advantage is that sparse matrix operations are particularly suited for UNIFIELD. With a few permutations we can achieve very dense packing of such matrices.

7.4 The UNIFIELD as a Stored Program Computer

UNIFIELD is a stored program computer in the general category of SIMD machines. A centralized unit decodes instructions and forms the control word (which is part of the microinstructions). Mask registers in each position allow for conditional execution of an instruction, whereas a variety of signals from the positions to the control unit (most notably overflow and underflow) allow for conditional machine level instructions (e.g., JUMP if underflow has occurred somewhere).

The claim that programming a parallel computer is a burden is actually not true in the case of UNIFIELD due to the fact that many of the tasks that would traditionally fall on the programmer are now part of the hardware (e.g., matrix transpose, rotations, etc.). It is true, however, that there are applications for which programming the UNIFIELD may be of great difficulty, for example implementation of a text editor that runs on the UNIFIELD. The fact is that this architecture is meant for processing of numerical data for large matrices; it is not intended for general purpose use (e.g., a multiuser environment running editors, etc.).

Image processing applications are of particular interest. With simple modifications to the line permuter, we can achieve operations such as convolution in time equal to that of regular permutations. The specific example can be implemented with a line permuter that uses threshold logic on the value of one position and its neighbors to determine the output of that position—the compacted notation guarantees that the results are valid. It is extremely important to realize that many operations are performed in a time independent of the matrix size and dependent only on r, p, and the number of successive permutations that are needed (normally a small number, if not 1). This gives the "slow" processing elements of UNIFIELD an advantage, because the number of operations that are necessary for a given task is reduced dramatically. Take, for example, the 90-degree rotation; for UNIFIELD I this operation will take 20 clock cycles, no multiplications, and no additions.

7.5 Implementation

As a proof of the UNIFIELD concept a $U\langle 8, 10, 2, 4, 32 \rangle$ is under development at the Information Engineering Laboratory of the Computer Science Department of the University of Illinois. This is a processor with an 8×8 matrix of 1 in 100-decimal representation numbers, four modules (two modules may be used as one double precision module for multiplication results), and 32 permutations. In addition, a data memory will be provided, not only to store partial results, but to facilitate the loading of data and mask patterns from a PDP 11/40 that is used as the front end of the machine. The machine was put into operation in the summer of 1986. The LS (low-power Shottky) subfamily of TTL was chosen for the implementation after cost-performance evaluation of the different options. The data memory is MOS, and the drivers and line permuters are FAST TTL (in order to ensure proper fan-out). Due to the constraints of the project, speed is not a concern, but reliable operation is. The machine is being used in order to evaluate the architecture and develop algorithms for a second generation implementation (Dollas, 1985).

7.6   Ideas for the Future of UNIFIELD

In practice, it might be desirable to use rather big arrays of buses with the appropriate permutation facilities. One approach is to use a mixture of (space-multiplexed) wires and a time-division scheme (Aurenz, 1986). Another idea is to use color carriers of densely spaced frequencies (Dollas, 1984). It might be possible to incorporate light switches in this so-called spectrum sample transmission. Research on the subject is presently being done in the Information Engineering Laboratory in the Department of Computer Science of the University of Illinois at Urbana-Champaign.

It is also quite possible—once one agrees to perhaps a quarter of a million (512×512) buses—to represent directly complex numbers or even quaternions. Certain problems in pattern recognition then become more amenable to calculation!

7.7   Summary of UNIFIELD

The UNIFIELD is a parallel machine that uses data flow into and out of shift registers to perform arithmetic. A parallel bus with hardwired permutations from the input to the output allows for transformations that are independent of the matrix size, and the overall architecture has minimal overhead for the control structure. Addition and subtraction are performed without any additional hardware, and even though these operations are not as fast as the comparable weighted binary, the high clock rates possible because of the natural absence of races make this scheme competitive. Virtually no time is lost for data transfer to and from processors because *data transfer and arithmetic operations are one and the same thing!*

8.   Summary and Outlook for Unary Processing

Unary Processing uses the simple counting of digits that have all the same weight. It has seen applications from finger counting to high-speed computing. Time interval counting suggested simple calculators and then general purpose computers (Babbage's machines). During the twentieth century, in what is often termed the "second industrial revolution," unary processing appeared in the simulation of organic functions; it then evolved into probabilistic and deterministic forms. The machines that have been built over the years (mainly in the Information Engineering Laboratory at the University of Illinois at Urbana-Champaign) are working proof of the soundness of this form of processing. It is interesting to note that the latest step in this "unary evolution," the pulse gear methods, has remarkable resemblance to the early steps. Indeed, one can find more than a casual similarity between Pascal's "Pascaline" calculator and the UNIFIELD computer.

The future of unary processing will undoubtably include larger and more powerful computers of some of the architectures that we described (stochastic, burst and pulse gear type), as well as new ones (a mix of the above with bundle processing might be attractive). Due to the novelty of these methods, it is not expected that they will be used for all computers but rather in specific areas, such as image processing, fault tolerant computing, and communication and control problems. The present trend in electronics is to use more than two states for logic. The obvious extension is to have states of powers of 2, in which all of the traditional weighted binary techniques and applications can be used: a less obvious extension is to have multistate logic, which is a space–domain homomorphism of the unary methods that we have discussed already. A great comeback of unary methods is expected with progress in the study of "chaotic systems" in physics; i.e., systems that are described deterministically but exhibit random behavior because of the finite precision of the initial values. Indeed, such applications (which include weather prediction) can be directly implemented with probabilistic unary machines or with hybrid unary/weighted binary machines. This comeback is expected during the 1990s, or the beginning of the new millenium.

REFERENCES

Afuso, C. (1968). Analog computation with random pulse sequences. Dept. Computer Science Report 255, University of Illinois, Urbana-Champaign.

Aurenz, S. A. (1986). On the design of low-cost permutation networks for parallel processing. M.S. thesis, Dept. Electrical and Computer Engineering, University of Illinois, Urbana-Champaign.

Batcher, K. E. (1974). STARAN parallel processor system hardware. *Proc. Nat'l. Computer Conf.* **3**.

Batcher, K. E. (1980). Design of a massively parallel processor. *IEEE Trans. Comput.* **C-29** (9), 1–9.

Bracha, E. (1975). BURSTCALC: A burst calculator. Dept. Computer Science Report UIUCDCS-R-75-769, University of Illinois, Urbana-Champaign.

Bracha, E. (1977). WALSHSTORE: The application of burst processing to failsoft storage systems using Walsh transforms. Dept. Computer Science Report UIUCDCS-R-77-878, University of Illinois, Urbana-Champaign.

Brown, A. W., and Mars, P. (1978). Some aspects of the design of a general purpose digital stochastic computer. *Proc. Int'l. Stochastic Computing*, Tolouse, France, pp. 167–191.

Coombes, D. (1970). SABUMA—safe bundle machine. Dept. Computer Science Report 412, University of Illinois, Urbana-Champaign.

Cutler, J. R. (1974). ERGODIC: Computing with a combination of stochastic and bundle processing. Dept. Computer Science Report UIUCDCS-R-74-630, University of Illinois, Urbana-Champaign.

Cutler, J. R. (1975a). Molecular stochastics: A study of direct production of Stochastic sequences from transducers. Dept. Computer Science Report UIUCDCS-R-75-723, University of Illinois, Urbana-Champaign.

Cutler, J. R., and Ficke, D. (1975b). A stochastic control system. Dept. Computer Science Report UIUCDCS-R-75-752, University of Illinois, Urbana-Champaign.

Dollas, A. (1984). Spectrum sample transmission: A new concept in wavelength division multiplexing. Dept. Computer Science Report UIUCDCS-R-84-1172, University of Illinois, Urbana-Champaign.

Dollas, A. (1985). UNIFIELD I specifications. Information Engineering Laboratory, Dept. Computer Science, University of Illinois, Urbana-Champaign.

Esch, J. W. (1969a). A display for demonstrating analog computations with random pulse sequences (POSTCOMP). Dept. Computer Science Report 312, University of Illinois, Urbana-Champaign.

Esch, J. W. (1969b). RASCEL, a programmable analog computer based on a regular array of stochastic computing element logic. Dept. Computer Science Report 332, University of Illinois, Urbana-Champaign.

Gaines, B. R. (1967a). Stochastic computing. *AFIPS Conf. Proc.* **30**, 149–156.

Gaines, B. R. (1967b). Stochastic computer thrives on noise. *Electronics* **7**, 72–79.

Gaines, B. R. (1974). The role of randomness in cybernetic systems. *Proc. Conf. Recent Topics in Cybernetics*, Cybernetics Society, London.

Gander, J. C. (1978). A simple stochastic implementation of the linear prediction filter. *Proc. 1st Int'l. Symp. Stochastic Computing*, Tolouse, France, pp. 193–201.

Ghest, C. (1971). Multiplying made easy for digital assemblies. *Electronics* **44.**

Gittleman, A. (1975). "History of Mathematics." Charles E. Merrill, Columbus, Ohio.

Glickman, J. (1985). Private conversations with C. O'Toole and A. Dollas.

Goldstine, H. H. (1972). "The Computer from Pascal to von Neumann." Princeton University Press, Princeton, New Jersey.

Hopcroft, H. E., and Ullman, J. D. (1979). "Introduction to Automata Theory, Languages, and Computation." Addison-Wesley, Reading, Massachusetts.

Jones, N. D. (1973). "Computability Theory: An Introduction." Academic Press, New York.

Loeckx, J. (1972). "Computability and Decidability." Springer-Verlag, New York.

Mars, P., and McLean, H. R. (1976a). High speed matrix inversion by stochastic computer. *Electronics Letters* **12** (18), 457–459.

Mars, P., and McLean, H. R. (1976b). Implementation of linear programming using a digital stochastic computer. *Electronics Letters* **12** (20), 516–517.

Mars, P., and Poppelbaum W. J. (1981). "Stochastic and deterministic averaging processors." IEE, London, Peter Peregrinus Ltd.

Marvel, O. E. (1970). TRANSFORMATRIX, an image processor. Dept. Computer Science Report UIUCDCS-R-70-393, University of Illinois, Urbana-Champaign.

Mirambet, P., Castanie, F., and Hoffmann, J. C. (1978). Application du calcul stochastique à la régulation de turbomachines. *Proc. 1st Int'l. Symp. Stochastic Computing*, Tolouse, France, pp. 249–260.

Mohan, L. P. (1976). The application of burst processing to digital FM receivers. Dept. Computer Science Report UIUCDCS-R-76-780, University of Illinois, Urbana-Champaign.

Mohan, L. P., (1975). Performance evaluation of the digital AM receiver. Dept. Computer Science Report UIUCDCS-R-75-757, University of Illinois, Urbana-Champaign.

Morrison, P., and Morrison, E. (1961). "Charles Babbage and His Calculating Engines." Dover Publications, Mineola, New York.

Needham, J. (1959). "The Heavenly Clockwork." Cambridge University Press, Cambridge, England.

Neville, R. G., and Mars, P. (1978). Hardware synthesis of stochastic learning automata. *Proc. 1st Int'l. Symp. Stochastic Computing,* Tolouse, France, pp. 364–365.

Pitt, D. A. (1978a). A new hardware approach to coefficient determination for the linear prediction of speech, Dept. Computer Science Report UIUCDCS-R-78-951, University of Illinois, Urbana-Champaign.

Pitt, D. A. (1978b). Bandwidth compression of speech using linear prediction and burst processing. *Proc. 1st Int'l. Symp. Stochastic Computing,* Tolouse, France, pp. 55–63.

Poppelbaum, W. J. (1968a). What is next in computer technology? Advances in Computers **9,** Academic Press, 1–22.

Poppelbaum, W. J. (1968b). Projects in the hardware research group of the Dept. Computer Science of the University of Illinois. Dept. Computer Science Report 281, University of Illinois, Urbana-Champaign.

Poppelbaum, W. J. (1972). "Computer Hardware Theory." Macmillan, New York.

Poppelbaum, W. J. (1973). A practicability program in stochastic processing. Proposal to the Office of Naval Research, Dept. Computer Science Report, University of Illinois, Urbana-Champaign.

Poppelbaum, W. J. (1974a). Statistical processors. Dept. Computer Science Report, University of Illinois, Urbana-Champaign.

Poppelbaum, W. J. (1974b). Applicability of stochastic-, bundle-, and burst-processing and the ARC information conveyor to the practical needs of the navy. Proposal to the Office of Naval Research, Dept. Computer Science Report, University of Illinois, Urbana-Champaign.

Poppelbaum, W. J. (1974c). A practicability program in stochastic processing, Appendix I. Proposal for additional work to be done in the area of a novel PCM transmission and processing system called burst processing, Dept. Computer Science Report, University of Illinois, Urbana-Champaign.

Poppelbaum, W. J. (1975). Application of stochastic and burst processing to communication and computing systems. Proposal to the Office of Naval Research, Dept. Computer Science Report, University of Illinois, Urbana-Champaign.

Poppelbaum, W. J. (1976). Statistical processors. Advances in Computers **17,** Academic Press, 187–230.

Poppelbaum, W. J. (1978). Burst processing: A deterministic counterpart to stochastic computing. *Proc. 1st Int'l. Symp. Stochastic Computing,* Tolouse, France, pp. 1–30.

Poppelbaum, W. J. (1979). Burst processing. Dept. Computer Science Report UIUCDCS-R-79-957, University of Illinois, Urbana-Champaign.

Poppelbaum, W. J. (1983). The UNIFIELD processor, a matrix computer using strings of "ones" to represent decimals. Information Engineering Laboratory, Dept. Computer Science, University of Illinois, Urbana-Champaign. (Revised November, 1984).

Poppelbaum, W. J., Afuso, C., and Esch, J. W. (1967). Stochastic computing elements and systems. *AFIPS, Proc. FJCC,* **30,** 149–156.

Ring, D. (1969). BUM—A bundle processing machine. Dept. Computer Science Report 353, University of Illinois, Urbana-Champaign.

Robinson, C. M. (1977). BURSTLOCK: A digital phase-locked loop using burst techniques. Dept. Computer Science Report UIUCDCS-R-77-872, University of Illinois, Urbana-Champaign.

Rohrbacher D., and Potter, J. L. (1977). Image processing with the STARAN parallel computer. *Computer* **10** (8), 54–59.

Russel, R. M. (1978). The CRAY-1 computer system. *Commun. ACM* **21** (1).

Ryan, L. D. (1971). System and circuit design of TRANSFORMATRIX. Dept. Computer Science Report UIUCDCS-R-71-435, University of Illinois, Urbana-Champaign.

Shannon, C. E., and McCarthy J., eds. (1956). "Automata Studies." Princeton University Press, Princeton, New Jersey.

Shaw, R. F. (1950). Arithmetic operations in a binary computer. *Rev. Sci. Instrum.* **21**

Siegel, H. J. (1979). Interconnection networks for SIMD machines. *Computer* **12** (6), 57–65.

Stenzel, W. J., Kubitz, W. J., and Garcia, G. H. (1977). A compact high-speed parallel multiplication scheme. *IEEE Trans. Comput.* **C-26**

Stifler, W. W., Jr., ed. (1950). "High-Speed Computing Devices." McGraw-Hill, New York.

Taylor, G. L. (1975). An analysis of burst encoding methods and transmission properties. Dept. Computer Science Report UIUCDCS-R-75-770, University of Illinois, Urbana-Champaign.

Tietz, L. C. (1977). BURSTLOGIC: Design and analysis of logic circuitry to perform arithmetic on data in the burst format. Dept. Computer Science Report UIUCDCS-R-77-895, University of Illinois, Urbana-Champaign.

Tse, B. K. P. (1974). BURP: A bundle repeater and restorer. Dept. Computer Science Report UIUCDCS-R-74-689, University of Illinois, Urbana-Champaign.

Turing, A. M. (1936). On computable numbers with an application to the entscheidungsproblem. *Proc. London Mathematical Society* **2** (42), 230–265. A Correction, *ibid.* **2** (43), 544–546.

Vernieres, F., Castanie, F., and Hoffmann, J. C. (1978). Analyseur spectral stochastique 1 Bit Large-Bande, *Proc. 1st Int'l. Symp. Stochastic Computing,* Tolouse, France, pp. 403–410.

Wells, D. K. (1977). Digital filtering using burst processing techniques. Dept. Computer Science Report UIUCDCS-R-77-871, University of Illinois, Urbana-Champaign.

Wo, Y. K. (1973). A novel stochastic computer based on a set of autonomous processing elements (APE). Dept. Computer Science Report UIUCDCS-R-73-556, University of Illinois, Urbana-Champaign.

Wolff, M. (1977). Transmission of analog signals using burst techniques. Dept. Computer Science Report UIUCDCS-R-77-838, University of Illinois, Urbana-Champaign.

Wolff, M. (1978). Digital encoding and decoding using burst techniques. *Proc. 1st Int'l. Symp. Stochastic Computing,* Tolouse, France, pp. 31–44.

Xydes, C. J. (1977). Application of burst processing to the spectral decomposition of speech. Dept. Computer Science Report UIUCDCS-R-77-870, University of Illinois, Urbana-Champaign.

Xydes, C. J. (1978). The decomposition of speech using burst processing. *Proc. 1st Int'l. Symp. Stochastic Computing,* Tolouse, France, pp. 45–54.

Zepf, K. (1906). "Grundzuge der Geschichte des Rechnens." Verlag der Hofbuchhandlung Friedrich Gutsch, Karlsruhe.

Parallel Algorithms for Some Computational Problems

ABHA MOITRA

Department of Computer Science
Cornell University
Ithaca, New York 14853

S. SITHARAMA IYENGAR

Department of Computer Science
Louisiana State University
Baton Rouge, Louisiana 70803

93

1. Introduction

In recent years we have witnessed a tremendous surge in the availability of very fast and inexpensive hardware. This has been made possible partly by the use of faster circuit technologies and smaller feature sizes; partly by novel architectural features such as pipelining, vector processing, cache memories, and systolic arrays; and partly by using novel interconnections between processors and memories, such as Hypercube, Omega network, Orthogonal Tree network, and others.

Our ability to design fast and cheap hardware, however, far outstrips our ability to utilize that hardware effectively to solve large problems quickly. This is mainly because a large problem may not be easy to decompose into smaller problems that could be solved in parallel, on account of data dependencies between the subproblems. The intrinsic parallelism of a problem can be defined as the product of the time required for solving it by the fastest parallel algorithm, and the number of processors required by that algorithm, divided by the time required by the best sequential algorithm. For a problem with high internal data dependency, the intrinsic parallelism would be very low.

Because of these data dependencies, processes solving related subproblems would need to communicate with each other. This communication could be via shared memory (with or without concurrent access), via a data bus, or via an interconnection network. Any specific scheme incurs an overhead in terms of time lost to contention, latency, or both, and additional overhead in hardware costs, which do not reduce dramatically with improved technology as does that of the underlying circuits. Further, a communication scheme that is good for one class of problems may not be good for another class, which only adds to our difficulty in finding a parallel algorithm.

Memory contention can slow down the execution of a parallel algorithm if the various processing elements must access the same variable at the same time; some systems must be devised so that only one processor can access a given variable at any one time (for example, LOCK and UNLOCK on MIMD machines). Also, if the number of logical processors is larger than the number of physical processors in the machine, some sort of scheduling must be done to determine where the extra processes will eventually be handled. The scheduling cost is the resource allocated to do this scheduling. For efficient scheduling, the extra logical processes should be saved until a processor is available, and the internal state of the logical processes should be monitored.

One factor that can vary greatly between machines and that influences execution speed is the cost of creating a new process. For example, if a single process created all the other processes, then the cost of constructing p processes is $O(p)$. On the other hand, if new processes are created dynamically by other existing processes, then in the best case the construction cost of

p processes is $O(\log p)$ if process creation corresponds to a binary tree configuration.

Examination of the above factors suggests two paradigms that can help improve parallel algorithms. The first is to design an algorithm with a large grain size and a smaller number of processes (grain size refers to the amount of processing done by an individual process). The second suggests that the optimal number of processes is a compromise between the gain provided by each process and the time lost to synchronization.

1.1 Models of Parallel Computation

The design of parallel algorithms becomes an important issue as numerous parallel architectures are developed. In fact, a considerable number of very different architectures for parallel computing are in existence. They range from special-purpose array processors to tree machines to loosely coupled networks of processors. Since the design and performance of a parallel algorithm depends very much on the architecture of the parallel machine, it is necessary to keep the architecture in mind when designing parallel algorithms. There is, however, no universal method for designing parallel algorithms. One approach to constructing parallel algorithms is to recognize parallelism in the existing sequential algorithms. This approach has been studied by several researchers (Keller 1973; Lee et al. 1985; Moitra and Iyengar 1986; Nicolau 1985; Shrira et al. 1983; Strom and Yemini 1985). We will therefore first examine briefly some parallel machine models of computations that have been proposed.

1.1.1 SIMD Machine

An SIMD (Single Instruction, Multiple Data) machine consists of an array of identical processors. All processors simultaneously execute the same instruction, supplied by the control unit, possibly on different data items. The execution of the instructions is synchronous in the sense that each processor executing the instruction in parallel must be allowed to finish before the next instruction is taken up for execution.

Different models are obtained, depending on whether the two types of conflicts are allowed or not. In the SIMD–SM model, reading and writing conflicts are not allowed; in SIMD–SM–R, simultaneous reading (but not writing) is allowed. In SIMD–SM–RW, simultaneous reading and writing is allowed; in case a number of processors attempt to write to the same location at the same time, different assumptions can be made about which process succeeds in writing. In the equality conflict resolution, simultaneous writing is permitted only when all processors attempt to store the same value. In priority conflict resolution, all the processors are linearly ordered according to some priority, and the processor with the highest priority attempting to write succeeds. In arbitrary conflict resolution, any arbitrary processor attempting to write succeeds.

1.1.2 MIMD Machine

MIMD stands for Multiple Instruction, Multiple Data; such machines consist of *processing elements* (PEs), which may be individually indexed. Each PE is capable of performing the standard arithmetic and logical operations. In addition each PE knows its index and has some local memory. The PEs operate asynchronously under the control of individual instruction streams. Different PEs can execute different instructions at any time. During the computation PEs communicate results to each other. In many MIMD models the time required to communicate data from PE to PE dominates the overall complexity of the algorithm. Several interprocessor communication models for MIMD computers have been proposed in the literature. The communication overhead of an algorithm varies from one communication model to the other; the shared memory (SM) model is well studied. This model has no communication delay. In a shared-memory computer there is a large common memory that is shared by all PEs. It is assumed that any PE can access any word in common memory in $O(1)$ time. When two or more PEs read from (write to) the same location simultaneously, we say that a read (write) conflict has occurred.

In the MIMD–TC model, the processors are attached tightly through a central switching mechanism to reach the global memory. Stone (1980) states that architectures based on the MIMD–TC model have limited numbers of processors because of the cost involved in the switching process. An example of this architecture is C.mmp, which has sixteen processors.

1.1.3 Tree Machine

The tree machine of Bentley and Kung (1979) consists of $O(n)$ processors of three types. A processor of type 1 is capable of broadcasting data it receives, processors of type 2 can combine their inputs in an elementary way. A processor of type 3 stores program and data of size $O(n)$.

1.1.4 Special-Purpose Parallel Machines

The advent of parallel processing (specifically VLSI) has led to the development of a number of special-purpose parallel machines to support directory structures. Leiserson (1979), Bentley and Kung (1979), Ottaman et al. (1982), and Atallah and Kosaraju (1985) proposed pipelined architectures based on a balanced binary tree. $O(n)$ PEs are used to support a search tree containing up to n elements. The machines vary in their wiring complexity and the variety of dictionary operations they support. Generally, all of them can perform the basic dictionary operations in $O(\log n)$ time. The complexity of the dictionary operation varies on the input pipeline intervals. The Atallah and Kosaraju (1985) machine provides $O(\log n)$ performance with a pipeline interval of $O(1)$ for a wide range of dictionary operations (n is the actual number of elements stored in the $O(n)$-PE machine). The above designs maintain the dictionary elements in some sorted order. Somani and Agarwal (1984) propose a binary tree machine with $O(n)$ PEs that does not require any sorted order for the dictionary elements. Their design supports all dictionary operations and provides an $O(\log n)$ time performance with constant pipeline interval. Tanaka et al. (1980) propose a pipelined architecture for maintaining a search tree of n elements with only $O(\log n)$ PEs. Fisher (1984) developed an architecture based on the Trie structure. In this design the number of PEs is proportional to the length of the maximum key; this scheme is advantageous when the dictionary keys are long. These pipelined architectures achieve only an $O(\log n)$ throughput improvement over the serial balanced-tree algorithms. When the number of records in the dictionary becomes greater than n these designs will not function, i.e., the hardware is tailored to the maximal possible number of elements in the tables. While the $O(n)$ PE architectures can efficiently handle operations beyond basic dictionary functions, they have no advantage over the $O(\log n)$ designs when only the basic operations are considered.

1.2   Techniques for Exploiting Parallelism in Algorithms

In most sequential algorithms some degree of parallelism exists; it is the task of the programmer to exploit it in the most efficient way. Since it is often the case that only one parallelization technique can be applied to an algorithm at a time, a careful examination of the algorithm must be made before a technique can be chosen. The speed-up ratio s, used for comparing the sequential algorithm with the parallel algorithm, is the time required for the sequential execution, divided by the time required for parallel execution. In the ideal case, s would be equal to the number of processors used in the parallel execution.

Data partitioning is one technique that can be applied to many algorithms. Data can be partitioned in two ways: statically and dynamically. In static partitioning, the data to be processed is partitioned into p processes, where p is the number of processes. Each processor handles one group of data, and each processor shares the same code. This type of partitioning is efficiently implemented on an SIMD machine. Dynamic partitioning allows data to be subdivided between active processors, as in the tree machine.

In some cases, computational partitioning can be performed on an algorithm. If several subprograms must be performed, and each of these subprograms is independent of the other subprograms, then each can be assigned its own processor. These processors have their own codes and execute independently, at their own speeds. Moitra (1986) discusses a general technique for data and computation partitioning to obtain distributed programs.

If several processors must make changes on a certain variable, memory contention can be minimized through localization. To decrease the access to these shared variables, a copy of the variable is made in the memory local to a processor. The processor uses this local variable to do its computations; then, if necessary, the global variable is updated at the end of the subprogram. It is possible in some cases to relax the control mechanism so that the parallel processor system is working asynchronously instead of synchronously. This method is called *relaxation* and involves replacing explicit synchronization with implicit synchronization to provide more flexibility.

A software pipeline is a software implementation of the pipeline machine discussed earlier. Each processor behaves like a pipeline segment, with items being passed down the line from one process to another. An item is said to be consumed by process i when process i is finished with it; when an item is consumed by process i, an item is produced for process $i + 1$. The output rate of the pipeline is dependent on the time spent in the slowest segment of the pipe, since this forms a sort of bottleneck behind which other items must wait before they can be processed. It is therefore wise to divide the algorithm into a number of processes that require approximately the same execution time. Synchronization is done by software also, most often using shared variables. When a process has consumed an item, it may set a flag in the shared memory, which the next process checks when it is free. If this flag is not set, meaning that the previous processes are not through with the item, the process continues checking the flag, essentially waiting until the item is available for processing. Synchronization cost can be said to be $O(1)$, since only two processes need to read or write into a given cell.

To sum up, it can be said that the amount of parallelism that can be achieved is dependent on all the above factors, with emperical evidence indicating that the granularity of the processes and communication requirements are usually the most critical and time-consuming for parallel algorithms.

For excellent surveys see Kung (1980) for a discussion on the structure and characterization of parallel algorithms, and Kuck (1976) where parallel processing of ordinary sequential programs is considered.

1.3   Computational Model Used

Observation 1. The parallel architectures mentioned above have some inherent drawbacks, namely the focus on a specific architecture does not provide insight into the logical structure of the algorithms. It also makes the transfer of an algorithm to a different architecture difficult.

Observation 2. Computational models for asynchronous parallelism are very abstract in nature (for example, Petri nets). This level of abstraction, while very powerful for structuring process interactions, often hides the actual computation process of the algorithm and makes the analysis of execution difficult.

Thus we must restrict ourselves to some specific but general model. We will mainly use the SIMD–SM model (and its various submodels) for the purpose of this paper. This choice is a natural one, since most parallel algorithms are indeed based on this model.

1.4   Paradigms for Organizing Parallel Computation

The design of parallel algorithms involves choosing appropriate data structures, allocating processors, and finally the algorithm to do the computation. All these three aspects can be combined under the heading of *computation organization.* Certain simple computation organizations are used frequently in the problems solved in the literature, and hence we will first identify these basic techniques in the form of paradigms. We will introduce three paradigms for computation organization.

1.4.1   Binary Tree Paradigm

Consider the problem of calculating a function F of n data items $(d_1, \ldots, d_n)$. If the function F is such that $(d_1, \ldots, d_n)$ can be calculated by combining the results $F(d_1, \ldots, d_{n/2})$ and $F(d_{n/2+1}, \ldots, d_n)$ then we can organize the computation of F in the form of a binary tree. The data forms the leaves of the binary tree, and the computation proceeds in steps. The processors are assigned so that all the computation at a level can be done as one step (and the same processors are reassigned for the next step). For a problem of size n, where n is a power of two, the number of processors required for the entire computation is $n/2$. If the processing at each step takes c units of time, then the entire computation takes $c * log\ n$ units of time. A simple illustration of this technique is the problem of computing the sum of n numbers that uses $O(n)$ processors and requires $O(\log n)$ time.

In the above description, notice that the computation proceeds from the leaves to the root, and that the entire problem is solved when the processor at the root does its computation. Most of the problems solved using the binary tree method are of this form. The binary tree method is more general, however, (see Dekel and Sahni 1983a), and lends itself to problems in which a number of passes over the computation tree have to be made, each odd pass from leaves to the root, and each even pass from the root to the leaves.

A simple illustration of this idea is the partial sums problem, where $S_j = \Sigma_{i=1}^{j} d_i$, $1 \leq j \leq n$ is to be calculated. Notice that in the first pass of the computation tree not all the S_j's are computed, but the remaining S_j's can be computed by making the second pass from the root to the leaves. In the second pass each vertex transmits to its children the sum of all the values to the left of each child.

1.4.2   Growing by Doubling

In the binary tree method, the first pass can be visualized in another way. At each step an (active) processor doubles the number of elements for which it has calculated the function F. Hence "growth" is achieved by doubling at each step. There are other ways in which this type of doubling technique can be used, even when there is no binary tree structure associated with the problem. A simple illustration is the problem of counting the number of elements in a linked list. This is done by associating a processor with each element of a list that maintains a pointer to an element further down the list; at each step the distance the pointer spans is doubled by setting the pointer to the value of the pointer belonging to the element pointed to on the previous iteration.

1.4.3   Spanning Tree for Graphs

A very important class of parallel algorithms present in the literature is the graph-theoretic. A large majority of graph-theoretic problems are solved sequentially by first finding a depth-first spanning tree. The construction of a depth-first spanning tree seems, however, to be inherently sequential, and hence cannot be done efficiently in a parallel model. Consequently, most of the sequential algorithms based on depth-first spanning trees are rather different from their parallel counterparts.

One way that graph-theoretic problems relying on depth-first spanning trees are converted into efficient parallel algorithms is by making use of any spanning tree (Tarjan and Vishkin, 1984). In general, an algorithm based on any arbitrary spanning tree is more complicated than the one based on a depth-first spanning tree, but this is a price that must be paid to obtain efficient parallel algorithms.

We now describe the spanning tree construction of Tarjan and Vishkin (1984), which is based on the connectivity algorithm of Shiloach and Vishkin

(1982). Each vertex v has a pointer field $D[v]$ through which it points to another vertex or itself. The algorithm proceeds in a number of iterations. Initially, $D[i] = i$ for $i = 1, \ldots, n$; i.e., all vertices are in component trees by themselves. At any iteration, the graph is always a forest of rooted trees plus self-loops that occur only in the roots; each one of these is called a *D-tree*. The algorithm proceeds by *hooking* one tree onto another. This has the effect of decreasing the number of trees, as well as increasing the size of individual trees. For efficiency, each rooted tree is kept so that each vertex is connected directly to the root; since the process of hooking violates this condition, the algorithm also performs *path compression* or *shortcutting*, in which a vertex is brought closer to the root. The D-pointers are therefore changed by two kinds of steps:

Step 1. Shortcutting: $D[i] = D[D[i]]$.
Step 2. Hooking: $D[D[i]] = D[j]$, where $D[i]$ is the root of a D-tree, j is a vertex in another D-tree, and (i, j) is an edge in the graph. That is, trees are hooked together. At this point simultaneous writing to the same location is used and it does not matter which one succeeds.

The edges used in the hooking step correspond to the edges in the spanning tree. This algorithm runs in $O(\log n)$ time using $O(n + m)$ processors.

1.5 Paradigms for Improving the Efficiency of Parallel Algorithms

The efficiency of any parallel algorithm A is measured by defining what is known as the *effective processor utilization*, or EPU, defined as

$$\text{EPU} = \frac{\text{complexity of the fastest sequential algorithm for problem}}{\text{number of processors used in } A * \text{time complexity of } A}$$

Note that $0 \leq \text{EPU} \leq 1$, and that an EPU equal to one is the best possible and corresponds to maximum speed-up. As an illustration, the EPU for the sum of n numbers algorithm in the previous section is $n/(n * \log n) = 1/\log n$.

In any parallel algorithm there is always a trade-off between the number of processors and the computation time (within some limits). For instance, for any algorithm a new version may be obtained by allocating the processing of a number of processors to a single processor, thereby reducing the number of processors required, at the expense of computation time. Notice, however, that for any such simple scheme the EPU remains constant.

There are times where reallocation of the processing to the processors can be done in such a way as to increase the EPU of the new version of the existing algorithm. We describe two such general techniques below.

1.5.1 Processor Reduction Without Increasing Time Complexity

Consider the problem of finding the sum of n numbers, discussed before. Suppose $p \leq n/2$ processors are available. To compute the lowest-level sum would require at most $\lceil n/2p \rceil$ time; the next higher level would require at most $\lceil n/4p \rceil$, and so on. The total time T required satisfies

$$T \leq \left\lceil \frac{n}{2p} \right\rceil + \left\lceil \frac{n}{4p} \right\rceil + \cdots + \left\lceil \frac{n}{2^{\lceil \log n \rceil}p} \right\rceil$$

$$\leq 1 + \frac{n}{2p} + 1 + \frac{n}{4p} + \cdots + 1 + \frac{n}{2^{\lceil \log n \rceil}p}$$

$$= \lceil \log n \rceil + \frac{n}{p}\left[\frac{1}{2} + \frac{1}{4} + \cdots + \frac{1}{2^{\lceil \log n \rceil}} \right]$$

$$\leq c_1 * \log n + c_2 * \frac{n}{p}$$

$$= O\left(\log n + \frac{n}{p} \right)$$

Notice that we can obtain a running time of $O(\log n)$ if $p = n/\log n$. That is, we have reduced the number of processors required while keeping the same time complexity. This type of improvement can be made for a number of problems; we call it the *processor reduction* or PR paradigm.

1.5.2 Time-Complexity Reduction Without Increasing the Number of Processors

Consider again the problem of finding the sum of n numbers. This problem, as we had indicated above, can be solved recursively by adding the sums of two smaller lists of numbers. This recursive structure was reflected in the algorithm of the previous section, where the recursion was unraveled all the way down. We now show how the time complexity can be reduced by unraveling the recursion only part of the way down; this will be done in such a way as to not increase the number of processors required.

Let the recursion be unraveled until we are left with blocks of size x whose sum has to be computed. Now, for each block we can allocate one processor to obtain the sum in time $O(x)$. The number of such blocks is n/x. Hence the computation time required is $T = O(x + \log(n/x))$. To minimize the time we require that $x = \log(n/x)$, to give us $n = x * 2^x$. When $n = x * 2^x$ we can compute the sum of n numbers in time $O(\log 2^x)$, and the number of processors required is 2^x. We call this technique the *time reduction* or TR paradigm. Another example of its usage is a sorting algorithm in Hirschberg (1978).

Notice that this technique allows us to decrease the time complexity as well as the number of processors required from that required in the algorithm of the previous section. This technique also yields a faster algorithm than the one by the PR paradigm, though this speed up is at the expense of the number of processors. For both of the algorithms in this section the product of the number of processors and the time complexity is the same; that is,

using paradigm PR, number of processors * time complexity

$$= \frac{n}{\log n} * \log n = n$$

using paradigm TR, number of processors * time complexity $= 2^x * \log 2^x$

$$= 2^x * x = n$$

Further, for both the algorithms obtained in this section the EPU $= 1$, the best possible that can be achieved theoretically.

There are two different assumptions that can be made about the number of processors available. Under *unbounded parallelism*, arbitrarily many processors are assumed to be available. Under *bounded parallelism*, a limited number of processors, independent of the problem size, are assumed to be available.

1.6 Organization and Scope of the Paper

Section 2 presents a survey of parallel algorithms for finding the connected and biconnected components of a graph. Section 3 discusses the various parallel algorithms for the minimum spanning tree problem. Section 4 discusses various other parallel graph algorithms for shortest path, maximum matching, planarity testing, maximal independent set, etc. Section 5 considers parallel algorithms for various nongraph-theoretic problems like arithmetic expression and polynomial evaluation, string matching, tree balancing, and alpha–beta search. Finally, section 6 presents some conclusions.

In our treatment of parallel algorithms we have excluded discussion on sorting and numerical algorithms, as well as any algorithms for VLSI and systolic arrays. An extensive amount of literature exists for parallel sorting and numerical algorithms, for instance, Bitton et al. (1984), Chen (1975), Dekel et al. (1981), Gentleman (1978), Lakshmivarahan et al. (1984), Sameh (1977). Kuck (1977) deals with parallel machine organization and programming, while Kuhn and Padua (1981) contains a collection of papers dealing with parallel processor taxonomies, pipeline, dataflow and array processors, compilers for translating sequential programs into parallel ones, operating systems for parallel computers, etc. Lee et al. (1985) deals with implementation details required for restructuring various nonnumerical programs for parallel processing.

The parallel algorithms we discuss are all deterministic, even though numerous randomized algorithms exist in the literature. Randomization can often achieve better efficiency than deterministic algorithms. The study of random algorithms is a current research focus and a lot more work needs to be done in this area.

In this paper we have attempted to give a survey of parallel algorithms for a class of computational problems. Undoubtedly, some algorithm may have been overlooked, but any such omissions were unintentional.

2.   Parallel Connectivity Algorithms

2.1   Parallel Connected Components Algorithms

The various parallel algorithms for finding the connected components of undirected graphs can be broadly classified according to two major criteria — the basic technique employed and the format of the input. The basic techniques used in these algorithms have been breadth-first search, transitive closure, and vertex collapse. The most common form of the input is adjacency matrix. The popularity of the adjacency matrix form of input in general stems from the fact that it allows graph-theoretic problems to be stated and solved in terms of matrix manipulation problems. This works very well for dense graphs, but for sparse graphs this may lead to inefficient algorithms, so quite often input in the form of adjacency lists is used. While most of the algorithms for finding connected components are very general, some of them are more suitable for sparse or dense graphs. As we shall see, this extra information about the sparsity of graphs allows for more efficient allocation of processors.

2.1.1   Breadth-First Search

Arjomandi and Corneil (1975) have proposed a technique for finding the connected components of a dense graph based on a breadth-first search of the given graph. The search starts from a vertex, and processors are assigned to edges emanating from that vertex. A vertex at a distance i from the start vertex is searched before any vertex at a greater distance from the start vertex. After all the vertices at distance i have been searched, the partial lists of all the new vertices at distance $i + 1$ are joined together, so that a new vertex at distance

$i+1$ can be picked efficiently for searching. When the average degree of each vertex in the graph is approximately greater than or equal to k, where k is the number of processors available, then the complexity of the resulting algorithm is near optimal and is $T/k + L\lceil \log k \rceil + 2n$, where T is the complexity of the optimal sequential breadth-first search algorithm and L is the distance of the vertex farthest away from the start vertex.

2.1.2 Transitive Closure

The basic idea of connected component (sequential) algorithms based on transitive closure is as follows. If the input is in the form of adjacency matrix A, then the transitive closure of A, call it B, can be obtained so that the element $b_{i,j}$ of B is one if and only if there is a path of length zero or more from vertex i to vertex j in the given graph. The component number of any vertex i is then just the smallest j such that $b_{ij} = 1$.

The first parallel algorithm for finding the connected components based on transitive closure is due to Reghbati and Corneil (1978). Their algorithm is essentially what is described above. On an SIMD–SM–R model the transitive closure of a $n \times n$ matrix can be obtained when n^3 processors are available by squaring the matrix $\log n$ times, which requires $O(\log^2 n)$ time; finding the first nonzero entry for each row can be done in $O(\log n)$ time. Hence the complexity of the algorithm is $O(\log^2 n)$ using n^3 processors on an SIMD–SM–R model.

The other algorithms based on transitive closure improve upon the efficiency of the transitive closure step. In Chandra (1976), the parallel matrix multiplication algorithm is used, thereby reducing the number of processors required from n^3 to $\lceil n^{\log 7}/\log n \rceil$.

In Kucera (1982) a stronger model, SIMD–SM–RW, is used. This allows n^2 processors to find the minimum of a set of n elements in constant time and hence allows the transitive closure of a binary matrix and the connected components to be computed in $O(\log n)$ time using n^4 processors.

2.1.3 Vertex Collapse

The input format is again in the form of an adjacency matrix. The basic idea is to combine adjacent vertices into "supervertices", which are then combined themselves. This process is repeated until no further collapses are possible, at which point each supervertex corresponds to a connected component. Some commonly used terminology is as follows: A *tree-loop* is a tree having directed edges, with an additional edge from the root to one of its descendants. A *club* is a tree-loop in which all the vertices other than the root are the sons of the root.

The first algorithm using the vertex collapse technique is due to Hirschberg (1976). The basic idea is to grow each connected component as a club, with the root of the club being the vertex with minimal label in that club. Figure 1 illustrates how this algorithm works. The algorithm proceeds by having each vertex identify the smallest numbered vertex it has seen so far that is in the same connected component (in Fig. 1 this relationship is indicated by solid arrows). Each iteration of the algorithm consists of three steps. In the first step, each vertex finds the lowest-numbered (new) neighboring root. In the second step, each root is linked to the root of the lowest-numbered neighboring root. In the third step, path compression is done so as to construct clubs.

---

algorithm Hirschberg;
Input: Adjacency matrix $A[n$ by $n]$
Output: Vector D of length n such that $D[x]$ is the smallest vertex y reachable from vertex x.
begin
1.   **for** all x **do** $D[x] = x$;
2.   **for** $\lceil \log n \rceil$ iterations **do**
      begin
3.   **for** all x
            do $C[x] = \min \{D[y] \mid A[x,y] = 1$ and $D[y] \neq D[x]\}$
                if none then $D[x]$;
4.   **for** all x
            do $C[x] = D[x] = \min \{C[y] \mid D[y] = x$ and $C[y] \neq x\}$
                if none then $D[x]$;
5.   **for** all x **do** $D[x] = C[x]$;
6.   **for** $\lceil \log n \rceil$ iterations **do**
            for all x **do** $C[x] = C[C[x]]$;
7.   **for** all x **do** $D[x] = \min \{C[x], D[C[x]]\}$;
      end;
end;

Algorithm Hirschberg has time complexity $O(\log^2 n)$ on n^2 processors, for an SIMD–SM–R model. Basically, both the path compression and finding the minimum require $O(\log n)$ time. Also, since each iteration reduces the number of clubs corresponding to a connected component by a factor of 2, until a single club corresponds to a connected component, $O(\log n)$ iterations are sufficient for the algorithm.

Hirschberg et al. (1979) improves upon the performance of the original Hirschberg algorithm by recognizing that the number of processors required can be reduced without increasing the time complexity. The idea is very similar to what we outlined as the PR paradigm in section 1.5.1 and amounts to having each processor assign values to $\log n$ elements instead of to one

Smallest numbered
vertex seen so for
which is in the same
connected component.

Iteration 1
  Find lowest-numbered
  (new)neighboring root.

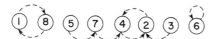

Connect roots.

Build new club.

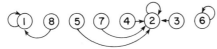

Iteration 2
  Find lowest-numbered
  (new)neighboring root.

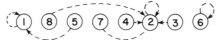

Connect roots.

Build new club.

FIG. 1. Vertex Collapse.

element; each processor can find the minimum of $\log n$ values instead of finding the minimum of two values. Both of these changes can be accomplished without increasing the time complexity, so the new algorithm has a complexity of $O(\log^2 n)$ using $n\lceil n/\lceil \log n \rceil \rceil$ processors on a SIMD–SM–R model.

Chin et al. (1981; 1982) improve upon the algorithm of Hirschberg et al. by considering in any iteration only those vertices that are nonisolated supervertices. This implies that the number of active vertices is reduced by a factor of at least two after each iteration, and therefore the same time bound $O(\log^2 n)$ can still be achieved by using $n\lceil n/\log^2 n \rceil$ processors on the SIMD–SM–R model. This reduction in the number of processors is essentially the PR paradigm.

Savage and Ja'Ja' (1981) develops two parallel connected components algorithms that provide improved performances one for dense and one for sparse graphs. For an undirected graph $G = (V, E)$ with $|V| \geq 2$, the diameter d of G is defined to be

$$d = \max \{d(v, w), 2\}; \, v,w \in V$$

where $d(v, w)$ is the length of the shortest path from v to w if it exists, otherwise $-\infty$.

The observation Savage and Ja'Ja' made is that it is not necessary to run the Hirschberg algorithm for $\lceil \log n \rceil$ iterations; rather it should be run until two consecutive iterations produce the same result. In that case the running time of the algorithm can be made $O(\log n * \min \{\log n, d/2\})$, where d is the diameter of the graph. When $d < 2 \log n$ (i.e., for dense graphs), this algorithm is faster than the original. When the graph is dense this algorithm requires $O(n^3/\log n)$ processors to obtain time complexity $O(\log n \log d)$.

When the graph is sparse, the number of processors required can be reduced by organizing the input in the form of the adjacency list rather than the adjacency matrix. Certain reorganization of the original Hirschberg algorithm then leads to an algorithm with time complexity $O(\log^2 n)$ using $O(m + n \log n)$ processors, where m is the number of edges in the graph.

Nath and Maheshwari (1982) considers the problem of finding the connected components on a weaker model that does not permit simultaneous reading from the same memory location by different processors. Their algorithm is based on the one due to Hirschberg et al. (1979), but it avoids read conflicts by organizing the intermediate data structure as a chain (which avoids read conflicts when children access nonroot parents) and by keeping multiple copies of data. This algorithm has complexity $O(\log^2 n)$ with n^2 processors on an SIMD–SM model.

Shiloach and Vishkin (1982) considers a stronger model, SIMD–SM–RW, where simultaneous reads as well as writes are allowed. In the latter case one

algorithm SV;
Input: Vertices are represented by the numbers $1, \ldots, n$. The edges are represented by a vector E of length $2m$ in which each edge (i, j) appears twice: once as the ordered pair $\langle i, j \rangle$ and once as the ordered pair $\langle j, i \rangle$.
Output: Vector D_{s_0} of length n, s_0 is the index of the last iteration. $D_{s_0}[n]$ is the representative vertex of the connected component containing vertex n.
Processor allocation: If $i \leq n$, processor P_i is allocated to vertex i. If $i > n$, processor P_i is allocated to the ordered pair $E[i - n] = \langle i_1, i_2 \rangle$ (this processor is denoted as P_{i_1, i_2}).

begin
1.   **for** $i \leq n$ **then**
      begin
2. $D_0[i] = i; Q[i] = 0; s = 1; s' = 1;$
      end;
3.   **while** $s' = s$ **do**
      begin
4.   **if** $i \leq n$ **then**
              begin
5. $D_s[i] = D_{s-1}[D_{s-1}[i]];$
6.   **if** $D_s[i] \neq D_{s-1}[i]$ **then** $Q[D_s[i]] = s;$
              end;
7.   **if** $i > n$
8.   **then if** $D_s[i_1] = D_{s-1}[i_1]$
9.   **then if** $D_s[i_2] < D_s[i_1]$
10.   **then begin** $D_s[D_s[i_1]] = D_s[i_2]; Q[D_s[i_2]] = s;$ **end**;
11.   **if** $i > n$
12.   **then if** $D_s[i_1] = D_s[D_s[i_1]]$ **and** $Q[D_s[i_1]] < s$
13.   **then if** $D_s[i_1] \neq D_s[i_2]$
14.   **then** $D_s[D_s[i_1]] = D_s[i_2];$
15.   **if** $i \leq n$ **then** $D_s[i] = D_s[D_s[i]];$
16.   **if** $i \leq n$ **and** $Q[i] = s$ **then** $s' = s' + 1;$
17. $s = s + 1;$
      end;
end;

processor succeeds, but which one is not known. This algorithm, SV, has complexity $O(\log n)$ using only $n + 2m$ processors, where $|E| = m$.

The processors are allocated by considering each undirected edge to be two directed edges, and each vertex and each directed edge is allocated one processor. In contrast to the Hirschberg algorithm, it is no longer required that each connected component be identified by its lowest-numbered member vertex; this allows the algorithm to utilize the power of this model by letting the vertices try simultaneous 'hooking' instead of connecting to minimum numbered neighboring root. This allows one of the two $\log^2 n$ factors to be replaced by a $\log n$ factor. The other $\log^2 n$ factor is replaced by a $\log n$ factor by reorganization that allows the path compression step to be done twice in each iteration rather than $O(\log n)$ times.

Awerbuch and Shiloach (1983) improved upon the results of Shiloach and Vishkin (1982) to obtain an $O(\log n)$ time complexity, connected components algorithm using $2m$ processors for the SIMD–SM–RW model (an arbitrary process succeeds in case of simultaneous writes).

Wyllie (1979) uses vertex collapse to obtain an $O(\log^2 n)$ algorithm using $O(n + 2m)$ processors on a synchronized MIMD–TC–R model. For sparse graphs this is a very efficient algorithm. A vertex x can be collapsed into vertex y by making any edge incident to x become incident to y instead. Each edge is viewed as a pair of two directed edges, and the input is in the form of an adjacency list matrix. This input is converted in constant time so that each vertex has a circular doubly linked list with a list header. The list consists of two types of elements: directed edge elements and dummy elements. At all times edge elements are separated by at least one dummy element. Each directed edge element contains (in addition to the forward and backward pointer) the number of vertices to which this directed edge is incident and a pointer to its 'brother' directed edge (the oppositely oriented directed edge representing the same undirected edge). The structure of the directed edge element allows for efficient collapse of two vertices into one vertex, and the use of dummy elements permits simultaneous collapse of different vertices. The various algorithms discussed for the connected components problem are summarized in Table I.

2.2 Parallel Biconnected Components Algorithms

For a connected undirected graph $G = (V, E)$, a vertex $a \in V$ is called an *articulation* point of G if there are vertices x and y in V, distinct from a, such that every path in G joining x and y contains a. The graph is biconnected if it contains no articulation points. A biconnected component of G is a biconnected subgraph H of G, which is not properly contained in any biconnected subgraph of G. There are a number of parallel algorithms for finding the biconnected components of an undirected graph. They are summarized in Table II.

Eckstein's (1979b) algorithm uses $O(d \log^2 n)$ time and $O((n + m)/d)$ processors on the SIMD–SM–R model where d is the diameter of the

TABLE I

PARALLEL CONNECTED COMPONENTS ALGORITHMS

Reference	Model	Complexity[a]	Processors
Arjomandi and Corneil (1975)	SIMD–SM–R	$T/k + L\lceil \log k \rceil + 2n$	k
Reghbati and Corneil (1978)	SIMD–SM–R	$O(\log^2 n)$	n^3
Chandra (1976)	SIMD–SM–R	$O(\log^2 n)$	$n^{\log 7}/\log n$
Kucera (1982)	SIMD–SM–RW	$O(\log n)$	n^4
Hirschberg (1976)	SIMD–SM–R	$O(\log^2 n)$	n^2
Hirschberg et al. (1979)	SIMD–SM–R	$O(\log^2 n)$	$n\lceil n/\lceil \log n \rceil \rceil$
Chin et al. (1981; 1982)	SIMD–SM–R	$O(\log^2 n)$	$n\lceil n/\log^2 n \rceil$
Savage and Ja'Ja' (1981)	SIMD–SM–R	$O(\log n \log d)$	$O(n^3/\log n)$
	SIMD–SM–R	$O(\log^2 n)$	$O(m + n \log n)$
Nath and Maheshwari (1982)	SIMD–SM	$O(\log^2 n)$	$n^2/\log n$
Shiloach and Vishkin (1982)	SIMD–SM–RW	$O(\log n)$	$n + 2m$
Awerbuch and Shiloach (1983)	SIMD–SM–RW	$O(\log n)$	$2m$
Wyllie (1979)	MIMD–TC–R	$O(\log^2 n)$	$n + 2m$

[a] d is the diameter of the graph; L is the distance of the vertex farthest away from the start vertex; T is the complexity of the optimal sequential breadth-first search algorithm.

graph. Savage and Ja'Ja' (1981) give two parallel algorithms, both based on the SIMD–SM–R model. The first algorithm uses $O(\log^2 n)$ time and $O(n^3/\log n)$ processors. The second algorithm uses $O(\log^2 n \log k)$ time and $O(mn + n^2 \log n)$ processors, where k is the number of biconnected components and hence is more suitable for handling sparse graphs.

The parallel algorithms of Tsin and Chin (1984) and Tarjan and Vishkin (1984) are both based on the following ideas. The sequential algorithm of Tarjan (1972) for finding the biconnected components of an undirected graph is based on manipulating the depth-first spanning tree of the original graph.

TABLE II

PARALLEL BICONNECTED COMPONENT ALGORITHMS

Reference	Model	Complexity[a]	Processors
Eckstein (1979b)	SIMD–SM–R	$O(d \log^2 n)$	$O((n + m)/d)$
Savage and Ja'Ja' (1981)	SIMD–SM–R	$O(\log^2 n)$	$O(n^3/\log n)$
	SIMD–SM–R	$O(\log^2 n \log k)$	$O(mn + n^2 \log n)$
Tsin and Chin (1984)	SIMD–SM–R	$O(\log^2 n)$	$O(n\lceil n/\log^2 n \rceil)$
Tarjan and Vishkin (1984)	SIMD–SM–RW	$O(\log n)$	$O(n + m)$
	SIMD–SM–R	$O(n^2/p)$	$p \le n^2/\log^2 n$

[a] d is the diameter of the graph and k is the number of biconnected components in the graph.

There is strong reason to believe, however, that depth-first search (Reif, 1985) is inherently sequential; i.e., it does not seem possible to implement it in polylog parallel time. Therefore, a new way of finding the biconnected components is devised, so that the problem of computing the biconnected components of the input graph can be reduced to the problem of computing the connected components of an auxiliary graph. The actual details of the algorithms by Tsin and Chin (1984) and Tarjan and Vishkin (1984) are, however, different.

The algorithm of Tsin and Chin (1984) uses $O(\log^2 n)$ time and $O(n\lceil n/\log^2 n\rceil)$ processors on the SIMD–SM–R model. Briefly, the Tarjan and Vishkin algorithms can be described as follows. First a sequential algorithm for finding the biconnected components is developed so that it makes use of any spanning tree (rather than a depth-first spanning tree). This sequential algorithm is then parallelized to yield an algorithm for the SIMD–SM–RW model that runs in $O(\log n)$ time and uses $O(n + m)$ processors. A second algorithm is also presented for the SIMD–SM–R model that uses $O(n^2/p)$ time and $p \le n^2/\log^2 n$ processors.

In comparing the algorithms due to Tsin and Chin and to Tarjan and Vishkin, notice that the algorithm of Tsin and Chin and the second algorithm of Tarjan and Vishkin are both optimal, since the time-processor product is $O(n^2)$ and the best sequential algorithm with adjacency matrix input is also $O(n^2)$. Also, by using a general simulation it is possible to convert the first algorithm of Tarjan and Vishkin so that it becomes one using $O(\log^2 n)$ time and $O(n + m)$ processors on the SIMD–SM–R model. For sparse graphs this has a much better performance than the algorithm of Tsin and Chin or the second algorithm of Tarjan and Vishkin.

3. Parallel Minimum Spanning Tree Algorithms

In this section we present several parallel minimum spanning tree algorithms for different types of parallel computational models. The problem of finding a minimum spanning tree of a weighted graph arises in many diverse applications, such as communications systems (where a minimum-cost spanning tree represents a communications network that connects all cities at minimal cost), transportation networks, data analysis, and operations research.

A minimum spanning tree of a weighted, connected, and undirected graph G is defined as a set of edges of the graph that connects all vertices and whose total edge weight is minimum. There are many different methods for constructing a minimum cost spanning tree. The following property is used to define the minimum cost method: Let $G = (V, E)$ be a connected, weighted, undirected graph. Let U be some proper subset of the set of vertices V. If (u, v) is an edge of minimum cost such that $u \in U$ and $v \in V - U$, then there is a minimum cost spanning tree that includes (u, v) as an edge. The proof that every minimum cost spanning tree satisfies the above property is given in Aho et al. (1974).

Traditionally, sequential methods to compute the minimum spanning tree of a weighted graph in parallel have focused on three classes of algorithms, all of which use greedy strategies. They are: Sollin's (1977) algorithm based on the lightest edge from each vertex method; Prim's (1957) and Dijkstra's (1959) algorithm based on the nearest neighbor method; and Kruskal's (1956) algorithm based on the lightest edge first method. For details on results related to the minimum spanning tree problem see Cook (1981), Kucera (1982), Chin et al. (1982), Awerbuch and Shiloach (1983), Hirschberg (1982), and Kwan and Ruzzo (1984). Among these minimum spanning tree algorithms, the Sollin algorithm is the most suitable candidate for parallel processing.

3.1   Parallel Sollin's Algorithm

The Sollin's algorithm for finding the minimum spanning tree is presented in the algorithm SOLLIN. Sollin's algorithm starts with the forest F_0 obtained by forming a tree with each vertex of the graph. In each iteration, the lightest edge incident on each tree is selected. All these edges are added to the existing forest F_i to form the new forest F_{i+1}. This process is continued until the forest F_i consists of a single tree. In the worst case this algorithm requires $\log n$ iterations. The direct implementation of Sollin's sequential algorithm requires $O(n^2 \log n)$ time. Researchers have also looked at efficient implementations of Sollin's algorithm on a sequential machine. Yao (1975) presents an algorithm with $O(n^2 \log \log n)$ time complexity for this problem; the Cheriton and Tarjan (1976) algorithm has time complexity $O(m \log \log n)$.

Parallel implementation of algorithm SOLLIN calls for suitable parallel implementation of lines 4 through 6. We now present the parallel versions of the algorithm SOLLIN for different types of computer configurations.

3.1.1   Sollin's Algorithm for an SIMD Machine

A number of researchers have implemented Sollin's algorithm on SIMD machines. Savage and Ja'Ja' (1981) and Nath and Maheshwari (1982) based their algorithms on Hirschberg's (1976) connected component algorithm to identify newly combined trees. The algorithm of Savage and Ja'Ja' (1981) achieves the time complexity of $O(\log^2 n)$ using $O(n^2)$ processors on the SIMD–SM–R model, while Nath and Maheshwari (1982) achieve time complexity $O(\log^2 n)$ using $n^2/\log n$ processors on the SIMD–SM model.

---

algorithm SOLLIN(G);
begin
1. $F_0 = (V, \phi)$; // begin with a forest F of n vertices of V //
2. $i = 0$;
3.   **while** there is more than one tree in F_i **do**
      begin
4.   **for** each tree T_j in forest F_i **do**
5.   choose the minimum weighted edge (u, v) joining some vertex u in T_j to a vertex v in some other tree T_k in forest F_i;
6.   form the forest F_{i+1} by joining all T_j and T_k of F_i with the corresponding selected edges;
7. $i = i + 1$;
      end;
end;

Chin et al. (1982) modifies Hirschberg's connected component algorithm to obtain $O(\log^2 n)$ using only $O(n\lceil n/\log^2 n\rceil)$ processors on the SIMD–SM–R model.

The technique used by Savage and Ja'Ja' (1981) is outlined in algorithm PSOLLIN–SIMD. In statements 1 and 2 of the algorithm each vertex is

---

algorithm PSOLLIN–SIMD;
begin
1.   **for** each vertex i **do**
2. $ROOT[i] = i$;
3. $over$ = false;
4.   **while** not($over$) **do**
      begin
5.   **for** each vertex i **do**
6. $NEAR[i] = j$ such that $(ROOT[i] \neq ROOT[j])$ and $(W[i, j] < W[i, k]$, for all $k \neq j)$
7.   **for** each component K of the forest F_t **do**
8.   choose vertex i such that $W[i, NEAR[i]]$ is minimum over all vertices of K;
9.   combine and create a new forest F_{t+1};
10.   **for** each vertex i **do**
11.   search $ROOT[i]$;
12.   **if** $ROOT[i] = ROOT[j]$ for all i, j **then** $over$ = true;
      end;
end;

---

represented as a single tree whose root is itself. The complexity of this task is constant with $O(n)$ processors. Statements 5 and 6 require finding n times the minimum of at most n numbers. The minimum of n numbers can be found in $\log n$ time using n processors. Thus the computation of statements 5 and 6 can be performed in $O(\log n)$ time using $O(n^2)$ processors. For each component K of the existing forest, the vertex i with minimum value for $W[i, NEAR[i]]$ is found in statements 7 and 8. Thus statements 7 and 8 can be executed in time $O(\log n)$ using $O(n^2)$ processors. Statements 10 and 11 find for each vertex i a representative component where vertex i belongs. This can be done in time $O(\log n)$ with $O(n^2)$ processors using Hirschberg's (1976) technique. Statement 12 checks whether each vertex belongs to the same component. This step requires $O(\log n)$ time, because the SIMD–SM–R machine model does not allow simultaneous writing into the same memory location. The time complexity of each iteration is $O(\log n)$, and there are $O(\log n)$ iterations. Thus the total time complexity of this algorithm is $O(\log^2 n)$ with $O(n^2)$ processors.

3.1.2   Sollin's Algorithm for an MIMD Machine

Deo and Yoo (1981) and Yoo (1983) present algorithms for the MIMD–TC model with the assumption that the number of available processors p is less than or equal to n. Each process handles approximately n/p vertices. The time required to compute the lightest edge incident on each vertex is $O(n^2/p)$ if a weight matrix is used. This step is repeated until a spanning tree is obtained. A detailed description of the algorithm presented in Yoo (1983) is given in algorithm PSOLLIN–MIMD. The function FIND and the procedure UNION used in this algorithm are for set operations. The function FIND(i) returns the set in which i is contained. The procedure UNION($r1, r2$) computes the set union of the sets $r1$ and $r2$.

In each iteration of algorithm POSLLIN–MIMD, every process examines n/p of the total vertices and finds a vertex nearest to a nontree neighbour. A single iteration therefore has complexity $O(n^2/p)$, and the entire algorithm has the time complexity of $O((n^2/p) \log n)$. When $p = n$ the time complexity becomes $O(n \log n)$ and the processor time product becomes $O(n^2 \log n)$. In the worst case the number of process creation becomes $(p \log n)$. The parallel version of Cheriton and Tarjan's (1976) minimum spanning tree algorithm is similar to the parallel version of Sollin's algorithm. For details see Deo and Yoo (1981).

3.2   Parallel Prim–Dijkstra Algorithm

The minimum spanning tree algorithm was first developed by Prim (1957) and its computer implementation was given by Dijkstra (1959). The algorithm

algorithm PSOLLIN–MIMD;

// parallel version of Sollin's algorithm for MIMD–TC macine //

process MAIN;

// initialization //

begin

1. $T = \phi; T_w = 0;$
2. $over = 0;$
3. **for** $i = 2$ **to** p **do**
4.   create TASKI(i);
5. call TASK1(1);
6. **while** $over < p$ **do** wait;
7. **for** $i = 1$ **to** n **do**
    begin
8. $j = V_j[i];$
9. $r1 = \text{FIND}[i]; r2 = \text{FIND}[j];$
10.   **if** $(r1 \neq r2)$ **then**
        begin
11. $T = T \cup \{(i, j)\};$
12. $T_w = T_w + V_{\min}[i];$
13.   call UNION($r1, r2$);
        end;
    end;
14. **while** there is more than one tree **do**
    begin
15. $over = 0;$
16.   **for** $i = 2$ **to** p **do**
17.   create TASK2(i);
18.   call TASK2(1);
19.   **while** $over < p$ **do** *wait*;
20.   **for** $i = 1$ **to** n **do**
        begin
21.   **if** $V_{\min}[i] \neq \infty$ **then**
            begin
22. $r1 = \text{FIND}(V_i[1]); r2 = \text{FIND}(V_j[i]);$
23.   **if** $r1 \neq r2$ **then**
                begin
24. $T = T \cup \{(V_i[i], V_j[i])\};$
25. $T_w = T_w + V_{\min}[i];$
26.   call UNION $(r1, r2)$;
                end;
            end;
        end;
    end;
end;

process TASK 1(k);
// computation process for finding the nearest vertex in PSOLLIN – MIND //
begin
1. **for** $i = k$ **to** n **by** p **do**
    begin
2. $TREE[i] = -1; m = 1;$
3. **for** $j = 1$ **to** n **do**
4. **if** $W[i, j] < W[i, k]$ **then** $m = j;$
5. $V_j[i] = m; V_{\min}[i] = W[i, m];$
    end;
6. lock(*over*); *over* = *over* + 1; unlock(*over*);
end;

---

process TASK 2(k);
begin
1. **for** $i = k$ **to** n **by** p **do**
2. $V_{\min}[i] = \infty;$
3. lock(*over*);
4. *over* = *over* + 1;
5. **if** *over* = p **then** *over* = 0;
6. unlock(*over*);
7. **while** *over* > 0 **do** wait;
8. **for** $i = k$ **to** n **by** p **do**
    begin
9. $r1 = \text{FIND}[i];$
10. **for** $j = 1$ **to** n **do**
    begin
11. $r2 = \text{FIND}[j];$
12. **if** $r1 \neq r2$ **then**
    begin
13. $a = \min\{i, j\}; z = \max\{i, j\};$
14. lock($V_{\min}[r1]$);
15. **if** $(W[i, j] < V_{\min}[r1]) \lor (W[i, j] = V_{\min}[r1]$ and
        $W(a, z) < \min\{V_i[r1], V_j[r1]\})$ **then**
        begin
16. $V_i[r1] = a; V_j[r1] = z; V_{\min}[r1] = W[i, j]$
        end;
17. unlock($V_{\min}[r1]$);
        end;
    end;
    end;
18. lock(*over*); *over* = *over* + 1; unlock(*over*);
end;

---

algorithm PRIM–DIJKSTRA;
// this algorithm finds the minimal spanning tree for a given graph //
begin
// initialization //
1. $T = \phi$; $T_w = 0$;
2. $NEAR[1] = 0$;
3.   **for** $i = 2$ **to** n **do**
      begin
4. $NEAR[i] = 1$;
5. $DIST[i] = W[1, i]$
      end;
// iteration step //
6.   **while** $|T| \le n - 1$ **do**
      begin
7.   choose j such that $DIST[j] = \min\{DIST[i] \,|\, NEAR[i] \ne 0\}$;
8. $T = T \cup \{(j, NEAR[j])\}$;
9. $T_w = T_w + DIST[j]$;
10. $NEAR[j] = 0$;
11.   **for** $i = 1$ **to** n **do**
12.   **if** $(NEAR[i] \ne 0)$ and $(W[i, j] < W[i, NEAR[i]])$ **then**
            begin
13. $NEAR[i] = j$;
14. $DIST[i] = W[i, j]$;
            end;
      end;
end;

(we name it PRIM–DIJKSTRA) works by starting with a forest consisting of n isolated vertices. Then a vertex is chosen arbitrarily from the forest to be the first vertex of the partial tree, and the tree is grown successively by bringing in the nearest neighbor from one of the isolated vertices. In other words, at an intermediate step an edge (u, v) is added to the current (partially formed) tree T if $T \cup \{(u, v)\}$ is also a tree and (u, v) is the lightest-weight edge with this property. This method is described in algorithm PRIM–DIJKSTRA.

The PRIM–DIJKSTRA algorithm uses the array W, which contains the weights of the edges. The arrays $NEAR$ and $DIST$ keep the current nearest neighbor and the corresponding weights of each vertex. T_w is the weight of the tree and T the set of edges in the tree at any stage during the execution of the algorithm. This algorithm has $n - 1$ iterations, and at each iteration a new edge is added to the partially built tree T_w. At each iteration the computation of the required edge can be performed in $O(n)$ time using the weight matrix as the data structure. Thus the minimum spanning tree can be computed in $O(n^2)$ time on a sequential machine.

We discuss two parallel implementations of the Prim–Dijkstra minimum spanning-tree algorithm. Bentley (1980) uses a tree machine to obtain a parallel version of the Prim–Dijkstra algorithm. Deo and Yoo (1981) present an MIMD version of the Prim–Dijkstra algorithm.

3.2.1 Prim–Dijkstra Algorithm for a Tree Machine

In this section we present the parallel version of the Prim–Dijkstra algorithm of Bentley (1980) for the tree machine. Initially we assume that there are n square processors. The initialization is implemented on the driver computer of the tree machine. The values are inserted into the tree machine by the pipeline process. The time required for implementation of this step is $O(n)$.

In each iteration the triangle processors compute the next edge to be added to the partially built minimum spanning tree. Thus the iteration step of the parallel algorithm consists of finding the minimum of n numbers in $O(\log n)$ time by letting the triangle processors compute the minimum of two incoming values. During each iteration the vertex nearest to the present partial tree is transferred down to the square processors in $\log n$ steps. If $W[i, j] < W[i, NEAR[i]]$, then the square processor i alters $NEAR[i]$ to j and

---

algorithm PRIM–TREE;
process DRIVER;
begin
1. **for** each vertex i **do**
    begin
2.   **if** $i = 1$ **then**
        begin
3. $NEAR[i] = 0$;
4. $DIST[i] = \infty$;
        end
5.   **else**
        begin
6. $NEAR[i] = 1$;
7. $DIST[i] = W[1, i]$;
        end;
8.   transmit $(NEAR[i], DIST[i])$ to the first broadcast processor in the tree machine;
    end;
end;

---

process SQUARE(i);
begin
1.   **repeat**
2.   receive(x, dx);
3.   **if** $NEAR[i] \neq 0$ **then**
        begin
4.   **if** $x = i$ **then**
          begin
5. $NEAR[i] = 0$;
6. $DIST[i] = \infty$;
          end
7.   **else**
8.   **if** $W[i, x] < DIST[i]$ **then**
          begin
9. $NEAR[i] = x$;
10. $DIST[i] = W[i, x]$;
          end;
        end;
11.   send ($NEAR[i]$, $DIST[i]$) to triangle processor;
12. **forever**;
end;

---

process TRIANGLE(i);
begin
1.   **repeat**
2.   (receive (x, dx) from left, receive (y, dy) from right);
3.   **if** $dx < dy$
4.   **then** send (x, dx)
5.   **else** send (y, dy);
6.   **forever**;
end;

$DIST[i]$ to $W[i, j]$. This step takes log n time. Since there are $n - 1$ iterations, the total time taken for the execution of the algorithm is $O(n \log n)$.

The same complexity of $O(n \log n)$ can be obtained by storing log n vertices with each square processor. Each square processor handles the corresponding vertices by finding the minimum and updating if necessary. The triangle proccesors find the minimum of $O(n/\log n)$ values, and each iteration still takes $O(\log n)$ time. Hence the total running time of algorithm PRIM–TREE remains $O(n \log n)$, with $O(n/\log n)$ processors. This reduction in the number of processors without increasing the time complexity is an instance of the PR paradigm described in section 1.5.1.

3.2.2 Prim–Dijkstra Algorithm For MIMD Machine

Deo and Yoo (1981) and Yoo (1983) present the parallel version of the Prim–Dijkstra algorithm for an MIMD machine. They assume p processors available with the machine where $2 \leq p \leq n$. For each of the $n - 1$ iterations of the Prim–Dijkstra algorithm p processes are created. Each process updates the distance of n/p of the nontree vertices, and all these processes synchronize after their computations. After synchronization another set of p processes is created for updating, thereby completing one iteration. The number of iterations is the same as for the sequential algorithm; hence if $p = n^{.5}$ the time complexity is $O(n^{1.5})$ on an MIMD–TC model with $O(n^{.5})$ processors. (The frequent number of synchronizations required and the contention for the global memory limits the number of processors that can be effectively utilized.) The details are presented in algorithm PRIM–MIMD.

---

algorithm PRIM–MIMD;
// parallel version of Prim–Dijkstra algorithm for minimal spanning tree //
// problem with p, $2 \leq p \leq n$, processors available //
process MAIN;
begin
// initialization //
1. $T = \phi$; $T_w = 0$;
2. $j = 0$; *over* $= 0$;
3.   **for** $i = 2$ **to** p **do**
4.   create TASK(i);
5.   call TASK(1);
6.   **while** $j < p$ **do** wait;
end;

---

process TASK(j);
begin
1.   **for** $i = j$ **to** n **by** p **do**
      begin
2. $NEAR[i] = 1$; $DIST[i] = W[1, i]$;
      end;
3. $NEAR[1] = 0$; $DIST[1] = \infty$;
4.   **while** $|T| < n - 1$ **do**
      begin

```
5.        lock(over);
6.        over = over + 1;
7.        if over = p then
          begin
8.            Vmin = ∞; over = 0;
          end;
9.        unlock(over);
10.       while over > 0 do wait;
11.       k = 1;
12.       for i = j to n by p do
13.          if (NEAR[i] ≠ 0) and (DIST[i] < DIST[k]) then k = i;
14.       lock(Vmin);
15.       if DIST[k] < Vmin then
          begin
16.           m = k; Vmin = DIST[k];
          end;
17.       unlock(Vmin);
18.       lock(over);
19.       over = over + 1;
20.       if over = p then
          begin
21.           T = T ∪ {(m, NEAR[m])}; Tw = Tw + Vmin;
22.           NEAR[k] = 0: over = 0;
          end;
23.       unlock(over);
24.       while over > 0 do wait;
25.       for i = j to n by p do
          begin
26.          if (NEAR[i] ≠ 0) and (W[i, m] < DIST[i]) then
             begin
27.              NEAR[i] = m; DIST[i] = W[i, m];
             end;
          end;
       end;
end;
```

Statements 10 and 24 of process TASK are two synchronization points in the iteration section of the algorithm. The global variable *over* is set to 0 before any process enters the synchronization block. For further details on the proof of correctness and implementation details see Yoo (1983).

TABLE III

PARALLEL MINIMUM SPANNING TREE ALGORITHMS

Reference	Model	Complexity	Processors
Savage (1977)	SIMD–SM–SR	$O(\log^2 n)$	$O(n^2/\log n)$
Bentley (1980)	Tree	$O(n \log n)$	$n/\log n$
Deo and Yoo (1981)	MIMD–TC	$O(n^{1.5})$	$n^{0.5}$
	MIMD–TC	$O((n^2 \log n)/p)$	$p \leq n$
Savage and Ja'Ja' (1981)	SIMD–SM–R	$O(\log^2 n)$	$O(n^2)$
Nath and Maheshwari (1982)	SIMD–SM	$O(\log^2 n)$	$n^2/\log n$
Kucera (1982)	SIMD–SM–RW	$O(\log n)$	n^5
Chin et al. (1982)	SIMD–SM–R	$O(\log^2 n)$	$n\lceil n/\log^2 n \rceil$
Hirschberg (1982)	SIMD–SM–RW	$O(\log n)$	$O(n^3)$
Hirschberg and Volper (1983)	SIMD–SM–RW	$O(\log n)$	$O(n^3)$
Yoo (1983)	MIMD–TC	$O(m)$	$O(m)$
Awerbuch and Shiloach (1983)	SIMD–SM–RW	$O(\log n)$	$2m$
Kwan and Ruzzo (1984)	SIMD–SM–R	$O((m \log n)/p)$	$p \log p \leq (m \log n)/n$
	SIMD–SM–R	$O((m \log n)/p)$	$p \leq \log n$
	SIMD–SM–R	$O((m \log n)/p)$	$p \leq m/\log n$

3.3 Parallel Kruskal's Algorithm

The development of data structures for graph problems has resulted primarily because of the parallel versions of Kruskal's algorithm. Initially the graph structure consists of a forest of isolated vertices. The edges are sorted in nondecreasing order of their weights, and every edge that connects two disjoint trees is added to the minimum spanning tree. In other words, edges that do not cause cycles with existing edges are selected. The termination of the algorithm takes place when the graph transforms to a single tree. Yoo (1983) has shown that an MIMD computer with $\lceil \log m \rceil$ processors can delete an element from an input of an m-element heap in constant time. This software pipeline technique is described in Yoo (1983).

Some other references to parallel minimum spanning tree algorithms in the literature are included in Quinn and Deo (1984). A number of different parallel minimum spanning tree algorithms are summarized in Table III.

3.4 Adaptive Parallel Algorithms

Recently, Kwan and Ruzzo (1984) have developed parallel algorithms for finding minimum spanning trees based on Prim's, Kruskal's, and Sollin's schemes, using the SIMD–SM–R model of computation. The run-time complexities of parallel algorithms based on all the above schemes have been shown to be $O((m \log n)/p)$, where n is the number of vertices, m is the number of edges, and p is the number of processors. The salient features of these algorithms are that their running time is a function of the number of processors and edges (and hence is adaptive) and makes use of some interesting algorithms for sorting and the union-find problems as intermediate steps. Furthermore, their parallel minimum spanning tree algorithm, based on Prim's scheme, improves the results obtained by Bentley (1980) and Deo and Yoo (1981) for sparse graphs. Since many applications of the minimum spanning tree problem in computer science involve the use of sparse graphs, the improvements obtained by Kwan and Ruzzo (1984) are quite significant.

4.   Other Parallel Graph Algorithms

There are numerous parallel graph algorithms in the literature. In this section we present some of the more interesting such algorithms. Some other parallel graph algorithms are also described in Quinn and Deo (1984).

4.1   Parallel Algorithms for Shortest Path Problems

Shortest path problems are perhaps the most important class of problems in the study of communication and transportation networks, and many efficient sequential algorithms have been developed for these problems. For an excellent taxonomy on the sequential shortest path algorithms, Deo and Pang (1984) may be referred to. Of relevance here are the so-called

 (i) single-source shortest path problem, where the aim is to find the shortest path or distance from a given vertex to all other vertices in a graph
(ii) the all-pairs shortest path, where the aim is to determine the shortest path or distance between every pair of vertices in a graph.

The shortest path algorithms are classified into two major categories, the label-setting type and the label-correcting type. For details on these types and for other classifications see Deo and Pang (1984). We first briefly outline the well-known algorithm for the single-source shortest path problem, due to Dijkstra (1959). This algorithm is of the label-setting category and is presented as algorithm SP.

The algorithm has a time complexity $O(n^2)$, where n is the number of vertices. The all-pairs shortest path problem can be solved by using the SP algorithm n times, for every $v \in V$. This and another algorithm, due to Floyd (1962), which makes use of matrix multiplication, have time complexity $O(n^3)$.

algorithm SP;
Input: A graph $G = (V, E)$ a source $s \in V$, and a function f from edges to nonnegative real numbers.
Output: A shortest path from s to every other vertex of V.
begin
1. $S = \{s\}$;
2. $D[s] = 0$;
3.   **for** each v in $V - S$ **do** $D[v] = f(s, v)$;
4.   **while** $S \neq V$ **do**
      begin
5.   pick a vertex w in $V - S$ such that $D[w]$ is a minimum;
6. $S = S \cup \{w\}$;
7.   **for** each v in $V - S$ **do** $D[v] = \min\{D[v], D[w] + f(w, v)\}$;
      end;
end;

The assumptions required for the parallel shortest path algorithms described in the literature are as follows:

(i) Edges in the graph may have positive, zero, or negative weights, but there are no negative weight cycles.
(ii) Edges in graphs must have nonnegative weights.

We now consider Kucera's method for solving the all-pairs shortest path problem when edges have nonnegative weights. The model of computation used is SIMD–SM–RW, where simultaneous writing is allowed only to specific memory locations that can contain only the number 0 or 1. All processes writing simultaneously in the same memory location must store the value 1.

The algorithm ALSP–Kucera makes use of a constant-time algorithm for finding the minimum of n numbers using $O(n^2)$ processors. The time complexity of the ALSP–Kucera algorithm is $O(\log n)$, using n^4 processors. Further, it is easy to see that Kucera's minimum finding algorithm can be used to parallelize Dijkstra's algorithm for the single-source shortest path problem in linear time using $O(n^2)$ processors. Other than these algorithms, Dekel et al. (1981) have obtained parallel algorithms for the all-pairs shortest path problem on the SIMD–Perfect-Shuffle and SIMD–Cube-Connected models. These algorithms have time complexity $O(\log^2 n)$ using $O(n^3)$ processors. Further, Levitt and Kautz (1972) have developed a parallel all-pairs shortest path algorithm having a linear time complexity using $O(n^2)$ processors on the

ABHA MOITRA AND S. SITHARAMA IYENGAR

algorithm ALSP–Kucera;
Input: Adjacency matrix $M[i, j]$ for graph G.
Output: Matrix $S[i, j]$ containing all-pairs shortest distances.
begin
1. $m[i, j] = M[i, j]$ for all i and j;
2.   **repeat** $\log_2 n$ times, the following steps:
3. $p[i, j, k] = m[i, j] + m[j, k]$ for all i, j, k;
4. $m[i, j] = \min \{m[i, j], p[i, 1, j], \ldots, p[i, n, j]\}$ for all i, j;
    end;
5. $S[i, j] = m[i, j], i \neq j$;
6. $S[i, i] = 0$;
end;

systolic array model. We given a summary of results on the parallel shortest
path algorithms in Tables IV and V.

It should be noted that Kucera's algorithm can be modified to yield an
$O(\log n)$ algorithm using $O(n^3)$ processors for the single-source shortest path
problem.

TABLE IV

PARALLEL ALL-PAIRS SHORTEST PATH ALGORITHMS

Reference	Model	Complexity	Processors	Weights
Savage (1977)	SIMD–SM–R	$O(\log^2 n)$	$n^3/\log n$	———
Kucera (1982)	SIMD–SM–RW	$O(\log n)$	n^4	nonnegative
Paige and Kruskal (1985)	SIMD–SM–RW	$O(\log n)$	$O(n^{3+\epsilon})$	arbitrary

TABLE V

PARALLEL SINGLE-SOURCE SHORTEST PATH ALGORITHMS

Reference	Model	Complexity	Processors	Weights
Mateti and Deo (1981)	MIMD	$O(n^2/p + np)$	p	arbitrary
Yoo (1983)	SIMD–SM–RW	$O(n)$	$O(n^2)$	arbitrary
	SIMD–R	$O(n \log n)$	$O(n)$	arbitrary
	SIMD	$O(mn)$	p	arbitrary
Paige and Kruskal (1985)	SIMD–SM	$O(nm/p + n \log p)$	$p \leq m$	arbitrary
	SIMD–SM–RW	$O(nm/p + n \log \log p)$	$p \leq m$	arbitrary
	SIMD–SM	$O(n^2/p + n \log p)$	$p \leq n$	nonnegative
	SIMD–SM–R	$O((m \log n)/p + n \log n)$	$p \leq d_{out}$	nonnegative
	SIMD–SM–RW	$O(n^2/p + n \log \log p)$	$p \leq n$	nonnegative

4.2   Parallel Matching Algorithms

For a given graph $G = (V, E)$, a set of edges of G is called a *matching* if no two of them have a vertex in common. *Maximum matchings* of a graph G is a matching with maximum cardinality. The matching is said to be *perfect* if it covers all the vertices. Various matching-related questions can be formulated for a given graph. For example:

1. Does a given graph have a perfect matching or not?
2. For a graph with a unique perfect matching, find the perfect matching.
3. Find a maximum matching for a given graph.

Various researchers have investigated these and related problems, but most of the work has been on randomized parallel algorithms, which we are not considering in this survey. We will therefore ignore some very important results of Karp et al. (1985), Mulmuley et al. (1986), and others and concentrate on deterministic parallel algorithms for matching-related problems.

4.2.1   Existence of Perfect Matching

Tutte (1947) gave necessary and sufficient conditions for the existence of a perfect matching in a graph $G = (V, E)$. This test is applied as follows. Let D be the adjacency matrix for G, i.e.,

$$d_{ij} = \begin{cases} 1 & \text{if } (v_i, v_j) \in E, \\ 0 & \text{otherwise} \end{cases}$$

Obtain Tutte Matrix T of G as follows from D: If $d_{ij} = d_{ji} = 1$, then replace these two entries by a unique indeterminate, say x_{ij} and its negative $-x_{ij}$, so that the entries above the diagonal get the positive sign. Then $|T| \neq 0$ if and only if there exists a perfect matching in G.

4.2.2   Unique Perfect Matching

If the graph G has a unique perfect matching, then Rabin and Vazirani (1984) have shown that the perfect matching can be obtained by an NC algorithm. (An algorithm is said to be in NC if the complexity is polylog with a polynomial number of processors.) The perfect matching is obtained by inverting the adjacency matrix D of the graph G. The problem of determining whether a graph G has a unique perfect matching has been solved by Kozen et al. (1985). They obtain an NC algorithm by using the matrix obtained by substituting $x_{ij} = 1$ for each indeterminate in Tutte matrix T of G.

Dekel and Sahni (1984) present a parallel algorithm for maximum matching in convex bipartite graphs. Their algorithm has time complexity $O(\log^2 n)$ with $O(n)$ processors, on the SIMD–SM model. They use that algorithm to derive parallel algorithms for scheduling problems.

4.3   Parallel Planarity Testing Algorithms

Ja'Ja' and Simon (1982) present two parallel planarity testing algorithms for the SIMD–SM–R model. The first algorithm has a complexity of $O(\log^2 n)$ on $O(n^4)$ processors, where the processors are bit processors that cannot add or multiply. The second algorithm has a complexity of $O(\log^2 n)$ on $O(n^{3.29}/\log^2 n)$ processors. Both algorithms are based on the idea of embedding triconnected graphs in a plane mesh, and on the fact that a graph is planar if and only if all its triconnected components are planar (see Tutte 1947). The triconnected components of a graph are found by using a technique that is a generalization of that used by Savage and Ja'Ja' (1981) to find the biconnected components of a graph.

4.4   Parallel Maximal Independent Set Algorithms

An *independent set* in a graph is a set of vertices, no two of which are adjacent. A *maximal independent set,* MIS, is an independent set that is not properly contained in any independent set. A sequential algorithm for the MIS problem is extremely simple and is given in MIS–SEQ.

---

algorithm MIS–SEQ;
Input. Graph $G = (V, E)$ with vertices $x_1, \ldots, x_n$.
Output. Set I contains a maximally independent set of vertices for graph G.
begin
1. $I = \phi$;
2.   **for** $i = 1$ **to** n **do**
3.   **if** $x_i \notin N(I)$ **then** $I = I \cup \{x_i\}$;
end;
where $N(I)$ is the neighborhood of any set $I \subseteq V$, defined as follows:
$N(I) = \{x_j \in V \mid \exists\, x_k \in I : (x_j, x_k) \in E\}$

It was conjectured by Valiant (1982) that the MIS problem may not have a fast parallel algorithm, despite the fact that it has a very easy sequential algorithm. Fast parallel algorithms (i.e., in NC), have however been devised for this problem. Karp and Wigderson (1985) have a parallel algorithm for the SIMD–SM model that runs in $O(\log^4 n)$ time on $O(n^3/\log^3 n)$ processors. The

---

algorithm MIS–KW;
begin
1. $I = \phi; H = V;$
2. **while** $H \neq \phi$ **do**
    //$I, N(I), H$ are disjoint and together exhaust vertex set V //
    begin
3. $S =$ an independent set in induced subgraph H;
4. $I = I \cup S$;
5. $H = H - (S \cup N_H(S))$;
    end;
end;

---

algorithm of Luby (1984) is for the SIMD–SM model and has complexity $O(\log^2 n)$ with $O(n^2 m)$ processors.

For the Karp and Wigderson (1985) algorithm, we first introduce some terminology. If $K \subseteq V$, then K is also used to denote the subgraph induced by K. This subgraph has vertex set K, and its edge set $E(K)$ consists of those edges of E that have both their end points in K. For $S \subseteq K$, $N_K(S) = N(S) \cap K$. An outline of a parallel algorithm (which, however, is not efficient) for the MIS problem is given in MIS–KW.

The important point is that Karp and Widgerson show S can be chosen in $O(\log^2 n)$ time so that $|S \cup N_H(S)| = \Omega(|H|/\log|H|)$. I and H can then be updated in $O(\log n)$ time. Therefore, the number of iterations is $O(\log^2 n)$ and the time complexity is $O(\log^4 n)$.

Luby (1985) develops three algorithms for the MIS problem. The first two algorithms are randomized algorithms and what is interesting is that these are used to develop a (deterministic) algorithm of complexity $O(\log^2 n)$ with $O(n^2 m)$ processors. Briefly, the derivation of the deterministic algorithm is as follows. In the first random algorithm, mutually independent choices (for adding a vertex to the independent set) are made, leading to a probability space with a large sample space. In the second random algorithm a new probability space with a smaller sample space is obtained by realizing that the choices need only be pairwise independent. This sample space contains only $O(n^2)$ points, so the deterministic algorithm is obtained by sampling in parallel all the points in the sample space.

4.5   Parallel Algorithms for Euler Circuits

A circuit (path) for a graph $G = (V, E)$ is an Euler circuit (path) if every edge in E appears exactly once. (For simplicity we will consider only the problem of finding Euler circuits.) A serial algorithm for this problem is as follows. For a directed graph the edges are partitioned into circuits, and these edge-disjoint circuits are combined to give a single Euler circuit by performing a number of 'switches'. These switches can be performed one by one and in any order. However, for an efficient direct parallelization we must be able to perform these switches in parallel.

Awerbuch et al. (1984) and Atallah and Vishkin (1984) both present parallel algorithms for finding Euler circuits for directed and undirected graphs. The time complexity of the Awerbuch et al. algorithm is $O(\log|E|)$ with $|E|$ processors on the SIMD–SM–RW model (in case of simultaneous writes any arbitrary processor can succeed). The time complexity of the Atallah and Vishkin algorithm is $O(\log|V|)$ with $|E| + |V|$ processors on the SIMD–SM–RW model (in case of simultaneous writes the lowest-numbered processor succeeds). In both cases, an auxiliary graph is constructed from G and that is used to obtain Euler circuits, but, the auxiliary graphs constructed by Awerbuch et al. and Atallah and Vishkin are different.

The algorithm of Awerbuch et al. for a directed graph proceeds as follows:

1. Generate an Euler partition $P = \{C_1, \ldots, C_m\}$.
2. Obtain a circuit graph $CG = (P, S)$ where $S = \{(e_i, e_j) | (e_i, e_j)$ is a switch with $e_i \in C_h, e_j \in C_k\}$.
3. Obtain CG', a sparse connected subgraph of CG.
4. Find a spanning tree T of CG'.
5. Execute the switches of T.

For undirected graphs, they first orient the edges appropriately and then use the algorithm described above.

The algorithm of Atallah and Vishkin for directed graphs proceeds as follows:

1. The edges of $G = (V, E)$ are partitioned into pairwise disjoint circuits, $C_1, \ldots, C_m$.
2. Auxiliary graph $G' = (V \overset{\bullet}{\cup} \{C_1, \ldots, C_m\}, E')$ is constructed where a vertex v_j in V and C_k are connected if v_j lies on circuit C_k in G.
3. Find a spanning tree T for G'.
4. From T construct a directed graph G'' by replacing each edge in T with two antiparallel edges.
5. Find an Euler circuit for G''.
6. Construct an Euler circuit for G from that of G''.

This algorithm for directed graphs can be used to obtain Euler circuits for undirected graphs by suitably orienting the edges of the input graph.

4.6 Miscellaneous Parallel Graph Algorithms

An undirected graph $G = (V, E)$ is called a *comparability* graph if its edges can be directed to obtain a transitively closed acyclic digraph H. Kozen et al. (1985) gives an NC algorithm that checks whether an undirected graph G is a comparability graph, and if so, it also obtains the transitive orientation of the edges.

If σ is a linearly ordered finite set, then an *interval* α of σ is any set of contiguous elements of σ. Two intervals intersect if and only if they have an element in common, and (α, I), where I is a set of intervals on α, is an *interval representation* of graph $G = (V, E)$ if there exists a bijection $f: V \rightarrow I$ such that $(u, v) \in E$ if and only if the intervals $f(u)$ and $f(v)$ intersect. Graph $G = (V, E)$ is an *interval graph* if and only if there exist α and I such that (α, I) is an interval representation of G. Kozen et al. (1985) gives an NC algorithm that checks whether a graph G is an interval graph, and if so it obtains an interval representation for it.

Ghosh (1986) describes parallel algorithms for connectivity problems in graph theory. In particular, algorithms for obtaining a fundamental set of cycles of a graph, for computing the bridges of a connected graph, and for strongly orienting a bridgeless graph are given. These algorithms have polylog complexity and require $O(n^3)$ processors. Atallah (1984) also discusses parallel algorithms for strongly orienting undirected graphs.

5. Other Parallel Algorithms

So far we have discussed various graph-theoretic algorithms, but in this section we consider some other interesting algorithms.

5.1 Parallel Algorithms for Evaluating
Arithmetic Expressions

Dekel and Sahni (1983b) consider the generation of the postfix form of an arithmetic expression, starting with its infix form. They also translate the postfix form into a binary tree representation. Their model is SIMD–SM, and it uses p processors. The input arithmetic expression can contain operands (constants and simple variables), operators (the binary operators $+, -, *, /, \uparrow$) and parentheses.

Their parallel algorithm originates from the standard priority-based sequential infix-to-postfix algorithm POSTFIX (Horowitz and Sahni, 1976). If the infix expression is in $E[1 \ldots n]$, then for every $E[i]$ define a value $AFTER[i]$ such that $E[i]$ immediately follows $E[AFTER[i]]$ in the postfix form of $E[1 \ldots n]$. Determination of $AFTER[i]$ is the first phase of the

---

algorithm POSTFIX(E, P, n, m);
// Translate the infix expression $E[1 \ldots n]$ into postfix form. The postfix //
// form is output in $P[1 \ldots m]$. "$-\infty$" is used as bottom of stack character //
// and has $ISP = 0$. //
begin
1. $STACK[1] = -\infty$; $top = 1$; $m = 0$;
2.   **for** $i = 1$ **to** n **do**
3.   **if** $E[i]$ is an operand **then**
          begin
4. $m = m + 1$; $P[m] = E[i]$;
          end
5.   **else if** $E[i] = $ ')' **then**
          begin
6.   **while** $STACK[top] \neq$ '(' **do**
              begin // unstack until '(' //
7. $m = m + 1$; $P[m] = STACK[top]$; $top = top - 1$;
              end;
8. $top = top - 1$;
          end
9.   **else**
          begin
10.   **while** $ISP[STACK[top]] \geq ICP[E[i]]$ **do**
              begin
11. $m = m + 1$; $P[m] = STACK[top]$; $top = top - 1$;
              end;
12. $top = top + 1$; $STACK[top] = E[i]$;
          end;
13.   **while** $top > 1$ **do**
          begin
14. $m = m + 1$; $P[m] = STACK[top]$; $top = top - 1$;
          end;
end;

---

parallel algorithm; in the second phase the actual postfix form is derived from the values of $AFTER[i]$.

The calculation of $AFTER[i]$ can be done by calculating $U[i]$, the index of the token that pops $E[i]$ from the operator stack, and $LU[i]$, the index of the last operator to be unstacked by $E[i]$. To calculate these values, each left parenthesis determines the position of its matching right parenthesis by doing a stable sort. This stable sorting can be done in $O(\log^2 n)$ time using n processors (Preparata, 1973). Now all the operators needed for the calculation of $U[i]$, $LU[i]$ can be linked together. $U[i]$ and $LU[i]$ (and hence the

AFTER value) can therefore be calculated in $O(\log^2 n)$ time using $O(n)$ processors. The calculation of the actual postfix form is done using the linked list defined by the *AFTER* values. This can be done using $O(\log n)$ time and n processors by recursively splitting the linked list. Thus the postfix form can be calculated in $O(\log^2 n)$ time using n processors on an SIMD–SM model.

They also give an alternative strategy for computing the values of U and LU. In that strategy a number of copies are made, to avoid read conflicts, and the algorithm has complexity $O(\log n)$ using $n^2/\log n$ processors on an SIMD–SM model.

Bar-On and Vishkin (1985) also present a parallel algorithm for obtaining the binary-tree representation of an arithmetic expression. The complexity of their algorithm is $O(\log n)$ using $n/\log n$ processors on an SIMD–SM–R model. Even though their model is more powerful than that used by Dekel and Sahni (1983b), the algorithm of Bar-On and Vishkin (1985) can be translated to obtain an algorithm for the SIMD–SM model with time complexity $O(\log^2 n)$ with $n/\log n$ processors. This translation can be obtained by using the simulations of Eckstein (1979a) and Vishkin (1983).

The heart of Bar-On and Vishkin (1985) algorithm consists of developing an efficient parentheses-matching algorithm. This is accomplished by using $n/\log n$ processors and allocating a segment of length $\log n$ to each processor. Each segment consists of some pairs of matching parentheses and some parentheses whose matches are in other segments. The matching pairs within a segment can be identified by making one pass through the segment. Matches for the remaining parentheses are found by performing a variant of binary search on a balanced binary tree that the algorithm constructs.

This parentheses-matching algorithm is used as follows. In the original expression, parentheses are introduced so that all subexpressions become simple expressions, where a simple expression is one in which all operators not enclosed by parentheses are of the same precedence. The parentheses-matching algorithm is then applied to this expression. At this point the original problem of obtaining a tree form for the input expression has been reduced to finding the tree form of a number of simple expressions. This can be done in a straightforward manner, and the result can then be combined to obtain the tree form of the original expression.

Apart from the parentheses-matching part, the remaining steps can all be done in $O(1)$ time using n processors, and therefore in $O(\log n)$ time using $n/\log n$ processors.

5.2   Parallel Algorithms for Polynomial Evaluation

Polynomial evaluation is a fundamental and widely used operation, and the problem of designing efficient parallel algorithms for it has received a great deal of attention in recent years. A polynomial can be expressed in a variety of ways—e.g., the power form, the root product form, the Newton form, and the orthogonal form. For details on the different representations, see Kronsjo (1979). Different representations lend themselves to different techniques for exploiting parallelism from the sequential polynomial evaluation algorithms.

Munro and Patterson (1973) developed optimal algorithms for polynomial evaluation, which use a large amount of parallelism. Their algorithms proceed by defining a recursive evaluation procedure for the polynomial. They ignore all memory access problems and assume the existence of k identical arithmetic processors, each of which can perform any one of the binary operations $+$, $-$, $*$, and $/$ in unit time. A lower bound of $2n$ arithmetic operations has been shown to be required for the evaluation of a general n-degree polynomial. When the degree of the polynomial exceeds $k\lceil \log k \rceil$, the Munro and Patterson algorithm is optimal within one time unit.

Hyafil (1978) presents a parallel evaluation algorithm for multivariate polynomials. Hyafil's algorithm shows that a polynomial P computed sequentially in $n\{+, -, *\}$ steps with degree d can be computed in parallel time $O((\log d)(\log n + \log d))$. The number of processors required for this algorithm is $n^{\log d}$, even when n and d are bounded polynomially in terms of the number of indeterminates. Valiant and Skyum (1981) present an improved version of the above algorithm for any multivariate polynomial. The time complexity is the same as for Hyafil's algorithm, but Valiant and Skyum's uses only $(nd)^{O(1)}$ processors. Another result that uses only a polynomial number of processors is the result of Csanky (1976) for evaluating the determinant.

There are other types of parallel polynomial evaluation algorithms in the literature. Recently Bini and Pan (1985) developed parallel polynomial division algorithms by preserving the full efficiency of the best sequential algorithms. This algorithm divides two polynomials of integer coefficients of degree at most m and can be accelerated by a factor of $\log m$. Bini and Pan further show that all the known algorithms for polynomial division can be represented as algorithms for triangular Toeplitz matrix inversion. For improving the efficiency of the determinant and of the inverse of the matrix see Pan and Galil (1985). Recent results on the algebraic complexity of computing polynomial zeros is described in Pan (1985).

5.3 Parallel String Matching Algorithms

The string matching problem consists of finding all occurrences of a given pattern in a given text. Galil (1984) presents families of parallel algorithms for this problem. For the SIMD–SM–RW model (the only simultaneous writes allowed are when processors attempt to write 0 simultaneously), his algorithms can be summarized as follows:

1. $O(n/p)$ time complexity for any number of $p \leq n/\log n$ processors;
2. constant time complexity for $p \leq n^{1+\epsilon}$ processors where $\epsilon > 0$;
3. time complexity $O(\log n/\log \log n)$ for n processors.

For the SIMD–SM–R model, Galil has an algorithm with $O(n/p)$ time complexity using any number $p \leq n \log^2 n$ processors.

All of Galil's algorithms solve the problem under the assumption that both the pattern and the text are over a given alphabet of fixed size. He develops these families of algorithms by first presenting a nonoptimal ($O(\log n)$ time with $O(n)$ processors) solution for the special case when the length of the text is twice the length of the pattern. Then he shows that the number of processors required can be reduced to $O(n/\log n)$ by using the four-Russian trick (Aho et al. 1974). Finally he shows how the restriction on the lengths of the pattern and text can be removed and still maintain optimality by appropriate assignment of processors. The resulting algorithms can then be modified to obtain optimal algorithms for the SIMD–SM–R model with the performance described above.

Vishkin (1985) also presents an optimal parallel algorithm for this problem. His algorithm has time complexity $O(n/p)$ for any number $p \leq n/\log n$ processors on an SIMD–SM–RW model. (In this paper the smallest numbered processor attempting to write succeeds; in a future paper Vishkin will show that these results are valid when simultaneous writes are allowed only if the processors attempt to write the same value.) In contrast to Galil's algorithms, the symbols are not constrained to be taken from an alphabet of fixed size. Briefly, Vishkin's algorithm works as follows:

1. Analyze the pattern so as to compute the following table. The ith entry in the table will indicate either that the suffix starting at position i of the pattern is a prefix of the pattern, or that it is not (in the later case it provides a counterexample).
2. This table allows us to infer for appropriate indices j_1 and j_2 in the text that an occurrence of the pattern cannot start at both j_1 and j_2. Therefore a sparse set of indices where an occurrence of the pattern may start can be obtained.
3. A character-by-character test is applied to the indices obtained in the previous step to determine whether an occurrence of the pattern in fact occurs at those locations.

5.4   Parallel Tree Balancing Algorithms

The task of balancing a binary tree is to adjust the left and right pointers of the vertices in the tree so that the height of the tree is minimized. In Moitra and

Iyengar (1986), an optimal parallel algorithm for obtaining route-balanced binary trees is derived. (In a route-balanced binary tree all the leaves at the highest level are located at the leftmost side of the tree.) In this section, unless otherwise stated, a balanced tree will mean a route-balanced binary tree. The balancing algorithm is systematically derived by starting from a recursive algorithm and transforming it first into an iterative algorithm and then into an optimal parallel algorithm. This parallel algorithm has time complexity $O(1)$ with n processors on an SIMD–SM model and can be described as follows.

The algorithm has two parts. In the first part a parallel in-order traversal of the binary tree is performed and the result is stored in an array $LINK$. In the second part a balanced tree is built from the array $LINK$. The parallel traversal can be done in constant time if additional information is stored with each vertex giving the number of vertices with values less than or equal to its own value.

To describe the building-up process we introduce some terminology. Let the $\langle i, j\rangle$th vertex refer to the jth vertex from the left on the ith level, if it exists in a binary tree. Also, let $VAL_N(\langle i, j\rangle)$ denote the number of vertices with data values less than or equal to the data value of the vertex $\langle i, j\rangle$ in a balanced tree of size N. It can be shown that

$$VAL_N(\langle i, j\rangle) = \min\{VAL_{2^n-1}(\langle i, j\rangle), [VAL_{2^n-1}(\langle i, j\rangle) + N - S + 1]/2\}$$

where $n = \lceil \log(N + 1)\rceil$, $VAL_{2^n-1}(\langle i, j\rangle) = 2^{n-i} + (j-1) * 2^{n-i+1}$, and $S = 2^n - 1 - N$. This gives a method of determining which cell in the array $LINK$ corresponds to the $\langle i, j\rangle$th vertex in the final balanced tree. To construct the balanced tree, a processor P_K is associated with $LINK[K]$, and it must do the following:

C1. Determine i, j such that $VAL_N(\langle i, j\rangle) = K$; that is, its final position in the balanced tree.

C2. If it has a left son, then determine $K1$ such that

$$VAL_N(\langle i + 1, 2 * j - 1\rangle) = K1.$$

C3. If it has a right son, then determine $K2$ such that

$$VAL_N(\langle i + 1, 2 * j\rangle) = K2.$$

Computations C2 and C3 can be done easily in constant time once computation C1 has been done. For simplicity consider the computation C1 when $N = 2^n - 1$. Note that if processor P_K is allocated to process the vertex with VAL equal to K, then P_K may correspond to different indices $\langle i + M, j\rangle$, $M = 1, 2, \ldots$, depending on the size of the balanced tree. The values $n - i$ and

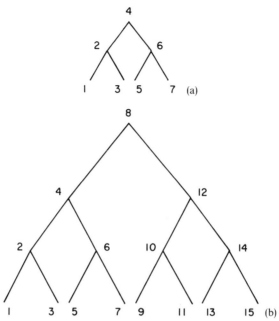

FIG. 2.   Vertex identification that is invariant over the size of the complete balanced binary tree. (a) Vertex with value 6 has $j = 2$, $n - i = 2$. (b) Vertex with value 6 has $j = 2$, $n - i = 2$.

j, however, are invariant over the size of the complete balanced binary tree, as shown in Fig. 2. If the values $n - i$ and j are permanently associated with each processor, then, computation C1 can also be done in constant time. Building up the balanced tree is given in algorithm COM-BAL.

---

algorithm COM-BAL;
// parallel growing algorithm for the construction of a balanced tree by //
// simultaneously executing processes $P_1, \ldots, P_N$, one for each cell in the //
// array $LINK$, where $N = 2^n - 1$ //
begin
1. **for** each P_K **do** in parallel   // h, j associated with each P_K //
    begin
2. $n = \lceil \log(N + 1) \rceil$;
3. $i = n - h$;
4.   **if** odd (K) **then**   // leaves //
        begin
5. $LSON[LINK[K]] = $ null;

6. $RSON[LINK[K]]$ = null;
            end;
7.   **if** even (K) **then**   // interior vertices //
            begin
8. $LSON[LINK[K]] = LINK[K - 2^{n-i-1}]$;
9. $RSON[LINK[K]] = LINK[K + 2^{n-i-1}]$;
            end;
        end;
end;

For arbitrary binary trees, cell $LINK[K]$ may correspond to different indices $\langle i, j \rangle$ and $\langle i', j' \rangle$ with $i \neq i'$ and $j \neq j'$ as the size of the tree changes, thereby making computation C1 expensive. The computation can, however, be reorganized so that a processor $P_{h'}$ sets up links for $LINK[h]$ where $h = \min\{h', [h' + N - S + 1]/2\}$. This allows for a simpler calculation of indices $\langle i, j \rangle$, but a direct implementation of this idea would require the use of $2^n - 1$ processors, where $n = \lceil \log(N + 1) \rceil$, for a tree of size N. To reduce the number of processors so that only N processors are required to grow a tree of size N, further reorganization of the computation has to be done. All the details are presented in algorithm BAL. This result can be extended to balance m-way trees, as discussed in Dekel et al. (1985).

---

algorithm BAL;
// parallel growing algorithm for the construction of a balanced tree by //
// simultaneously executing processes $P_1, \ldots, P_N$ //
begin
1.   **for** each P_K **do** in parallel
        begin
2. $n = \lceil \log(N + 1) \rceil$; $i = n - h$; $S = 2^n - 1 - N$;
3. $K = 2^{n-i} + (j - 1) * 2^{n-i+1}$; $K' = (K + N - S + 1)/2$;
4.   **if** $K' > K$ **then** $K' = K$;   // $K' = VAL_N(\langle i, j \rangle)$ //
5.   **if** odd (K) and $(K = K')$ **then**   // leaves on the highest level //
            begin
6. $LSON[LINK[K']]$ = null; $RSON[LINK[K']]$ = null;
            end;
7.   **if** odd (K) and $(K \neq K')$ **then**   // reorganization of computation //
            begin
8. $K = K + S$; $K' = (K + N - S + 1)/2$;
9.   **if** $K' > K$ **then** $K' = K$;
            end;

10.   **if** even (K) **then**
      begin
11. $K1 = 2^{n-i+1} + (2 * j - 2) * 2^{n-i}$ // set up left link //
12. $K1' = (K1 + N - S + 1)/2$
13.   **if** $K1' > K1$ **then** $K1' = K1$ // $K1' = VAL_N(\langle i + 1, 2 * j - 1\rangle)$ //
14.   **if** odd $(K1)$ and $(K1 \neq K1')$ // odd $(K1) \Rightarrow K'$ on level $n - 1$ //
15.   **then** $LSON[LINK[K'']] =$ null
16.   **else** $LSON[LINK[K']] = LINK[K1']$;
17. $K2 = 2^{n-i-1} + (2 * j - 1) * 2^{n-i}$ // set up right link //
18. $K2' = (K2 + N - S + 1)/2$
19.   **if** $K2' > K2$ **then** $K2' = K2$ // $K2' = VAL_N(\langle i + 1, 2 * j\rangle)$ //
20.   **if** odd $(K2)$ and $(K2 \neq K2')$ // odd $(K2) \Rightarrow K'$ on level $n - 1$ //
21.   **then** $RSON[LINK[K']] =$ null
22.   **else** $RSON[LINK[K']] = LINK[K2']$;
        end;
      end;
end;

5.5   Parallelism In Alpha−Beta Algorithms

Efficient search of trees is fundamental to many areas of study, such as artificial intelligence, operations research, and computer science at large. Most AI problems, especially game-playing programs, use heuristic information to direct the search that is relevant to the goal.

It has been well documented in Berliner (1978) that an important component of search trees in game playing is the speed at which the search is conducted. The focus of this section is to explore parallelism in the alpha−beta search algorithm used extensively in game trees. We first present definitions necessary for the formulation of the alpha−beta search algorithm (Knuth and Moore, 1975; Nilsson, 1980; Slagle and Dixon, 1969; Pearl, 1982). Then we describe a technqiue developed by Finkel, and Fishburn (1982) to exploit parallelism in alpha−beta search algorithms.

5.5.1   Definitions and Formulation of the Alpha−Beta Search Algorithm

Decision and game trees have been used extensively in AI problems such as chess-playing programs. Since the size of the decision or game tree encountered in such problems is very large, it becomes physically impossible to completely search a tree. Thus it becomes important to develop an efficient method for searching and/or pruning the tree; for more details see Knuth and Moore (1975), Nilsson (1980), and Slagle and Dixon (1969).

We restrict the word *game* to mean a two-person, zero-sum, perfect information, play strictly alternating between two players. Each player, on his move, is allowed to choose a move from only a finite number of possible moves. The game is characterized by a set of positions and by a set rules for moving from one position to another.

If, from a given state or position P, a player is allowed to move to any of the possible $P_1, \ldots, P_k$ positions, then in the corresponding game tree one would find a connecting branch from vertex P to each of the $P_1, \ldots, P_k$ vertices. There are two procedures for assigning a static value to the vertices of a decision or game tree, the minimax procedure and the negamax procedure.

In the minimax procedure, even-level vertices $(0, 2, 4, \ldots)$ (the root is at level 0) are called MAX vertices and odd-level vertices $(1, 3, \ldots)$ are called MIN vertices. Player 1 moves from MAX vertices and player 2 moves from MIN vertices. Note that this notation of naming the vertices and assigning each player to even or odd vertices is arbitrary and is chosen by convention. Having named the vertices, a static evaluation function is used to preassign a value to the terminal vertices. After assigning these values, the values for all other nonterminal vertices up to the root are calculated. The procedure used is as follows:

For each MAX vertex, the value assigned is the maximum value of its sons.
For each MIN vertex, the value assigned is the minimum value of its sons.

This procedure is used repeatedly until the value of the root vertex is calculated. The thinking behind this procedure is that each player wants to maximize its own gain and minimize its loss to the other player. In the minimax procedure we always evaluate the game position from any one of the player's viewpoints.

In the negamax procedure there is no differentiation between MAX and MIN vertices. It assigns a static value to a terminal vertex, say $f(p)$, from the point of view of a player whose turn it is to make a move. The value from the other player's point of view is $-f(p)$. If there are more than one possible moves, one needs to select the best move, which will result in the greatest possible gain when the game ends. Thus the value assigned to a nonterminal vertex is the maximum of the negative of its sons. Remember that the value assigned to a terminal vertex is from the point of view of the player whose turn it is to make a move, and that the players strictly alternate. The negamax approach is useful when it is undesirable to deal with two or more separate cases.

5.5.2 Pruning Strategy

Having described the basic background material, let us now describe one of the possible pruning strategies. As remarked earlier, the size of a decision or game tree is extremely large in most AI applications, making pruning desirable. The basic thinking behind pruning is as follows: If we can somehow determine that a given vertex can never improve the value of its parent, it is not necessary to continue the search beyond that vertex. The subtree below that vertex can be cut off, thus pruning the entire tree.

It is obvious that the negamax procedure as described above is not efficient, as it makes no attempt to use the information content of vertices processed earlier. Thus our line of thinking should necessarily include the use of that information to improve the basic negamax procedure. We illustrate this point by the example in Fig. 3, in which we use the information available from earlier vertices to prune the tree. In Fig. 3a the negamax procedure tells us that $m = \max\{3, -n\}$, where $n = \max\{-2, \ldots\}$.

Hence $n \geq -2$, so whatever may be the value of n, we will always get $m = 3$. Thus we need not search the vertex n and everything below vertex n. This gives shallow cutoffs. Following this argument for more than one level gives us deeper cutoffs. Consider the subtree below and inclusive of vertex k in Fig. 3b, where $k = \max\{-j, \ldots\}$ and $j = \max\{-2, \ldots\}$. This gives us two possible cases, viz $k > -j$ or $k = -j$.

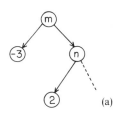

(a)

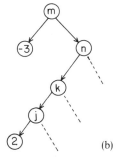

(b)

Fig. 3.   Pruning of search tree: (a) shallow cutoff: (b) deeper cutoff.

Consider $k > -j$. This means that the value of k is not determined by vertex j but by siblings to the right of vertex j. Thus the subtree rooted at vertex j can be cut off.

Consider $k = -j$. Since $j \geq -2$, we get $k \leq 2$. Now $n \geq -k$ and therefore $-n \leq 2$. Since $m = \max\{3, -n\}$ and $-n \leq 2$, we get $m = 3$, which is independent of the value of n. Thus the subtree rooted at vertex n can be cut off.

5.5.3 Definition of Alpha–Beta Bounds

Previous examples illustrate that by using the information obtained from earlier vertices, we can prune the decision or game tree to a considerable extent.

Using two bounds α and β, we get the alpha–beta search algorithm as described by Knuth and Moore (1975):

```
1.   function alphabeta (p : position; α, β : integer) : integer;
2.        var i, d : 1 ... MAXCHILD;
                succ : array [1 ... MAXCHILD] of position;
     begin
4.   determine the successor position succ[1], ..., succ[d];
5.   if d = 0 then return (static_value (p));          // terminal vertex //
6.   for i = 1 to d do
     begin
7.      α = max {α, −alphabeta (succ[i], −β, −α)};
8.      if α ≥ β then return (α);                       // cutoff //
     end;
9.   return (α);
     end;
```

We can thus summarize the characteristics of the function alphabeta as follows:

a) For a given position p and for values of α, β with $\alpha < \beta$,
   1. if negamax$(p) \leq \alpha$ then alphabeta $(p, \alpha, \beta) \leq \alpha$;
   2. if negamax$(p) \geq \beta$ then alphabeta $(p, \alpha, \beta) \leq \beta$;
   3. if $\alpha < $ negamax$(p) < \beta$ then alphabeta $(p, \alpha, \beta) = $ negamax(p).
b) The pair (α, β) is called the window for the search.
c) The alpha–beta search algorithm is strongly serial in the sense that the earlier work is used in deciding cutoffs at the later stages.

5.5.4   Parallelization of Alpha–Beta Search Algorithm

Attempts aimed at a parallel version of alpha–beta include the parallel "aspiration search" by Budet (1978), "mandatory-work-first" by Akl et al. (1982), and tree-splitting algorithms by Finkel and Fishburn (1982) and by Kumar and Kanal (1984). We now look more closely at the algorithm of Finkel and Fishburn.

Finkel and Fishburn (1982) present a parallel version of the alpha–beta search algorithm. This tree-splitting algorithm speeds up the search of a large tree of potential continuations by dynamically assigning subtree searches for parallel execution. The root processor evaluates the root position. Each of the interior processors evaluates the position assigned to it by generating successors, queuing them for parallel execution to its slave processor. A processor tree is used in the execution of this parallel algorithm. Thus a processor that is at the kth level in the processor tree corresponds to the position at level k in the lookahead tree used by the game-playing expert system. The terminal processor evaluates its position using a serial alpha-beta algorithm. Thus on completion of its slave's evaluation (or at cutoff) the master can evaluate its position. The masters inform their working slaves about the updated narrow window as they receive information from their slaves.

As is clear from the above discussion, there are two algorithms, viz the leaf algorithm and the interior algorithm. We now describe these algorithms in more detail.

5.5.5   The Leaf Algorithm

We can describe the interaction of algorithm Leaf with its master either by remote procedure calls or by the message-passing or shared memory form. In the algorithm below the master calls the function leaf$\alpha\beta$ remotely (line 11) and interrupts the active slaves to inform them of updated windows, by invoking the asynchronous procedure update (line 2).

5.5.6   The Interior Algorithm

As we described earlier, the slaves report to the master. The creation and coordination of the slaves is done by the master. We now give this algorithm and discuss how it works.

The Interior algorithm generates all successors of the position to be evaluated (as indicated in line 15). If there are a sufficient number of slaves available, then each slave is assigned to evaluate one of the positions.

---

algorithm Leaf;

1. α, β : **array** [1 ... MAXDEPTH] **of integer**; // global arrays //

2.   **asynchronous procedure** update (*newα, newβ* : **integer**);
    // the asynchronous procedure update is called by my master to //
    // inform me of new window (*newα, newβ*) //

3.   **var** *tmp* : **integer**;

4.   *k* : 1 ... MAXDEPTH;

    begin

5.   **for** $k = 1$ **to** MAXDEPTH **do**

      begin   // update arrays α and β //

6. $\alpha[k] = \max \{\alpha[k], new\alpha\}$;

7. $\beta[k] = \min \{\beta[k], new\beta\}$;

8. $tmp = new\alpha$;

9. $new\alpha = -new\beta$;

10. $new\beta = -tmp$;

      end; // update //

    end;

11.   **function** leaf$\alpha\beta$(*p* : position; α, β : **integer**) : **integer**;

    begin

12. $\alpha[1] = \alpha$;

13. $\beta[1] = \beta$;

14.   **return**(alphabeta(*p*, 1));

    end;

15.   **function** alphabeta(*p* : position; *depth* : **integer**) : **integer**;

16.   **var** *succ* : **array** [1 ... MAXCHILD] **of** position;   // successors //

17.   *succno* : 1 ... MAXCHILD;   // which successors //

18.   *succlim* : 1 ... MAXCHILD;   // how many successors //

    begin

19.   determine the successors *succ*[1], ..., *succ*[*succlim*];

20.   **if** *succlim* $= 0$ **then return** (static_value(*p*));

21.   **for** *succno* $= 1$ **to** *succlim* **do**

      begin   // evaluate each successor //

22. $\alpha[depth + 1] = -\beta[depth]$;

23. $\beta[depth + 1] = -\alpha[depth]$;

24. $\alpha[depth] = \max \{\alpha[depth], -\text{alphabeta}(succ[succno], depth + 1)\}$;

25.   **if** $\alpha[depth] \leq \beta[depth]$ **then**

           return($\alpha[depth]$);   // a cutoff has occurred //

      end; // for *succno* //

26.   **return**($\alpha[depth]$);

27.   **end**; // alphabeta //

```
algorithm Interior;
1.    var g1α, g1β : integer;              // global variables //
2.        q : integer;                     // variable used for the depth of tree //
3.    asynchronous procedure update(newα, newβ : integer);
          // update is called asynchronously by my master to inform me of the //
          // new window (newα, newβ) //
      begin
4.        atomically do
          begin
5.            g1α = max {g1α, newα};
6.            g1β = min {g1β, newβ};
          end; // of atomically do //
7.        for all salveid do slaveid.update(−g1β, −g1α);
      end; // update //
8.    function interiorαβ(p : position; α, β : integer) : integer;
9.    var succ : array [1 ... MAXCHILD] of position; // for denoting successors //
10.       succno : 1 ... MAXCHILD;             // the number of successors //
11.       succlim : 1 ... MAXCHILD;            // limit on number of successors //
12.       tmp : array [1 ... MAXCHILD] of integer;
13.       g : integer;
      begin
14.       g1α = α; g1β = β;
15.       determine the successors succ[1], ..., succ[succlim];
16.       if succlim = 0 then return(static_value(p));
17.       if depth(succ[1]) < q
18.           then g = interiorαβ
19.           else g = leafαβ;
20.       parfor succno = 1 to succlim do              // parallel operation //
          begin
21.           slaveid = idle_slave( );
22.           if g1α < g1β then
              begin
23.               tmp[succno]-slaveid.g(succ[succno], −g1β, −g1α);
24.               if tmp[succno] > g1α then
                  begin
25.                   atomically do g1α = max {tmp[succno], g1α};
26.                   for all salveid do salveid.update(−g1β, −g1α);
                  end;
              end;
          end; // of parfor //
27.       return(g1α);
      end; // interiorαβ //
```

Otherwise a queue is formed. Although there are several ways of forming the queue, the queue is implemented as a *parallel for* loop (starting at line 20). One of the following actions is taken when one of the slaves returns:

1. If the returned value causes the value of current α to increase, then all active slaves are informed of the updated value (line 26).
2. If α increases beyond β, then a cutoff has occurred. Since a nonpositive, updated window is now sent to slaves (line 26), the slaves get terminated. The queue of waiting successor positions (line 22) is emptied.
3. On an update interrupt from the master, the new window is transmitted to the slaves.

When all successors are evaluated, the final value is returned to its master (line 27).

5.5.7 Optimizations

There are several ways in which this algorithm can be optimized:

1. The majority of the time, a master is waiting for messages from the slaves. This waiting time can be used for subtree searches, but since slaves have further slaves below them to help, masters are slower than slaves. Hence only deep masters can use this optimization.
2. One can group several higher-level masters onto a single processor.
3. The root processor can send a special window $(-\alpha - 1, \alpha)$ instead of $(-\beta, -\alpha)$. The narrower window speeds up the search.

Finkel and Fishburn (1983) discuss some improved speed-up bounds for parallel alpha–beta search.

6. Conclusions

The design of parallel algorithms for various parallel computer architectures is motivated by factors such as speed and the need to solve complex problems of practical interest. With the continuing decrease in hardware cost, the objective is to trade the number of processors for a gain in computational speed. The advent of commercial multiprocessors has sparked considerable interest in the study and development of parallel algorithms. An extensive study of parallel algorithms for useful computational problems calls for a systematic and thorough investigation of research efforts spanning more than a decade. The attempt we have made here is to illustrate and emphasize the following needs:

1. to systematize the study of parallel algorithms and the design process;
2. to survey the various techniques employed in exploiting the inherent parallelism in problems;
3. to unify parallel algorithms by means of well-defined paradigms;
4. to present a bird's-eye view of some of the current research efforts in the area of concurrent algorithms.

These are expected to result in a better understanding of the working, as well as the development, of parallel algorithms. In view of the ongoing Fifth-Generation Computer Project and the increased use of high-speed supercomputers, a detailed study of the techniques for the design of parallel algorithms becomes quite important.

Because of the growing number of parallel computer architectures and the algorithms developed on these for a large class of problems, it has become increasingly difficult for a user to select a particular parallel algorithm for any given application. In fact, we feel that such a choice is usually decided by factors such as ease of implementation of the algorithms and cost-effectiveness of the computers. What could best be done under such circumstances is to identify some of the inherent, invariant features of the parallel algorithms and base one's judgement on a critical analysis of these.

The notions of time and space complexity carry forward from the sequential algorithmic domain and are indeed helpful in making an appropriate choice of a parallel algorithm. It is often difficult to analyze the complexity of parallel algorithms on MIMD machines, however, because of the close interleaving and the indeterminacy of communication and synchronization costs. Such asynchronicity has benefits in the ease of design of parallel algorithms, usually from an efficient sequential version, and in more generality. The synchronous models of parallel computation, such as the SIMD machines, have come to be accepted as useful models because of their simple structures and amenability to formal analysis. In fact, the complexity classes with regard to parallel computation have been mostly for the synchronous models of computation. Still, it should be observed here that, unlike the case of sequential algorithms, there is no "satisfactory" model of parallel computation.

A large number of results on developing efficient parallel algorithms have enriched the complexity classes and thrown open newer issues. The notion of P-completeness is a useful analogue of NP-completeness, in the sense that, just as deterministic polynomial-time sequential algorithms are unlikely for NP-complete problems, polylog parallel-time algorithms are unlikely for P-complete problems. The class NC (Nick's class) characterizes the problems having efficient parallel algorithms. Though it is known that NC is a subset of

P, it is widely believed that the inclusion is proper. Problems such as depth-first search, unification etc., are examples of problems in P not known to be in NC. Further, they are not likely to be in NC, because they have been shown to be P-complete. The question is whether P-complete problems can be efficiently parallelized in some sense.

Recently, Vitter and Simons (1986) have proposed some new complexity classes for parallel algorithms, called PC and PC*. These classes of problems do not have speed-ups comparable to those in NC. The speed-up is usually by a constant factor or proportional to the number of processors used. Another important point to be observed is that the parallel algorithms in the literature have been mostly on problems in P. This is understandable, since for NP-hard algorithms we cannot devise a polynomial-time parallel algorithm with a polynomial number of processors, unless P = NP. Browning (see Mead and Conway, 1980) has proposed a tree machine with an exponential number of processors, and using this he has developed polynomial-time algorithms for some NP-complete graph problems. It is to be borne in mind that quite a large number of useful problems are NP-complete. Though we cannot expect to achieve a significant speed-up by parallel algorithms for these problems, such a study has not been undertaken so far in a systematic way. It is possible to achieve some useful results in the speed-up for these problems using a polynomial number of processors. Research efforts are needed in this direction.

We can view the paradigms discussed here at two different levels: the abstract and the concrete (relatively). At the abstract level the paradigms for the design of parallel algorithms can be split up into three categories:

1. parallelizing existing sequential algorithms;
2. deriving by formal means a parallel algorithm from a sequential algorithm (this is a special case of (1) above, with the emphasis here on the derivation technique);
3. using elegant characterizations and identifying computationally efficient properties.

In this setting, almost all MIMD algorithms fall in category 1. This includes the algorithm of Prim and Dijkstra and that of Kruskal for the minimum spanning tree problem. Algorithms such as the parallel connected components, parallel biconnected components, maximum matching, and maximal independent set fall into category 3. Parallel algorithms for balancing trees, as in our section 5, typify category 2. At the concrete level we discuss paradigms like the binary tree method, growing by doubling and spanning trees for graphs.

We have also substantiated these techniques with suitable examples. We would like to emphasize here that there is no universal method for designing parallel algorithms. Usually the trick lies in identifying the right formulation of the problem amenable to parallelization and the use of one or more of the technique we have elucidated.

ACKNOWLEDGMENTS

We thank our graduate students S. V. N. Rao, Chandrasekhran, and Girish Kumthekar for their contributions in this paper. Comments by Professors Kraft and Bastani helped in revising the paper.

REFERENCES

Aho, A., Hopcroft, J., and Ullman, J. (1974). "The Design and Analysis of Computer Algorithms." Addison–Wesley, Reading, Mass.

Akl, S. G., Barnard, D. T., and Doran, R. J. (1982). Design, analysis, and implementation of a parallel tree search algorithm. *IEEE Trans. Pattern Anal. Mach. Intell.* **PAMI-4,** 192–203.

Arjomandi, E., and Corneil, D. G. (1975). Parallel computations in graph theory. *Proc. 16th Annu. Symp. Foundations Comput. Sci.,* 13–18.

Atallah, M. J. (1984). Parallel strong orientation of an undirected graph. *Inf. Process. Lett.* **18,** 37–39.

Atallah, M. J., and Kosaraju, S. R. (1985). A generalized dictionary machine for VLSI. *IEEE Trans. Comput.* **C-35** (2), 151–155.

Atallah, M., and Vishkin, U. (1984). Finding Euler tours in parallel. *J. Comput. Syst. Sci.* **29** (3), 330–337.

Awerbuch, B., and Shiloach, Y. (1983). New connectivity and MSF algorithms for Ultracomputer and PRAM. *Proc. 1983 Int. Conf. Parallel Process.,* 175–179.

Awerbuch, B., Israeli, A., and Shiloach, Y. (1984). Finding Euler circuits in logarithmic parallel time. *Proc. 16th Annu. ACM Symp. Theory Comput.,* 249–257.

Bar-On, I., and Vishkin, U. (1985). Optimal parallel generation of a computation tree form. *ACM Trans. Program. Lang. Syst.* **7** (2), 348–357.

Baudet, G. M. (1978). The design and analysis of algorithms for asynchronous multiprocessors. Ph.D. dissertation, Carnegie–Mellon University, Pittsburgh, Pennsylvania.

Bentley, J. L. (1980). A parallel algorithm for constructing minimum spanning trees. *J. Algorithms* **1** (1), 51–59.

Bentley, J. L., and Kung, H. T. (1979). A tree machine for searching problems. *Proc. 1979 Int. Conf. Parallel Process.,* 256–266.

Berliner, H. J. (1978). A chronology of computer chess and its literature. *Artif. Intell.* **10** (2), 201–214.

Bini, D., and Pan, V. (1985). Parallel polynomial division can be accelerated preserving full efficiency of the best sequential algorithms. Tech. Rep. 85-3, Computer Science Dept., State University of New York at Albany.

Bitton, D., DeWitt, D. J., Hsaio, D. K., and Menon, J. (1984). A taxonomy of parallel sorting. *ACM Comput. Surv.* **16** (3), 287–318.

Chandra, A. K. (1976). Maximal parallelism in matrix multiplication. IBM Tech. Rep. RC 6193, Thomas J. Watson Research Center, Yorktown Heights, N.Y.

Chen, S. (1975). Speedups of iterative programs in multiprocessing systems. Ph.D. dissertation, Univ. Illinois at Urbana–Champaign.

Cheriton, D., and Tarjan, R. E. (1976). Finding minimum spanning trees. *SIAM J. Comput.* **5** (4), 724–742.

Chin, F. Y., Lam, J., and Chen, I.-N. (1981). Optimal parallel algorithms for the connected component problem. *Proc. 1981 Int. Conf. Parallel Process.*, 170–175.

Chin, F. Y., Lam, J., and Chen, I.-N. (1982). Efficient parallel algorithms for some graph problems. *Commun. ACM* **25** (9), 659–665.

Cook, S. A. (1981). Towards a complexity theory of synchronous parallel computation. *L'Enseignement Mathematique* **XXVII**, 99–124.

Csanky, L. (1976). Fast parallel inversion algorithms. *SIAM J. Comput.* **5** (4), 618–623.

Dekel, E., and Sahni, S. (1983a). Binary trees and parallel scheduling algorithms. *IEEE Trans. Comput.* **C-32** (3), 307–315.

Dekel, E., and Sahni, S. (1983b). Parallel generation of postfix and tree forms. *ACM Trans. Program. Lang. Syst.* **5** (3), 300–317.

Dekel, E., and Sahni, S. (1984). A parallel matching algorithm for convex bipartite graphs and applications to scheduling. *J. Parallel Distrib. Comput.* **1**, 185–205.

Dekel, E., Nassimi, D., and Sahni, S. (1981). Parallel matrix and graph algorithms. *SIAM J. Comput.* **10** (4), 657–675.

Dekel, E., Peng, S., and Iyengar, S. S. (1985). Optimal parallel algorithm for constructing and maintaining a balanced m-way search tree. Tech. Rep. CS-209, Dept. Mathematical Sciences, Univ. Texas at Dallas. Dallas, Texas.

Deo, N., Pang, C. Y. (1984). Shortest path algorithms: Taxonomy and annotation. *Networks* **14** (2), 275–324.

Deo, N., and Yoo, Y. B. (1981). Parallel algorithms for the minimum spanning tree problem. *Proc. 1981 Int. Conf. Parallel Process.*, 188–189.

Dijkstra, E. (1959). A note on two problems in connexion with graphs. *Numer. Math.* **1**, 269–271.

Eckstein, D. M. (1979a). Simultaneous memory access. Tech. Rep 79-6, Dept. of Computer Science, Iowa State Univ. of Science and Technology, Ames, Iowa.

Eckstein, D. M. (1979b). BFS and biconnectivity. Tech. Rep. 79-11, Dept of Computer Science, Iowa State Univ. of Science and Technology, Ames, Iowa.

Finkel, R. A., and Fishburn, J. P. (1982). Parallelism in alpha–beta search. *Artif. Intell.* **19**, 89–106.

Finkel, R. A., and Fishburn, J. P. (1983). Improved speedup bounds for parallel alpha–beta search *IEEE Trans. Pattern Anal. Mach. Intell.* **PAMI-5** (1), 89–92.

Fisher, A. L. (1984). Dictionary machines with a small number of processors. *Proc. 11th Annu. ACM Conf. Comput. Architecture,* 154–156.

Floyd, R. W. (1962). Algorithm 97: Shortest path. *Commun. ACM* **5** (6), 362.

Galil, Z. (1984). Optimal parallel algorithms for string matching. *Proc. 16th Annu. ACM Symp. Theory Comput.*, 240–248.

Gentleman, W. M. (1978). Some complexity results for matrix computations on parallel processors. *J. Assoc. Comput. Mach.* **25** (1), 112–115.

Ghosh, R. K. (1986). Parallel algorithms for connectivity problems in graph theory. *J. Comput. Math.* **18**, 193–218.

Hirschberg, D. S. (1976). Parallel algorithms for the transitive closure and the connected component problems. *Proc. 8th Annu. ACM Symp. Theory Comput.*, 55–57.

Hirschberg, D. S. (1978). Fast parallel sorting algorithms. *Commun. ACM* **21** (8), 657–661.

Hirschberg, D. S. (1982). Parallel graph algorithms without memory conflicts. *Proc. 20th Allerton Conf.*, 257–263.

Hirschberg, D. S., and Volper, D. J. (1983). A parallel solution for the minimum spanning tree problem. *Proc. 17th Annu. Conf. Inf. Sci. Syst.*, 680–684.

Hirschberg, D. S., Chandra, A. K., and Sarwate, D. V. (1979). Computing connected components on parallel computers. *Commun. ACM* **22** (8), 461–464.

Horowitz, E., and Sahni, S. (1976). "Fundamentals of Data Structures." Computer Science Press, Woodland Hills, Calif.

Hyafil, L. (1978). On the parallel evaluation of the multivariate polynomials. *Proc. 10th Annu. ACM Symp. Theory Comput.*, 193–195.

Ja'Ja', J., and Simon, J. (1982). Parallel algorithms in graph theory: Planarity testing. *SIAM J. Comput.* **11** (2), 314–328.

Karp, R. M., and Wigderson, A. (1985). A fast parallel algorithm for the maximal independent set problem. *J. Assoc. Comput. Mach.* **32** (4), 762–773.

Karp, R. M., Upfal, E., and Wigderson, A. (1985). Constructing a perfect matching in random NC. *Proc. 17th Annu. ACM Symp. Theory Comput.*, 22–32.

Keller, R. M. (1973). Parallel program schemata and maximal parallelism I: Fundamental results. *J. Assoc. Comput. Mach.* **20**, 514–537.

Knuth, D. E., and Moore, R. W. (1975). An analysis of alpha–beta pruning. *Artif. Intell.* **6** (4), 293–326.

Kozen, D., Vazirani, U. V., and Vazirani, V. V. (1985). NC algorithms for comparability graphs, interval graphs, and testing for unique perfect matching. *Fifth Conf. Foundations Software Tech. and Theoretical Comp. Sci.*, 496–503.

Kronsjo, L. (1979). "Algorithms: Their Complexity and Efficiency," John Wiley and Sons Ltd.

Kruskal, J. B. (1956). On the shortest subtree of a graph and the traveling salesman problem. *Proc. Am. Math. Soc.* **7**, 48–50.

Kucera, L. (1982). Parallel computation and conflicts in memory access. *Inf. Process. Lett.* **14** (2), 93–96.

Kuck, D. J. (1976). Parallel processing of ordinary programs. Advances in Computers **15**, Academic Press, 119–179.

Kuck, D. J. (1977). A survey of parallel machine organization and programming. *ACM Comput. Surv.* **9**, 29–59.

Kuhn, R. H., and Padua, D. A. (1981). "Tutorial on Parallel Processing." IEEE Computer Society Press.

Kumar, V., and Kanal L. N. (1984). Parallel branch and bound formulations for understanding and synthesising AND/OR TREE search. *IEEE Trans. Pattern Anal. Mach. Intell.* **PAMI-6** (6), 768–778.

Kung, H. T. (1980). The structure of parallel algorithms. Advances in Computers **19**, Academic Press, 65–112.

Kwan, S. C., and Ruzzo, W. L. (1984) Adaptive parallel algorithms for finding minimum spanning trees. *Proc. 1984 Int. Conf. Parallel Process.*, 439–443.

Lakshmivarahan, S., Dhall, S. K., and Miller, L. L. (1984). Parallel sorting algorithms. Advances in Computers **23**, Academic Press, 295–354.

Lee, G., Kruskal, C. P., and Kuck D. J. (1985). An empirical study of automatic restructuring of nonnumerical programs for parallel processors. *IEEE Trans. Comput.* **C-34** (10), 927–933.

Leiserson, C. E. (1979). Systolic priority queues. Tech. Rep. CMU-CS-79-115, Dept. of Computer Science, Carnegie–Mellon University, Pittsburgh, Pennsylvania.

Levitt, K. N., and Kautz, W. T. (1972). Cellular arrays for the solution of graph problems. *Commun. ACM* **15** (9), 789–801.

Luby, M. (1985). A simple parallel algorithm for the maximal independent set problem. *Proc. 17th Annu. ACM Symp. Theory Comput.*, 1–10.

Mateti, P., and Deo, N. (1981). Parallel algorithms for the single source shortest path problems. Tech. Rep. CS-81-078, Computer Science Dept., Washington State Univ., Pullman, Wash.

Mead, C. A., and Conway, L. A. (1980). "Introduction to VLSI Systems." Addison–Wesley, Reading, Massachusetts.

Moitra, A. (1986). Automatic construction of CSP programs from sequential nondeterministic programs. *Sci. Comput. Program.* **5**, 277–307.

Moitra, A., and Iyengar, S. S. (1986). Derivation of a parallel algorithm for balancing binary trees. *IEEE Trans. Software Eng.* **SE-12** (3), 442–449.

Mulmuley, K., Vazirani, U. V., and Vazirani, V. V. (1986). Matching is as easy as matrix inversion. To appear in *Combinatorics.*

Munro, I., and Patterson, M. (1973). Optimal algorithms for polynomial evaluations. *J. Comput. Syst. Sci.* **7**, 189–198.

Nath. D., and Maheshwari, S. N. (1982). Parallel algorithms for the connected components and minimal spanning tree problems. *Inf. Process. Lett.* **14** (1), 7–11.

Nicolau, A. (1985). Uniform parallelism exploitation in ordinary programs. *Proc. 1985 IEEE Int. Conf. Parallel Process.*, 614–618.

Nilsson, N. J. (1980). "Principles of Artificial Intelligence." Tioga Publishing Co., Palo Alto, Calif.

Ottaman, T. A., Rosenberg, A. I., and Stockmeyer, L. J. (1982). A dictionary machine for VLSI. *IEEE Trans. Comput.* **C-31** (9), 892–897.

Paige, R. C., and Kruskal, C. P. (1985). Parallel algorithms for shortest path problems. *Proc. 1985 IEEE Int. Conf. Parallel Process.*, 14–20.

Pan, V. (1985). Complexity of computing polynomial zeros. Tech. Rep. 85–27, Computer Science Dept., State University of New York at Albany, Albany, New York.

Pan, V., and Galil, Z. (1985). Improving the efficiency of parallel algorithms for the evaluation of the determinant and of the inverse of a matrix. Tech. Rep. 85-5, Computer Science Dept., State University of New York at Albany, Albany, New York.

Pearl, J. (1982) The solution for the branching factor of alpha–beta pruning algorithms and its optimality. *Commun. ACM* **25** (8), 559–563.

Preparata, F. P. (1973). New parallel sorting schemes. *IEEE Trans. Comput.* **C-27** (7), 669—673.

Prim, R. C. (1957). Shortest connection networks and some generalizations. *Bell Syst. Tech. J.* **36**, 1389–1401.

Quinn, M. J., and Deo, N. (1984). Parallel graph algorithms. *ACM Comput. Surv.* **16** (3), 319–348.

Rabin, M. O., and Vazirani, V. V. (1984). Maximum matchings in general graphs through randomization. Tech. Rep. 15-84, Center for Research in Computing Technology, Harvard University, Cambridge, Mass.

Reghbati (Arjomandi), E., and Corneil, D. G. (1978). Parallel computations in graph theory. *SIAM J. Comput.* **2** (2), 230–237.

Reif, J. H. (1985). Depth-first search is inherently sequential. *Inf. Process. Lett.* **20** (5), 229–234.

Sameh, A. H. (1977). Numerical parallel algorithms—A survey. *In* "Tutorial on Parallel Processing" (R. H. Kuhn and D. A. Padua, eds.), pp. 412–427. IEEE Computer Society Press,

Savage, C. (1977). Parallel algorithms for graph theoretic problems. Ph.D. dissertation, University of Illinois, Urbana, Ill.

Savage, C., and Ja'Ja', J. (1981). Fast, efficient parallel algorithms for some graph problems. *SIAM J. Comput.* **10** (4), 682–691.

Shiloach, Y., and Vishkin, U. (1982). An $O(\log n)$ parallel connectivity algorithm. *J. Algorithms* **3** (1), 57–67.

Shrira, L., Francez, N., and Rodeh, M. (1983). Distributed k-selection : From a sequential to a distributed algorithm. *Proc. Second Annu. ACM Symp. Principles of Distributed Computing*, ACM, New York, 143–153.

Slagle, J. R., and Dixon, J. D. (1969). Experiments with some programs that search game trees. *J. Assoc. Comput. Mach.* **16** (2), 189–207.

Sollin, M. (1977). An algorithm attributed to Sollin. *In* "Introduction to the Design and Analysis of Algorithms" (S. E. Goodman and S. T. Hedetniemi, eds.), Sect. 5.5. McGraw-Hill, New York.

Somani, A. K., and Agarwal, V. K. (1984). An efficient VLSI dictionary machine. *Proc. 11th Annu. ACM Int. Symp. Comput. Architecture*, 142–150.

Stone, H. S. (1980). Parallel computers. *In* "Introduction to Computer Architecture" (H. S. Stone, ed.), Chap. 8. Science Research Associates, Chicago, Ill.

Strom, R., and Yemini, S. (1985). Synthesizing distributed and parallel programs through optimistic transformations. *Proc. 1985 IEEE Int. Conf. Parallel Process.*, 632–642.

Tanaka, Y., Nozoka, Y., and Masuyama, A. (1980). Pipeline searching and sorting modules as components of data flow database computer. *Proc. IFIP*, 427–432.

Tarjan, R. E. (1972). Depth first search and linear graph algorithms. *SIAM J. Comput.* **1** (2), 146–160.

Tarjan, R. E., and Vishkin, U. (1984). Finding biconnected components and computing tree functions in logarithmic parallel time. *Proc. 25th Annu. Symp. Foundations of Comput. Sci.*, 12–20.

Tsin, Y. H., and Chin, F. Y. (1984). Efficient parallel algorithms for a class of graph theoretic problems. *SIAM J. Comput.* **13** (3), 580–599.

Tutte, W. T. (1947). The factorization of linear graphs. *J. London Math. Soc.* **22**, 107–111.

Valiant, L. G. (1982). Parallel computation. *Proc. 7th IBM Symp. Math. Foundations of Comput. Sci.*

Valiant, L. G., and Skyum, S. (1981). Fast parallel computation of polynomials using few processors. *Lecture Notes in Computer Science,* **118.** Springer-Verlag, New York, 132–139.

Vishkin, U. (1983). Implementation of simultaneous memory address access in models that forbid it. *J. Algorithms* **4** (1),45–50.

Vishkin, U. (1985). Optimal parallel pattern matching in strings. *Lecture Notes in Computer Science, 194.* Springer-Verlag, New York, 497–508.

Vitter, J. S., and Simons, R. S. (1986). New classes for parallel complexity : A study of unification and other complete problems in P. *IEEE Trans. Comput.* **C-35** (5), 403–418.

Wyllie, J. C. (1979). The complexity of parallel computations. Ph.D. dissertation, Cornell Univ., Ithaca, NY.

Yao, C.-C. (1975). An $O(|E|\log\log|V|)$ algorithm for finding minimum spaning trees. *Inf. Process. Lett.* **4** (1), 21–23.

Yoo, Y. B. (1983). Parallel processing for some network optimization problems. Ph.D. dissertation, Washington State Univ., Pullman, Wash.

Multistage Interconnection Networks for Multiprocessor Systems

S. C. KOTHARI

Computer Science Department
Iowa State University
Ames, Iowa 50011

1. Introduction

Over the last two decades computer technology has advanced dramatically in terms of performance, cost, and reliability. As a notable example of progress, super computers have steadily gone up in speed from mega flops (floating point operations per second) to giga flops—an increase by a factor

155

of 10^3. The increase in speed has been a result of an equally dramatic improvement in integrated circuit (IC) technologies. With present research on new fabrication methods, there is every reason to expect this advancement to continue. The current work on fabrication using ultrathin layers of dissimilar materials (gallium compounds) holds a promise of switching devices that are 10 times faster than the present silicon based devices. However, the advance already achieved has pushed the technology close enough to fundamental physical limits, such as the speed with which information can travel inside a computer. This has brought an awareness of the limitations in the engineering of high performance computer systems based on high speed IC technologies. There is growing consensus that, in the future, significant increases in the performance of computer systems will come mainly from the use of multiple processors that work in parallel on a single task. A highly parallel multiprocessor system is now economically feasible. The same technology that pushed the performance of computer systems to its present level has also brought down the hardware cost to a level where it is also feasible to construct a multiprocessor system by interconnecting hundreds or even thousands of processors.

Computer architecture concepts, such as pipelining and array processing, have traditionally been very successful in improving performance. The multiprocessor systems pose new challenges and call for new innovations in computer architecture. Parallel processing requires a careful partition of a computational task into processes that can be assigned to different processors for better resource utilization and higher performance. Almost always the processes must communicate with each other for successful completion of the task. The communication requirement is a dominant factor that determines the performance in many applications. The communication requirement depends on the specific algorithm being used to partition the task and the available interconnection between processors. The interconnection network that connects the processors thus becomes a critical part for performance of a highly parallel multiprocessor system.

In a multiprocessor system, an interconnection network is used to connect processors and/or memory modules. A time-shared bus is the simplest form of interconnection network, but it cannot provide the performance required in multiprocessor systems of today. A crossbar switch is an alternative used in the earlier systems. It has a separate switching gate for each input-output connection, and thus, the delay to connect inputs to outputs is only the delay of a single switching gate. A crossbar switch with N inputs and N outputs requires N^2 switching gates. Thus, for large systems with hundreds and possibly thousands of processors, the required large number of switching gates prohibits the use of a crossbar switch as an interconnection network. The hardware cost of such a switch is enormous and can easily dominate the cost of the entire system. Also, because of constraints such as restriction on the number of pins for a single chip, the VLSI implementation of a large crossbar switch is not feasible. This has turned the attention to multistage interconnection networks (MINs). The idea behind a multistage interconnection network is to connect several stages of smaller crossbar switches to provide the required interconnection network.

The reduction in hardware achieved by using MINs can be significant. As noted earlier, a crossbar switch with N inputs and N outputs requires N^2 switching gates. By contrast, for important classes of MINs, such as the rearrangeable networks and the unique path property (UPP) networks, the total number of switching gates is of order $N \log N$. The reduction in hardware entails a sacrifice in communication speed of an interconnection network. The communication speed is reduced for two main reasons: the number of stages through which the information must pass and the time needed for setting the network control. The number of stages in most MINs is of order $\log N$. The delay due to set-up time can be considerably higher and can become a limiting factor for a MIN. However, there are MINs such as digit controlled networks where the set-up time is also of order $\log N$, making such MINs very desirable in multiprocessor systems.

The earliest MINs for computer system applications were proposed in the early 1970s. These MINs include the data manipulator and the banyan networks. The research connected to MINs, however, goes back to the 1950s long before their application to computer systems. This work was in connection with switching exchanges for telephone systems. A milestone in the earlier research on MINs is the work by Benes (1962) who proposed the well-known rearrangeable network often referred to as the Benes network.

In the last decade, there has been intense research activity in interconnection networks because of their importance in high performance multiprocessor computer systems. Some examples of multiprocessor systems using MINs include the Butterfly parallel processor, the NYU ultracomputer, the IBM research prototype RP3, and STARAN by Goodyear Aerospace Corporation.

This paper provides a survey of MINs emphasizing the underlying topological design principles. We have relied heavily on the existing literature on MINs; however, the literature is so vast that it is not possible to discuss it here in its entirety. The arrangement of the paper is as follows: An overview section is included in the beginning to provide a bird's-eye view of the field and establish the basic terminology. The next three sections deal with important classes of MINs, and Sections 6 and 7 deal with performance analysis and VLSI implementation of MINs, respectively. The paper ends with a brief section for the conclusion.

2. Overview

This section provides the basic terminology and the general framework that is to be used throughout the paper. The important design parameters for multistage interconnection networks are also discussed and a classification of MINs is given.

2.1 Basic Terminology

A multistage interconnection network consists of a sequence of switching stages, each of which consists of several switches. The switching stages are connected with interstage links between successive stages. The most common switch used in a MIN is a crossbar switch. A crossbar switch of size $p \times q$, has p inputs and q outputs. A crossbar switch in which the number of inputs is the same as the number of outputs is called a *square* switch. A crossbar switch can connect its inputs to its outputs in a one-to-one manner in any order. The inputs or outputs of a crossbar that are not yet connected are called either idle or free. In a crossbar, any free input can be connected to any free output. A schematic of a 4×4 crossbar switch is shown in Fig. 1. The hardware cost of a $p \times q$ crossbar switch is measured as pq, which is the number of switching gates inside the switch.

A MIN with M inputs and N outputs is called a network of size $M \times N$. The stages in a network are numbered starting from one. The first and the last stages are called input and output stages, respectively. The switches in each stage are labeled in sequence starting from zero. The terms *spread* and *fanout* are also used in relation to a network or a switch to refer to the number of

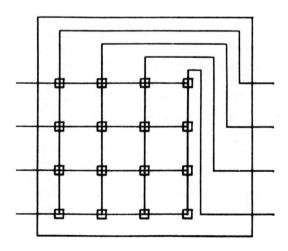

Fig. 1. 4×4 crossbar switch.

inputs and the number of outputs, respectively. A MIN is normally assumed to have the following characteristics:

- All the switches in given stage are of identical size.
- The outputs of every switch in one stage are connected one-to-one, to the inputs of switches in the next stage.
- The inputs of the network are connected to the inputs of switches in the first stage.
- The outputs of the network are connected to the outputs of switches in the last stage.
- *Full access:* every input of the network can be connected to every output of the network through the switching stages.

The interconnection pattern between two successive stages is specified by the function Λ. The function Λ is specified using the format Λ (*stage, switch, output*) where the first parameter indicates the stage number, the second parameter indicates the switch label, and the third parameter indicates the output label of the switch. The function Λ applied to (i, t, j) specifies the switch in stage $(i + 1)$ that is connected to the jth output of switch t, in stage i.

A MIN connects its inputs to outputs by an appropriate setting of the switches. A *state* of a switch corresponds to the interconnection of its inputs to outputs in a specific order. Thus, a $p \times p$ crossbar switch has a factorial of p different states. In a MIN the switches may also be equipped with broadcast states. The four states—straight, exchange, lower broadcast, and upper broadcast—for a 2×2 switch are shown in Fig. 2. Hardware implementations of switches are discussed in (Gecsei, 1977; Premkumar *et al.*, 1980; Jansen and Kessels, 1980; Patel, 1981).

A *state* of a MIN is defined as a vector representing the states of its switches. A *connection* of a MIN is defined as a one-to-one mapping of its inputs to

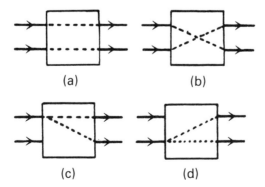

FIG. 2. Four states of a 2×2 switch. (a) straight (b) exchange (c) upper broadcast (d) lower broadcast.

outputs, and a *partial connection* refers to a connection of a subset of inputs. A state of a MIN is called a *valid* state if it corresponds to a connection of the MIN; otherwise, the state is called an *invalid state*. If the MIN uses square switches in each stage, then it has no invalid states. There may be invalid states when nonsquare switches are used. Section 6 gives an example of a MIN that has invalid states.

A connection of an $N \times N$ MIN can be represented by a permutation of N elements. A permutation is said to be *passable* (or *realizable*) by a MIN if there is a connection of the MIN that is represented by that permutation.

2.2   Design Parameters of MINs

The design of a MIN can be thought of as a multilayer process. The network topology, functional characteristics of a switch, and the control strategy can be viewed as three different layers of MIN design. The topology layer deals with the number of stages, the number of switches in a stage, the size of a switch, and how switches in successive stages are connected. Networks with a given topology can have different characteristics based on the functions provided at the switch level. Moreover, networks with the same topology and identical switches may have different characteristics on account of their control strategies. The three layers of MIN design are not independent but strongly influence each other. Other considerations that affect the MIN design include VLSI implementation, partitionability, reconfigurability, and data alignment requirements. The following parameters are fundamental in design of MINs.

2.2.1   Network Topology

Intuitively, the topology is the layout of the network. The network topology is determined by the number of stages, the number and size of switches in each stage, and the interconnection pattern connecting the switches in successive stages. The topology of a MIN can be depicted by a graph where nodes represent switches and edges represent interconnection links. In general, the topology of a MIN may be formally defined as the pair (S, Λ) where $S = (S_1, S_2, \ldots, S_n)$, n is the number of stages, $S_i = p_i \times q_i$ gives the size of a switch at stage i, and Λ is the interconnection function for interstage links as described earlier. Network topologies are further classified as *static* or *dynamic*. In a static topology, each switch is connected to a resource such as a processor. In the dynamic case, only the switches in the input-output stages of the network are connected to other resources.

Topological Equivalence.   Let (S^1, Λ_1) and (S^2, Λ_2) be the topologies of interconnection networks $N1$ and $N2$, respectively. The MIN $N1$ is topologically equivalent to MIN $N2$ if $S^1 = S^2$ and there exists a one-to-one mapping

Φ that maps a switch t at stage i of $N1$ to the switch $\Phi(i, t)$ at stage i of $N2$, such that the following *equivalence condition* holds:

$$\Phi(i + 1, \Lambda_1(i, t, j)) = \Lambda_2(i, \Phi(i, t), j')$$

for some output j' of the switch $\Phi(i, t)$. The function Φ is called an *equivalence function*. The equivalence condition implies that up to a repositioning of switches and renumbering of their outputs the two networks are identical. The topological equivalence has the following important implications:

1. With similar control structure, equivalent networks can simulate each other and the routing information for one network can be directly used by its equivalent network.

2. Under the same routing algorithm, equivalent networks have identical performance and fault tolerance characteristics.

3. The sets of permutation passable by equivalent networks are co-sets of each other, i.e., if P_1 and P_2 are respectively sets of permutations passable by two equivalent networks, then there exist permutations π and τ such that $P_1 = \pi \circ P_2 \circ \tau$. The physical implication of the preceding condition is that, with appropriate hardwire link permutations at input and output stages, or by an appropriate logical renaming of inputs and outputs, a MIN can pass exactly the same set of permutations as another equivalent network. The process of logical renaming is called *reconfiguration*. The reconfiguration technique increases the combinatorial capability of a MIN without changing the hardware organization.

A MIN is called a *unique path property (UPP) network*[1] if there is exactly one path in the network from every input to every output. Several known UPP networks have been shown to be topologically equivalent (Wu and Feng, 1980a). The discussion of topological equivalence of specific MINs follows in Section 3.

The topology of a MIN is a key parameter that affects its performance, fault tolerance, reliability, partitionability, and VLSI implementation. The performance of a MIN is commonly measured by its *bandwidth* (BW) and *combinatorial power* (CP), which are discussed in Section 6. The reliability of a network is quantified by measures such as *terminal reliability* (TR). The *fault tolerance* is usually measured in terms of the number and types of faults that can be tolerated by a network. The reliability and fault tolerance are discussed in Section 5. The *partitionability* of a MIN is the ability to partition the network into independent subnetworks of different sizes. Each subnetwork in the partition has to have all the interconnection capabilities of a complete

---

[1] The term *banyan network* is also used in the literature.

network of that same type, built to be of smaller size as the subnetwork. The partitionability is closely related to the concept of *block structure* of a MIN which is discussed in Section 3.

2.2.2 Input-Output Arrangement

The inputs and outputs for dynamic topologies of interconnection networks can be arranged in three different ways: two-sided, one-sided and folded. The two-sided topologies have separate input and output links. They are further subdivided into *connectors* and *concentrators* (Pinsker, 1973; Mason, 1977). Connectors have an equal number of input and output links whereas concentrators have more input links than output links.

The one-sided topologies have no distinction between input and output links, i.e., a processor uses the same link for input and output. The one-sided topologies include the *full switch* and the *partitioner*. A full switch is an interconnection network that is capable of performing an arbitrary partitioning of terminals into disjoint subsets, each of size two, so that the terminals in each subset are interconnected. A partitioner is a generalized full switch where the sizes of the disjoint subsets can be arbitrary.

The folded topologies recirculate links from the output side to the input side, and each processor node has at least one input link and one output link. Examples of folded networks include the single-stage shuffle-exchange network (Stone, 1971).

2.2.3 Control Strategies

Control strategies deal with routing of data from input to output through a MIN. The objective of a control strategy is to route with minimal delay. The control function may be managed by a central computer or it may be distributed. The distributed control structure can be of different types, such as (a) *stage control:* one control line per stage, (b) *switch control:* one control line per switch, or (c) *partial stage control:* a type of control that is a combination of the stage and switch type controls. The most desired routing scheme involving switch control is the *destination tag algorithm* (DTA) first proposed by Lawrie (1975). The DTA requires a proper labeling of outputs (destinations), and routing is based on output labels called the *destination tags*. The DTA can be implemented on a class of networks called *delta networks*. The delta networks provide a simple form of control called the *digit control* where each switch is controlled by a digit. The delta networks are discussed in Section 3. The basic idea behind DTA is that a switch at stage i is controlled by the ith digit of a destination tag. The detailed description of DTA is also given later using the omega network as an example. Depending on the routing algorithm, the set-up delay for the control varies significantly and may be of a higher order of magnitude than the number of stages. But in the case of the DTA, the delay is of the same order as the number of stages, namely $O(\log N)$ for an $N \times N$ MIN. On the other hand, the delay of the looping algorithm for the Benes network is $O(N \log N)$, whereas the number of stages is only $O(\log N)$.

The actual routing can be implemented by using two quite different methods: *circuit switching* and *packet switching*. In circuit switching, a physical path is actually established between an input (source) and an output (destination), and the path is held till data is transmitted from the source to the destination. In packet switching, data is put in a packet and routed through the network without establishing a physical connection path. In general, circuit switching is more suitable for bulk data transmission, and packet switching is more efficient for short data messages. A third method called *integrated switching* combines both circuit switching and packet switching. The routing process can be pipelined with each stage of a MIN corresponding to a stage in the pipeline.

The other issues that have to be dealt with by control strategies are the resolution of *conflicts* and rerouting in case of faults in a network. A *conflict* is said to occur when two or more desired input-output connections require a common link in routing through the network. A conflict can be viewed as a situation where two or more inputs require a connection to the same output of a switch. Thus, in case of a conflict, the output is not available for at least one connection. In case of a fault, an output of a switch cannot be used because either the link connected to the output or the switch at the next stage is faulty. The basic control problems in a conflict or a fault can thus be viewed as similar, and after the detection phase, conflicts and faults can be treated similarly by the control strategy.

2.2.4 Functional Characteristics of a Switch

The functional characteristics of a switch include the size, the number of possible states for the switch, routing logic, fault detection capability, communication protocols, and data storage buffers. A typical switch in a MIN has to provide a combination of some or all of the above functions. In a MIN with distributed control, the switches are required to provide more functions and accordingly they are more complex compared to switches in a MIN with centralized control.

In terms of the number of states, the crossbar represents a typical switch used in a MIN. The routing logic in a switch provides the capability to calculate the correct state for the switch based on the routing information. For multipath MINs, the routing logic also deals with resolution of conflicts and alternate routing in case of faults. The commonly used routing information consists of appropriate digits of the destination tag. In a distributed form of control, the switches also may be equipped with capability to detect faults at the next stage. Switches also need protocol hardware for handshaking to ensure the correct transfer of data and may include buffers to store the blocked requests for later routing. One additional effect of such buffers is to improve the performance of the network.

2.2.5   VLSI Design

With VLSI design techniques, it is feasible to implement a MIN using a small number of VLSI chips. Due to the current limitations of VLSI technology, the entire network cannot usually reside on a single chip. The problem then is to partition the desired MIN into a number of modules, each of which can be implemented on a single chip. In this respect, block structure of a MIN is a desired feature for VLSI implementation. The objectives in a VLSI implementation are to minimize the number of modular types and optimize the area required, and also the delay. Section 7 discusses these issues in more detail.

2.3   Classification of MINs

An interconnection network which at a time, connects an input to at most one output is called a *permutation network*. Permutation networks can be divided into the following four classes, based on their functionality:

1. *Nonblocking.* Any free input can be connected to any free output without affecting the existing connections.
2. *Rearrangeable.* Any free input can be connected to any free output; however, the existing connections may require rearrangement of paths.
3. *Blocking (UPP).* There is a unique path between every input-output pair. In this case, a connection between a free input-output pair is not always possible because of conflicts with the existing connections.
4. *Multipath.* Extension of blocking networks with multiple paths to reduce conflicts and provide fault tolerance.

Nonblocking networks are studied in Clos (1953) and Cantor (1971). The Clos network is a well-known example of a nonblocking network. Rearrangeable networks were studied by Benes (1962), and a well-known example is the Benes network. The nonblocking and the rearrangeable class of networks provide *full combinatorial capability* (FCC); i.e., they can realize any arbitrary permutation. Another class of interconnection networks with FCC is the so called cellular interconnection array. These three classes of networks are grouped together as FCC networks and discussed in Section 4. The realization of FCC is a positive aspect of these networks; however, the control algorithms for FCC networks require considerable set-up time, which degrades the overall rate of data transfer through the network.

TABLE I

FREQUENTLY USED PERMUTATIONS IN PARALLEL PROCESSING

Permutation	Definition	Applications
Perfect shuffle	$\sigma^{(n)}: (x_{n-1}x_{n-2}\cdots x_1 x_0) \rightarrow (x_{n-2}x_{n-3}\cdots x_0 x_{n-1})$	Fast Fourier Transform, parallel sorting
Segment shuffle	$\gamma_{j,i,l,m,h}: (\hat{x}_5, \hat{x}_4, \hat{x}_3, \hat{x}_2, \hat{x}_1) \rightarrow (\hat{x}_5, \hat{x}_4, \hat{x}_3, \hat{x}_2, \hat{x}_1)$ where $\hat{x}_5, \hat{x}_4, \hat{x}_3, \hat{x}_2, \hat{x}_1$ are substrings of $x = x_{n-1}x_{n-2}\cdots x_0$ with lengths $j, l, m, h, n - (j + l + m + h)$ respectively.	
Unshuffle	$U^{(n)}: (x_{n-1}x_{n-2}\cdots x_1 x_0) \rightarrow (x_0 x_{n-1}\cdots x_2 x_1)$	
Flip permutations	$\tau_s^{(n)}: x \rightarrow x \oplus a, 0 < a < N$	partial differential equations on multimesh region image warping
Cyclic shifts	$\pi_\delta^{(n)}: x \rightarrow (x + b) \bmod N, 0 < b < N,$	
Cyclic shifts within segments	$\delta_{j,e}^{(n)}: (\hat{x}_2, \hat{x}_1) \rightarrow (\hat{x}_2, \pi_e^{n-j}(\hat{x}_1))$ where,	"divide and conquer" techniques
Permutive shifts	$\lambda_{a,b}^{(n)}: x \rightarrow (ax + b) \bmod N, 0 < a, b < N, a\ odd$ $\hat{x}_2 = (x_{n-1}x_{n-2}\cdots x_{n-j})$ and $\hat{x}_1 = (x_{n-j-1}x_{n-j-2}\cdots x_0)$	parallel load and store operations on matrices
Bit-switches	$\xi_{j,k}^{(n)}: (x_{n-1}\cdots x_j\cdots x_k\cdots x_0) \rightarrow$ $(x_{n-1}\cdots x_k\cdots x_j\cdots x_0)$	
Bit reversal	$\rho^{(n)}: (x_{n-1}x_{n-2}\cdots x_0) \rightarrow (x_0 x_1\cdots x_{n-1})$	Fast Fourier Transform
Bit reversals within segments	$\alpha_{j,k}^{(n)}: (\hat{x}_2, \hat{x}_1) \rightarrow (\hat{x}_2, \rho^{n-j}(\hat{x}_1))$ where $\hat{x}_2 = (x_{n-1}x_{n-2}\cdots x_{n-k})$ and $\hat{x}_1 = (x_{n-k-1}x_{n-k-2}\cdots x_0)$	
Exchange	$\eta_j^{(n)}: (x_{n-1}\cdots x_j\cdots x_0) \rightarrow$ $(x_{n-1}\cdots x_j\cdots x_0 \oplus x_j), 0 \le j \le n - 1$	

Since the speed of data transfer through the interconnection network is of prime importance, the nonblocking and rearrangeable networks have been in disfavor for use in multiprocessor systems. Research has proceeded in two directions to alleviate the problem of inefficient control algorithm. In one approach, researchers have investigated the possibility of a simpler control algorithm for classes of permutations frequently used in parallel processing applications (Nassimi and Sahni, 1982). These permutations are listed in Table I. The other approach has been to design networks with simple and efficient control algorithms at the cost of reduced combinatorial power. The second approach has the advantage that the networks can be designed using roughly half the hardware with half the number of stages compared to the networks with full combinatorial power. The second approach has led to the design of the so called blocking networks that are characterized by the unique path property, namely the existence of a unique path between every input-output pair. The well-known examples of blocking networks with UPP are sw-banyan (Goke and Lipovski, 1973), omega (Lawrie, 1975), flip (Batcher, 1976), indirect binary cube (Pease, 1977), generalized cube (Siegel, 1979), and baseline (Wu and Feng, 1980a).

The UPP leads to blocking and impairs the full access capability of the network even when there is a single link or a switch fault. The shortcomings of UPP have led to the design of multipath MINs. Multipath MINs provide multiple paths between input-output pairs. The digit control structure of delta networks is essentially retained in multipath MINs by innovative extensions of the delta network topology. The use of multiple paths for alternate routing can considerably enhance the performance and the fault tolerance of a multipath MIN over a UPP network. The multipath MINs have become a very attractive class of networks because of their simple control strategies combined with enhanced performance and fault tolerance. The IADM (Mcmillen and Siegel, 1982), gamma network (Parker and Raghavendra, 1982), and kappa network (Kothari et al., 1985b), are some of the examples of multipath MINs.

3. Unique Path Property Networks

In this section the general properties of unique path property networks are discussed followed by comparative study of specific MINs. A multistage interconnection network is a UPP network if there is one and only one path between any input-output pair.

First, we discuss a characterization of UPP networks. Consider a network of size $M \times N$; i.e., with M inputs and N outputs. Let n be the number of stages in the network and $p_i \times q_i$ be the size of the switches at stage i. The inputs and outputs are numbered in sequence starting with zero and the stages are numbered starting with one at input stage.

A path from input to outputs forks into q_i distinct paths at a switch in stage i for $1 \leq i \leq n$. Thus, the total number of paths through the network, from any input to outputs is $q_1 q_2 \cdots q_n$. Since there is exactly one path from any input to an output, the total number of paths from any single input to outputs is the same as the number of outputs, which is N. Thus, if the network has UPP then necessarily $N = q_1 q_2 \cdots q_n$. This discussion can be summed up by the following characterization of UPP.

Theorem 3.1. *A MIN of size $M \times N$ with n stages and $p_i \times q_i$ switches at stage i for $1 \leq i \leq n$, has UPP if and only if $N = q_1 q_2 \cdots q_n$, and the MIN has full access capability (i.e., existence of a path from every input to every output).* ∎

3.1 Block Structure

Intuitively, the term *block structure* refers to formation of blocks in a MIN such that the interconnection links are localized to switches in a block. The concept of a block for UPP networks was introduced by Wu and Feng (1980a) to describe the baseline network with 2×2 switches. The block structure of a MIN is a fundamental concept that provides insights into its properties, such as partitionability, control, and fault tolerance. Block structure is also important for the VLSI layout of the network because it provides a basis for modular design. The relationship of block structure to other properties of MINs is discussed later. A formal description of block structure for UPP networks is given here.

Definition. A *block* at level i of an n stage UPP network is a UPP subnetwork with $n - i + 1$ stages consisting of switches from each stage j, for $i \leq j \leq n$. We will use the terminology "B(i) block" to refer to a block at level i. ∎

Definition. A B(j) block is said to be a *sub-block* of a B(i) block if $i < j$ and the B(j) block is a subnetwork of the B(i) block. ∎

Definition. An $M \times N$ UPP network with n stages and $p_i \times q_j$ switches at stage i, is said to be *block-structured* if each B(i) block has q_i distinct B(i + 1) sub-blocks for $1 \leq i \leq n - 1$. ∎

Note that the B(1) block is the entire network. The blocks of an 8×8 baseline network are shown in Fig. 3. The block structure in a UPP network is not necessarily explicit in its layout. For the baseline network shown in Fig. 3, the block structure is explicit; later Fig. 4 shows an 8×8 omega network for which the block structure is not explicit. The block structure of a network can be conveniently represented by a block tree diagram (BTD).

Definition. A *block tree diagram* (BTD) of an n stage block-structured UPP network is a tree of depth n such that (a) for $1 \leq i \leq n$, nodes at level i are identified with B(i) blocks of the network and (b) for $1 \leq i < n$, there exists an edge from a B(i) node X to a B(i + 1) node Y if and only if Y is a sub-block of X. ∎

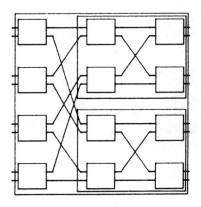

FIG. 3.   Block structure of 8 × 8 baseline network.[a]

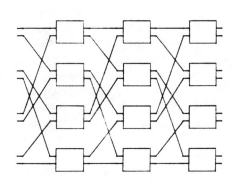

FIG. 4.   8 × 8 omega network.

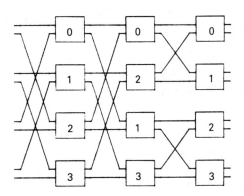

FIG. 5.   Reconfiguration of 8 × 8 omega network.[b]

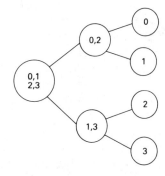

FIG. 6.   Block tree diagram for 8 × 8 omega network.

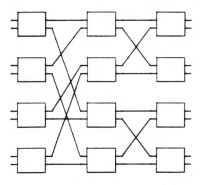

FIG. 7.   An example of unidirectional block structure.[c]

[a] The outer boxes show the blocks.
[b] The numbers identify switches in omega network and its reconfiguration.
[c] There is no block structure from right to left.

Note that the switches in the first stage of a B(i) block are actually from stage i of the original network. At times the switches in the first stage of B(i) are listed in the corresponding node of the BTD to illustrate the block structure of a MIN. The block structure of an 8×8 omega network and its BTD are illustrated Fig. 5 and Fig. 6. For a block-structured UPP network, each switch in a B(i) block must be connected through its q_i outputs to all of its B(i + 1) sub-blocks. This property of interconnection links is referred to as the *distributive property of interconnection links for UPP networks*. The distributive property ensures existence of a unique path in a block-structured network.

Remark. Block structure is a directional property of a MIN as is clear from the use of stage numbers in the definition of block structure. An example of a MIN with unidirectional block structure is shown in Fig. 7; the MIN has a block structure going from left to right but there is no block structure in the reverse direction. Many of the standard UPP networks, such as omega, baseline and other networks listed in Table III have block structure in both directions.

3.2   Case Study: The Omega Network

This section presents the omega network as a typical example of a network with digit control. Currently the omega network is used as an interconnection network in several multiprocessor systems. The destination tag algorithm, data alignment requirement, and routing conflicts for the omega network are discussed in this section.

The omega network and a primary *memory system* for an array processor were proposed by Lawrie (1975) for parallel processing of matrix operations. The primary memory system stores an array to provide *parallel access* to rows, columns, diagonals, etc. The omega network connects processors to memory modules providing necessary *data alignment* functions for array processing algorithms. The primary memory system utilizes a *generalized skewing scheme* for storing an array. The scheme requires $2N$ memory modules to store a two-dimensional array A of size $N \times N$. An element a_{jk} of the array is stored in memory module $k\delta_1 + j\delta_2 \bmod(2N)$. A generalized skewing scheme satisfies parallel access requirements if $\delta_1 = 2$ and δ_2 is odd. The generalized skewing scheme is illustrated in Table II, for $N = 4$, $\delta_1 = 2$, and $\delta_2 = 3$.

3.2.1   *Data Alignment Requirements*

Data alignment involves making one-to-one connections in proper order between processors and memory modules to ensure proper access of data. An alignment requirement can be represented by a permutation that defines the

TABLE II

PRIMARY MEMORY SYSTEM FOR PARALLEL ACCESS OF ARRAY

Memory modules							
0	1	2	3	4	5	6	7
a_{00}		a_{01}		a_{02}		a_{03}	
	a_{13}		a_{10}		a_{11}		a_{12}
a_{21}		a_{22}		a_{23}		a_{20}	
	a_{30}		a_{31}		a_{32}		a_{33}

mapping between the processors and the memory modules. The alignment requirements depend on the memory system and a particular algorithm. A MIN has to provide suitable permutation functions for subsequent alignment of data for processing.

Let us consider the standard matrix multiplication algorithm to illustrate the need for data alignment. Assume that an array is stored using a specific generalized skewing scheme discussed earlier. From the example shown in Table II, it is clear that the rows and the columns are not stored in the same order. In order to multiply ith elements of a row and of a column, the elements of the row and the column have to be aligned. A number of data alignment requirements for array processing are identified by Lawrie (1975) and they are shown to be satisfied by the omega network.

3.2.2 Omega Network

An omega network of size $N \times N$ ($N = 2^n$) consists of n stages. Each stage consists of an interstage connection using perfect shuffle followed by $N/2$ switches of size 2×2, as shown in Fig. 4. Several options in the actual design of an omega network using different switches are discussed in Lawrie (1975).

3.2.3 Control for the Omega Network

The omega network is an example of a delta network with digit control. A destination tag algorithm is illustrated in Fig. 8 for an 8×8 omega network. The DTA can be used with any delta network. With DTA, the delay involved in control is of the order $O(\log N)$ which is the same as the delay introduced by the number of stages. Thus, the DTA does not require any delay of higher order for the control than the actual delay to pass data through the MIN.

First, consider connecting input (source) S to output (destination) D. Let $S = s_1 s_2 \cdots s_n$ and $D = d_1 d_2 \cdots d_n$ be binary tags for input and output, respectively. Starting at input, the first switch in stage 1 to which S is connected is set to connect to the upper output if $d_1 = 0$ or the lower output if $d_1 = 1$. An example of a connection using DTA is shown in Fig. 8 for $S = 010$ and $D = 110$. The process is carried through the successive stages, setting the switch at stage i to connect to the upper output if $d_i = 0$ or the lower output if $d_i = 1$. The proper connection is thus made using the ith digit of the destination tag at the stage i.

3.2.4 Routing Conflicts in the Omega Networks

In order to set up a particular one-to-one mapping of inputs to outputs, the DTA is followed simultaneously for all input-output pairs. For simultaneous connection of inputs to outputs, there may be *routing conflicts*. In absence of conflicts, the UPP implies a unique setting of the state of the network for each passable permutation of inputs to outputs.

Because there is one and only one path between any input-output pair, a routing conflict arises whenever there is a pair of input-output connections that causes a conflict. Thus, it is important to analyze the conflicts caused by a pair of input-output connections. The characterization of such conflicts follows.

Let $S^i = s_1^i s_2^i \cdots s_n^i$, $S^j = s_1^j s_2^j \cdots s_n^j$, be input tags and $D^i = d_1^i d_2^i \cdots d_n^i$, $D^j = d_1^j d_2^j \cdots d_n^j$, be output tags in binary. A pair of connections (S^i, D^i) and (S^j, D^j) will involve conflict if and only if they share a common interconnection link. Suppose the output links at each switching stage are numbered starting from zero. For links in the path connecting S^i to D^i, the output

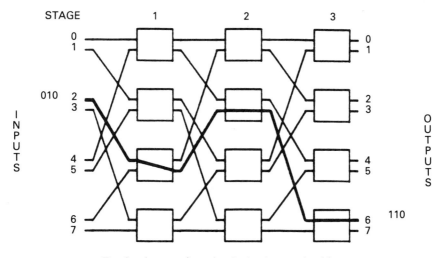

FIG. 8.   A connection using destination tag algorithm.

link number at stage k is given by $s_{k+1}^i s_{k+2}^i \cdots s_n^i d_1^i d_2^i \cdots d_k^i$. Thus, there is a conflict if and only if $d_1^i d_2^i \cdots d_k^i = d_1^j d_2^j \cdots d_k^j$ and $s_{k+1}^i s_{k+2}^i \cdots s_n^i = s_{k+1}^j s_{k+2}^j \cdots s_n^j$ for some k.

3.3   Comparative Study of UPP MINs

In this section, specific UPP MINs are discussed and compared. The MINs that are presented here are omega, flip, indirect binary cube, generalized cube, and baseline. The discussion in this section is largely based on Siegel (1979) and Wu and Feng (1980a). The networks are assumed to be of size $N \times N$ ($N = 2^n$) and constructed with 2×2 switches. All the UPP networks considered here have $\log_2 N$ stages. The number of switches in each stage is $N/2$ and the number of links between two successive stages is N. Thus, the hardware complexity, excluding the control hardware, is the same for each of these MINs. The most important common aspect of these networks is that they are topologically equivalent (Wu and Feng, 1980). Topologically these networks belong to a class of networks called *delta* networks.

3.3.1   Delta Networks

The design of a delta network is proposed by Patel (1981) using a demultiplexer tree for each input to connect it to any one of the outputs. Among the UPP networks, delta networks are characterized by the property that the path from any input to an output is *digit controlled;* i.e., a crossbar switch of size $p \times q$ in a delta network connects an input to one of its q outputs depending on a single base-q digit of the destination tag. In most common examples of delta networks switches are of size 2×2, a destination address is expressed as a binary tag and each digit of a tag is used to control a switch. The omega network is an example of a delta network and a routing algorithm based on digit control was illustrated earlier.

Delta Networks and Block Structure: Topological design and the digit control of delta networks can be easily explained in terms of the block structure of the network. The exact relationship between delta networks and the block structure is characterized by the following two theorems (Kruskal and Snir, 1982):

Theorem 3.2.   *If a UPP network is digit controlled from inputs to outputs then it has block structure from inputs to outputs.*   ■

Theorem 3.3.   *A UPP network with n stages is digit controlled from inputs to outputs if (a) it has block structure from inputs to outputs and (b) corresponding output ports of all switches in a B(i) block are connected to the same B(i + 1) sub-block.*   ■

An important implication of these results is that in order to realize digit control, a MIN must have block structure. Recently, several designs of fault-tolerant multipath MINs with digit control have been proposed. The concept of block structure plays an important role in the design and control of these MINs, as discussed later in Section 5. In view of condition (b) of Theorem 3.3, the digit control at a switch in stage i corresponds to selecting a specific $B(i + 1)$ sub-block from a $B(i)$ block. The digit controlled routing can be easily explained by a block tree diagram. The leaves of a BTD corresponds to switches connected to destinations. The digit controlled routing is to select the correct path through BTD where each edge is labeled by a single digit such that the address tag for a leaf is the concatenation of edge labels along the path.

A summary of well-known UPP networks is given in Table III and the topologies are shown in Fig. 9. The function Λ (stage, switch, output) introduced in Section 2 is used to describe the topology. The permutation Π_i and Π_0 denotes the link permutations at input and output stages, respectively. For switches with two states (cross and straight) the switch type is given as *2-function;* for switches with four states (cross, straight, lower broadcast, and upper broadcast) the switch type is given as *4-function.* The control structure is identified as switch control, stage control, or partial stage control. The flip network used in the multiprocessor system STARAN developed at Goodyear Aerospace Corporation (Batcher, 1976) is a noted example that provides two different control structures: *Flip control* is a stage control that specifies flip permutations, and *shift control* is a partial stage control, with i control lines for stage i, that specifies shift permutations. The actual details of the control structures for the flip network and how it specifies the permutations are given by Batcher (1976).

3.3.2 Topological Equivalence and Reconfiguration

The MINs listed in Table III are shown to be topologically equivalent and the equivalence functions to map them to the baseline network are given in Wu and Feng (1980). As an example, the equivalence function Φ to map omega network to the baseline is as follows:

$$\Phi(i, t) = t_{i-1}t_{i-2} \cdots t_1 t_i t_{i+1} \cdots t_l$$

where $l = n - 1$ and $t = t_l \cdots t_2 t_1$ is a binary label of a switch in the omega network. The omega network with the new configuration is shown in Fig. 6, where the labels on switches indicate their original positions in the omega network. A MIN can be reconfigured to perform permutations passable by an equivalent MIN. Thus, the flexibility in choice of a MIN is greatly increased if reconfiguration techniques are used. In fact, it has been shown that arbitrary permutation is realizable using reconfiguration in one pass of a baseline network (Wu and Feng, 1980b).

TABLE III

DESCRIPTION OF UPP MINS OF SIZE $N \times N$ $(N = 2^n)$*

Network	Topology $\Lambda(i, t, \delta) =$	Link permutations at end stages	Switch type	Control structure
Omega	$t_{m-1}t_{m-2}\cdots t_1\delta$	$\Pi_i(j) = j_{n-1}j_{n-2}\cdots j_1 j_n$ identity for output	4-function	Individual switch control
Flip	$\delta t_m t_{m-1}\cdots t_2$	$\Pi_o(j) = j_1 j_n \cdots j_2$ identity for input	2-function	Two control mechanisms: flip and shift
Indirect binary n-cube	$t_m t_{m-1}\cdots t_{i+1}\delta t_{i-1}t_{i-2}\cdots t_1$	$\Pi_o(j) = j_1 j_n \cdots j_2$ identity for input	2-function	Individual switch control
Generalized cube	$t_m t_{m-1}\cdots t_{m-i+2}\delta t_{m-i}\cdots t_1$	$\Pi_i(j) = j_1 j_n \cdots j_2$ identity for output	Optional	Optional
Baseline	$t_m t_{m-1}\cdots t_{m-i+2}\delta t_{m-i+1}t_{m-i}\cdots t_2$	Identity for both the end stages	Optional	Optional

* $m = n - 1$, $\delta = 0$ or 1, switch label: $t = t_m t_{m-1}\cdots t_1$ (in binary), $j = j_n j_{n-1}\cdots j_1$

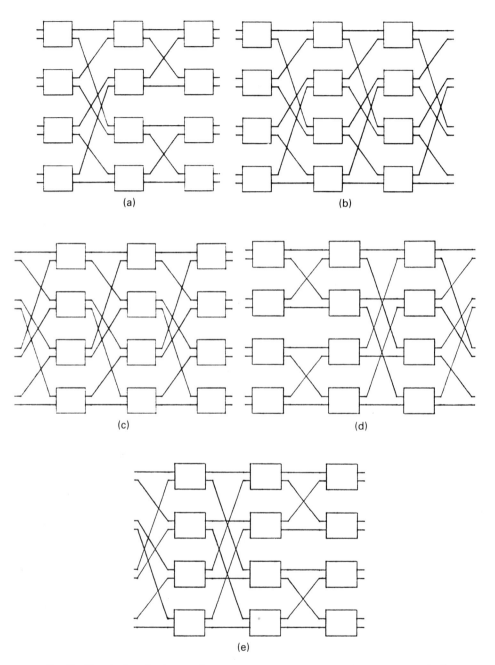

FIG. 9.   Topologies of unique path property (UPP) MINs.   (a) baseline network   (b) flip
network   (c) omega network   (d) indirect binary cube   (e) generalized cube.

3.3.3 Universality

An UPP network cannot provide the full set of permutations from inputs to outputs. The term *universality* relates to the capability of a MIN to realize an arbitrary permutation by using multiple passes through the network or multiple copies of the network. The multiple copies of the network may be connected in series or parallel. The multiple passes, of course, entail a sacrifice in speed but provide capability to realize more permutations.

The determination of the minimum number of passes through a network to realize an arbitrary permutation is difficult (Parker, 1980); the actual specification of the control algorithm is even more difficult. For more information on universality the reader can refer to Wu and Feng (1981). The other related aspect of the universality is the relationship between UPP networks and the rearrangeable Benes network. The following result from Kruskal and Snir (1982) establishes the relationship between delta networks and Benes network:

Theorem 3.4. *A network is a Benes network if and only if it consists of a delta network G followed by GR (the reversal of delta network) where the last stage of G is identified with the first stage of GR.* ∎

Similar results about universality of a network followed by its reversal, using MINs with 2 × 2 switches, are discussed in Agrawal (1983).

4. Full Combinatorial Capability Networks

A permutation network is said to have *full combinatorial capability* (FCC) if it realizes all input-output permutations. In this section, we discuss three important classes of interconnection networks that have FCC.

4.1 Topology of Rearrangeable Networks

A rearrangeable network of size $N \times N$ is constructed as a cascade of three stages. The first and the last stage consist of m subnetworks of size $d \times d$ and the middle stage consists of d subnetworks of size $m \times m$, where $N = dm$ is a factorization. Each of the subnetworks is itself a network with FCC, in particular each subnetwork can be a crossbar switch or a rearrangeable network. There are many options for the size of a network used in the three-stage cascade depending on the choice of d and m. The interstage link connections in a three-stage cascade are subject to the condition that for each $d \times d$ network in the first and the last stage, its d links must have one-to-one connections to the d distinct $m \times m$ networks in the middle stage. This condition is referred to as the *distributive property of interstage links for rearrangeable networks* (Kothari and Lakshmivarahan, 1983). The distributive property ensures that for each network in the first or the last stage, there is a link to connect to any network in the middle stage. There are again several options for interstage link connections, the only basic requirement is the distributive property. However, in practice, the interstage link pattern is chosen to be symmetric for better layout of the circuit.

In practice, a rearrangeable network is constructed by using $d \times d$ crossbar switches with a suitable choice of d for implementation. The value of N is chosen to be a power of d and the three-stage cascade topology is applied iteratively until the size of each subnetwork reduces to $d \times d$. An example of an 8×8 rearrangeable network with $d = 2$ is shown in Fig. 10a. There are several conceptual similarities in topology between a rearrangeable network and a UPP network with block structure. A block structure can be defined for a rearrangeable network where a block is defined as a subnetwork in the middle stage of the three-stage cascade. In both cases, the topology can be iteratively defined in terms of blocks. Also, in both cases the concept of the distributive property of interstage links is similar; namely, it corresponds to distribution of links from each switch to all the blocks. In one case, the distributive property is important for unique path property; in the other case, it is important for the full combinatorial capability. The important difference in the two topologies is that in case of UPP network each iterative step involves a cascade of two stages, whereas in rearrangeable topology each iterative step involves a cascade of three stages. If N is a power of two, in both cases, $\log_2 N - 1$ iterations are required in constructing a network using 2×2 switches. For the rearrangeable topology, two stages of 2×2 switches are created in each iterative step, but in the last step, three stages of 2×2 switches are created. Thus, for $N = 2^n$, a rearrangeable network of size $N \times N$ has $(2n - 1)$ stages with $N/2$ switches of size 2×2 in each stage. Such a rearrangeable network is also called a Benes network. The Benes network of size $N \times N$ uses $N(2 \log_2 N - 1)/2$ switches of size 2×2. From Sterling's well-known formula for the approximation of a factorial, it follows that the number of switches has to be of order $O(N \log N)$, thus the Benes network does provide the optimal order of growth for the number of switches to realize all the $N!$ permutations.

4.2   A Control Algorithm for Rearrangeable Networks

In this section, a control algorithm is described for a Benes network. The objective of a control algorithm is to determine settings for switches in order to connect the N inputs to N outputs according to a given permutation. The following algorithm, called *looping algorithm,* has the set-up time of order $O(N \log N)$. The looping algorithm as presented here is from Anderson (1977). Another important control algorithm for Benes network, called *self-routing algorithm,* has the set-up time of order $O(\log N)$. The set-up time for the looping algorithm is considerably higher and thus imposes a serious limitation

S. C. KOTHARI

(a) Benes network

(b) Clos network

INPUTS

(c) Cellular interconnection array

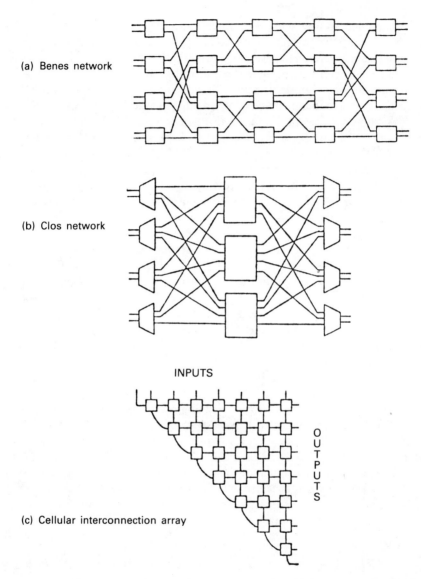

FIG. 10. Full combinatorial capability (FCC) networks. (a) benes network (b) clos network (c) cellular interconnection array.

in its use. On the other hand, although the self-routing algorithm can realize only a subset of the total number of permutations, this subset includes a rich class of permutations used in parallel processing. The name *self-routing* comes from an important feature whereby control is implemented at switches using digits of destination tags. Thus, self-routing is an analog of destination tag algorithm discussed earlier for UPP networks. For more details on the self-routing algorithm, the reader may refer to Nassimi and Sahni (1982).

4.2.1 Looping Control Algorithm

Let P be an arbitrary permutation of N elements that maps i to $P(i)$ for $0 \leq i \leq N - 1$. The looping algorithm is an iterative procedure that determines the control to realize a permutation P. It follows the iteration used to define the topology of the network. The iterative procedure, when applied to a Benes network of size $N \times N$, determines the switch settings for the first and the last stage and produces two permutations of size $N/2$, each to be realized by the networks in the middle stage of the iterative topology. The two networks will be referred to as blocks and labeled as 0 and 1, as shown in Fig. 11b. For simplicity, the iterative procedure is explained as six steps applied to determine the control of the network. During the course of following discussion, refer to Fig. 11 for an example of the looping algorithm.

Step 1. The permutation P is represented by an array of size $N \times N$ such that the (i, j)-th entry is X if and only if $P(i) = j$.

Step 2. The $N \times N$ array is viewed through a grid of size $N/2 \times N/2$ in order to construct a graph using X's as nodes (see Fig. 11a). Each row of the grid corresponds to two adjacent rows of the array and similarly for columns. The graph is constructed by connecting a pair of X's if they belong to the same row or column of the grid.

Step 3. Label the X's by 0 or 1 so that no two adjacent X's connected by an edge in the graph have the same labels. (The labels are shown as subscripts in Fig. 11a.) The label indicates the block in the middle stage of the iterative step, that is to be used in connecting the input-output pair corresponding to the particular X. In the next step, 0 and 1 will also be used to label straight and cross states of a switch respectively.

Step 4. First, note that the two X's in the ith column of the grid correspond to the two inputs of ith switch in the first stage; the first X (the X in column $2i$ of the array) corresponds to the input $2i$ and the second X corresponds to the input $2i + 1$. Set the ith switch in the first stage to the same state as the label of the first X in the ith column of the grid. This setting of switches connects an input to the block labelled

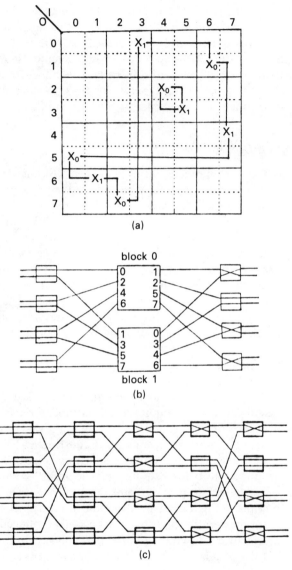

FIG. 11.   An example of looping algorithm for a Benes network.   (a) Determination of con-
trol settings for first iteration. Given permutation: $P = \begin{pmatrix} 0 & 1 & 2 & 3 & 4 & 5 & 6 & 7 \\ 5 & 6 & 7 & 0 & 2 & 3 & 1 & 4 \end{pmatrix}$ (b) Control
setting resulting from the first iteration of the looping algorithm. Permutations to be realized in
second iteration: $P_0 = \begin{pmatrix} 0 & 1 & 2 & 3 \\ 2 & 3 & 1 & 0 \end{pmatrix}$ $P_1 = \begin{pmatrix} 0 & 1 & 2 & 3 \\ 3 & 0 & 1 & 2 \end{pmatrix}$ (c) A complete setting of switches to
realize P.

d if the corresponding X has the label d. The inputs to the two blocks are numbered according to the connections just described (Figure 11b).

Step 5. This step is similar to Step 4. The switches in the last stage are set by using X's in the rows of a grid instead of columns as in Step 4. The outputs of the two blocks are now numbered according to the output connections made through the last stage.

Step 6. At this point, the switch settings for the first and the last stages are known and the purpose of this step is to determine the permutations to be performed by each of the two blocks in the middle stage. The permutation P is decomposed into two subpermutations of half the original size, to be performed by each block. These subpermutations are induced by the original permutation according to the numbering done in Steps 4 and 5, on the inputs and outputs of each middle block. The permutations P_0 and P_1 (Figure 11b) to be performed by the blocks are now determined by mapping the subpermutations to permutations on $0, 1, \ldots, N/2 - 1$.

4.2.2   Brief Description of the Iteration

In the second call of the iteration, the six steps are applied to two networks of size $N/2$ each, to determine the switch settings of the second and the last but one stage of the original network. As a result four permutations of size $N/4$ each are produced. The ith iterative call requires application of the iterative procedure to 2^{i-1} networks of size $N/2^{i-1}$ each. The ith iterative call determines the switch settings for the ith stages from the input and output side of the network. The number of iterative calls is $\log_2 N$. The last call determines the switch settings in the stage numbered $\log_2 N$.

4.3   Clos Networks and Cellular Interconnection Arrays

In this section, the Clos network (Clos, 1953), and cellular interconnection arrays (Kautz *et al.*, 1968) are discussed as examples of FCC MINs. The Clos network is a well-known example of nonblocking networks mentioned in Section 2.

4.3.1   Clos Networks

The Clos network and the rearrangeable network share the same basic idea of a 3-stage iterative topology. In fact, the idea was first used by Clos to construct nonblocking networks. The Clos network differs from the rearrangeable network in the number and the size of the switches in each stage.

The Clos network of size $N \times N$ has m switches of size $d \times r$ in the first stage, m switches of size $r \times d$ in the third stage, and m switches of size $r \times r$ in the middle stage. The number r is required to be at least $(2d - 1)$ and $N = md$ is a factorization of N. Thus, compared to the rearrangeable network, the Clos network has more switches and also nonsquare switches in the first and the last stages of the iterative topology. The links in a Clos network must also have the distributive property, as discussed earlier in the case of a rearrangeable network. The following principle is involved for determining the number of switches required in the middle stage: Suppose a connection is to be established from input i to output j. A sufficient number of intermediary switches is required to permit the $(d - 1)$ inputs other than i on the particular input switch and the $(d - 1)$ outputs other than j on the particular output switch to have connections to separate intermediary switches. One additional switch for the desired connection between i and j is also required. Thus, $2(d - 1) + 1$ intermediary switches are required. An example of a Clos network is shown in Fig. 10b.

4.3.2   Cellular Interconnection Arrays

Cellular interconnection arrays provide another class of nonblocking networks. Several different array topologies have been proposed. A triangular interconnection array of size $N \times N$ consists of $N(N - 1)/2$ switches of size 2×2. A representative 8×8 nonblocking network in the form of a triangular array is shown in Fig. 10c.

5.   Multipath MINs

Multipath MINs have been proposed as an improvement over UPP networks to provide better fault tolerance and higher bandwidth. There is a drawback with UPP networks; namely, a single failure of a switch or a link makes connections between several inputs and outputs impossible. The multipath MINs are designed to overcome this drawback by providing multiple paths between an input-output pair. A rearrangeable network also provides multiple paths, but control algorithms for them involve considerable set-up delay. The control algorithms for multipath MINs are simpler and more efficient. In most cases, the topology of a multipath MIN can be seen as an extension of the topology of a UPP network. In general, multipath MINs have better performance than the corresponding UPP MINs because alternate paths can also be used to resolve conflicts in the network.

In this section, basic topologies and fault-tolerance characteristics of multipath MINs are discussed. There are numerous multipath MINs proposed in recent years and it is not possible here to go into their details. Instead, we have chosen to discuss in detail only two examples of multipath MINs. Our selections were based on how well they serve as illustrations rather than their importance.

5.1 Topology of Multipath MINs

First we discuss various ways to extend the topology of a UPP network to provide multiple paths between an input-output pair. Consider a $M \times N$ UPP network with n stages and $p_i \times q_i$ switches at stage i for $1 \leq i \leq n$. It was noted in Section 3 that the number of paths from any single input to outputs is $q_1 q_2 \cdots q_n$ and an essential condition for UPP is $N = q_1 q_2 \cdots q_n$. If $q_1 q_2 \cdots q_n > N$, then there are multiple paths from each input to at least some of the output. Suppose q_i's are chosen such that $R = \dfrac{q_1 q_2 \cdots q_n}{N}$ is an integer. Then, on average, there are R multiple paths between an input-output pair. The number R is called the *redundancy* of the multipath network. A multipath MIN with redundancy R is called *balanced* if there are exactly R paths between each input-output pair. There are several ways to extend the topology of a UPP network to a multipath network topology. The following provides a list of different types of extensions of UPP network topology with corresponding examples of multipath networks:

1. *Add extra stage(s).* An example is the extra stage cube network that is discussed by Adams and Siegel (1982a).

2. *Increase the number of interstage links by providing bigger size switches.* An example is a dilated banyan network where each link from a UPP network is duplicated.

3. *Use multiple copies of a network.* An example is a replicated banyan network where multiple copies of a UPP network are used to connect inputs to outputs.

4. *Introduce links between switches at the same stage.* An example is the network with cross links (Kothari *et al.*, 1985c).

5.1.1 Multipath MINs with Digit Control

In Section 3, it was noted that there is a close relationship between digit control and block structure for a UPP network. We provide here an illustration to show that the block structure can also be effectively used to design a multipath MIN with digit control. The illustration starts with a well-known topology for a multipath network. Then we relate the topology to an underlying UPP network and its block structure. The relationship with block structure provides a better understanding of the topology of the multipath network. We conclude the illustration with another multipath network where the topological design is based on block structure. A comparison of two networks shows that proper use of block structure in topological design can provide a balanced network with digit control and better fault tolerance.

The starting point for the illustration is the well-known topology that is used the in the IADM network (McMillen and Siegel, 1982) and also in the gamma network (GN) (Parker and Raghavendram 1982). The topology for an $N \times N$ ($N = 2^n$) network has $n + 1$ stages. In the first and the last stage, it has 1×3 and 3×1 switches, respectively, and 3×3 switches are used in the remaining stages. The topology of the GN for $N = 8$ is shown in Fig. 12. The three outputs of a switch are denoted as U (for upper output), M (for middle output), and L (for lower output). The link mapping for the topology is defined as $\Lambda(i, upper, t) = t - 2^i \pmod{N}$, $\Lambda(i, middle, t) = t$, and $\Lambda(i, lower, t) = t + 2^i \pmod{N}$. A reconfiguration of the GN topology is shown in Fig. 13. The UPP network topology underlying the GN is shown in Fig. 14 where either the U or the L link is selectively omitted from each switch of the GN. The UPP network is called the modified baseline network (MBN). The block structure of the GN is explicitly seen in Fig. 13. By comparing the topologies in Fig. 13 and Fig. 14, it is evident that the U and L links of each switch in the GN are duplicate links to the same block at the next stage, thus providing alternative paths in the network. The middle link connects to a different block and is not duplicated. Thus, there is an asymmetry in the duplication of links at the block level. One undesirable consequence of the asymmetry is that no rerouting around a middle link is possible. Another undesirable feature of the topology is a lack of proper identification of outputs of a switch, based on their connections to blocks at the next stage. Such an identification is crucial for digit control. The topological design of the GN was not based on block structure. An alternative topology can be designed on the basis of the block structure of MBN by providing duplicate links from a switch to both the blocks at the next stage. This is indeed the case with the kappa network (KN) shown in Fig. 15. Unlike the GN, rerouting around any single link is always possible in the KN. Also, the interstage links in the KN are laid out in such a way that there is a clear identification of outputs of a switch, based on the block structure—the upper two links of a switch always connect to an upper sub-block at the next stage; similarly, the lower two links of a switch always connect to a lower sub-block. For the KN of size $N \times N$ ($N = 2^n$) with $n + 1$ stages, a destination tag has n binary digits. The ith digit of

---

(*Footnotes for Figures 13 and 14*)

[a] U, L, and M refer to upper, middle, and lower output links of a switch in GN.

[b] MBN is the UPP network underlying GN and KN.

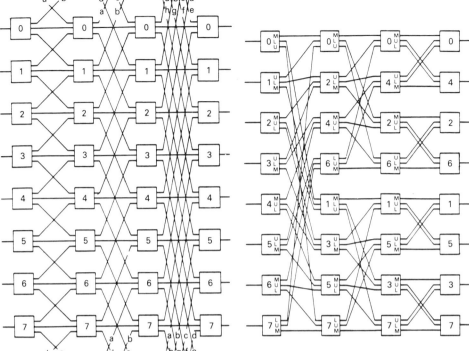

FIG. 12.   8 × 8 gamma network (GN).

FIG. 13.   Reconfiguration of 8 × 8 GN to show block structure.[a]

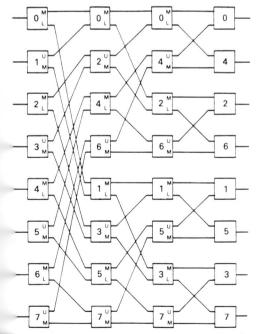

FIG. 14.   8 × 8 modified baseline network (MBN).[b]

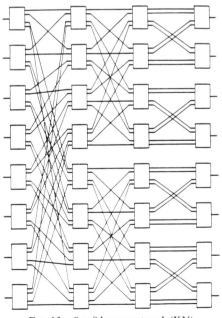

FIG. 15.   8 × 8 kappa network (KN).

the destination tag is used for the control of the switch at stage i. If a digit is zero (one) then any one of the two upper (lower) links can be used. This clearly provides digit control for routing. The KN is discussed in more detail in Kothari *et al.* (1985b).

5.2   Control Strategies and Fault Tolerance

This section provides a general discussion of control strategies and fault tolerance for multipath MINs. We present the notion of a redundancy graph that is useful to determine the fault tolerance of a MIN.

5.2.1   Control Strategies

The control strategies for routing through the network are broadly classified as static or dynamic. In static control, a fault in the network has to be located before the routing can proceed. Thus, there are two distinct phases, one to locate the fault and the other to actually set up a path. In absence of faults, a multipath network with static control operates as the underlying UPP network and does not provide any better performance than the UPP network. The extra hardware is passive until a fault occurs. The advantage of static control is that it requires only a small amount of additional hardware compared to the underlying UPP network. The extra stage cube (Adams and Siegel, 1982a), is an example of static control. Although dynamic control requires more hardware than static control, it has several advantages. In dynamic control, alternate paths are selected as and when a fault or a conflict is encountered during the setting up of a path. Thus, there is no separate fault diagnosis phase associated with routing. The extra hardware is not passive in the absence of faults, but it is used to resolve conflicts, thus providing improved performance. The dynamic control may or may not involve back-tracking. If the topology provides alternate paths at each stage, then back-tracking is not necessary. If alternate paths are provided only at a subset of stages, then in order to select an alternate path, it is necessary to backtrack up to a stage where an alternate path is available. The modified omega network (Padmanabhan and Lawrie, 1983), is an example of dynamic control with backtracking, whereas the kappa network is an example of dynamic control without backtracking.

5.2.2   Fault Detection

Most of the multipath MINs with dynamic control, assume switches that can detect the inaccessibility of any of its output ports and signal the presence of the fault back to the switches in the previous stage. Thus, such a switch can keep functioning (with reduced capability) in the presence of faults. If a switch failure is total, the switch at the earlier stage can detect the failure condition from the absence of proper handshaking.

5.2.3   Fault Tolerance

In multipath MINs, failures may occur in switches or links. If an input-output port or a multiplexer/demultiplexer directly connected to such a port is faulty, then the associated processor or the memory module has no access to the MIN. Consequently, the input and output ports and the multiplexers and demultiplexers are assumed to be fault-free. This implies that the input and output ports and the multiplexers and demultiplexers connected to them must be designed to be very robust.

Once a fault is detected in the network, the routing strategy should use an alternate path that excludes the location of the fault. Thus, the fault tolerance of a MIN is dependent on existence of such paths and a routing strategy that is capable of utilizing them. The fault tolerance of a MIN is often measured in terms of the number and types (switch or link) of faults that can be tolerated while retaining full access. The fault tolerance of a MIN is often studied using a *redundancy graph*. A redundancy graph is a flow graph of all possible paths between an input-output pair with switches as nodes and interstage links as edges. For a multipath MIN with balanced topology, the redundancy graphs for all input-output pairs are identical. The fault tolerance is easily characterized from the redundancy graph for a MIN with balanced topology. The gamma network does not have a balanced topology. For an 8 × 8 GN, the number of multiple paths varies from 1 to 5 depending on the input-output pair (Parker and Raghavendra, 1982). The kappa network has a balanced topology. For an 8 × 8 KN, $R = 8$; the redundancy graph is shown in Fig. 16.

5.3   Reliability Analysis

In this section, we present a measure of the reliability that is commonly used for multistage interconnection networks. The particular measure that is presented here is called *terminal reliability*. The purpose of terminal reliability

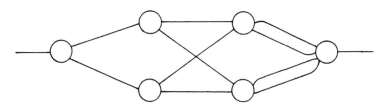

FIG. 16.   Redundancy graph of 8 × 8 kappa network (KN).

analysis is to determine the effect of switch faults on the availability of at least one path between a given input-output pair. The link faults are not considered in terminal reliability analysis. As noted earlier, the input and output ports and the demultiplexers and multiplexers directly connected to these ports are assumed to be fault-free. The terminal reliability is defined as the probability that there is at least one fault-free path between a given input-output pair.

Consider a MIN of size $N \times N$ ($N = 2^n$) with l stages. Let (S, D) be a given pair of input-output. The following notation is used in the analysis:

p: the probability a switch in the MIN is not faulty.
$R(i)$: the probability at least one fault-free path is available
from a switch S_{i-1} at stage $i - 1$ to output D
given that S_{i-1} is fault-free for $2 \le i \le l$.

As an illustration, we present the terminal reliability analysis for $N \times N$ kappa network in which case $l = n + 1$.

If a switch S_n at stage n is fault-free then there is always a fault-free path from S_n to the given output because the multiplexer connected to the output is assumed to be fault-free; thus, $R(n + 1) = 1$. Also, since the demultiplexer connected to the input is assumed to be fault-free, the terminal reliability is given by $R(2)$. Now, starting from $R(n + 1)$, we can compute $R(2)$ by using a recurrence relation between $R(i)$ and $R(i + 1)$. The recurrence relation depends on the topology of the network, and it can be easily established from the redundancy graph for the given input-output pair. In the case of the KN, there are two alternatives at each stage in setting up a path between any input-output pair—this is shown in Fig. 16 for $N = 8$. It then follows that the recurrence relation in the case of the KN is:

$$R(i) = pR(i + 1) + (1 - p)pR(i + 1) \text{ for } 2 \le i \le n$$

The values for terminal reliability for the KN are given in Table IV.

TABLE IV

TERMINAL RELIABILITY ASSUMING $p = 0.9$

Network size (N)	delta	GN	KN
16	0.656	0.859	0.970
32	0.590	0.844	0.961
64	0.531	0.830	0.951
128	0.478	0.815	0.942
256	0.430	0.801	0.932
512	0.387	0.787	0.923

6.   Performance Analysis

In this section, combinatorial power (CP), path blockage (PB), and bandwidth (BW) are discussed as three different measures of performance of a MIN.

6.1   Combinatorial Power

For a MIN of size $N \times N$, combinatorial power is defined as the ratio of the number of permutations passable in a single pass to the total number of permutations of N. A passable permutation is a simultaneous connection of N inputs to N outputs through the network.

If CP $\neq 1$, then a problem of practical interest is to determine if specific permutations are passable by a MIN. Thus, a more refined and more useful measure than CP would be a characterization of permutations passable by a MIN. The characterization must be such that it can be easily applied to check if a given permutation is passable. Although there has been some work to characterize permutations passable by a MIN (Adams and Siegel, 1982b; Varma and Raghavendra, 1985a), in general, characterization is a difficult problem. For UPP networks with nonsquare switches and for multipath networks, even the computation of CP is a difficult problem. The computation of CP for UPP networks with square switches and nonsquare switches is discussed.

6.1.1   Computation of CP for a UPP Network with Square Switches

In this case, there is a one-to-one correspondence between states of the network and permutations passable by the network. In other words, corresponding to each permutation there is a unique way to set the switches and, conversely, each state of the network corresponds to a unique permutation. Thus, the number of permutations passable by the MIN is the same as the number of different states for the network. A UPP network of size $N \times N$ ($N = 2^n$) with switches of size 2×2 has $(N \log_2 N)/2$ switches. Assuming that each switch is a crossbar and has two states, the total number of states for the MIN is $N^{N/2}$ and the CP is $N^{N/2}/N!$.

6.1.2   Computation of CP for UPP Networks with Nonsquare Switches

UPP ensures that corresponding to every permutation passable by a MIN there is a unique state of the network that realizes that permutation. However, each state of the network does not necessarily correspond to a permutation. A state of a MIN is called *valid* if it corresponds to a passable permutation; otherwise, the state is called *invalid*. The problem of computing the CP then reduces to counting the number of valid states of a MIN. The problem can be transformed to a matrix enumeration problem (Roberts and Kothari, 1982). The computation of CP is illustrated for a two-stage 8×8 expanding and contracting SW-banyan shown in Fig. 17.

The two stages are made of 2×4 and 4×2 switches labeled S_1 to S_4, and S_5 to S_8, respectively. A state of a 2×4 switch is defined by a connection of its two input ports to any two of its four output ports; thus, there are 12 distinct states for each switch. The states are similarly defined for a 4×2 switch, which also has 12 distinct states. The total number of states for the network is then given by $(12)^8$—only a fraction of these states are valid. Since there is a unique state corresponding to every passable permutation, a maximum of 8! states would be valid if all permutations were realizable, but many are not. For example, there is no way to connect all inputs "straight through" so that inputs, 0, 1, ..., 7 go to outputs 0, 1, ..., 7, respectively.

Figure 17 shows a valid state for the MIN by indicating a set of possible connections for S_1 to S_8 with dashed lines. The constraints that imply valid states for this network can be represented in terms of a 4×4 matrix. To

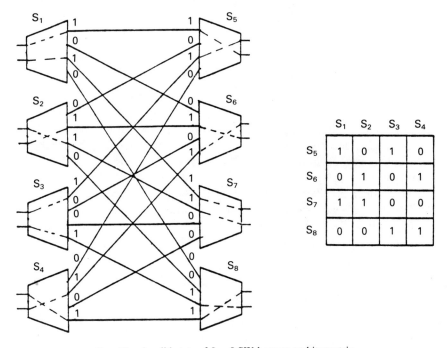

FIG. 17.   A valid state of 8×8 SW-banyan and its matrix.

demonstrate the constraints for this example, all of the output ports for switches S_1 to S_4 (refer to Fig. 17) are marked with a one (1) or zero (0) to denote the links that are being used. These sets of ones and zeros are arranged in a matrix shown in Fig. 17. In the matrix, each column corresponds to a switch at the first stage, and each row corresponds to a switch at the second stage. Note that each row sum as well as each column sum is equal to two. These sums are not accidental but occur because each of the switches can have only two active ports for inputs and outputs. In other words, the column sums represent the fact that only two outputs are active on S_1 to S_4; the row sums likewise represent the fact that only two inputs are active on S_5 to S_8. To construct a valid connection for this network, a first step could be to choose active output ports for S_1; choosing these ports (and marking with one or zero) would also determine which of the top input ports on each of S_5 to S_8 are active. The interdependence of the constraints on port choices is expressed by the following matrix problem: Fill the 4×4 matrix so that all elements are zero or one and the row and column sums are equal to two.

When the number of ways to fill the matrix is determined, the CP for this network can be easily calculated. For each matrix, or a valid choice of active ports of switches, each of the switches S_1 to S_8 can be set in two ways. Thus, if $W(4)$ denotes the number of 4×4 matrices that meet the constraints previously given, then the number of realizable connections for the network is given by 2^8 times $W(4)$. Thus, CP for this network is given by $2^8 W(4)/(8!)$, where $W(4)$ turns out to be 90. The computation of CP for the expanding and contracting SW-banyans is discussed in Roberts and Kothari (1982).

6.2 Path Blockage

The path blockage for a MIN is defined as the number of connections between free input-output pairs that are rendered impossible (become blocked) by any single connection of an input to output made on an otherwise idle network.

The concept of path blockage was introduced by DeGroot (1983) who used examples to show that expanding and contracting SW-banyans provide higher performance in terms of less path blockage. We give here a formula to compute PB for UPP networks, based on the number of stages and the size of a switch in each stage. For an UPP network of size $N \times N$ with n stages and switches of size $p_i \times q_i$ at stage i for $i = 1, 2, \ldots, n$, path blockage PB is given by:

$$PB = \sum_{i=1}^{n-1} p_1 p_2 \cdots (p_i - 1) q_{i+1} \cdots q_n - p_1 p_2 \cdots p_{n-1} + 1$$

It follows that for UPP networks with n stages and $N/2$ switches of size 2×2

in each stage, path blockage is $PB = 2^{n-1}(n - 2) + 1$. For example in an 8×8 omega network, when input 2 is connected to output 6 then the connections between the input-output pairs (6, 4), (6, 5), (6, 7), (0, 7), (4, 7) are blocked.

6.3   Bandwidth

In this part, a performance analysis of a crossbar switch and a UPP network is presented with respect to bandwidth. The bandwidth is expressed in number of connection requests accepted per cycle. A cycle is defined as the time for a request to propagate through the MIN plus the time to access memory and return through the network to the source. The presentation is based on the model given in Patel (1981). The model makes several assumptions to simplify the analysis. There have been simulation studies that support the model (Patel, 1981). Recently, a similar performance analysis has also been done for several multipath MINs. The following assumptions are commonly made in a performance analysis of a crossbar switch or an UPP network:

1. Each processor generates random and independent requests; the requests are uniformly distributed over all memory modules.
2. At the beginning of every cycle, each processor generates a new request with probability m; i.e., the request rate at each of the inputs is m.
3. The requests that are blocked (not accepted) are ignored; i.e., the requests issued at the next cycle are independent of the requests blocked.

In addition to these three assumptions, the following are commonly made in performance analysis of multipath MINs.

4. A multipath MIN is assumed to be fault-free.
5. The probability of a request on an output link of a $p \times 1$ switch at the last stage of a multipath MIN is computed using one of the following two assumptions: Let w denote the probability of a request on an input link of a $p \times 1$ switch, then the probability of the request on an output link is assumed to be either (a) pw or (b) $1 - (1 - w)^p$. Both of these assumptions have been used in the literature.

The two ways of computation based on the fifth assumption ultimately give two different bounds for the bandwidth of a multipath MIN. In some cases, the two bounds differ significantly and may be far from the accurate value. This suggests the need for further analysis of multipath MINs by simulation and analytic techniques.

Next we present the performance analysis for a crossbar switch and an UPP network using the following notation and definitions. The network is assumed to be of size $M \times N$.

$R(i)$: the probability there are i requests at inputs of a network.

$E(i)$: the expected number of requests accepted by an $M \times N$ network given i requests at inputs.

The bandwidth and the probability of acceptance of a request (P_A) are defined as follows:

$$BW = \sum_{i=0}^{M} R(i)E(i) \quad \text{and} \quad P_A = \frac{BW}{mM}$$

6.3.1 Analysis of a Crossbar Switch

Consider an $M \times N$ crossbar switch with M inputs and N outputs. Two requests are in conflict in a crossbar switch if and only if the requests are to the same output. Therefore, in the case of a crossbar, memory conflicts (two requests for the same destination) are analyzed rather than the network conflicts. Recall that m is the probability that a processor generates a request during a cycle, then $R(i)$ is given by:

$$R(i) = C_i^M (1 - m)^{M-i} m^i$$

where C_i^M denotes a binomial coefficient. The probability that an output link has a request, given that there are i requests at inputs, is $1 - (1 - \frac{1}{N})^i$. Then $E(i)$ is given by:

$$E(i) = N \left[1 - \left(1 - \frac{1}{N} \right)^i \right]$$

On simplifying, the following expressions for the bandwidth and the probability of acceptance of requests are obtained in case of a crossbar switch:

$$BW = N \left[1 - \left(1 - \frac{m}{N} \right)^M \right] \quad \text{and} \quad P_A = \frac{N}{mM} \left[1 - \left(1 - \frac{m}{N} \right)^M \right]$$

6.3.2 Analysis of a UPP Network

The analysis of a UPP network given here is identical to the analysis of delta networks in Patel (1981). In fact, the analysis of delta networks does not use any special properties of delta networks and is equally applicable to UPP networks in general.

Consider a UPP network of size $p^n \times q^n$ constructed from $p \times q$ crossbar switches. The performance analysis of a UPP network is done by applying the results of previous analyses to each $p \times q$ crossbar switch in the network. Given the request rate at each of the inputs of a $p \times q$ crossbar switch, the request rate at each of its outputs is obtained by dividing the BW by q, the number of outputs. Let $p_{in}(j)$ denote the request rate at each of the input links

TABLE V

PROBABILITY OF ACCEPTANCE OF A REQUEST
ASSUMING $m = 1$

Network size (N)	delta	GN	KN
16	0.4498	0.608	0.642
32	0.3993	0.578	0.633
64	0.3594	0.551	0.624
128	0.3271	0.526	0.617
256	0.3004	0.504	0.610
512	0.2778	0.483	0.603

of stage j of the network for $1 \le j \le n$. Similarly, let $p_{out}(j)$ denote the request rate at each of the output links of stage j. Then, $p_{out}(j)$ can be computed from $p_{in}(j)$ by using the formula for the bandwidth of a crossbar switch. We get the following relation:

$$p_{out}(j) = 1 - \left(1 - \frac{p_{in}(j)}{q}\right)^p \quad \text{for} \quad 1 \le j \le n$$

Since $p_{out}(j) = p_{in}(j + 1)$, the preceding equation can be used iteratively starting at stage 1 with $p_{in}(1) = m$. Then, the following expressions for the BW and the probability of acceptance of a request are obtained for the UPP network:

$$BW = q^n p_{out}(n) \quad \text{and} \quad P_A = \frac{q^n p_{out}(n)}{p^n m}$$

The values of P_A for the GN (with unrestricted routing), the KN, and the delta network are reported in Table V.

In this part, we have discussed the basic model for performance analysis of MINs. Recently, the model has been extended in several directions to include: (a) buffering at switches (Dias and Jump, 1981; Kumar and Jump, 1984), (b) multipath MINs, and (c) locality of references (Pfister and Norton, 1985).

7. VLSI Implementation

The VLSI layout of a MIN entails mapping the network into a planar grid so that switch nodes are mapped one-to-one to intersections of the grid lines and links are mapped one-to-one to paths consisting of line segments of the grid. The paths are allowed to cross, but they cannot share line segments. Depending on the fabrication technology, the model assumes one or multiple planar layers of metal interconnections. With present technology, two layers are common in which one layer provides for all horizontal paths and the other layer provides for all vertical paths.

7.1 Performance Criteria

Two important parameters in VLSI implementation are area and delay. The area of a layout is defined as the area of the smallest rectangle containing all the switch nodes and links. The time delay includes the switching delay of logic, gates and path delay due to inductance and capacitance. An important measure of VLSI performance is the space-time product measure. The results based on the space-time product measure differ significantly from those obtained with more traditional measures based on the number of switching gates and delays calculated by the number of stages. A comparison between a MIN and a crossbar switch, assuming implementation on a single VLSI chip, is done by Franklin (1981). The comparison concludes that the difference between the two networks using the space-time product measure is much less than that predicted by traditional measures, and for reasonable size, the two have roughly comparable VLSI performance. A problem of practical importance is to find a layout of a network with minimal area. The layout of a crossbar and certain UPP networks are studied for minimal area requirement in Hoey and Leiserson (1980) and Wise (1981). It was found that the locality of edges between switch nodes is a key to effective layout since long edges require a significant amount of area.

7.2 Control Structures

A major implementation constraint for a large VLSI based interconnection network is the number of pins available on a chip. The number of pins depends on the number of input and output ports, data lines per port, and control lines. One way to solve the pin limitation problem is to partition a large network into small subnetworks that can be implemented individually by a VLSI chip. Another approach to solving the pin limitation problem is to slice the network to create a set of network planes with each plane handling one or more bits. But this bit slicing procedure can lead to synchronization problems, especially where message routing through the network is via local control logic at each switch node. If several messages arrive close together in time and request the same output, then it is possible that the output word will contain bits from a number of input sources, thus causing an error. This situation is referred to as *word inconsistency*. The pin limitation and partitioning is studied in Franklin *et al.* (1982).

A broader question related to the partition problem is the timing control to synchronize the data movement in the network. Two approaches, asynchronous and clocked, have been investigated for timing control. The asynchronous scheme uses self-timed, handshaking protocols while the clocked scheme uses a global clock. In particular, clocked designs have usually been preferred due to their relative simplicity and lower hardware cost. However, for large systems clocked control is difficult to implement because of the inevitable problems of clock skews and delays. The clocked control also becomes more difficult if the final size and configuration of the system is not known in advance. This happens to be the case when the MIN is required to be modular and expandable to support a wide range of multiprocessor systems. Thus, the asynchronous control tends to be more advantageous when a system becomes large or when the size of the system cannot be predicted in advance. In general, the design of control logic is simple for clocked systems, but there is a clock distribution problem. On the other hand, for asynchronous schemes the design of the control logic is difficult, but there is no clock distribution problem. The control schemes are modeled for MINs and equations for time delay have been developed by Wann and Franklin (1983).

8. Conclusion

We have attempted to introduce the reader to important aspects of multistage interconnection networks for parallel computer systems. The interconnection networks are considered to be of primary importance in determining the power of a parallel computer. A multistage interconnection network is an efficient solution to provide dynamically reconfigurable interconnections among the components of a parallel computer. We have emphasized the topological design of a network. The topology of a network has major impact on the design of routing algorithm, the possible interconnection patterns, the fault tolerance and many other important properties of the network. Other features such as pipelining, arbitration to resolve conflicts, switching methodology and capability to combine concurrent requests to the same memory location are used to enhance the capability of a multistage interconnection network.

REFERENCES

Adams, G. B., III, and Siegel, H. J. (1982a). The extra stage cube: A fault-tolerant interconnection network for supersystems. *IEEE Trans. Comput.* **C-31** (5), 443–454.
Adams, G. B., III, and Siegel, H. J. (1982b). On the number of permutations performable by the augmented data manipulator network. *IEEE Trans. Comput.* **C-31** (4), 270–277.
Agrawal, D. P. (1982). Testing and fault tolerance of multistage interconnection networks. *Computer* **15** (4), 41–53.
Agrawal, D. P. (1983). Graph theoretical analysis and design of multistage interconnection networks. *IEEE Trans. Comput.* **C-32** (7), 637–648.

Anderson, S. (1977). The looping algorithm extended to base 2^t rearrangeable switching networks. *IEEE Trans. Commun.* **COM-25** (10), 1057–1063.

Batcher, K. E. (1976). The flip network in STARAN. *Proc. 1976 Int'l Conf. Parallel Processing*, pp. 65–71.

Benes, V. E. (1962). On rearrangeable three-stage connecting networks. *Bell System Tech. J.* **41** (9), 1481–1492.

Benes, V. E. (1965). "Mathematical Theory of Connecting Networks." Academic Press, New York.

Bhuyan, L. N., and Agrawal, D. P. (1983). Design and performance of generalized interconnection networks. *IEEE Trans. Comput.* **C-32** (12), 1081–1090.

Cantor, D. G. (1971). On nonblocking switching networks. *Networks* **1** (4), 367–377.

Chin, C., and Hwang, K. (1984). Connection principles for multipath packet switching networks. *IEEE Trans. Comput.*, Special issue on Parallel Processing, **C-33** (11), 99–108.

Ciminiera, L., and Serra, A. (1982). A fault-tolerant connecting network for Processor systems. *Proc. 1982 Int'l. Conf. Parallel Processing*, pp. 113–122.

Clos, C. (1953). A study of nonblocking switching networks. *Bell System Tech. J.* **32** (3), 406–424.

DeGroot, D. (1983). Expanding and contracting SW-banyan networks. *Proc. 1983 Int'l Conf. Parallel Processing*, pp. 19–24.

Dias, D. M., and Jump, J. R. (1981). Analysis and simulation of buffered delta networks. *IEEE Trans. Comput.* **C-30** (4), 273–282.

Feng, T., and Wu, C. (1981). Fault diagnosis for a class of multistage interconnection networks. *IEEE Trans. Comput.* **C-30** (10), 743–758.

Franklin, M. A. (1981). VLSI performance comparison of banyan and crossbar communication networks. *IEEE Trans. Comput.* **C-30** (4), 283–291.

Franklin, M. A., Wann, D. F., and Thomas, W. J. (1982). Pin limitations and partitioning of VLSI interconnection networks. *IEEE Trans. Comput.* **C-31** (11), 1109–1116.

Gecsei, J. (1977). Interconnection networks from three-state cells. *IEEE Trans. Comput.* **C-26** (8), 705–711.

Goke, L. R., and Lipovski, G. J. (1973). Banyan networks for partitioning multiprocessing systems. *Proc. 1st Int'l Symp. Computer Architecture*, pp. 21–28.

Gotlieb, A., Grishman, R., Kruskal, C. P., McAuliffe, K. P., Rudolph, L., and Snir, M. (1983). The NYU ultra computer—Designing an MIMD shared memory parallel computer. *IEEE Trans. Comput.* **C-32** (2), 175–189.

Hoey, D., and Leiserson, C. E. (1980). A layout for the shuffle-exchange network. *Proc. 1980 Int'l Conf. Parallel Processing*, pp. 329–336.

Jansen, P. G., and Kessels, J. L. W. (1980). The DIMOND: A component for the modular construction of switching networks. *IEEE Trans. Comput.* **C-29** (10), 884–889.

Joel, A. E., Jr. (1968). On permutation switching networks. *Bell System Tech. J.* **67**, 813–822.

Kautz, W. H., Levitt, K. N., and Waksman, A. (1968). Cellular interconnection arrays. *IEEE Trans. Comput.* **C-17** (5), 443–451.

Kothari, S. C., and Lakshmivarahan, S. (1983). A condition known to be sufficient for rearrangeability of the Benes class of networks with 2×2 switches is also necessary. *Proc. 1983 Int'l Conf. Parallel Processing*, pp. 76–79.

Kothari, S. C., Lakshmivarahan S., and Peyravi, H. (1985a). A new upper bound on the number of stages required for the universality of shuffle-exchange networks. *Proc. Annual Conf. on Information Sciences and Systems*, pp. 515–520.

Kothari, S. C., Prabhu, G. M., and Roberts, R. (1985b). The kappa network, with fault-tolerant destination tag algorithm. Iowa State University Technical Report 85–20, Computer Science Department, Ames, Iowa.

Kothari, S. C., Prabhu, G. M., and Roberts, R. (1985c). Multipath network with cross links. Iowa State University Technical Report 85–22, Computer Science Department, Ames, Iowa.

Kruskal, C. P., and Snir, M. (1982). Some results on packet-switching networks for multiprocessing. *Proc. Annual Conf. on Information Sciences and Systems*, pp. 305–310.

Kruskal, C. P., and Snir, M. (1983). The performance of multistage interconnection networks for multiprocessors. *IEEE Trans. Comput.* **C-32** (12), 1091–1098.

Kumar, M., and Jump, J. R. (1984). Performance enhancement in buffered delta networks using crossbar switches and multiple links. *J. Parallel and Distributed Computing* **1** (1), 81–103.

Lang, T., Valero, M., and Alegre, I. (1982). Bandwidth of crossbar and multiple-bus connections for multiprocessors. *IEEE Trans. Comput.* **C-31** (12), 1227–1234.

Lawrie, D. H. (1975). Access and alignment of data in an array processor. *IEEE Trans. Comput.* **C-24** (12), 1145–1155.

Leiserson, C. E. (1985). Fat-trees: Universal networks for hardware-efficient supercomputing. *Proc. 1985 Int'l. Conf. Parallel Processing*, pp. 393–402.

Lenfant, J. (1978). Parallel permutations of data: A Benes network control algorithm for frequently used permutations. *IEEE Trans. Comput.* **C-27** (7), 637–647.

Lev, G., Pippenger, N., and Valiant, L. G. (1981). A fast parallel algorithm for routing in permutation networks. *IEEE Trans. Comput.* **C-30** (2), 93–100.

Lillienkamp, J. E., Lawrie, D. H., and Yew, P. C. (1982). A fault-tolerant interconnection network using error correcting code. *Proc. 1982 Int'l. Conf. Parallel Processing*, pp. 123–125.

McMillen, R. J., and Siegel, H. J. (1982). Performance and fault tolerance improvements for the inverse augmented data manipulator network. *Proc. 9th Int'l. Symp. Computer Architecture*, pp. 63–72.

Masson, G. M. (1977). Binomial switching networks for concentration and distribution. *IEEE Trans. Commun.* **C-25** (9), 873–883.

Nassimi, D., and Sahni, S. (1982). Parallel algorithms to set up the Benes permutation network. *IEEE Trans. Comput.* **C-31** (2), 148–154.

Opferman, D. C., and Tsao-Wu, N. T. (1971). On a class of rearrangeable switching networks–Part I: Control algorithm; Part II: Enumeration studies of fault diagnosis. *Bell System Tech. J.* **50** (3), 1579–1618.

Padmanabhan, K., and Lawrie, D. H. (1983). A class of redundant path multistage interconnection networks. *IEEE Trans. Comput.* **C-32** (12), 1099–1108.

Parker, D. S. (1980). Notes on shuffle/exchange-type switching networks. *IEEE Trans. Comput.* **C-29** (3), 213–222.

Parker, D. S., and Raghavendra, C. S. (1982). The gamma network: A multiprocessor interconnection network with redundant paths. *Proc. 9th Int'l. Symp. Computer Architecture*, pp. 73–80.

Patel, J. H. (1981). Performance of processor-memory interconnections for multiprocessors. *IEEE Trans. Comput.* **C-30** (10), 771–780.

Pease, M. C. (1977). The indirect binary n-cube microprocessor array. *IEEE Trans. Comput.* **C-26** (5), 548–573.

Pfister, G. F., and Norton, V. A. (1985). Hot spot contention and combining in multistage interconnection networks. *Proc. 1985 Int'l. Conf. Parallel Processing*, 790–797.

Pfister G. F., Brantley, W. C., George, D. A., Harvey, S. L., Kleinfelder, W. J., McAuliffe, K. P., Melton, E. A., Norton, V. A., and Weiss J. (1985). The IBM research parallel processor prototype (RP3): Introduction and architecture. *Proc. 1985 Int'l. Conf. Parallel Processing*, pp. 764–771.

Pinsker, M. (1973). On the complexity of a concentrator. *Proc. 7th Int'l. Teletrafic Conf.*, 318/1–318/4.

Pradhan, D. K., and Kodandapani, K. L. (1980). A uniform representation of single and multiple interconnection network used in SIMD machines. *IEEE Trans. Comput.* **C-29** (9), 777–790.

Premkumar, U. V., Kapur, R., Malek, M., Lipovski, G. J., and Horne, P. (1980). Design and implementation of the banyan interconnection network in TRAC. *AFIPS Conf. Proc.* **49**, 643–653.

Raghavendra, C. S., and Parker, D. S. (1984). Reliability analysis of an interconnection network. *Proc. 4th Int'l. Conf. Distr. Comp. Systems*, pp. 10–20.

Raghavendra, C. S., and Varma, A. (1985). INDRA: A class of interconnection networks with redundant paths. *Real Time Systems Symposium*, Austin, Texas, pp. 155–164.

Reddy, S. M., and Kumar, V. P. (1984). On fault-tolerant multistage interconnection networks. *Proc. 1984 Int'l. Conf. Parallel Processing*, pp. 155–164.

Reddy, S. M., and Kumar, V. P. (1985). On multipath multistage interconnection networks. *Proc. 5th Int'l. Conf. Distr. Comp. Systems*, pp. 210–217.

Roberts, R. and Kothari, S. C. (1982). On computing the combinatorial power of SW-banyan networks. *Proc. 18th Hawaii Int'l. Conf. System Sciences*, pp. 1–10.

Shen, J. P. (1982). Fault tolerance analysis of several interconnection networks. *Proc. 1982 Int'l Conf. on Parallel Processing*, pp. 102–112.

Shen, J. P., and Hayes, J. P. (1984). Fault-tolerance of dynamic-full-access interconnection networks. *IEEE Trans. Comput.* **C-33** (3), 241–248.

Siegel, H. J. (1977). Analysis techniques for SIMD machine interconnection and the effects of processor address masks. *IEEE Trans. Comput.* **C-26** (2), 153–161.

Siegel, H. J. (1979). A model of SIMD machines and a comparison of various interconnection networks. *IEEE Trans. Comput.* **C-28,** 907–917.

Siegel, H. J. (1980). The theory underlying the partitioning of permutation networks. *IEEE Trans. Comput.* **C-29** (9), 791–801.

Siegel, H. T., ed. (1981). Interconnection networks for parallel and distributed processing. *IEEE Trans. Comput.*, Special issue **C-30** (4).

Siegel, H. J. (1984). "Interconnection Networks for Large-Scale Parallel Processing: Theory and Case Studies." Lexington Books, Lexington, Massachusetts.

Siegel, H. J., and McMillen R. J. (1981). The multistage cube: A versatile interconnection network. *Computer* **14** (12), 65–76.

So, K. M., and Narraway, J. J. (1979). On-line fault diagnosis of switching networks. *IEEE Trans. Circuits and Systems* **CAS-26** (7), 575–583.

Stone, H. S. (1971). Parallel processing with the perfect shuffle. *IEEE Trans. Comput.* **C-20** (2), 153–161.

Tzeng, N. F., Yew, P. C., and Zhu, C. Q. (1985). A fault-tolerant scheme for multistage interconnection network. *Proc. 1985 Int'l. Conf. Parallel Processing*, pp. 474–479.

Varma, A. and Raghavendra, C. S. (1985a). On permutations passable by the gamma network. *Proc. 18th Hawaii Int'l. Conf. System Sciences*, pp. 10–20.

Varma, A., and Raghavendra, C. S. (1985). Realization of permutations on generalized Indra networks. *Proc. 1985 Int'l. Conf. Parallel Processing*, pp. 328–333.

Varma, A., and Raghavendra, C. S., (1985). Performance analysis of a redundant-path interconnection network, *Proc. 1985 Int'l. Conf. Parallel Processing*, pp. 474–479.

Waksman, A. (1968). A permutation network. *J. ACM* **9** (1), 159–163.

Wann, D. F., and Franklin, M. A. (1983). Asynchronous and clocked control structures for VLSI-based interconnection networks. *IEEE Trans. Comput.* **C-32** (3), 284–293.

Wise, D. S. (1981). Compact layout of banyan/FFT networks. *Proc. CMU Conf. VLSI Systems and Computations*, Computer Science Press, pp. 186–195.

Wu, C., ed. (1981). Interconnection networks. *Computer*, Special issue **14** (12).

Wu, C., and Feng, T. (1980a). On a class of multistage interconnection networks. *IEEE Trans. Comput.* **C-29** (8), 694–702.

Wu, C., and Feng, T. (1980b). A software technique for enhancing performance of a distributed computer system. *Proc. Compsac 80*, pp. 274–280.

Wu, C., and Feng, T. (1981). Universality of the shuffle-exchange network. *IEEE Trans. Comput.* **C-30** (5), 324–332.

Wu, C., and Feng, T. (1984). Tutorial: Interconnection networks for parallel and distributed processing. IEEE Publication.

Fault-Tolerant Computing[1]

WING N. TOY

[1] This chapter is based in part on portions of Chapter 8 of "Computer Hardware/Software Architecture," by Wing Toy and Benjamin Zee (Prentice-Hall, 1986), and "Microprogrammed Control and Reliable Design of Small Computers," by George D. Kraft and Wing N. Toy (Prentice–Hall, 1981).

ADVANCES IN COMPUTERS, VOL. 26

1. Introduction

System reliability has been a major concern from the inception of electronic digital computers. There are two approaches to increased reliability: fault avoidance (fault intolerance) and fault tolerance. Fault avoidance uses high-reliability components, conservative design practices, and extensive design reviews to eliminate design flaws. Its objective is to reduce the possibility of a failure. Failures will eventually occur, even with the most careful fault avoidance, hence the term "fault intolerance." On the other hand, fault tolerance uses additional components (redundancy)—hardware, software, or both—to bypass the effects of failures. Both techniques are usually employed in high-reliability systems.

The term *fault-tolerant computing* is defined as the ability to compute in the presence of errors. In the past, fault-tolerant computer systems occupied a relatively narrow niche in the commercial market. Most were and still are designed to provide solutions for specialized applications, but fault-tolerant computing is beginning to play an important part in the design of commercial computers, for several reasons. These include the dramatic advances in VLSI technology, the high cost of maintaining sophisticated equipment, a wider field of applications, and user demands for better reliability. As computers have continued to take over more and more tasks critical to the successful operation of hospitals, manufacturing plants, power plants, banks, and offices, the demand for fault tolerance and the scope of fault-tolerant systems has increased substantially in the past few years.

A dramatic improvement in hardware reliability has been made with the advent of semiconductor technology. Meanwhile, software complexity, and with it software failure, increases at an unexpectedly high rate. Fault-tolerant computing includes protection against both hardware and software faults. At present, some progress has been made in software fault tolerance, but it still remains a challenge.

This chapter gives an overview of fault-tolerant computing design, including both hardware and software techniques. The emphasis is directed toward practical applications rather than theory. Some commercial fault-tolerant computer systems are included to illustrate the various techniques being deployed to achieve fault tolerance.

2. Reliability Estimation

Reliability estimation is a process of predicting from available failure-rate data the achievable reliability of a part, subsystem, or system and the probability of meeting its objectives for a specified application. These calculations are most useful in the early design stages of a project. The use of pure numerical values for the reliability of various components will generally provide little benefit in evaluating the initial system design. Such figures can be extremely valuable, however, when it is necessary for a designer to select from a number of alternative designs. It enables the designer to make a selection based on a particular type of system redundancy and its associated reliability.

2.1 Failure Rate

When an item no longer works as intended it has failed to perform its required function. An item may be any part, subsystem, system, or equipment that can be individually evaluated and separately tested. Well-defined failures that are both sudden and complete are referred to as *catastrophic failures*. They are unpredictable and may not be evident during normal testing procedures. Failures that take place gradually in equipment that remains operational are classified as *degraded failures* and are often partial (i.e., the equipment will function correctly part of the time). Degraded failures are the result of aging, which causes certain characteristics of the equipment under consideration to deviate beyond specified limits. In many instances, failures of this type cause intermittent or marginal conditions that are extremely difficult to isolate. Techniques of "stressing" the operating conditions to force partial failures to become complete failures have been used to identify the weak components before they become troublesome to a working system.

The failure pattern of equipment placed in service can be naturally categorized into three periods of operation. At the very beginning, any inherently weak parts that are the result of improper design, improper manufacture, or improper usage usually fail fairly soon. The early failure rate, although relatively high, decreases progressively and eventually levels off as the weak components are replaced. This situation is illustrated in Figure 1 and is called the *early life period* of a system. The diagram in Figure 1 is commonly referred to as the "bathtub curve", which is divided into three periods. Many early failures can be sorted out by the burn-in test or by 100-percent inspection. Such a practice is common to eliminate all "weaklings" by subjecting components to tests under accelerated conditions. Similarly, systems are operated for a period of time under varying conditions to ensure the detection of early failures or of potential ones. This practice is certainly a must for equipment aboard airborne missiles and satellites, which are nonrepairable during missions. This type of inspection is also highly desirable

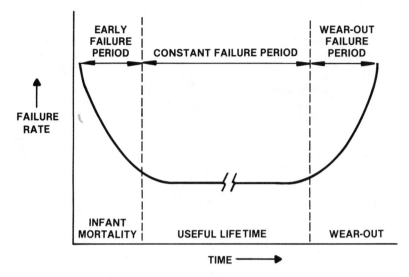

FIG. 1.   Typical bathtub curve of failure rate versus time.

for repairable equipment, such as undersea transatlantic amplifiers, whose repair is a major undertaking and very expensive. For low-cost small computers, a 100-percent burn-in of components may not be economically feasible. However, a certain amount of stressing of components—i.e., by varying the power-supply voltages or increasing the clock rate—may identify marginal components in a working system.

After the early failures have been replaced, the components settle down to a long, relatively steady period at an approximatly constant failure rate. During this period the failure rate is usually low and is unlikely to be due to any single cause. This means the failures from a wide variety of causes occur at random and at a uniform rate, without any obvious pattern. The normal working life of a system occurs during this interval, which is also called the *useful life period* of a system.

In the *wear-out period* the components rapidly deteriorate, with each one eventually wearing out. The failure rate, as indicated in Figure 1, rises again. Wear-out failures can be avoided by replacing components before they reach this period. As an example, the wear-out period for automobile batteries usually begins at the end of the warranty. The item must then be replaced to ensure continued reliable service.

Human life characteristics closely follow the bathtub curve shown in Figure 2. The first part of the curve is normally referred to as the "infant mortality" period. Infants unfortunate enough to be born with physical defects or weaknesses generally die in the early years of life. After the tenth year, the death rate drops to its lowest level, and a majority of those who sur-

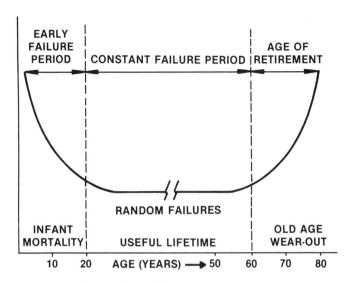

FIG. 2. Human life characteristics.

vive live to old age. The deaths occurring during the second period are attributed to a wide variety of causes on a random basis at a constant rate. In the sixtieth and seventieth years, the curve rises as people begin to die of natural causes. This is the period of old age. The risk of death continues to increase with age until everyone in the group is dead.

2.2 Reliability Calculations with Constant Failure Rate

The constant failure rate represented by the useful life portion of Figure 1 implies that the probability of failure is independent of age. This simply means that old equipment still operating is just as good as new equipment that has been recently installed. For any constant failure rate, the value of reliability depends only on time. A reliability function that is characterized by a constant failure rate is the negative exponential distribution. The negative exponential distribution has the form

$$R = e^{-\lambda t} \tag{2.1}$$

where λ = failure rate and t = time.

It is assumed that when a system commences operation (begining its mission time at $t = 0$) all components are operational. By this assumption, $R(0) = 1$. Since all components must fail in infinite time, $R(\infty) = 0$. The importance of the negative exponential distribution is that the reliability is independent of when time $t = 0$ is defined. If an item of equipment has a failure rate of λ, its reliability for the period of time t is $e^{-\lambda t}$. If, at the end of this time, the item is still in the same operating condition, its reliability for the next time period of equal duration is still $e^{-\lambda t}$. During the interval when the equipment failure rate is relatively constant, the negative exponential function is a good representation of the reliability of the equipment.

A physical system normally consists of many different types of components (i.e., intergrated circuits, connectors, switches, etc.). Typically, each type of component has a different instantaneous failure rate. One means of characterizing a physical system is to treat each component as being in *series* with the other components in the system. Consequently, when a single component fails, the entire system fails. The reliability function of the entire system is represented by the product of the individual reliability functions for each component. In making this statement, it is assumed that the reliability of each component is independent of all others. The overall system reliability function may be represented by the expression

$$R_T = R_1 R_2 R_3 \cdots R_n \tag{2.2}$$

If the reliability function for each component is given by an exponential distribution function, then the above equation becomes

$$R_T = e^{-\lambda_1 t} e^{-\lambda_1 t} e^{-\lambda_3 t} \cdots e^{-\lambda_n t} \tag{2.3}$$

Collecting terms and simplifying Eq. (2.3) yields the following expression:

$$R_T = e^{-(\lambda_1 + \lambda_2 + \lambda_3 + \cdots + \lambda_n)t} \tag{2.4}$$

For a *series interconnection* of components whose individual reliability functions are exponential, the failure rate for the total system is the sum of the individual failure rates of all components.

2.3   Mean Time Between Failures

The *mean time between failures* (MTBF) may be regarded as the average time an item may be expected to function before it fails. There is no certainty that the item will not break down before the end of this period or, for that matter, that it will not function longer. However, the interval between failures for a piece of equipment is given by its MTBF.

In general, the MTBF of a system may be treated as the integral of the reliability function of the overall system:

$$\text{MTBF} = \int_0^\infty R(t)\, dt \tag{2.5}$$

The MTBF can also be visualized intuitively by supposing a particular unit has a constant failure rate of 10^{-6} failures per hour. If this unit is tested and replaced by an identical one every time it fails, the unit will fail, on the average, once every 10^6 hours. Therefore, the MTBF is equal to 10^6 hours. This is just the reciprocal of the constant failure rate for the exponential function, where $\lambda = 10^{-6}$ failure per hour.

The MTBF is a quantitative measure of reliability. It gives the average time interval during which equipment is expected to operate without a failure. In some literature this interval is also referred to as the *mean time to failure* (MTTF). Technically speaking, MTTF and MTBF are not identical. MTBF can be defined, in an alternative form, as

$$MTBF = MTTF + MTTR \qquad (2.6)$$

where MTTR is the *mean time to repair*. If a component or a system is repaired instantenously when a failure is experienced, the MTBF and MTTF are the same quantity. In general, MTTF and MTBF have been used interchangeably, since MTTR is usually very small in comparison with MTTF.

2.4 Repair Rate

The *repair rate*, or the *reciprocal of the repair time*, is another factor that materially affects the reliability and maintainability of a system. When one unit in a duplicated system is defective, the system depends on the second unit to continue operation. If the defective unit is repaired quickly, the chance of the complete system going down becomes quite small, because the second unit will operate in such a manner as to preserve the integrity of the system's operation. Since the system is vulnerable only during the time it takes to repair the defective unit, a short repair time can tremendously increase the system's reliability.

The system repair time may be divided into two separate intervals called the *passive repair time* and the *active repair time*. The passive repair time is the time interval measured from the time a fault is first recognized in the system until the time that maintenance personnel arrive to initiate repair work. This interval is determined entirely by administrative and logistic support provided by the user of the system.

The active part of the repair time is the actual time required by the maintenance personnel to isolate, diagnose, repair, and verify that the trouble condition is corrected. This time is directly affected by the equipment design. The active repair time can be reduced by improvement of both the hardware and software designs, with an eye toward minimizing the maintenance skills required to support the system. In view of the continued increase in labor costs, this is a particularly worthwhile philosophy to observe.

2.5 Repairable Dual Redundancy System

The dual redundancy structure is one of the more commonly employed architectures to provide real-time continuous control. This technique has been used successfully in electronic telephone switching systems for the past twenty-five years. The important steps to achieve high reliability in a dual

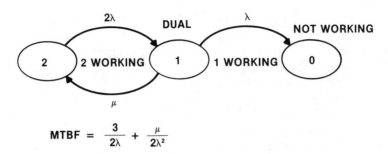

$$\text{MTBF} = \frac{3}{2\lambda} + \frac{\mu}{2\lambda^2}$$

FIG. 3.   Markou-process model; fits the assumption that failure rates are constant.

configuration are fault detection, fault recovery, and repair. Both units are monitored continually, so that faults in the backup (standby) are found just as quickly as those in the on-line unit. This is accomplished by running the on-line and standby units in the synchronous match mode of operation. Every operation in both units is performed in step, with key outputs compared for error detection. If a mismatch occurs, each unit goes through the fault recognition program to determine which half of the system is faulty. The suspected unit is removed from service and the system continues to function.

A dual redundancy system can be said to be vulnerable to total system failure only when the original active unit has failed and is undergoing repair. Reliability is therefore related not only to the failure rate, but also to the repair rate, or the rate at which the failure is corrected.

The MTBF derived from the Markov model for the dual system with repair, as shown in Figure 3, is given by (Kraft and Toy, 1981).

$$\text{MTBF} = \frac{3}{2\lambda} + \frac{\mu}{2\lambda^2} \tag{2.7}$$

where μ is the repair rate, or the reciprocal of mean time to repair (MTTR), and λ is the failure rate of one module.

2.6   Repairable TMR (Triple-Modular Redundant) System

The standard TMR operates in the synchronous mode as in the dual system, but the TMR architecture has inherent fault-masking capability. Error detection and correction are done in a single step without any disturbance to the system's operation. This unique property is the strength of the TMR structure. Recovery from a fault in one module is automatic. Transient errors are corrected automatically. These attributes are realized by having three modules rather than two.

When one module becomes faulty, the remaining two continue to function as in a dual system with only error detection capability. If a second module

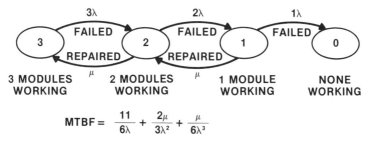

$$MTBF = \frac{11}{6\lambda} + \frac{2\mu}{3\lambda^2} + \frac{\mu}{6\lambda^3}$$

FIG. 4. Markou model of TMR 3-2-1.

becomes faulty before the first one is completely repaired, the third module continues system operation. The system is down only when the second and the third modules fail during repair. The MTBF is extended substantially over the dual system. The Markov model of the TMR system is shown in Figure 4. In the 3, or normal state, all three modules are fault-free and fully operational. As long as the modules are fault free, the system remains in this state. Since λ is the failure rate for one module and there are three modules in the system, the probability of transition from state 3 to state 2 is 3λ. When one module fails, the system goes to state 2. Upon repair, with a probability of repair rate μ, it is restored to state 3. Should another module fail before the repair is completed, the system degrades from state 2 to state 1. The transition back to the previous state is by repairing defective modules, one by one. The trapping state, state 0, is when the last module fails, bringing the system down completely. Notice that the number of λ decreases by one with each state. This corresponds to the number of working modules. The MTBF calculation is the time that the system takes to reach the 0 state. If the repair time is short, the possibility of moving out of state 2 to state 1 is very small, and the possibility of moving from the 1 to the 0 state is exceedingly small. The solution to this MTBF follows the similar procedure outlined in Siewiorek and Swarz (1982). The result is

$$MTBF = \frac{11}{6\lambda} + \frac{2\mu}{3\lambda^2} + \frac{\mu^2}{6\lambda^3} \qquad (2.8)$$

2.7 MTBF Comparisons

Table 1 shows the MTBF calculations for the single, dual, and TMR configurations. λ is the failure rate of a single module; assume it has a value of 10^{-4}, one failure in 10^4 hours. The MTBF for a nonredundant system is, then, $1/10^{-4}$, 10^4 hours, or approximately one year. In the dual system the MTBF is dominated by the second term, which varies inversely with λ^2. Assume the repair rate μ is 0.125 (repair time equals eight hours). The MTBF is calculated

TABLE I

MTBF OF SINGLE, DUAL, AND TMR CONFIGURATIONS

System	MTBF	MTBF, years
Simplex	$\dfrac{1}{\lambda}$	1
Dual 2-1	$\dfrac{3}{2\lambda} + \dfrac{\mu}{2\lambda^2}$	625
TMR 3-2	$\dfrac{5}{6\lambda} + \dfrac{\mu}{6\lambda^2}$	208
TMR 3-2-1	$\dfrac{11}{6\lambda} + \dfrac{2\mu}{3\lambda^2} + \dfrac{\mu}{6\lambda^3}$	260,400

to be 625 years, a substantial increase in reliability, compared with a nonredundant simplex system. This is an upper bound, however, and decreases substantially by imperfect coverage when a fault occurs in the system. This problem is discussed in the next section. In the TMR case, the MTBF is increased to a phenomenal value of 260,000 years. Again, as in the case of the dual system, the MTBF will be reduced considerably because of imperfect coverage.

2.8   Effect of Coverage

The dynamic redundancy technique generally requires two sequential steps: detection and correction. A fault is first detected, and then recovery action reconfigures a fault-free operational state. The important factor in dynamic redundancy is the concept of coverage, i.e., its ability to recover successfully from a fault. In the dual system, the ability to isolate the faulty unit depends heavily on both hardware and software support to diagnose and pinpoint the defective module. The inadequacy of the recovery program to configure a working system around the faulty unit reduces the coverage factor.

The coverage factor can be included in the reliability modeling as shown in Figure 5 for the dual configuration. It is assumed that not all faults are recoverable and that c is the coverage factor denoting the conditional probability that the system recovers, given that a fault has occurred. The transition probability is $2\lambda c$ from state 2 to state 1 and $2\lambda(1 - c)$ to state 0. A fault occurring in the normal working state can take the system down, depending upon the coverage factor. The calculation based upon the Markov model, as shown in Figure 5 for the dual structure, from Trivedi (1982), is

$$\text{MTBF} = \frac{\lambda(1 + 2c) + \mu}{2\lambda[\lambda + \mu(1 - c)]} \tag{2.9}$$

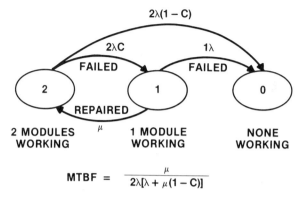

$$\text{MTBF} = \frac{\mu}{2\lambda[\lambda + \mu(1 - C)]}$$

FIG. 5.   Effect of imperfect coverage of a dual system.

TABLE II

MTBF OF DUAL AND TMR WITH COVERAGE CONFIGURATIONS,
$(\mu = 0.125 \ \lambda = 10^{-4})$

System	MTBF, years			
	$c = 1$	$c = 0.99$	$c = 0.95$	$c = 0$
Dual 2-1	625	50	10	0.5
TMR 3-2	208	—	—	—
TMR 3-2-1	260,400	20,833	4,167	208

Notice the factor of $(1 - c)$ in the denominator has a great influence in the value of MTBF. Table II shows that if c has the value of 0.99, or 99%, the MTBF is reduced from 625 years $(c = 1)$ to 50 years. This is a substantial reduction in reliability. If $c = 0.95$, the MTBF is further reduced to 10 years. The coverage factor is very important in reliability calculations.

For the TMR structure, including the coverage factor, the calculation is quite "messy," involving many terms. Reliability modeling programs have been widely used to facilitate these calculations. One such program is the ARIES (Automated Reliability Interactive Estimation system) (Ng and Avizienis, 1977; Makam and Avizienis, 1982).

3.   Availability

The *availability* of equipment may be defined as the probability of the equipment operating satisfactorily at any point in time while being used under stated conditions. The concept of availability is used in measuring the system's effectiveness. Both reliability and maintainability are combined in the concept of availability. This relationship may be expressed as follows:

$$\text{availability} = \frac{\text{total time}}{\text{total time} + \text{total downtime}}$$

$$= \frac{\text{total time}}{\text{total time} + (\text{number of failures} \times \text{MTTR})} \tag{3.1}$$

$$= \frac{\text{total time}}{\text{total time} + (\lambda \times \text{total time} \times \text{MTTR})}$$

$$= \frac{1}{1 + \lambda \times \text{MTTR}} \quad \text{if} \quad \text{MTTR} = \frac{1}{\lambda}$$

$$= \frac{\text{MTTF}}{\text{MTTF} + \text{MTTR}}$$

where the reliability function is assumed to be an exponential distribution $R(t) = e^{-\lambda t}$.

Since MTTF is a measure of reliability and MTTR, a measure of maintainability, a trade-off between the two can be arranged to realize a given availability. As the MTTF (reliability) increases, the MTTR can also. This means a more reliable system can tolerate a longer repair time. A trade-off might be made in which ease of maintenance and/or repair would be enhanced at the expense of reliability, to retain the same availability.

4. Application Reliability Requirements

Reliability requirements vary considerably from application to application. For example, the reliability objectives of an electronic telephone switching office designed for use in telephone applications are (1) a total system downtime of no more than three minutes per year with a mean time to repair (MTTR) of four hours; and (2) no more than 0.01 percent of the calls should be lost or handled incorrectly during the system's operation (Downing et al., 1964). Satisfactory operation, in this case, is not 100 percent reliability; a few incomplete or wrong connections are permissible, since the customer is expected to immediately redial and obtain the correction. On the other hand, a malfunction in critical equipment, such as underwater amplifiers in the transatlantic cable system, may cause an entire system to become inoperative. In this case, satisfactory operation requires all amplifiers to be working. This situation can be compared to a chain of Christmas lights connected in series; when one light is defective, none of the others will be energized.

The length of time of operation for a telephone switching system is simply the life span of the equipment that makes up the system. The switching system must function continuously, without interruption, until the equipment is replaced at the end of its life, or for any other reason. Since service must be provided twenty-four hours a day, there can be no scheduled system downtime for repair or maintenance. The reliability objective of three minutes downtime per year and the MTTR of four hours can be translated into system availability of 99.9996%.

In contrast, the application of critical aircraft control, as in the case of the SIFT (software-implemented fault tolerance) (Wensley, *et al.*, 1978) and FTMP (fault-Tolerant multiprocessor) (Hopkins, *et al.*, 1978) projects, demands ultra-high reliability. The design specifications require that the system must experience less than 10^{-9} failure in a ten-hour mission time with an MTTR of ten hours. The availability factor is equal to 99.9999999%.

The reliability requirements to a large degree determine the architecture of the system, the type and amount of redundancy, and the cost. Dual redundancy proves to be adequate to meet the telephone application. On the other hand, for critical aircraft control, triplication and sparing are necessary to achieve the high degree of reliability.

5. Fault Classification

There are three major categories of error sources in a system: *design mistakes, physical faults*, and *human operator interaction faults* (Avizienis, 1972). These error sources contribute to system failures. Although design mistakes occur in both hardware and software, software errors are much more predominant and are also difficult to eliminate from the system. Physical faults, on the other hand, are generally the result of component aging or environmental influences that cause certain characteristics of the equipment to deviate beyond the specified limits. These faults are referred to as *hardware faults*. Inappropriate operator actions at control and maintenance panels may destroy the sanity of the system. Operator inputs normally have high priority, with many systems fatally vulnerable to inappropriate commands and typographical errors.

System failures are functionally classified as *hardware, software*, and *procedural*. The three types of system failures are closely related to the categories of error sources. Physical faults occur in just the hardware. Design mistakes, although they occur in the hardware, mostly cause software system failures. Procedural errors are usually caused by mistakes made by the system's operator. The percentages of system downtime attributed to each category depend on system hardware configuration, redundancy structure, software complexity, and human-to-machine interface. For example, Figure 6 shows the field experience for AT&T's 1ESS processor. The percentages in this

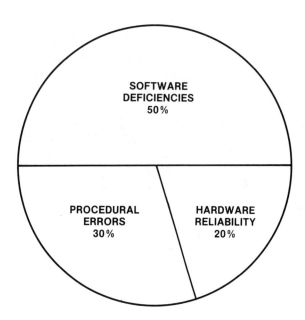

FIG. 6.   Causes of system outages for AT&T 1ESS processor. Based on data from Staehler and Watters (1976).

figure represent the fractions of total downtime attributable to the various causes (Staehler and Watters, 1976) Software faults account for 50 percent of the downtime, compared to 20 percent attributable to hardware and 30 percent caused by procedural errors.

These percentages are reasonable because the 1ESS processor is duplicated. If one of the units fails, its duplicate is switched in, thus maintaining continuous operation. Meanwhile, the defective unit is repaired. It is rare that a hardware fault occurs in the duplicated unit during the repair interval, but when it does happen, the entire system fails. The redundancy structure tolerates a single hardware fault, but simultaneous hardware faults (one in each processor during the repair interval) cause system outages and contribute to the percentage of system downtime attributed to hardware faults.

Procedural errors account for about 30 percent of the downtime. This figure is comparable to those experienced in commercial computer sytems. In transaction-based computer systems, such as Tandem, the proportion between hardware and software faults, indicated in Figure 6, is considerably different from those of ESS systems (Wallace and Barnes, 1984). This is due to the proportion of hardware and software for two diverse applications. In ESS systems, the vast amount of software (many millions of lines of codes), constant updates, and frequent feature additions contribute to the complexity and volatility of software components in the system. In transaction-based machines, the application requires a large data base, hence a large number of disk drives. The hardware dominates in this type of application. As a result, many of the system failures are attributed to hardware faults. Procedural faults are approximately the same for both systems.

5.1 Hardware Faults

Reliability is often thought of as the qualitative judgment of the performance of a device or system. The reliability of hardware components may be measured quantitatively, though, because components fail at statistically predictable rates. The engineering definition of reliability—the probability that a component will perform a required function under controlled conditions for a specified period of time—becomes appropriate for analyzing component faults. Statistical analysis generally assumes that the hardware being tested is initially free of faults and that it deteriorates with time.

In addition to normal device failures, environmental conditions (radiation), design faults (mistakes), and inadequate margin (timing problems) all contribute to hardware faults. Design mistakes, as in the case of software faults, are more difficult to measure quantitatively. The reliability calculations discussed previously have been based mainly on device faults.

5.2 Software Faults

In contrast with hardware faults, no software failures result from aging. Software faults are caused by errors in the specifications and in their implementation. There are many special cases that the software architect may overlook or handle improperly.

The basic elements of software are structures whose behavior does not change with time. Software faults result from design errors by incorrect combinations of instructions. The interactions between instructions are much more complicated than the interconnections of hardware components. A physical machine has a relatively small number of distinct internal states, compared with a software system. Software architects usually assume that the hardware designs are correct. The software design, however, has an enormous number of different states to consider; even after extensive validation efforts, the correctness of the design of a large software system cannot be assumed. There are no available techniques for measuring the number of software faults in a program, and every change to a software system creates a new system that has different reliability properties from the original one. The correction of a software error may have side effects in other parts of the system that increase rather than decrease the total number of errors. Obviously, correcting a software error is not as simple as correcting a hardware error, by just replacing a faulty component with a good one, but once the software faults are corrected, they do not recur as do those caused by hardware.

Software faults are not predictable, except that they exist in every system. Several definitions of software reliability are in use. One definition states that software reliability is the probability that a software system will perform its intended functions for a specified number of input cases under state input conditions. Since the sequence of code executed depends on the values of the input parameters, the probability of obtaining the correct result also depends on the input data. This definition is probabilistic, because of the uncertainty in the selection of input parameters when the system is in operation. Exhaustive testing of all possible input cases is usually not possible. Thus some software faults manifest themselves only when untested input cases occur in the actual operation of the system.

For a large software system, exhaustive testing is usually unfeasible. Some programs always contain residual errors that survive the design, development, and testing stages. The occurrence of software errors in the development of the program may be expected to follow a decreasing pattern (Figure 7). Initially, the system contains a large number of software faults. As the system is used more frequently and is operated at its full capacity, major errors are detected

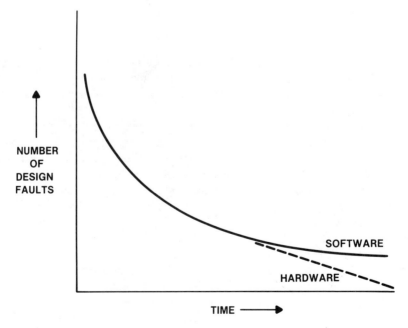

FIG. 7.   Software faults in a large system.

and corrected, thereby reducing the total number of faults within it. The number continues to decrease asymptotically with time to a limit of some fixed positive number. One may expect a number of software faults monotonically decreasing toward zero, since faults are constantly detected and removed from the program. This is the case for the hardware design faults, as shown in the dotted line in Figure 7, because the hardware design becomes stable with time. Software, however, is so easily changed that it rarely becomes stable. Each software change introduces new errors, so that the value of the lower limit is a function of the rate at which new capabilities are added to the software. The process of correcting a detected error may unintentionally introduce some subtle errors in other parts of the program. Another reason for constant software faults is that a large portion of the program is not tested or exercised. Faults in this portion of the code remain latent for indeterminable amounts of time.

The behavior of the system with several major software releases may follow a pattern similar to that of Figure 8. Each release represents a major revision and update of the program specifications and modifications of the software module to include new features. If more of the residual type of software faults are detected and corrected before a program is released for field or commercial

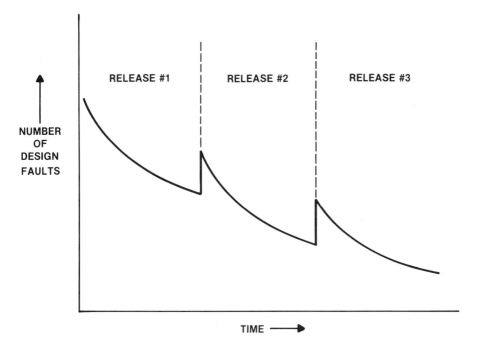

FIG. 8. Software faults in a multiple release program.

use, the peaks of the curve are reduced and the product becomes more reliable. This is the objective of the evaluation and validation process.

5.3   Procedural Faults

Human errors by maintenance personnel and operators also cause system failures. Procedural faults, also referred to as *interaction faults*, are caused by inputs to the system through operator–machine interfaces during operation or maintenance that are not appropriate to the current state of the system. These errors are statistically unpredictable and occur at an unpredictable rate. They may be caused by inadequate and incorrect documentation (for example, user's manuals), or simply by not following instructions in the relevant operating manuals. For example, an operator may mistakenly remove a busing cable between the central processing unit and the main store, completely disrupting the entire system. It is probably impossible to anticipate and provide safeguards against all possible procedural faults.

The problem of procedural faults has continuously remained a great concern to users of information processing systems. Several approaches help avoid interaction faults. Many companies have extensive operator training and explicit and complete operation and maintenance manuals. Another approach reduces the number of errors by having operators work on more sophisticated and user-friendly systems; their sophistication also includes the replacement of control panels by more intelligent microprocessor-based consoles. Including well-established protocols into the design of the operator– machine communication interfaces may screen operator inputs for many types of mistakes, but procedural faults still enter systems at high rates.

The occurrence of interaction faults may be expected to follow a decreasing pattern similar to that of software faults (Figure 7). In the early stage, there are a considerable number of interaction errors resulting from inadequate or incorrect documents and inexperienced operators. As these shortcomings are corrected, the procedural errors decrease asymptotically with time. Shortcomings in the software to deal with the operator procedures are also corrected to improve the robustness of the system. Interaction faults continue to decrease to a fixed number, however, since human operators are not perfect. There is also continual turnover of operators, which tends to perpetuate procedural errors.

6.   Effect of System Utilization

The failure rates or reliability curves for the hardware, the software, and the procedural operator-to-machine interfaces all are high in the early-life period. These faults decrease and settle to a constant level as the system matures.

Weak hardware components are replaced, design errors are corrected, and procedural interaction is refined. The wear-out phase is present only in the hardware component curves, since each component eventually wears out and is replaced.

Software reliability must take the operating environment into account. A large program contains so many possible flow paths that exhaustive testing is not feasible. Consequently, large programs are not expected to be completely fault free. Many of their faults are not detected until a specific combination of input variables occurs. The probability of exposing these latent or dormant faults increases with system use. There is a distinct relationship between failure rate and system use for both hardware and software faults. The statistical study done at Stanford Linear Accelerator Center (SLAC) of their computer complex, which consists of two IBM 370/168s and one IBM 360/91 in a triplex mode, shows an increased system failure rate with higher levels of use (Butner and Iyer, 1980). The failure rates are the lowest during nonworking hours. They increase rapidly as the working day begins (8:00 A.M.) and peak before and after lunch hour. The end of the working day is made apparent by a significant decrease in the failure rates. This study shows the direct relationship between the failure rates and the amount of use a particular module or subsystem receives.

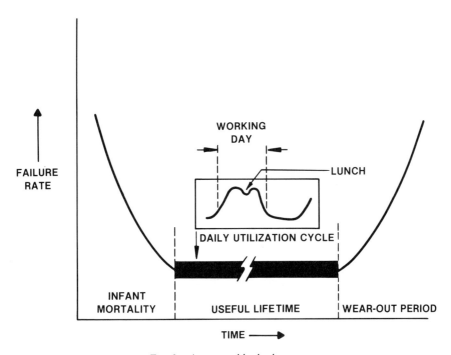

FIG. 9. Augmented bathtub curve.

Other studies support this relationship between systems' activity and their failures (Castillo and Siewiorek, 1980). These observations indicate that the overall failure rate is composed of two separate quantities. The first is the inherent failure rate as determined through the classical reliability models. The second is the induced failure rate, which depends on system utilization and is cyclic on a daily basis. The classic bathtub curve may be augmented to incorporate this cyclic effect (Figure 9) (Butner and Iyer, 1980).

7. Redundancy Techniques

If a computer were fault free, the hardware and software would always behave predictably. The perfect computer has not been built, however, and failures in both hardware and software do occur. Hardware failures may affect the control sequence or data words within the machine. This results in errors of two types:

1. The program sequence is unchanged, but the failure affects the final results.
2. The program sequence is changed, and the program no longer executes the specified algorithm.

Software faults are the results of improper translations or implementations of the original algorithms. The flow of instruction execution deviates from the correct control sequence. In many instances, unfortunately, hardware and software faults are indistinguishable. Systems therefore need to be tolerant of faults and able to compute correctly in their presence, regardless of their sources.

A good way of making computers tolerant of faults is by making parts of them redundant. Redundancy allows computers to bypass errors so that the final results are correct. This is known as *protective redundancy* and consists of combinations of hardware, software, and time. *Hardware redundancy* consists of additional circuits that detect and correct errors. *Software redundancy* consists of additional programs that reestablish an error-free working system under trouble conditions. It may include fault detection and diagnostic programs to periodically test all logic circuits of the computer for hardware faults. *Time redundancy* consists of a retrial of an erroneous operation. It includes the repetition of a program or segment of a program immediately after the detection of an error. The retrial is often done by hardware. For example, hardware logic may initiate the automatic reread of a memory location in which a parity failure is detected.

Although protective redundancy is functionally classified into three separate types, one type may encompass one or both of the other types. In the case of software redundancy, the control program requires both memory space (hardware) and execution (time). Each of these types of redundancy and their various combinations have been employed in the design of fault-tolerant computers; the choice of emphasis depends on the user application and the associated reliability requirements.

7.1   Hardware Redundancy

There are two types of hardware redundancy: static and dynamic. The static approach uses massive replication of components, circuits, and subsystems. Error correction occurs automatically. Dynamic redundancy requires additional parts or subsystems to serve as spares. Both static and dynamic redundancy techniques are used in complex computer installations.

7.1.1   Static Hardware Redundancy

In systems where the most-frequently encountered type of failure in a component is an open circuit, paralleling two of the components introduces redundancy. Figure 10a shows a parallel connection of diodes. The failure of a single open-circuit diode does not influence the circuit operation. If most failures are short-circuits, a series configuration is necessary to compensate for them (Figure 10b). If the probability of failure is equal for both modes, a combination of series and parallel arrangements is the best method for correcting single errors (Figure 10c).

Failure detection is extremely difficult when static redundancy is applied at the component level, since the component failure is masked out by the redundant hardware. If the fault is not susceptible to masking and causes an error, it will go undetected and not be corrected. For a repairable system design, this method of fault correction is undesirable from the viewpoint of fault isolation; i.e., a fault may not necessarily be recognized at the system level and isolated to a specific unit.

On the circuit and subsystem level, von Neumann's original concept of majority logic has been widely studied and enlarged upon by many reliability designers, particularly for military applications. This technique involves triplication of the functional blocks and the use of voter circuits (Figure 11). Voter circuits restore the proper output when a fault is present in one of the functional blocks. To safeguard against failures in the voter circuit, majority logic is applied to them as well.

Error correction codes are another type of static hardware redundancy. Techniques based on error correction codes employ additional hardware and

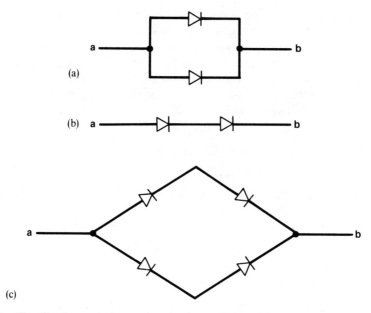

(a)

(b)

(c)

FIG. 10. Circuits employing static redundancy: (a) Parallel redundant circuit; (b) Series redundant circuit; (c) Series-parallel redundant circuit.

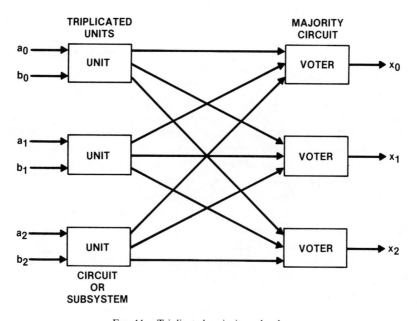

FIG. 11. Triplicated majority redundancy.

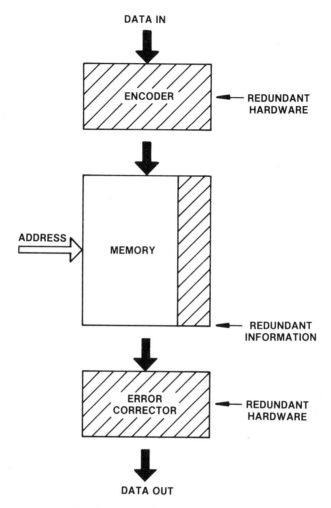

FIG. 12. Redundancy in an error correction scheme.

information (data), for example Hamming correction codes. Figure 12 shows functionally the redundant hardware and information for error correction in a memory system.

7.1.2 Dynamic Hardware Redundancy

Dynamic redundancy, also referred to as *selective redundancy*, requires judicious choices to give the most effective protection against failures. In response to an error, the faulty unit is automatically (or manually) replaced with a good unit to correct the trouble. The selected circuit, before its use, may be active (powered) or passive (unpowered). There are three necessary steps in the dynamic redundancy procedure: error detection, diagnosis, and fault recovery. The foremost step in the procedure is detecting the error quickly. If the fault-detection logic points to a fault within a single replaceable unit, the second step (diagnosis) is not needed, but if the fault-detection logic embraces a number of replaceable units, diagnosis must be initiated to pinpoint the faulty unit. During diagnosis the fault is analyzed by either special hardware or software diagnostics; the result of the analysis assigns the fault to a specific device or unit. The third and final step is the recovery action of eliminating the fault by replacing the offending unit with a working unit. In addition, for a real-time control system, if the error occurs in the middle of an operation some program rollback is necessary to discard the bad data and to recover as much good data as possible.

7.2   Software Redundancy

Redundant software protects the system from hardware and software faults by additional programs and instructions at both the macro and micro levels. If the hardware of a computer were fault free, some degree of software redundancy would still be necessary to ensure reliability (Avizienis, 1975).

Like hardware redundancy, there are two types of software redundancy. Static software redundancy employs extensive replication. Replicated (separate) programs are written and executed concurrently on separate hardware facilities. Fault detection is performed by comparison. When more than two programs exist, majority decision by software provides the means of immediate error detection and correction. This is a software equivalent of the triple-modular redundant (TMR) system.

Dynamic software redundancy is frequently used in conjunction with dynamic hardware redundancy. When the system detects a failure, error recovery is required to configure the system around the faulty component. Software copies of the state of each system component are made from time to time during normal system operation. To correct the erroneous states of the machine caused by a failure, the system rolls back to the latest software copy of the states.

A rollback operation makes use of the concept of *checkpoint*. A checkpoint is a scheduled point in the execution sequence when the system saves its states. Program rollback forces execution to restart at the last checkpoint and then begin processing the data saved; it assumes the data is unmutilated. Error recovery must therefore involve both hardware and software to ensure continuity of operation or at least to minimize the disturbance of the system.

N-version programming is an example of static software redundancy (Chen and Avizienis, 1978; Avizienis and Kelly, 1984). Different versions of a program are written and run concurrently on separate hardware. Their outputs are compared before any action is taken. If one of the versions of the program disagrees with the others, the results of the majority are used, as it is in the triple-modular redundant hardware structure. If one version of a program is faulty, it is not necessary to take it out of service, since it is likely that versions of other programs will later agree. The only error recovery that may be necessary is to make the data used by the faulty program consistent with that used by the other versions. This may be done by copying the data used by one of the other versions. If the fault is in the hardware, the correct result of the majority is used. The N version (independently written programs) provides protection against both hardware and software faults, but the amount of effort to write N versions of a program and the amount of processing power required for running the N versions are about N times the effort and processing power needed for a simplex program.

Rather than expending N times the effort in program development, a more effective approach is to develop a single reliable program using highly structured and formal models to prove the correctness of the software. By developing formal techniques to ensure that the programs operate correctly, the difficult problems of writing multiple versions of the program, testing them, administering and maintaining the program package, and updating changes are thus avoided. This approach is taken in the software-implemented fault tolerance (SIFT) system designed by Stanford Research Institute for real-time aircraft control (Wensley, 1972; Weinstock, 1980). As the name implies, reliability depends primarily on software mechanisms. The system software is proven mathematically to be correct and is run independently by a number of computer elements. The correct output is chosen by a majority vote implemented by software, in contrast to the hardware voters used in triple-modular redundancy structures.

7.3   Time Redundancy

Time redundancy, or *retrial*, is another form of redundancy. Retrial is used to correct errors caused by transient faults. By repeating programs or parts of programs, retrials correct errors caused by transient faults. The system architecture must make several decisions about the retrial (Avizienis, 1972);

1. where the retrial must begin to ensure correction of the error;
2. the probability (and necessity) of correcting the error that caused the fault, by the rollback action;
3. what the cost/benefit ratio is for the rollback, in terms of real-time, hardware usage, and software constraints;
4. whether the operating system will permit the rollback;
5. the consequences of the rollback in the real world.

The machine must be restored to the state of the rollback point; all actions and data changes made after the rollback point as a result of program execution must be restored. Singular events in a real-time system that represent output commands to initiate irreversible actions should not be repeated; for example, an I/O operation in the process control of drilling or cutting a machined part should not be made twice. If such an event is repeated because of a rollback, serious consequences in the real world may result. Provisions to handle singular events must be incorporated into the rollback procedure.

The use of time redundancy in data transfer or I/O communication is much easier and is more effective in correcting transient errors than the use of hardware and software redundancy. For example, if the data received contains an error, the error check circuitry can initiate a retry. The source or sender retransmits the same data. If no error is detected in the retrial, the system proceeds as if nothing had happened. The event is recorded for later analysis. It is completely transparent to the software.

8.   Hardware Fault Detection Techniques

Both the static and the dynamic redundancy structures described in the previous sections are methods of providing spare parts to enable the system to tolerate failures. When static redundancy is used, the spare units (components, circuits, or subsystems) are permanent parts of the system. They correct errors or mask them to prevent them from propagating throughout the system. The masking function takes place automatically; corrective action is immediate and "wired in." Static types of redundancy have been used primarily in military applications that require high reliability for a short duration, and more recently in commercial applications (see Section 13.3).

Dynamic redundancy, in which additional subsystems serve as spares within the system, has been employed in commercial applications. The major components are fault detection, fault diagnosis (isolation), recovery, and repair. The most important component in dynamic redundancy is fault detection (Figure 13). If all errors were detected and the appropriate techniques were applied to recover from them, no fault would lead to a system failure. This type of coverage cannot be achieved in practice.

The speed of fault detection facilitates the process of fault location and error containment. It is important to perform the next step, fault handling or isolation, as quickly as possible so that faults do not propagate extensively and are contained within a specified unit. Delayed detection can corrupt important data throughout the entire system. The speed of detection is also important for locating the source of an error: the longer the delay, the harder it is to unwind the system and find the source. Inaccurate diagnosis prevents the working

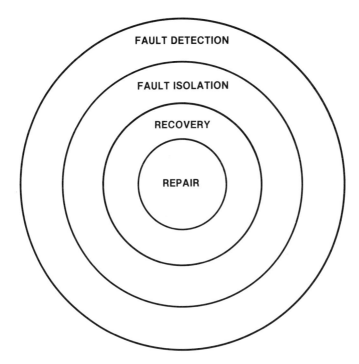

FIG. 13. Components of fault tolerance.

spares from replacing defective units. Furthermore, the speed of detection directly affects system recovery.

In general, error detection is accomplished through the use of hardware, firmware, and software. The type of checking circuitry used depends on the logical structure of the machine, as well as on the operational and functional use of the data and the control signals.

The hardware error-detection circuitry incorporated in a computer system can take many forms. Most of these detection techniques fall into these broad classifications (Anderson and Lee, 1981):

- replication checks
- coding checks
- timing checks
- exception checks

Error detection may be strategically located within a functional unit or at the interface (Figure 14). There are benefits to be gained when detection is done internally at the earliest possible stage, which is during the system activity that

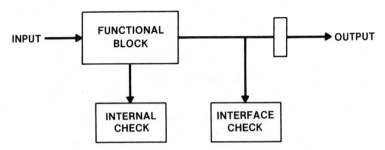

FIG. 14.   Placement of error detection.

generates the results. Internal or early checks minimize the amount of system activity and erroneous transition caused by a fault. There is less time for damage to spread within the system, and the actions necessary for fault isolation and error recovery are more likely to be simple. On the other hand, interface or last-moment checks are deployed before any results from a functional unit are transmitted to another functional unit. This prevents any errors from propagating externally to another functional unit and simplifies the more difficult problem of global recovery. The error is contained within the level in which it is detected.

8.1   Replication Checks

Replication checking is one of the most complete methods for detecting errors in a computer system. It is also the most expensive redundancy technique, because of the hardware required for it. Rapid advances in VLSI and microprocessor technology, however, are beginning to make this type of redundancy cost effective for many applications that require high reliability.

Replication checks detect hardware faults. They are based on the assumption that the design of the system is correct and that component failures occur independently. A replication-check system has an identical copy of a circuit (or subsystem) processing input signals in parallel with the original circuit. The two sets of outputs are then compared by a simple match circuit. No faults in either version of the circuit can remain undetected if the system design is correct and the components fail independently.

Replication checks are made at the circuit or subsystem level. The choice of level is influenced to a large degree by the overall fault-tolerant design; the architect must consider reliability, cost, and performance objectives. The arrangement of arithmetic logic units (ALUs) exemplifies replication checking at the circuit level (Figure 15). ALU 1 is duplicated and the outputs of the two ALUs are matched after each ALU operation. The outputs from ALU I are used as the actual source of the ALU results sent to the rest of the processor

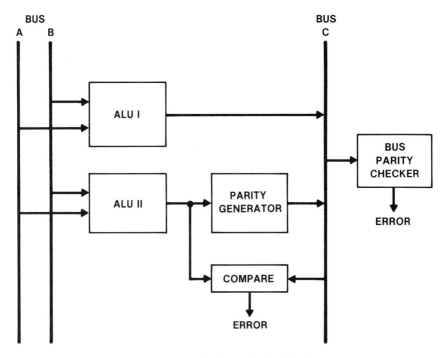

FIG. 15. Replication at the circuit level.

logic. When the outputs from ALU 1 are gated onto the output bus, the data is moved into the comparator and matched against the outputs of ALU 11. This completely checks the results of the ALU operation. The parity of the result is generated from the outputs of ALU II.

In the AT&T electronic switching systems replication checks are made at the subsystem level. The approach adopted by the designers of the 1ESS, 1A ESS, 2ESS, and 4ESS switching systems is based on the duplication and match philosophy (Toy, 1978). In this approach, both central processing units handle the same input information and run in synchronism with each other. Critical outputs from each machine are matched against one another at the completion of each internal machine control operation. Only one CPU, called the on-line machine, actually handles the call processing. The second CPU functions as a standby to the on-line CPU, so that matching may be performed. Peripheral equipment is controlled by the on-line CPU. When the outputs from the two CPUs do not match, a fault detection program is called to determine which CPU is faulty. Figure 16 shows the 2ESS system configuration, a much simpler structure than that of the later 1A ESS switch. There is only one matcher in the 2ESS switch; it is located in the nonduplicated maintenance center (Beuscher et al., 1969). The matcher always compares the

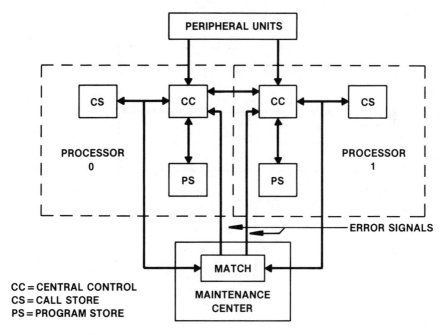

FIG. 16.   2ESS match access.

call store input registers in the two CPUs when call store operations are performed synchronously. A fault in almost any part of either CPU quickly results in a mismatch in the call store input register. This occurs because almost all the data manipulation performed in both the program control and the input–output control involves processed data returning to the call store. The call store input is the central point where data is eventually funneled through to the call store. By matching the call store inputs, an effective check of the system equipment is provided. Compared to the more complex matching of the 1A ESS CPU, error detection in the 2ESS CPU is not as fast, since only one crucial node in the processor is matched. Four are matched in the 1A ESS processor (Budlong et al., 1977). Certain faults in the 2ESS processor go undetected until errors are propagated into the call store. This interval is usually no more than tens or hundreds of microseconds. During such a short interval, the fault affects only a single telephone call. The duplication and match approach is cost effective and practical, since the spare unit is required only for uninterrupted service.

Replication in a system need not be limited to duplication. Multiple copies of a system module may be used, as in the case of triple-modular redundancy systems. When three or more copies of a system module are employed, the comparison check is referred to as *voting*. Voting ensures that erroneous output is suppressed in favor of, or masked by, the majority output. Higher orders of redundancy make error correction possible, by identifying which copy of the module is erroneous. The error detection capability is the same whether the unit is duplicated or triplicated. Note, however, that an error check based solely on duplication and matching does not identify which copy of the system unit contains the fault.

An example of replication checks in a triple-modular redundant system is the Fault Tolerance Multiple Processor (FTMP) developed for aircraft computers (Hopkins *et al.*, 1978). FTMP is a multiprocessor system consisting of a number of processing modules, global memory modules, and input–output modules connected together by multiple buses. Specialized hardware enables three modules of the same type to be configured to operate in what is termed a *triad*. Figure 17 shows a simplified view of a triad of FTMP modules logically connected and operated as TMR units. All activity is conducted by triads of modules and buses. A module triad is formed by associating any three identical modules with one another. This means that any module may serve as a spare in any triad. One triad of bus lines is always active for each of the buses in the system. Each module has access to all the bus lines and contains a decision element to select the correct version of three bus lines. There are five bus lines, three of which (depicted as solid lines in the figure) are enabled. They are connected to a voter in each module, thus constituting a TMR element. The other two bus lines (dotted lines) are not enabled and serve as spares. The three active bus lines carry three independently generated versions of data, each coming from a different member of the triad that is transmitting the data (solid line to the bus) on one specific bus line.

The replication checks based on identical copies of a subsystem do not detect the consequences of design faults. Design faults affect all copies of the unit; hence they are not detectable by replication. Formal design verification techniques must be employed to ensure that there are no design faults in the structure that could bypass the protection provided by the replication.

8.2   Coding Checks

Error detection codes are formed by the addition of check bits to a data word. The error detection capability of this approach is a direct function of the number of check bits included in a word. There are two types of coding checks: separate and nonseparable. *Separable* checks, including parity checking and arithmetic codes, are characterized by the addition of check bits to data words. *Nonseparable* checks, such as m-out-of-n code, are coded in specialized formats.

Parity checking is the most widely used type of coding check, because it requires a minimum number of check bits yet provides good error-detection

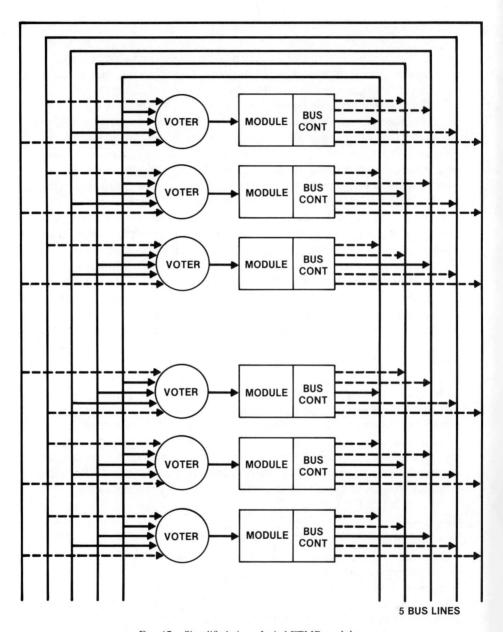

FIG. 17.   Simplified view of triad FTMP modules.

capability. Parity checking, a type of separable error-detection code, is accomplished by assigning a parity bit to a data word. An odd-parity check requires that both the check bit and the total number of bits in the ones state in the data word be odd numbers. An even-parity check requires that the check bit and the total number of bits in the ones state in the data word be even numbers. For example, data words 10110100 and 10101000 contain, respectively, four ones (an even number) and three ones (an odd number). For an odd-parity check, the check bit must be set to one in the first data word and zero in the second data word; that is, to 101101001 and 101010000, respectively. In this example, the check bit occupies the least significant bit position of each data word. For an even-parity check the check must be set to zero in the first data word and to one in the second data word. Any single-bit errors or odd multiple-bit errors are detectable by a single parity check bit. Faults caused by an even number of erroneous bits are not detected by the parity checks, however, since an even number of errors appears transparent to the parity check logic. Parity checking is used extensively in data paths and memory systems in electronic switching systems (Toy, 1978).

Another type of separable code used for error detection is arithmetic codes (Avizienis, 1971). These are based on remainder theorems for residue arithmetic. The major difference between the two code categories is that residue codes are preserved under arithmetic operations. For residue codes the operands (x, y) and their check symbols (x', y') are handled separately; (x, y) generates the result z, while (x', y') generates check result z'. The checking algorithm computes the residue from the result z and compares it with the check result z'. If the two values match, no error is detected. A disagreement between the two values is considered a fault, either in the main arithmetic unit or in the check circuit. Arithmetic codes are rarely used in LSI and VLSI fault-tolerant system design, since the present trend is toward inexpensive hardware and single-chip CPUs. It is much more economical to duplicate and compare results for error detection (Toy, 1978; Gallaher and Toy, 1981).

The *fixed-weight* or *m-out-of-n* code is an important type of nonseparable coding check. In coding theory the *weight* of a code word is defined as the number of its nonzero components. Therefore a fixed-weight code has a fixed number of ones. The unique property of the fixed-weight coding check is its ability to detect all unidirectional multiple-bit errors. This type of error occurs when a fault causes all data bits in the code word to either change from the zero state to the one state or vice versa. Unidirectional errors cause the code word to have a different weight, making the errors detectable by the checking logic. Errors that cause transitions in the states of the data bits in both directions simultaneously are not always detectable using fixed-weight coding checks.

Encoded binary signals used in a computer system represent two types of information: data and control. The data signals in turn represent a variety of entities, including numbers, characters, addresses, and labels. These entities may be used directly, without modification, or may be operated on by any of the arithmetical or logical functions available on the processor, to compute specific values needed by the currently executing program. Separable error detection codes (systematic codes) such as parity allow the original data to be determined without any additional decoding. This characteristic is quite convenient for processing and handling data signals within the computer system. For control functions the binary encoded signals may similarly employ separable error detection codes, but these signals are usually decoded at their destinations (e.g., the logic gates that generate each of the control signals). Therefore nonseparable error detection codes with special characteristics are more effective for detecting errors on individual control signals. M-out-of-n codes have been employed extensively in the 3ESS processor (Cook et al., 1973) and the (Avizienis et al., 1971).

A *cyclic* code is a type of separable code that forms a code word from any cyclic shift of the code. Cyclic codes are easy to encode and decode using linear feedback shift registers, so they are quite commonly used for checking serial data streams. These codes have been developed to provide efficient error detection for blocks of data. For instance, a cyclic-redundancy code check is used in the disk stores of the 1A ESS switching system (Ault et al., 1977) and in the 3B2OD disk system (Hagland and Peterson, 1983). A detailed mathematical treatment of error detection techniques using coding schemes is given by Peterson and Weldon (1972).

8.3 Timing Checks

Hardware checking procedures such as replication and coding techniques are designed to detect physical circuit faults in the arithmetic logic units, the data path(s), the control sections, and one or more specific subsystems. In general, hardware error checks are not capable of detecting software faults. Even when two processors are running in synchronism and are matched for error detection, the same error may appear in the program executing in the on-line machine and in the copy of the program executing in the standby machine. The error can therefore go undetected.

Timing checks are an effective form of software check for detecting errors in duplicated programs, if the specification of a component includes timing constraints. The operating system normally oversees and coordinates the activities of the system. For some applications, such as in the control of a telephone office, the operating system is cyclic in nature; that is, its program always returns to its basic starting point upon completion of the scheduled tasks. The main program is normally exercised and debugged thoroughly before it is integrated into a system load. It is rare, however, that every conceivable path in the program has been checked under all possible conditions. Consequently, some of the less-frequently traversed branches of the main program may contain subtle logic faults that may sidetrack the main flow of the execution sequence so that it never returns to the main program. This situation, of course, may also result from undetected hardware faults and program bugs.

A hardware timer, also referred to as a *watchdog* timer, is used in telephone switching systems to guard against program faults from which the system cannot recover. The concept is relatively simple. A hardware timer runs continuously in the processor and is periodically reset by the main program if nothing unusual occurs to deflect the latter from its normal execution sequence. If for some reason (such as a software bug or a hardware fault) the execution sequence never returns to the main program, the timer is not reset. It then issues a high-priority interrupt request and takes the necessary action to reinitialize the system. When a redundant standby processor is provided in the system, the timer interrupt may automatically cause control to switch to the standby machine in an attempt to recover from the system error.

Circuit operations, particularly those involved in communication between two functional units, also use timing checks. For example, in memory access the data transfer between the CPU and the main store is usually done asynchronously by handshaking. When a memory read operation is initiated, the CPU waits for a response signal from the memory control unit, indicating that the addressed data word is ready to be transferred. If, for certain reasons such as a hardware fault in the control logic, the response signal is not generated, the CPU will wait indefinitely. Since the normal memory read operation only takes a certain amount of time, a hardware timer can be used to detect errors.

In the nonstop Tandem computer, timing checks are integrated into the operating system as one of the major error detection measures (Katzman, 1978). Each processor sends a special message every second to all the other processors in the system. Each processor then checks every two seconds whether messages have been received from the other processors. If a message is not received, the corresponding processor is assumed to have failed and appropriate action is taken. Timing checks are also made for all input–output operations.

Although timeout signals from a hardware timer indicate a problem in the system, their absence does not necessarily mean that the system is performing satisfactorily. Timing checks on a circuit function are not complete system checks. They reveal the presence of faults, but not their absence. Consequently, computer architects use timing checks to supplement other checks, to cover a higher percentage of faults in a system.

8.4   Exception Checks

Programs run in protected environments following sets of prescribed constraints. If the programs are fault free, they observe the constraints and perform the specified functions accordingly, but design faults in the software often violate these constraints and thus may adversely affect the entire system. Some hardware detection circuits are usually designed into the system to recognize the design faults and handle them as exceptions. Exception handling therefore refers to detecting and responding to abnormal or undesired events.

These constraints may be attributed to either the hardware or the software. Some hardware examples are:

- improper address alignment
- unequipped memory locations
- unused opcode
- stack overflow

These constraints usually result from the inability of the hardware to provide the service needed by the software. Take, for example, the case of improper address alignment. In many modern computers integer data types of 8, 16, 32, and 64-bit sizes (byte, half-word, word, double word) are supported by their instruction set. It is convenient and simpler from the hardware viewpoint to have these data types aligned on the word boundary that matches the layout of the main memory (Figure 18). By aligning the data types on word

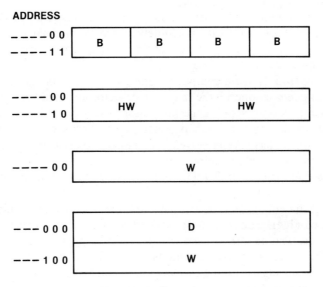

FIG. 18.   Data-type layout.

boundaries, deviations from the format are detected as exceptions of improper address alignment. A hardware constraint, of course, places an additional burden on the programmer to observe predefined constraints. As hardware costs continue to decrease, it is appropriate to reduce or eliminate some of the hardware constraints. For example, the VAX 11/780 has integer data types of 8, 16, 32, and 64 bits. The system has been generalized so that these data types occupy 1, 2, 4, and 8 contiguous bytes, starting on any arbitrary byte boundary. Considerations like this are becoming increasingly prevalent in modern computer design.

The software structure also places certain constraints on the system to enhance its robustness and provide a protected environment for application programs. Some software exception checks are:

- illegal execution of privilege instructions
- out-of-range address
- memory access violation
- illegal operands
- invalid arithmetic operations, such as overflow, underflow, and division by zero

The detection of an error raises an exception, which is followed by the automatic invocation of the appropriate exception handling facility. In many cases, the exception is attributable to a design fault in the program.

9. Software Detection Techniques

The need for developing software mechanisms for detecting software errors is increasingly apparent if reliable systems are to be built. Hardware mechanisms, though technologically well advanced, can detect and isolate faults in the hardware but are not proficient in analyzing software faults. Early software detection schemes rely on hardware protection mechanisms such as exception checks to indicate when program errors occur. This reliance on hardware mechanisms is inefficient, though, because often by the time a software error causes a hardware exception, it has propagated to affect an unnecessarily large area. The original error may compound itself so severely that it goes undetected and uncorrected. In large systems the approach of detecting software errors based on the principle that they eventually cause hardware exceptions is unfeasible (Kopetz, 1979). Better software error-detection capabilities are needed, but designing them is not easy, because software faults are not as distinct as hardware component failures. They must be detected rapidly during program execution, especially in real-time systems.

In many cases a process stops rather than continues, resulting in a wrong operation, since many of the results are damaging and irrevocable. Unlike hardware component failure rates, there are no reliable statistics on the behavior and distribution of various software faults. Design faults are extremely difficult to characterize and enumerate in terms of expected failure modes. Software error detection can only be carried out by recognizing the *abnormal* behavior of the system. A set of standards for normal behavior is thus required, to check deviations from it. By checking the reasonableness of the program behavior at various stages of computation, errors are detected early enough to restrict the propagation of bad data.

There are several general techniques for observing the behavior of a computer system to detect malfunctions (Morgan and Taylor, 1977; Yau and Cheung, 1975):

- *Function of a process.* The reasonableness of the outputs for a given set of inputs is checked at the functional block level. Certain performance measures may be used to indicate whether the system is functioning properly. When the applied workload is normal but measurements that characterize the performance of the system (such as response time, throughput, and time required to perform a standard function) fall outside established threshold values, the system probably has one or more errors.
- *Control sequence of a process.* The sequence of computations made by an executing process is referred to as its *control sequence.* Each computation changes various system states, and system abnormalities may be detected.
- *Data of a process.* The integrity of the system's data and its structure can be observed while the system executes the program sequence. Mutilation of system data can also be caused by software or hardware trouble.

A *process* is defined here to mean a self-contained portion of a computation which, once initiated, is carried out to its completion without the need for additional input.)

9.1 Functional Checking

The functional aspects of a process may be checked by verifying the reasonableness of the outputs for a given set of inputs. When the relationship between the inputs and outputs is one to one, *reversal* checks may be used to check the correctness of the process. A reversal check takes the outputs from the system and computes what the inputs should have been. The calculated inputs are then compared to the actual ones to check for error conditions. In the AT&T 1A ESS switching system, a simple reversal check is applied to a magnetic-tape write operation by reading the data written onto the tape and comparing it to the original data. Well-defined mathematical functions often lend themselves to reversal checks. For example, if the output is the solution of a set of mathematical equations, its correctness may be verified by substituting the output in the equation and checking for consistency. In some cases, there may be a simple relationship between the output variables. The output can be verified by checking this relationship. For example, the output of a sorting program may be tested to ensure that it is indeed sorted (ordered) and contains the correct number of elements.

In many other cases, the correctness of the output can only be verified by an algorithm that is just as complicated as the original algorithm and is therefore subject to design faults of its own. This situation further complicates system reliability. A rigorous check on the correctness of the output is impractical, so only the reasonableness of the output is checked. An unreasonable output usually indicates the presence of errors, but not vice versa.

Timing checks, as mentioned in Section 8.3, are also used to check given processes. A timing check is a classic way of easily observing the internal performance of a system while detecting bottlenecks and infinite loops. The procedure is to set the interval timer to sound an alarm after an adequate time elapses for the system to perform its function unless something goes wrong. If the timer interrupt occurs before the system has reset it, the interrupt handler must assume that the process has not been carried out properly. Again, it is a check for reasonableness. The lack of a timeout does not imply the absence of errors.

Software functional checking is analogous to a black-box approach in testing a hardware system, examining the relationship between the inputs and the corresponding outputs. Software functional checking, however, is neither efficient nor effective. A better approach to error detection is achieved when a direct access of an internal structure monitors its internal behavior, including its control sequence and the dynamic behavior of critical or global variables.

9.2 Control Sequence Checking

When each task represents a well-defined set of operations, the correct sequence in which these operations are executed determines the proper output of a process. Any deviation from the specified execution sequence produces a faulty output. A software fault that causes an incorrect execution sequence is called a *control fault*. A control fault may cause the following consequences:

- execution of an infinite loop
- execution of a program loop an incorrect number of times
- traversal of an illegal or wrong branch.

These types of error conditions can be detected by various schemes designed for sequence checking. The three types of control sequence that have been implemented are *branch-allowed checks*, the *relay-runner scheme*, and the combined watchdog timer and relay-runner scheme.

A branch-allowed check is a means of detecting the execution of an improper branching operation. This type of check is implemented in several AT&T electronic switching systems (Gallaher and Toy, 1981). As shown in Figure 19, a check bit called the branch-allowed (BA) bit is assigned to each word in the main memory. If the BA bit contains a zero, the contents of that location in main memory may not be referenced by any branch instructions.

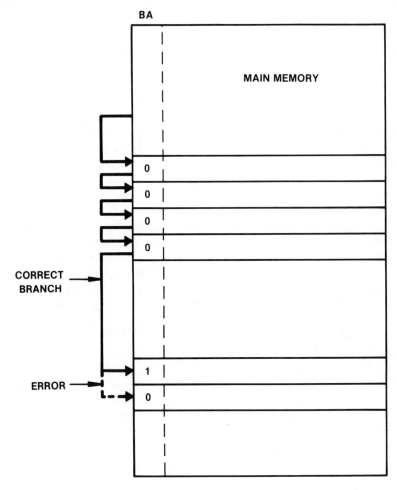

FIG. 19. Branch-allowed check.

The location, however, may be referenced by the program counter (PC) in its normal sequential addressing mode (that is, the mode in which the PC is incremented by one to point to the location of the next instruction). If the BA bit contains a one, the contents of that location may be referenced by any branch instruction located anywhere in main memory. If a branch instruction is being executed in a normal processing sequence, the BA bit of the target location is checked to see whether a branching operation can reference the contents of the target location. If the BA bit is in the zero state, an improper branch has been executed and the BA checking logic indicates that an error has occurred.

The relay-runner scheme also provides protection against illegal jumps that may be caused by software errors or hardware malfunctions (Ramamoorthy *et al.*, 1974). *In this scheme a baton,* which is similar to a password, is carried along with the transfer of control and checked at the appropriate points. When an illegal branch is taken, control does not have the valid baton value. The error is detected at the next checkpoint. Figure 20 shows a flow diagram of the relay-runner scheme. A piece of the program is partitioned into functional blocks separated by relay checkpoints. These checkpoints are conditional statements to test whether the program flow carries the valid, up-to-date baton code. The application program enters the first of a series of baton codes in a specified address, for example, CODE1. When program execution reaches the first relay checkpoint, the instruction compares the content at CODE1 with a preset code number. If they agree, the content of CODE1 is cleared to zero and a new baton code is stored in location CODE2. If the codes do not agree, an error-trap routine is invoked and normal execution terminates. The process of checking and updating the baton code is performed at various strategic points throughout the program. The scheme is analogous to a relay race, in which one runner does not proceed until receiving a baton from the previous runner.

The combined watchdog timer and relay-runner scheme (Kraft and Toy, 1981) combines the effectiveness of the watchdog timer operation for detecting infinite program loops with the ability of the relay-runner scheme to detect faults in the control structure of program sequencing. Although the operation of a hardware timer is simple to implement in most processors (see Section 8.3), additional safeguards to program sequencing and generating timer reset signals are provided by the relay-runner scheme. The hardware timer must be reset only when the system is performing properly; otherwise the timer should be allowed to request a recovery action. For example, the program may be segmented, with relay checks inserted at the appropriate points (Figure 21). In addition, a marker keeps track of the number of checkpoints the program has traversed. The timer is activated at the first program segment. Before a reset timer is generated, the program must pass through each checkpoint success-fully and have gone through a correct number of checkpoints. The second

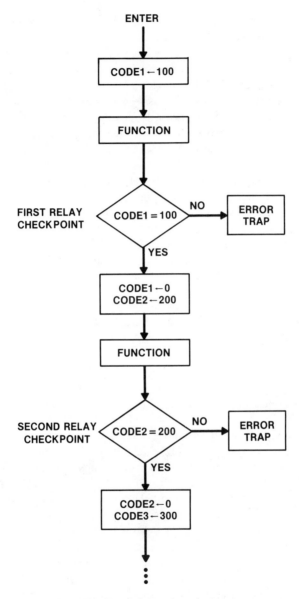

Fig. 20.   Relay-runner scheme.

check is redundant, in that the relay-runner scheme ensures that all segments are sequenced correctly. If the program jumps ahead by one or more program segments, the baton code will not match the code number at the next checkpoint. If the program backtracks one or more segments, the old baton

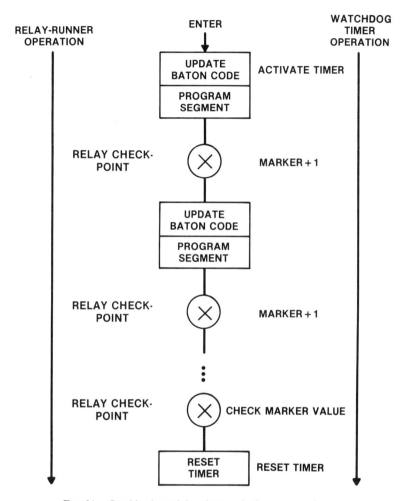

FIG. 21. Combined watchdog timer and relay-runner scheme.

value has been reset to zero; the relay-point check will also detect this condition.

9.3 Data Checking

Software errors, as previously indicated, may be caused by residual software design faults, as well as by hardware faults. Each can result in the mutilation of memory. Although "data" usually refers to the information items to be processed by the program, it refers generally to all information stored in main memory. This means both program instructions and data. Text containing the program instructions may be checked by a functional check or a control sequence check, as described in previous sections. The integrity of the data value of the instructions may be easily protected by coding techniques such as Hamming correction codes and maintaining a checksum of the content of a piece code. The Hamming correction code is very effective in ensuring the integrity of data values for both instructions and data as they are used and processed.

Besides instructions, data checks may be performed by in-line program checks or by independent software error detection programs, called *audits*. In-line checks include code in the system to check the validity of data structures each time they are processed by the system routines. If data structures are checked before they are used, errors previously introduced by system components are identified immediately after they are modified, and the routine causing an error is usually identified. For example, if an item is inserted in a linked list, a check can be made on the link in the opposite direction to verify its integrity after the insertion. Properly constructed tests can detect many errors with a small amount of processing. On the other hand, extensive checking often introduces an unacceptable overhead and substantially degrades performance.

Another effective in-line check covers parameters passed to the system routine by user programs. It is quite possible that an error in one routine will cause another routine to fail, because of an invalid parameter. This conceals the original source of the error. Since checking all the parameters passed between system routines would undoubtedly consume too much overhead, a more structured check with adequate error detection capability may be applied, as is done in the SUE operating system (Sevcik *et al.*, 1972). This approach takes advantage of the levels of structure of the program environment; parameters are checked as they pass from a higher to a lower level. User programs, for example, are at a higher level than system supervisory programs. The checks are not made in the reverse direction, nor are parameters checked between routines on the same level. A balance between error checking and the overhead of in-line checking is achieved with this straightforward procedure.

An alternative to in-line checking is auditing. Audits are integrated in the system software, and thus normally consume only a small portion of the total processing capacity of the system. The system invokes audits periodically to run routine checks. Audits may be invoked manually when trouble is suspected. Audit programs check for inconsistencies in the data structures, which usually reflect erroneous system operations. They do not anticipate problems or determine their causes. Thus they are fast, thorough error-detection mechanisms.

Several techniques used by audit programs are similar to those for in-line checking. These techniques include consistency checks, linkage checks, integrity checks, and time-out checks. *Consistency checks* are made on redundant information stored as backup records. For example, if the program and critical data are stored in main memory, a backup recovery copy is placed on a low-cost disk system. When changes are made, records are kept of both previous and changed versions. The comparison of the updated backup record with the main memory provides a means for detecting an error is the main memory. Correction is done by simply overwriting mutilated data from the secondary storage. Furthermore, if necessary, the previous version of the program may be reloaded to allow more drastic initialization.

Linkage checks verify that registers associated with facilities are validly linked together, by using the redundancy inherent in the linkage structure. For example, when a doubly linked list is audited, redundancy permits the last entry on the list to be identified by the previous one and the next entry. Similarly, a loop-around check may be made of registers linked in a circular list.

Integrity checks are made on state data associated with facilities. These checks are done by verifying the consistency of the data with the actual states of the resources. Error-detecting codes may be employed to code the state of facilities.

Time-out checks locate facilities that may be falsely put into the busy state. If an absolute limit is placed on the holding time of a facility, the facility may be examined at a period equal to the maximum holding time. If the audit finds a facility in the nonidle state longer than the maximum time allowed, it assumes that the facility is lost and can be idled and therefore restores it to the operational state.

Audit programs sample, rather than continuously observing the system's behavior; hence they require less overhead than in-line checks. They do not, however, provide as timely a detection of errors as do in-line checks. Many routines may access invalid data before an audit program determines that an error has occurred. Subsequent operations with the erroneous data may cause other system data to become corrupted, making recovery more difficult and drastic. The relatively low overhead of audit programs, allows them to check on the other hand, the system more extensively than in-line checks.

10. Fault Recovery

Recovery is the most complex and difficult function of all systems (Toy, 1978). Shortcomings of either hardware or software design to detect faults when they occur has a direct effect on the system's ability to recover. When faults go undetected, the system remains impaired until the trouble is recognized. Another kind of recovery problem can occur if the system is unable properly to isolate a faulty subsystem and configure a working system around it. The many possible system states that may arise under trouble conditions make recovery a complicated process.

The more rapidly an error is detected, the easier it is to determine which component is faulty and thereby perform fault recovery. Rapid error detection and good error containment are therefore fundamental to successful fault recovery.

10.1   Classification of Recovery Procedures

There are three classes of recovery procedures: full recovery, degraded recovery, and safe shutdown (Avizienis, 1978). The recovery procedures may be invoked automatically—with no known interaction between the maintenance operator and the system—or manually. Manually initiated recoveries may make use of extensive program—controlled sequences. The three classes of recovery procedures are described below.

● *Full Recovery.* In a real-time facility, the system providing continuous service must remain operational even in a faulty environment. This means that trouble symptoms must be recognized quickly and faulty units repaired with little or no interference from the user's standpoint. To provide full system capability at all times, appropriate spare subsystems must be available as replacement units for defective ones. A full recovery procedure usually requires all five aspects of fault-tolerant computing: fault detection, fault isolation, system recovery, fault diagnosis, and repair. The sequence of events is depicted in Figure 22. Before any system action, the fault must be detected. The objective of fault isolation is to identify the subsystem (for example, a memory module, a processor unit, an input–output channel controller, etc.) where the fault occurred. By using automatic program-controlled switching, the system is reconfigured by interchanging the faulty subsystem with its corresponding spare. The recovery procedure is then initiated to restore the system to its original computing capability with no loss of hardware or software features. The period of interrupted service during the recovery procedure is minimized and is hardly noticeable to the user. Diagnosis and repair, the most time-consuming tasks of the recovery procedure, may be deferred and interleaved with normal system operation (Figure 22).

● *Degraded recovery.* This is also referred to as a *graceful degradation* operation. As in the case of full recovery, all the steps involved with fault tolerance (detection, isolation, system recovery, diagnosis, and repair) must be included in the procedure. The sequence of events shown in Figure 22 also applies to a degraded recovery, except that no subsystem is switched in. Instead, the defective component is taken out of service and the system is returned to a fault-free state of operation. Selected computing functions in systems using degraded recovery are allowed to operate so that their real-time

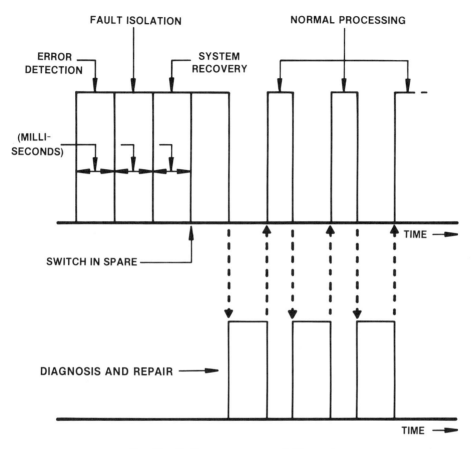

FIG. 22. Fault recovery sequence (with spare).

performance characteristics fall below a normally accepted standard until repairs are made.

• *Safe shutdown.* This is often called a *fail-safe* operation. It occurs as the limiting case of degraded recovery, when the system computing capability has degraded below a minimally acceptable threshold of operation. The goals of safe shutdown are

1. to avoid damaging any system elements or stored software modules (programs or data) that may still be compromised after degraded operation has been allowed to take place
2. to terminate interaction with any associated systems (users) in an orderly manner
3. to deliver diagnostic and shutdown messages to designated users, systems, and maintenance personnel.

The safe shutdown category is similar to a system without any redundancy (Figure 23). Action to isolate the fault must be initiated to determine its identity and location. The normal system operation, which had been momentarily interrupted at the time of fault detection, must now be suspended through diagnosis and repair. The system must then be recovered to a hardware state and program point where normal processing can be resumed.

All three types of fault recovery require certain operations to take place after the fault is detected. A comparison of Figures 22 and 23 illustrates some of the maintenance advantages of hardware redundancy. First, the time-consuming task of diagnosis and repair may be deferred and interleaved with normal system processing on a time-shared basis after the system has been restored to the operational state. Second, the availability of a spare permits the fault-free machine to interrogate and diagnose the faulty machine. This type of testing is easily made automatic under program control. Otherwise it is necessary to have an operator manually force the machine through the diagnostic and recovery steps.

10.2 Reconfiguration

In redundant systems, an ensemble of spares or multiple functional units ensures a continuously working system. The simplest structure is a duplex configuration, in which every functional unit is duplicated. If one of the units fails, the duplicated unit is switched in and continuous operation is maintained while the defective unit is repaired. Should a fault occur in the duplicated unit during the repair interval, the whole system will of course go down, but if the

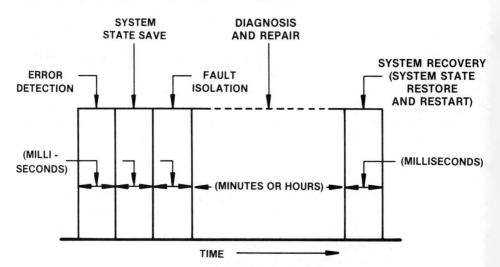

FIG. 23. Fault recovery sequence (without spare).

repair interval is relatively short, the probability of simultaneous faults occurring in the two identical units is quite small.

The capability of the system to dynamically reconfigure its modules into a working system provides the continuous operation required for many critical real-time applications. In general, hardware redundancy at the subsystem level is essential to fault tolerance and ease of repair. Several structures have been used successfully to achieve high availability by means of dynamic reconfiguration. Figure 24a shows the simplest duplex structure. The CPU and its associated bus are duplicated. One machine is in the active mode and controls the system; the spare is strictly a standby unit. In this arrangement, standby machines do not produce or contribute any useful work except in emergencies. Figure 24b shows a load-sharing arrangement in which both CPUs are actively performing concurrent operations. The faulty processing unit is switched out of service when a hardware error that reduces the

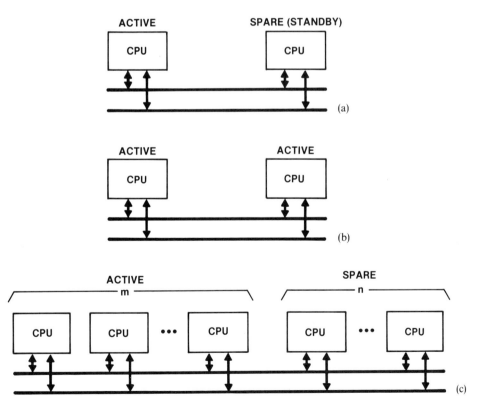

FIG. 24. Dynamic redundant structures: (a) Duplex—spare; (b) Duplex—active; (c) Multiprocessors—roving spares.

performance capabilities of the system is detected. If the application can tolerate this sort of degradation, the multiple active configuration provides better overall system performance than a simple duplex system.

The approach of combined multiple processors with standby spares is shown in Figure 24c. Demands for performance and reliability are ideally met by this structure. It is modular, in that the system can grow gracefully by adding processing modules. High reliability is met by the number of roving spare modules provided in the pool. If one of the active modules fails, a roving spare is substituted and the system recovers to its fullest capability. Full performance is maintained until all the spares are exhausted.

The active-standby duplex structure, as shown in Figure 24b, is quite simple and straightforward. Because of its simplicity, this redundancy structure has been used throughout the ESS processors (Toy, 1978). For medium and small ESS processors, Figure 25 shows a system structure containing several functional units that are treated as a single entity. The structure consists of two store communities, program store (PS) and call store (CS). The program store is in read-only memory and contains the call processing, maintenance, and

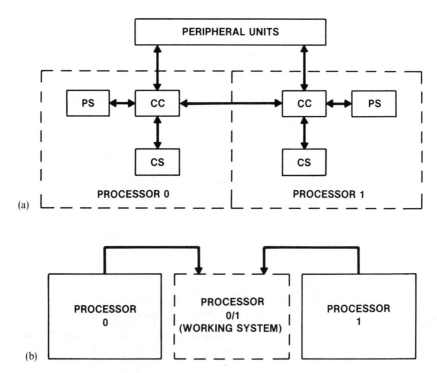

FIG. 25. Single-unit duplex configuration. (a) Processor structure. (b) Two possible configurations.

administration programs. It also contains long-term translation and system parameters. In this arrangement the complete processor is treated as a single functional block and is duplicated. This type of single-unit duplex system has two possible configurations: Either processor 0 or processor 1 can be assigned as the on-line working system while the other unit serves as a standby backup (active redundancy). The single-unit duplex configuration has the merit of being very simple in terms of the number of switching blocks in the system. This configuration simplifies not only the recovery program, but also the hardware interconnections, because the additional accesses required to make each duplicated block capable of switching independently into the on-line system configuration are eliminated. In the large 1ESS switching system, which contains many components, the mean time to failure (MTTF) becomes too low to meet standard reliability requirements. To increase the MTTF, either the number of components (failure rate) or the repair time must be reduced. The single-unit duplex configuration can be partitioned into a

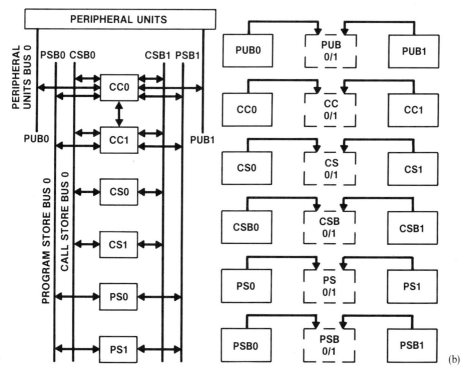

FIG. 26. Multiunit duplex configuration. (a) Processor structure. (b) Sixty-four possible configurations.

multiunit duplex configuration (Figure 26). In this arrangement, each subunit contains a small number of components and can be switched into a working system. The system will fail only if a fault occurs in the redundant subunit while the original is being repaired. Since each subunit contains fewer components, the probability of simultaneous faults occurring in a duplicated pair of subunits is reduced. A working system is configured with a fault-free $CCx-CSx-CSBx-PSx-PSBx-PUBx$ arrangement, where x is either subunit 0 or subunit 1. This means there are 2^6 or 64 possible combinations of system configurations. Reconfiguration into a working system under a trouble condition may be an extensive task, depending on the severity of the fault. For example, the processor may lose its ability to make proper decisions. This problem is addressed in the 1A ESS processor by an autonomous hardware processor configuration circuit in each CC to assist in assembling a working system (Budlong *et al.*, 1977).

10.3   Software Recovery

The objective of error recovery is restoring the system to a consistent state from an erroneous one, thus allowing the system to function properly. There are three error recovery strategies: backward error recovery, forward error recovery and resets (Anderson and Lee, 1981). The *backward error recovery* technique, also called *rollback-and-retry*, involves validating and saving the system state (for example, saving the contents of registers within a processor and of main memory in a reliable backup storage) at various stages during program execution. As shown in Figure 27, the points during execution at which system states are saved are called *recovery points*. If an error is detected, the backward recovery technique reestablishes the system to a previously recorded state and restarts the program execution. If does not precisely identify the source of the error, and after each backward recovery the work that has been discarded must be repeated.

The rollback and retry recovery technique is not suitable for hardware faults, because the same error conditions result. For the backward recovery to work in this situation, the rollback must be done in fault-free hardware. For example, in the Tandem computer system the program is made up of process pairs (Bartlett, 1978). One of the processes is considered primary, with all program execution done in it. The other process is the backup process, consisting of the recovery point and periodic updates of the backup process. The checkpoint is data located in different processor hardware. The checkpoints ensure that the backup process has all the information needed to take over control in the event of a failure of the primary process.

In the case of a software fault, a different strategy is needed. Software reconfiguration can overcome the problem of repeating the same errors by

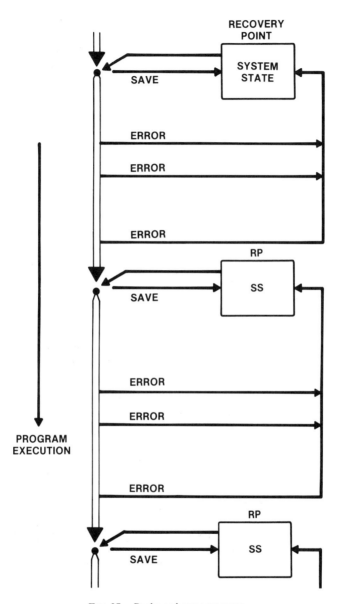

FIG. 27.   Backward error recovery.

replacing a suspected software module with an alternative version. Figure 28 shows the *recovery block scheme*, which is a structured method of combining three techniques: the use of error detection routines, backward recovery, and the use of multiple versions of software modules (Horning *et al.*, 1974).

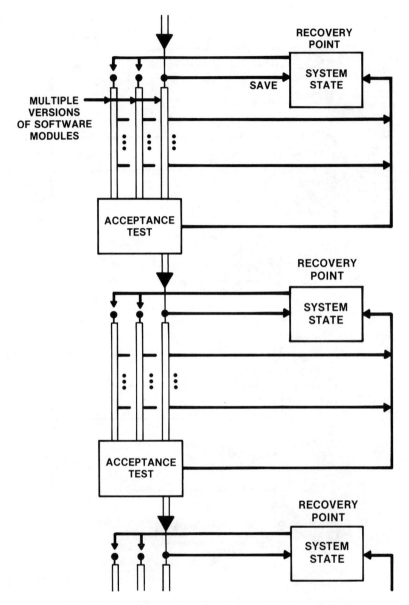

FIG. 28.   Software reconfiguration (recovery block approach).

Multiple versions of software modules produce the same or similar computational results by using an acceptance or validation test as a criterion for
determining the acceptability of the execution results of software modules or
object blocks. If the acceptance test fails, the process rolls back to the recovery

point and makes another try with an alternative object block. An imperfect design of an object block is thus bypassed.

In contrast, *forward error recovery* techniques have the system itself make further use of its present erroneous state to obtain another state (Figure 29). Forward error correction is usually highly application dependent. It relies heavily on knowledge of the nature of the fault and its consequences. For example, a real-time control system in which an occasional missed response to a sensor input is tolerable can recover by skipping its response and proceeding

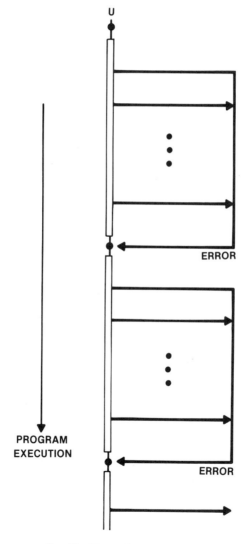

FIG. 29.   Forward error recovery.

immediately to the following input samples. Although forward recovery must be designed specifically for each system, it recovers from faults efficiently when the faults are known and their full consequences anticipated (Anderson and Randell, 1979).

The most drastic approach to recovery from unanticipated damage caused by system faults is a fixed *reset*. A reset is a comprehensive approach to

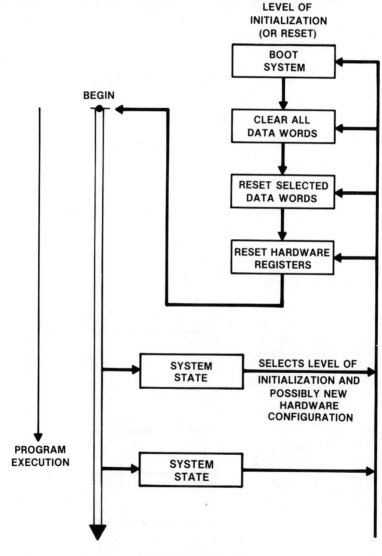

FIG. 30.   Reset recovery.

recovery because it places the system in a predefined (fixed) state. Resets are designed primarily to reduce the effects of failures, rather than to prevent their occurrence. An example of this is the telephone switching system, in which some telephone calls are lost, yet the system continues to provide service. Figure 30 shows a reset arrangement consisting of a set of initialization states to which the system may be reset. The actual reset level used for a particular error condition is selected by the system state at the occurrence of the error. If the error is caused by a hardware failure, for example, the selection includes a new hardware configuration to ensure a successful recovery.

In the 2ESS switching system there are six levels of initialization programs for system recovery (Kennedy and Quinn, 1972). The levels are similar to those shown in Figure 30. At level 1 hardware registers are reset. Levels 2 through 5 incrementally clear call data from the system and reset the corresponding data structures. All transient data in the call stores are cleared at level 6. The level of initialization is done successively, in increasing order of severity, until no further errors are detected.

11. Fault Diagnosis

Whereas fault detection determines whether a circuit is operating correctly, fault diagnosis localizes the failure to a replaceable unit. The replaceable unit may be a component, a circuit, or a subsystem. The fault diagnosis routine uses fault detection hardware and test sequences to help locate the defective unit. If fault detection identifies a single entity as the source of the fault, diagnosis may not be necessary, since the fault can be corrected simply by replacing the entity. If the detection circuit is less specific, however, the fault diagnosis routine may be required to further isolate the offending unit.

The modern packaging technique of using LSI and VLSI circuits to implement both memories and processors has encouraged the use of large-size circuit boards. Fault resolution does not need to be as precise when the standard repair procedure is to replace the circuit board containing the fault. First, a processor is typically implemented on one or two large circuit boards. If a fault occurs and is isolated to one of the two processor boards, repair by replacement is a quick, simple, and cost-effective approach to servicing the faulty unit. The cost of replacing an entire circuit board is justified when one considers the advantages of faster repair times and the savings realized by not having to develop additional fault diagnosis hardware and software.

When the detailed fault resolution requirement is relaxed because of the use of large boards in the processor's implementation, a basic problem still exists. That is, after the faulty unit has been replaced, the integrity of the replacement unit must be verified to ensure that it does not have a fault itself. The complete system, including the replacement unit, must be exercised exhaustively to ensure that the difficulty has been corrected. This may often amount to a complete diagnostic test sequence being applied to the repaired system. Even though the processor hardware incorporates additional logic to act as an aid in detecting faults and isolating the faults to a specific unit in the processor, a complete evaluation of the hardware by the processor diagnostic program is still required.

Test generation for digital logic circuits has been studied extensively since the mid 1960s. The objective of these studies has been to develop a systematic procedure that allows a designer to derive a set of tests that exposes all possible faults in a logic circuit. The basic philosophy observed by designers of such test sequences is to apply an input sequence (test vectors) to a specific logic circuit that causes the output(s) to differ from those in a normal, fault-free condition. The identification of the appropriate test sequences for a complex LSI logic circuit can be a highly laborious procedure, even with the use of sophisticated computer programs. There are essentially four techniques that are used extensively: the path sensitizing technique, the D-algorithm technique, the Boolean difference technique, and Poage's technique. These procedures are described in considerable detail in several excellent references (Breuer and Friedman, 1976; Chang *et al.*, 1970).

One of the most important aspects of diagnostic design in the early planning stage is the specification of features to be incorporated in the hardware (such as test points, observation points, private control points, signature analysis, level-sensitive scan design) the diagnostic uses to evaluate the hardware. These features must be specified and agreed on during the hardware design phase by both the logic designer and the diagnostic programmer.

With the high cost of labor, the concept of remote and centralized maintenance appears attractive for many installations. In this approach, the expertise necessary to perform system maintenance is concentrated at a central location. Instead of dispatching technicians to the site of a faulty machine, faults are diagnosed remotely. Standard telephone lines are used as the data links to the centralized maintenance facility. Computer systems such as the VAX 11/780, IBM 4300, IBM System/38, and HP 3000 Series 33 all provide remote diagnostic capabilities (Digital Equipment Corp, 1977; Durniak, 1979; Nelson, 1978).

12. Reliability Validation

One of the more difficult tasks of maintenance design is fault recovery and diagnosis. Its effectiveness in recovery from a fault and diagnostic resolution can be determined by simulation of the system's behavior in the presence of a specific fault. By means of simulation, design deficiencies can be identified and corrected prior to field use of the system. It is necessary to evaluate the system's ability to detect faults, to automatically recover back into a working system, and to provide diagnostic information (i.e., the location of the fault). Fault simulation is therefore, an important aspect of maintenance design.

There are essentially two techniques used for simulating the faults of digital systems: physical simulation and digital simulation. Physical simulation is a process of inserting faults into a physical working model. When compared with digital simulation, this method produces more realistic behavior under fault conditions. In addition, a wider class of faults can be applied to the system, such as a blown fuse or shorted backplane interconnection. However, fault simulation cannot begin until the design has been completed and the equipment is fully operational. Furthermore, it is not possible to introduce faults to interior points of the logic (i.e., integrated circuits).

Digital fault simulation is a means of predicting the behavior under failure of a processor modeled in a computer program. The computer used to execute the program, called the host, is generally different from the processor being simulated, called the *object*. Digital fault simulation provides a high degree of automation and excellent access to interior points of logic, permitting designers to monitor the signal flow. Another advantage of this method is that it allows diagnostic test development and evaluation to proceed well in advance of unit fabrication. The cost of computer simulation can be quite high for a large, complex system.

Physical simulation was first employed by the Bell System to generate diagnostic data for the ESS field test (Tsiang and Ulrich, 1962). Over 50,000 known faults were purposely introduced into the central control (CC) to be diagnosed by its diagnostic program. Test results associated with each fault were recorded, sorted, and then printed in dictionary format to formulate a trouble-locating manual (TLM). Under trouble conditions it was possible for maintenance personnel to determine which circuit packs might contain the defective component, by consulting the TLM. Using this dictionary technique the average repair time was kept low and maintenance was made much easier.

The experience gained by using physical fault simulation in this field test was applied and extended in the development of the No. 1ESS (Downing *et al.*, 1964). Each plug-in circuit pack was replaced, one at a time, by a fault simulator, which introduced every possible type of single fault. The system's reaction was then recorded on magnetic tape. This was done for all circuit packs in the system. In addition to diagnostic data for TLMs, additional data was collected to determine the adequacy of hardware and software in fault detection and system recovery. Deficiencies were corrected to improve the overall maintenance of the system.

A digital logic simulator called LAMP (Logic Analyzer for Maintenance Planning) (Chang *et al.*, 1974) was designed for the No. 1A ESS development. It played an important role in the development of the 1A processor's hardware and diagnostics. The simulator is capable of simulating a subsystem with as many as 65,000 logic gates. All classic faults for standard logic gates are simulatable as logic nodes stuck at 0 or stuck at 1. Before physical units are available, digital simulation can be extremely effective in verifying the design, evaluating diagnostic access, and developing diagnostic tests. Both fault simulation techniques were integrated for the development of the 1A processor to take advantage of each method's strengths simultaneously. The use of complementary simulation allows faults to be simulated physically (in the system laboratory) and logically (on a computer). Most of the deficiencies of each simulation technique are compensated for by the other technique. They complement one another—hence the term *complementary simulation*. The complementary method provided both a convenient method for validating the results and more extensive fault simulation data than would have been available if either process was used individually (Goetz, 1974).

13.   Examples of High-Reliability Real-Time Systems

In fault-tolerant computing, commercial applications are growing. Much of the earlier work was focused in two major areas, the aerospace and telephone systems. Extremely high reliability is required for aerospace to ensure a high probability of success during a relatively short mission time in which repair is not possible. On the other hand, for telephone applications, high availability is

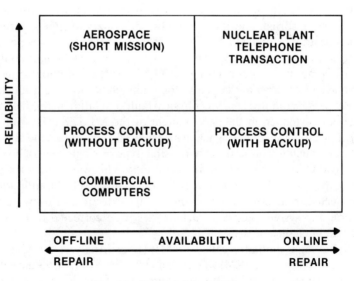

FIG. 31.   Commercial applications.

required even in the presence of a fault while repair is being done on the system. These two applications, plus the rapid expansion of on-line transaction-based applications in recent years represent the upper half in Figure 31. At the bottom, in a typical commercial computer or a process control without backup, where redundancy is minimal, the system must be shut down to await repair when a fault occurs in the machine. During the repair interval the system is not available to the user. If higher availability is required, a backup machine is provided, as is currently done in the process control industry. The switching of the backup into service under trouble conditions is usually under manual control. This trend is currently changing because of the lower cost of integrated circuits, and because of users' needs for greater reliability, particularly in process control applications.

The following sections discuss representative systems that are available commercially for three specific applications: electronic telephone switching systems, on-line transaction-based systems, and process control applications.

13.1   Electronic Telephone Switching Systems

The computer control of the Bell System Electronic Switching Systems (ESS) has been commercially deployed since the 1960s. At the core of every ESS is a single high-speed central processing unit. To establish an ultrareliable switching environment, redundancy of system components and duplication of the processor itself has been the approach taken to compensate for potential machine faults. Without this redundancy a single component failure in the processor might cause a complete failure of the entire system. With duplication, a standby processor takes over control and provides continuous telephone service.

When the system fails, the fault must be quickly detected and isolated. Meanwhile, a rapid recovery of the call-processing functions [by the redundant component(s) and/or processor] is necessary to maintain the system's high availability. Next the fault must be diagnosed and the defective unit repaired or replaced. The failure rate and repair time must be such that the probability is very small for a failure to occur in the duplicated unit before the first one is repaired.

Figure 32 shows the trend of processors for electronic switching systems for the past three decades. The first-generation processors, the No. 1 and the No. 2, were designed specifically for controlling large (several thousand to 65,000 lines) and medium (1000 to 20,000 lines) telephone offices. The predominant cost of these systems, as in most early systems, was the cost of hardware. The advent of silicon integrated circuits in the mid-1960s was the technological advance needed for dramatic performance improvements and cost reductions in hardware. Integrated circuits led to the development of the

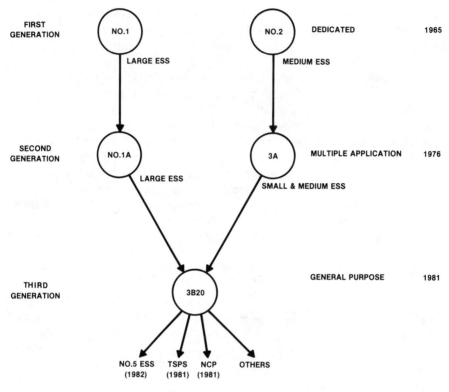

FIG. 32.   ESS processors.

second generation of processors, the No. 1A and the No. 3A. These processors, unlike the first-generation machines, were designed for multiple
applications. The third generation, the 3B20D processor, is a general-purpose
system. Its versatile processing base fulfills the varied needs of telecommuni-
cations systems.

Even with duplication, troubles must be found and corrected quickly to
minimize the exposure to system failure due to multiple troubles. All units are
continually monitored so that troubles in the standby units are found just as
quickly as those in the on-line units. This is accomplished by running the on-
line and standby units in the synchronous and match mode of operation.
Synchronization requires that the clock timing signals be in close tolerance, so
that every operation in both halves is performed in step with key outputs
compared for error detection. Figure 33 shows the duplex-synchronous and
match configurations for the first-generation processors (the No. 1 and the
No. 2) and the second-generation processor (the No. 1A). If a mismatch
occurs, an interrupt is generated, causing the fault-recognition program to

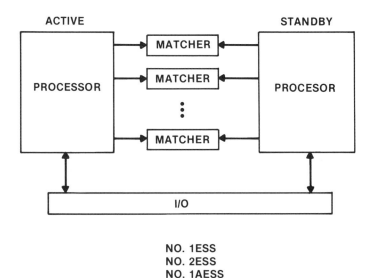

FIG. 33. Duplex-synchronous and match configuration.

run. The basic function of this program is to determine which half of the system is faulty. The suspected unit is then removed from service and the appropriate diagnostic program is run to pinpoint the defective circuit pack.

The synchronous and match mode arrangement of the No. 1, No. 2, and No. 1A processors provides excellent detection and coverage of faults. There are many instances, however, (e.g., periodic diagnostics, administration changes, recent change updates, etc.), when the system is not run in the normal match mode. During these periods, the system is vulnerable to faults, which may go undetected. The rapid advances in integrated circuit technology make possible the implementation of self-checking circuits in a cost-effective manner. Figure 34 shows architecture for the No. 3a and the 3B20D. It operates in the nonmatched mode of duplex operation. Self checking includes error detection circuitry as an integral part of the processor. Faults occurring during normal operation are discovered quickly by detection hardware. This eliminates the need to run the standby system in the synchronous and match mode of operation and the need to run the fault recognition program to identify the defective unit when a mismatch occurs. Normal operation requires the on-line processor to run and process calls while the standby processor is in the halt state, with its memory updated for each write operation. For the read operation, only the on-line memory is read, except when a parity error occurs during a memory read. This results in a microprogram interrupt, which reads the word from the standby store in an attempt to bypass the error.

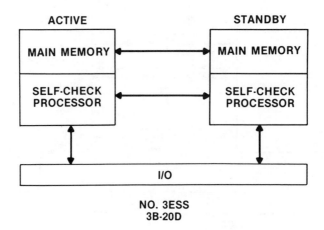

F8ɢ. 34.   Duplex, self-check hardware.

The successful deployment and field operation of many electronic switching systems and processors (notably the No. 3A) have contributed to the design of the 3B20D (Gallaher and Toy, 1981). Previous systems have demonstrated the simplicity and robustness of duplex configuration, which forms the basic structure for both the hardware and software architecture of the 3B20D. Figure 35 shows the general block diagram of the 3B20D processor. The central control (CC), the memory and the I/O disk system are duplicated and grouped as a switchable entity. Although each CC may access each disk system, this capability mainly provides a valid data source for memory reloading under trouble conditions. The processors are not run in the synchronous and match mode of operation, as in early systems (Bell System Technical Journal, 1968; 1969; 1977). Both stores (on-line and standby) are kept current, however, by memory update hardware that acts concurrently with instruction execution. When memory data is written by the CC, the on-line memory update circuit writes into both memories simultaneously. Under trouble conditions the memory of the standby processor contains up-to-date information and a complete transfer of memory from one processor to another is not necessary.

The direct memory access (DMA) circuits interface directly with the memory update circuit to have access to both memories. A DMA write also updates the standby memory. Communication between the DMA and the peripheral devices is accomplished by using a high-speed dual serial channel (DSCH). The duplex dual serial bus selector (DDSBS) allows both processors to access a single I/O device. For maintenance purposes the duplex 3B20D central controls are interconnected by the maintenance channel (MCH). This high-speed serial path provides diagnostic access at the microcode level. It

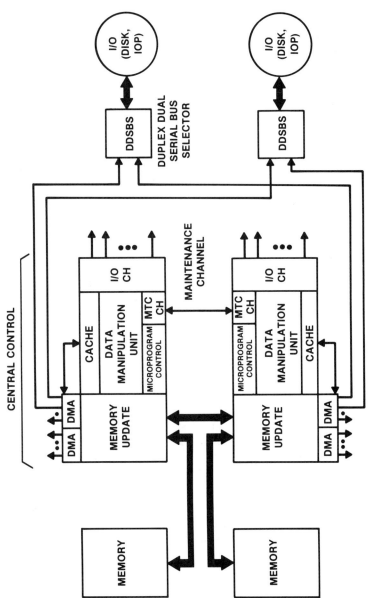

Fig. 35. 3B-20D processor general block diagram.

transmits streams of microinstructions from the on-line processor to exercise the standby processor. Other microinstructions from an external unit help diagnose problems.

The 3B20D processors have been in commercial operation since September 1981. Several hundred systems are providing real-time, high-availability telecommunication services. The performance of the 3B20D improved tremendously during the first two years of operation. Figure 36 shows the results of field data accumulated over many machine operating hours (Wallace and Barnes, 1984). When the first system began commercial service, outages occurred because of software and hardware faults that could only be corrected with field experience. The sharp inverted spikes shown in the figure were caused by combinations of design faults that showed up under unusual sets of system conditions. The one for May 1982, for example, resulted from a hardware problem (noisy power supply) that forced a recovery that was too drastic for the fault. The curve in the figure shows that the availability factor improved as the processor design matured and the operating personnel gained experience.

Figure 37 shows downtime data for three AT&T processors, including the 3B20D (Wallace and Barnes, 1984). The experience gained in the design and field operation of earlier electronic switching systems (notably the 1A and the 3A processors) have contributed to the design of the 3B20D. The reliability (downtime) curves shows that each processor approached its downtime objective more quickly than its predecessor. The data has been smoothed and fit to an exponential decaying function for the comparison.

13.2   On-Line Transaction Processing Systems

The demand for fault-tolerant, high-availability computers is growing at a very rapid pace. This is due to an increasing demand for on-line processing applications. As on-line systems gain increasing importance, system downtime becomes less and less tolerable, since the main stream of the customer's business is on-line. The loss of an on-line system, even for a short-time, will be much more costly than a failure of a traditional batch system. A typical on-line processing application is characterized by many individual users concurrently requiring access to large data bases. The response time is on the order of seconds and the processing of transactions must be error-free.

On-line fault-tolerant computers have been commercially available since Tandem Computers shipped its first NonStop system. It was not until 1982 that another company, Stratus Computer, entered into the market. Since then, there are more than a dozen other companies competing in the fault-tolerant on-line processing market. The first two companies, Tandem and Stratus, are emerging as the leaders in this market place. Each employs a different

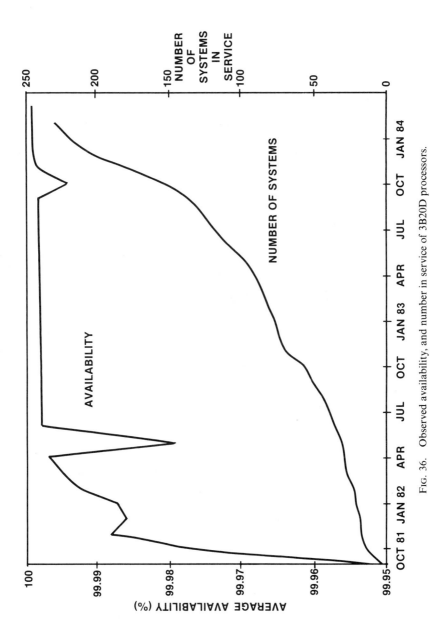

Fig. 36. Observed availability, and number in service of 3B20D processors.

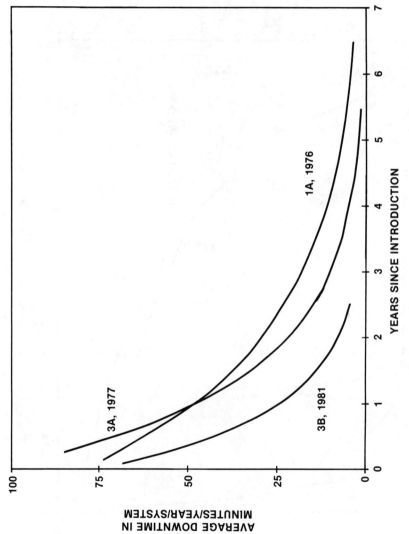

FIG. 37.   Downtime versus time since introduction for three high-availability processors.

approach to achieving fault tolerance. Tandem uses the software-intensive approach, requiring specialized software to reduce the amount of hardware at the expense of performance. This is understandable, since VLSI and microprocessor technology was at its infancy during the time period when Tandem entered the market. Stratus, on the other hand, takes advantage of mature microprocessor technology, using a hardware-intensive approach to achieve fault tolerance. A short description of the Tandem system and the Stratus system is presented in the following sections.

13.2.1   Tandem System (Katzman, 1978; Bartlett, 1978; Serlin, 1984)

The block diagram of a Tandem system in Figure 38 represents a typical four-processor system. A Tandem system can be configured from a minimum of two up to a maximum of sixteen processors. Each processor has its own private memory unit and I/O channels. All device controllers are dual-ported, so that in the event of a processor failure there is an alternate path to all peripherals. The disk can be duplicated or mirrored and is handled by two (or more) dual-ported controllers connected to two dual-ported disk drives, as shown in the figure, giving eight separate paths to any file in the data base.

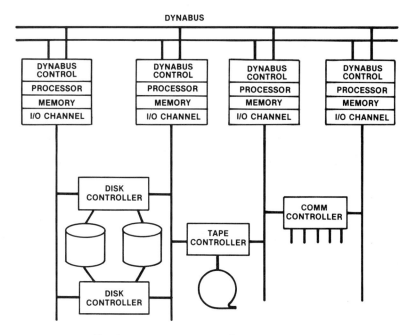

Fig. 38.   Tandem Computers four-process system.

With disk mirroring, the system automatically maintains two identical copies of designated disk drives. Should a disk drive fail, the data base can still be recovered from its mirrored copy. The processors communicate over a high-speed, duplexed, 16-bit parallel bus system call Dynabus. It is capable of transferring data at a rate of 13 megabytes per second. In addition, a processor can communicate on either Dynabus, providing an aggregate bandwidth of 26 megabytes per second.

Each executing program or process is backed up by another processor. The operating system creates a backup copy of a process in another processor. The data area and execution point of the backup process are synchronized to the primary process at essential points, so that the backup always knows what the primary is doing. This procedure, known as checkpointing, is done periodically by the primary process with the checkpoint messages that define the state of the process at critical points in the computation. The operating system in each processor wakes up the relevant backup process upon discovering that its corresponding primary has failed. The backup can then resume the task from the state defined in the last checkpoint.

Checkpointing is conceptually simple, but its efficient application requires a high degree of programming skill and understanding of system details. This checkpointing must be done as part of the application program. It is now managed automatically by the Pathway Transaction Processing system and the Transaction Monitoring Facility (TMF), both of which are part of Tandem's distributed data base management system.

13.2.2   Stratus/32 System (Serlin, 1984; Johnson, 1985)

Stratus's system uses extensive hardware for error detection and spare units for continuous operation. The approach of their implementation is termed "pair and spare." Each functional unit is duplicated (paired) on one circuit board. For self-checking the pair of identical circuits receives identical inputs, with the outputs compared for error detection. A miscompare generates an error signal and disconnects the pair; the spare continues the operation without missing a beat. The pair and spare concept employs quadruplication of hardware: units are duplicated for self-checking and again for spare. This degree of redundancy is economically feasible because of the continual decrease in the cost of off-the-shelf commercial devices. The Motorola 68000 microprocessor that is the heart of the processor circuit board has dropped from $200 in 1983 to around $15 in 1985. The hardware-intensive approach of this implementation has proved to be a reasonable way to design a fault-tolerant computer.

Figure 39 shows the Stratus pair-and-spare architecture. Every functional unit, except the tape controller, has a spare doing the same operation

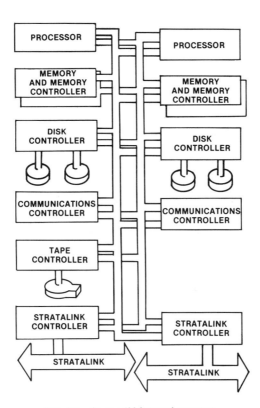

FIG. 39. Stratus/32 internal structure.

though not simultaneously. The processor contains two MC68000 pairs, one that runs the operating system and the second for the user program. There are a maximum of two memory controllers per processor, with each controlling up to 2 megabytes of main memory. Data transfer within a module takes place over a bus within a transfer rate of 16 megabytes/second. Between modules, data is transmitted over a duplex local area network called Stratalink.

The Stratus architecture is attractive from the viewpoint that it requires no recovery from a fault. The operation continues with the spare subsystem. Since no recovery is required, neither are software checkpointing and "I'm alive" broadcasts. The tradeoff for hardware is simplification of the software and an increase in performance.

13.3 Process Control Systems

In the process control area, benefits derived from government-sponsored projects are migrating into the commercial market. A considerable amount of work and accomplishments in triple-modular redundancy (TMR) were done at Stanford Research Institute and Draper Laboratory under separate contracts from NASA to develop a highly reliable computer system for critical aircraft control, during the 1970s. At Stanford Research Institute the key element was the use of software to vote and correct in a TMR configuration, known as the SIFT (software-implemented fault tolerance) project (Wensley, 1972; Weinstock, 1980). At Draper Laboratory, the FTMP (fault-tolerant multiple processors) project employed hardware voter circuits to vote and correct outputs as compared with the software approach (Hopkins *et al.*, 1978). John Wensley, one of the original contributors to the SIFT architecture, left Stanford Research Institute in 1978 and formed the August Computer Company; he designed its product based upon the SIFT architecture. Recently, in 1983, Triconex Corporation (a second company) was formed to compete in the process control market using TMR architecture with hardware voting. Figure 40 traces the TMR technology from government-sponsored project into the commercial market.

Triple-modular redundancy provides a triplication of all essential functional units. Three separate processors are independent of each other, with each processing the complete algorithm. In a process control environment, each processor module scans the values of all inputs. It then accesses the data

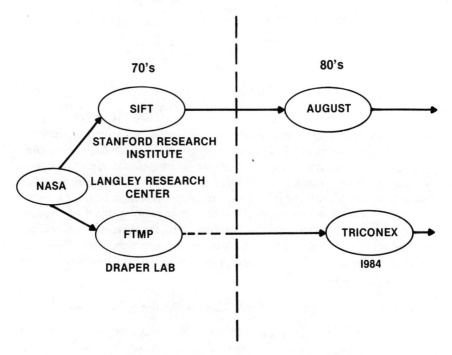

FIG. 40.   High-reliability process control applications.

from the other two modules and compares them. If a discrepancy is found, by a simple two-out-of-three vote, the majority-voted data is used in each of the modules. This voting corrects any error from the input circuitry. The control algorithm is then computed independently by each processor module and the results again compared and voted. The majority output is sent to the external world.

Both August and Triconex employ similar TMR implementations. The following sections briefly describe the architecture of each.

13.3.1   August System (Wensley, 1985)

Figure 41 shows a functional block diagram of the early August Series 330 system. At the left of the figure, analog and digital inputs are brought into the system via the termination panels, which provide signal conditioning, noise immunity, and overvoltage protection. The inputs are converted to logic-level signals at the termination panel. Each of the preprocessed logic inputs fans out to three independent input circuits in the process interface module (PIM). These input boards contain triplicated input channels and independently powered bus structures, each of which interfaces with one of the control computer modules (CCMs) in the control system. The normal flow of the control in the CCMs begins with each CCM scanning the values of all inputs. It then reads from the other CCMs the values they have obtained and carries out, by software, a two-out-of-three vote that corrects any errors produced by any faults in the process interface module. Following this vote and correction, the inputs are processed independently by the control algorithm by each CCM. Before sending these signals to the output circuits, the CCMs once again carry out another vote, this time to remove any possible arithmetic

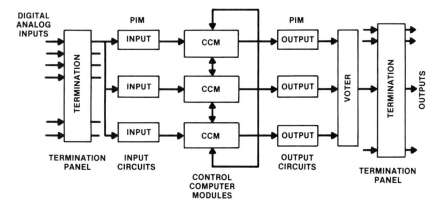

FIG. 41.   August 330 functional diagram.

errors. These outputs are then sent to the output circuits in the respective peripheral interface module (PIM) where a final hardware vote takes place to correct any error possibly caused by a failure in the PIM. From the PIM, the resultant output is routed to the destination via the termination panel.

Each of the three control computer modules is packaged on an individual board. An Intel 8086 microprocessor provides the control sequence with up to 1 megabyte of RAM memory and up to 320 kilobytes of EPROM. A communication channel to each of the CCMs provides data transfer to each of the other two CCMs. This link makes it possible for each CCM to vote and correct errors on the input and output data. A defective board can be pulled off-line for repair.

13.3.2   Tricon-1 System (Toy, 1985a; 1985b)

In the Tricon-1 design, Triconex Corporation also uses three independent I/O buses, each one connecting a National 32016 main processor (MP) to an I/O processor. This system goes beyond the August System; it triplicates not just the paths from the main processor to the logic level point, but also those from the I/O point to the sensors and motors. Hardware voters are used rather than software voting for both inputs and outputs, hence greater performance is achieved. Intelligent I/O deloads the main processors by preprocessing the inputs prior to sending the data to the MP.

Figure 42 shows the Tricon-1 functional block diagram. The MP is triplicated, with a high-speed Tribus connection from each to the other two for communication, data transfer, voting, and error correction. Each MP is packaged on a 15-by-15-inch board with its own memory, 128 kilobytes of EPROM for the operating system, and 256 kilobytes of static RAM for the user programs and a separate I/O bus to its own I/O circuitry. The I/O processor scans input points independently, passes the data to the MP, and by means of the Tribus the data from the other MPs are obtained, voted, and corrected before each MP processes the data. After processing the MPs, again by means of the Tribus, perform the output voting before each sends the outputs to the I/O board. At the output circuits, the data are again voted and corrected by hardware before being output to the destination devices. All three independent I/O circuits are packaged on one 15-by-15-inch board. A spare slot adjacent to each I/O circuit card is provided for on-line repair. If one of the three I/O channels or legs becomes defective, majority vote continues to provide correct outputs. To replace the defective board, a spare card (if not already present as a "hot" spare) must then be inserted into the adjacent slot. The operating system recognizes that a spare is present and automatically switches operation to the adjacent I/O card. When this is done, the defective

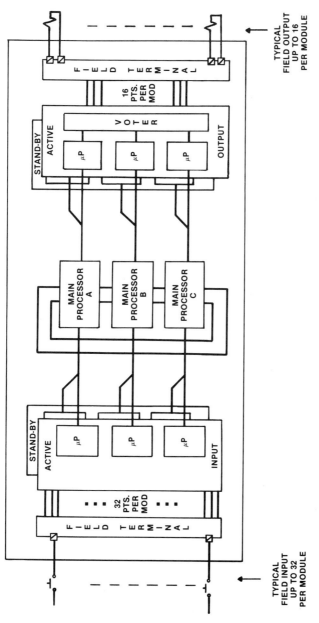

FIG. 42. Tricon triplicated architecture.

card can then be pulled out for repair. In the case of the MPs, each one is packaged on a single board and can be pulled out for repair without disturbing the system's operation.

The power supplies are duplicated for each housing or chassis. Either one of the duplicates can power all three MPs and up to six I/O cards. Moreover, extensive use of CMOS circuitry eliminates the need for cooling fans, a frequent source of failures.

14. Conclusion

Fault-tolerant computing is defined as the ability to compute correctly in the presence of a failure, regardless of its source. Errors are attributed to hardware faults, software faults, and procedural faults. To achieve fault tolerance, redundancy in hardware or software or both is required so that errors are bypassed and the final results correct.

A great deal of work in the area of fault-tolerant computing has been done in the past twenty years; much of it is support for the U.S. space program (Avizienis, 1978) and in special applications such as electronic telephone switching systems (Briley and Toy, 1977). More recently, fault tolerance is expanding into on-line transaction processing systems (Serlin, 1984) and into process control systems (Laduzinsky, 1985; Machulda, 1985). Reliability is of primary importance in these applications. A large collection of design techniques has been developed for implementing these systems, including the following (Rennels, 1980):

1. duplex self-checking configuration (Toy, 1978)
2. triple-modular redundancy (TMR) with voting (Lyons and Vanderkulk, 1962)
3. error correction codes for concurrent processes (Peterson and Weldon, 1972)
4. software-implemented fault tolerance (Wensley, 1972)
5. fault-tolerant memory systems (Carter and McCarthy, 1976; Sarrazin and Malek, 1984)

The choice of these techniques must be appropriate to the requirements of the system in terms of reliability objective, available technology, user needs, and cost–benefit trade-offs.

As improved integrated circuit technology becomes available and users demand greater reliability, maintenance features are even being integrated into general-purpose computer designs. Most fault-tolerant techniques developed for space and other real-time high-reliability applications are directly applicable to the designs of reliable and highly maintainable computer systems.

It is now economically feasible to duplicate, triplicate, and even quadruplicate hardware components to realize high reliability and performance in a distributed processor arrangement. This is evidenced by the commercial product offerings of the AT&T 3B20D computer (duplication), the August and Triconex computers (triplication), and the Stratus computers (quadruplication). The trend of the future will be more of the nonstop or high-availability type of computer systems.

REFERENCES

Anderson, T., and Lee, P. A. (1981). "Fault-Tolerance Principles and Practice." Prentice–Hall, Englewood Cliffs, N. J.

Anderson, T., and Randell, B. (1979). "Computing Systems Reliability." Cambridge University Press, Cambridge, England.

Arnold, T. F. (1973). The concept of coverage and its effect on the reliability model of a reparable system. *IEEE Trans. Comput.* C-22, 251–254.

Arsenault, J. E., and Roberts, J. A. (1980). "Reliability and Maintainability of Electronic Systems." Computer Science Press, Potomac, Maryland.

Ault, C. F., Brewster, J. H., Greenwood, T. S., Hagland, R. E., Reed, W. A., and Rolund, M. W. (1977). Memory systems. *BSTJ* 56 (2), 181–206.

Avizienis, A. (1971). Arithmetic error codes: Cost and effectiveness studies for applications in digital systems designs. *IEEE Trans Comput.* C-20 (11), 1322–1331.

Avizienis, A. (1972). The methodology of fault-tolerant computing. *First USA–Japan Comput. Conf. Proc.*, 405–413.

Avizienis, A. (1975). Fault-tolerance and fault-intolerance: Complementary approaches to reliable computing. *Proc. Int. Conf. Reliable Software*, Los Angeles, pp. 458–464.

Avizienis, A. (1978). Fault-tolerance: The survival attribute of digital systems. *Proc. IEEE* 66 (10), 1109–1125.

Avizienis, A., and Kelly, J. P. J. (1984). Fault tolerance by design diversity: Concepts and experiments. *Computer* 17 (8), 67–80.

Avizienis, A., Gilley, G. C., Mathur, F. P., Rennels, D. A., Rohr, J. A., and Rubin, D. K. (1971). The STAR (self-testing and repairing) computer: An investigation on the theory and practices of fault-tolerant computer design. *IEEE Trans. Comput.* C-20 (11), 1312–1321.

Bartlett, J. F. (1978). A non-stop operating system. *Proc. Hawaii Int. Conf. System Sci.*, pp. 103–117.

Bell System Technical Journal (1964). No. 1 ESS description. *Bell System Tech. J.* 43 (5), pp. 1831–2282.

Bell System Technical Journal (1969). No. 2 ESS description. *Bell System Tech. J.* 48 (8), pp. 2607–2905.

Bell System Technical Journal (1977). No. 1A processor description. *Bell System Tech. J.* 56 (2), pp. 119–325.

Beuscher, H. J., Fessler, G. E., Huffman, D. W., Kennedy, D. J., and Nussbaum, E. (1969). Administration and maintenance plan. *BSTJ* 48 (8), 2765–2864.

Breuer, M. A., and Friedman, A. D. (1976). "Diagnosis and Reliable Design of Digital Systems." Computing Science Press, Woodland Hill, CA.

Briley, B. E., and Toy, W. N. (1977). Telecommunication processors. *Proc. IEEE* **65** (98), 1305–1312.

Browne, T. E., Quinn, T. M., Toy, W. N., and Yates, J. E. (1969). No. 2 ESS control unit system. *BSTJ* **48**, 2619–2668.

Budlong, A. H., Delugish, B. G., Neville, S. M., Nowak, J. S., Quinn, J. L., and Wendland, F. W. (1977). 1A processor—Control system. *BSTJ* **56**, 135–180.

Butner, S. E., and Iyer, R. K. (1980). A statistical study of reliability and system load at SLAC. *Proc. FTCS* **10**, 207–212.

Carter, W. C., and McCarthy, C. E. (1976). Implementation of an experimental fault-tolerant memory system. *IEEE Trans. Comput.* **C-25** (6), 557–568.

Castillo, X., and Siewiorek, D. P. (1980). Workload, performance, and reliability of digital computing systems, *Proc. FTCS* **11**, 84–89.

Chang, H. Y., Manning, E. G., and Metze, G. (1970). "Fault Diagnosis of Digital Systems." Wiley Interscience, New York.

Chang, H. Y., Smith, G. W., and Walford, R. B. (1974). LAMP: System description. *Bell System Tech. J.* **53**, 1431–1450.

Chen, L., and Avizienis, A. (1978). *N*-version programming: A fault-tolerance approach to reliability of software operation. *Proc. FTCS* **8**, 3–9.

Cook, R. W., Sisson, W. H., Storey, T. F., and Toy, W. N. (1973). Design of a self-checking microprogram control. *IEEE Trans. Comput.* **C-22**, 255–262.

Digital Equipment Corp. (1977). "VAX 11/780, Technical Summary." Digital Equipment Corp., Maynard, MA.

Downing, R. W., Nowak, J. S., and Tuomenoksa, L. S. (1964). No. 1 ESS maintenance plan. *Bell System Tech. J.* **18**, 1961–2019.

Durniak, A. (1979).Computers, *Electronics* **52** (10), 164–177.

Gallaher, L. E., and Toy, W. N. (1981). Fault-tolerant design of 3B20 processor. *NCC-81 Proc.*, Chicago, pp. 41–48.

Goetz, F. M. (1974). Complementary fault simulation. *Proc. 3rd Ann. Texas Conf. Comput. Systems*, Univ. Texas, pp. 941–945.

Hagland, R. E., and Peterson, L. D. (1983). 3B20D file memory systems. *BSTJ* **62** (1), 235–254.

Hopkins, A. L. Jr., Smith, T. B. III, and Lala, J. H. (1978). FTMP—A highly reliable fault-tolerant multiprocessor for aircraft. *Proc. IEEE* **66** (10), 1221–1239.

Horning, J. J., Lauer, H. C., Melliar–Smith, P. M., and Randell, B. (1974). A program structure for error detection and recovery. *Lect. Notes Comput. Sci.* **16**, Springer Verlag, pp. 171–187.

Johnson, K. (1985). Stratus/32 systems. *Proc. Nat. Commun. Forum* **39**, 738–740.

Katzman, J. A. (1978). A fault-tolerant computing system. *Proc. Hawaii Int. Conf. System Sci.*, pp. 85–105.

Kennedy, P. J., and Quinn, T. M. (1972). Recovery strategies in the No. 2 ESS. *Digest of Papers, 1972 Int. Symp. Fault-Tolerant Comput.*, Newton, MA, pp. 165–169.

Kopetz, H. (1979). "Software Reliability." Springer Verlag, New York.

Kraft, G. D., and Toy, W. N. (1981). "Microprogrammed Control and Reliable Design of Small Computers." Prentice–Hall, Englewood Cliffs, N. J.

Laduzinsky, A. J. (1985). Programmable controller delivers fault tolerance using twelve microprocessors. *Cont. Eng.* **32** (2) 76–77.

Lyons, R. E., and Vanderkulk, W. (1962). The use of triple-modular redundancy to improve computer reliability *IBM J. Res. Dev.* **6** (2), 200–209.

Machulda, J. (1985). Fault tolerant control: You can afford it. *In Tech* **32** (8), 105–108.

Makam, S. V., and Avizienis, A. (1982). ARIES81: A reliability and life-cycle evaluation tool for fault-tolerant systems. *Proc. FTCS* **12**, pp. 267–274.

Morgan, D. E., and Taylor, D. J. (1977). A survey of methods of achieving reliable software. *Computer* **10** (2), 44–51.

Nelson, D. L. (1978). A remote computer troubleshooting facility. *Hewlett–Packard J.* **Sept., ed.,** 13–15.

Ng, Y. W., and Avizienis, A. (1977). ARIES—An automated reliability estimation system. *Proc. 1977 Annual Reliability and Maintainability Symposium,* Philadelphia, PA, pp. 108–113.

Peterson, W. W., and Weldon, E. J. Jr. (1972). "Error-Correcting Codes." MIT Press, Cambridge, MA.

Ramamoorthy, C. V., Cheung, R. C., and Kim, K. H. (1974). Reliability and integrity of large computer programs. Memo No. ERL-M430, Electronics Research Laboratory, College of Engineering, University of California, Berkeley.

Rennels, D. A. (1980). Distributed fault-tolerant computer systems. *Computer* **13** (3), 55–65.

Sarrazin, D. B., and Malek, M. (1984). Fault-tolerant semiconductor memories. *Computer* **17** (8), 49–56.

Serlin, O. (1984). Fault-tolerant systems in commercial applications. *Computer* **17** (8), 19–30.

Sevcik, K. L., Atwood, J. W., Brushcow, N. W., Holt, R. C., Horning, J. J., and Tsichritzis, D. (1972). Project SUE as a learning experience. *AFIPS, Proc. FJCC* **41** (1), 331–339.

Siewiorek, D. P., and Swarz, R. S. (1982). "The Theory and Practice of Reliable System Design." Digital Press.

Staehler, R. E., and Watters, R. J. (1976). 1A Processor—An ultra-dependable common control. *Int. Switch. Symp. Rec.*

Toy, W. N. (1978). Fault-tolerant design of local ESS processors. *Proc. IEEE* **66** (10), 1126–1145.

Toy, W. N. (1985a). Fault recovery strategy of TRICON-1. *Proc. ISA/85 Internat. Conf.,* Philadelphia, pp. 979–990.

Toy, W. N. (1985b). Fault-tolerant design of TRICON-1. *Proc. Nat. Commun. Forum* **39,** 735–738.

Trivedi, K. S. (1982). "Probability and Statistics with Reliability, Queuing, and Computer Science Applications." Prentice–Hall, Englewood, Cliffs, N.J.

Tsiang, S. H., and Ulrich, W. (1962). Automatic trouble diagnosis of complex logic circuits. *Bell System Tech. J.* **41,** 1177–1200.

Wallace, J. J., and Barnes, W. W. (1984). Designing for ultrahigh availability: The UNIX RTR operating system. *Computer* **17** (8), 31–39.

Weinstock, C. B. (1980). SHIFT: System design and implementation. *Proc. FTCS* **10,** 75–77.

Wensley, J. H. (1972). SIFT—Software implemented fault tolerance. *Fall Joint Comput. Conf. Proc.,* pp. 243–253.

Wensley, J. H. (1985). Redundant modules may be best for control systems. *Comput. Des.* **April ed.** 738–740.

Wensley, J. H., Lamport, L., Goldberg, J., Green, M. W., Levitt, K. N., Melliar–Smith, P. M., Schostak, R. E., and Weinstock, C. B. (1978). The design and analysis of a fault-tolerant computer for aircraft control. *Proc IEEE* **60** (10), 1240–1254.

Yau, S. S., and Cheung, R. C. (1975). Design of self-checking software. *Proc. Int. Conf. Reliable Software,* Los Angeles, pp. 450–457.

Techniques and Issues in Testing and Validation of VLSI Systems

H. K. REGHBATI

School of Computing Science
Simon Fraser University
Burnaby, British Columbia, Canada

1. Introduction

A very large scale integrated (VLSI) circuit is commonly defined as a single chip that contains more than 100,000 devices. Generally, the metal-oxide-semiconductor (MOS) technology is being used with a minimum feature size in the 1–2 micron range. The advent of VLSI systems, while making significant contributions to the cost effectiveness of many products, is presenting challenges not previously faced by design and test engineers.

This article is about the techniques and tools that may help us solve the VLSI design validation and testing crisis of the 1980s. There are many reasons why a particular chip may not work. These range from very low-level

ADVANCES IN COMPUTERS, VOL. 26

problems, such as two signals shorted together because they were too close to each other, to high-level bugs in algorithms. In another dimension, VLSI circuits may fail due to production problems or bonding errors.

While computer-aided design and test (CADT) is an explosively growing area in many engineering disciplines, VLSI-CADT is certainly the most widely used and best developed CADT branch. New CADT tools are continually being developed to cope with the ever-increasing problems of VLSI complexity. The bristling richness of this rapidly growing field unfolds in the rest of this article with sections on some of the major techniques and issues.

Fabrication of VLSI circuits and sources of failure are introduced in the next section. In Section 3, design validation tools are discussed. Testing of VLSI chips is the topic of Section 4; design for testability techniques are described in Section 5; and built-in self-test is discussed in Section 6.

2.   Integrated Circuit Fabrication and Yield

The integrated circuit (IC) was invented by Kilby in 1958. The first ICs were phase-shift oscillators and flip-flops, fabricated in germanium substrates. The individual components in these circuits were isolated in mesa-shaped regions that had been etched in the substrate by using black wax (applied by hand) to mask the active regions. The individual devices were interconnected by wire bonding. These first working units were used for the first public announcement of the "Solid Circuit" (integrated circuit) concept in March 1959. Other critical developments around the same time included the first modern diffused bipolar transistor by Hoerni. This transistor was based on the planar diffused process, a cornerstone of modern IC fabrication, that uses silicon dioxide as a barrier to impurity diffusion. In 1958, a patent was filed on the first use of p-n junctions for device isolation, and, in 1959, a patent was filed for an IC that used evaporated aluminium metallization over an oxide layer to provide interconnections.

From these early primitive forms, ICs have evolved into complex electronic devices containing hundreds of thousands of individual components on a single chip of silicon. The first ICs were based on contributions from many different fields, including device physics, materials science, and chemistry. Interdisciplinary contributions continue to be sought today in the development of new IC technologies.

The MOS-IC technology has led the industry in increasing the on-chip circuit density and started the movement towards high density integrated circuits. A brief overview of the MOS-IC fabrication technology is given in Section 2.1, then process monitoring is discussed in Section 2.2, and the issue of IC fabrication yield is the topic of Section 2.3.

2.1   IC Fabrication Technology

The implementation of an IC chip involves three major steps: design, mask making, and fabrication. The architecture of the chip originates at the "design house," where the system-level specification of the chip is transformed to a layout description. The basic task of the fabrication process is to map the layout structures onto the silicon surface in specified layers. The first step in this process is photolithography, which converts the layout description into a set of masking plates containing exact images of the structures in either opaque or transparent shades. This job is carried out at "mask houses." The actual fabrication of the chip is done in a "fab house," that makes "prints" of the masks onto the silicon wafers. The wafers are then tested and diced and the functioning chips are then packaged.

Silicon transistors and integrated circuits are manufactured starting with pure slices, or wafers, of single-crystal silicon, 100 or 125 mm in diameter and about 0.2 mm thick. The thickness is determined by the need to provide enough mechanical strength so that the wafer cannot be easily broken. The thickness necessary to meet the electronic requirements is 10 μm or less.

After processing, each wafer is sawed into hundreds or thousands of identical rectangular chips, typically between 1 and 10 mm in size on each edge. IC chips may contain as few as 10 devices (transistors, resistors, diodes, etc.) to as many as 100,000 or more. The processing sequence that forms the devices and circuits is comprised of a sequence of pattern definition steps interspersed with other processes, such as oxidation, etching, controlled introduction of desired elements (doping), and material deposition. Simple examples of such sequences will now be described.

The process of pattern transfer and pattern definition is repeated 4 to 12 times during the fabrication of an integrated circuit wafer. Each of these so-called masking steps requires that the wafer be coated with a photosensitive emulsion, known as photoresist, and then be optically exposed in desired geometric patterns using a previously prepared photographic plate. After development of the photoresist (which removes the photoresist in the selected areas), a specified process such as etching or doping is carried out in the patterned areas of the wafer. This entire pattern transfer process is known as photolithography, or optical lithography.

Steady improvements in optical lithography have made it possible to reduce the smallest surface dimensions on an IC chip from about 25 μm in 1960 to about 2 μm today. (A hair from your head is about 50 μm in diameter.) The cost per logic gate or memory cell is reduced as more devices and circuits are formed per unit chip area. Furthermore, smaller devices have smaller capacitances and hence can switch faster, leading to better circuit performance. Minimum feature sizes less than 1 μm are feasible from the standpoint of device operation, but cannot be achieved with optical lithography because the wavelength of light is about 0.4 μm. To overcome this limation of optical lithography, electron beam lithography, or x-ray lithography should be used.

2.1.1 MOS-IC Fabrication Process

The process sequence for fabrication of n-channel MOS integrated circuits is illustrated in Figure 1. Although more advanced NMOS and CMOS processes require seven to twelve masking steps, the simplest process for forming NMOS circuits requires these five steps:

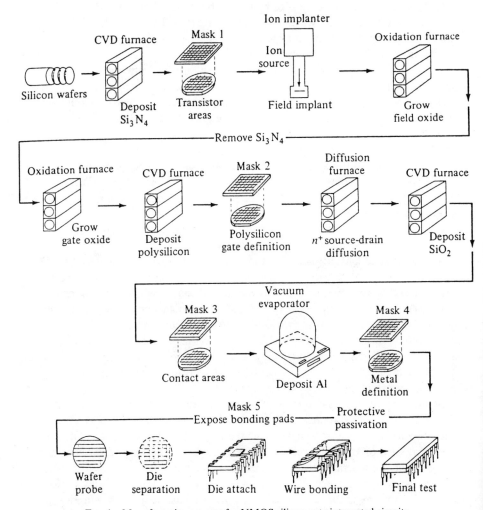

FIG. 1   Manufacturing process for NMOS silicon-gate integrated circuits.

1. A Chemical Vapor Deposition (CVD) process deposits a thin layer of silicon nitride (Si_3N_4) on the entire wafer surface. The first photolithographic step defines areas where transistors are to be formed. The silicon nitride is removed outside the transistor areas by chemical etching. Boron (p-type) is implanted in the exposed regions to suppress unwanted conduction between transistor sites. Next, a layer of silicon dioxide (SiO_2) about 1 μm thick is grown thermally in these inactive, or field, regions by exposing the wafer to oxygen in an electric furnace. This is known as a selective, or local, oxidation process. The Si_3N_4 is impervious to oxygen and thus inhibits growth of the thick oxide in the transistor regions.

2. The Si_3N_4 is next removed by an etchant that does not attack SiO_2. A clean thermal oxide about 0.1 μm thick is grown in the transistor areas, again by exposure to oxygen in a furnace. Another CVD process deposits a layer of polycrystalline silicon (poly) over the entire wafer. The second photolithographic step defines the desired patterns for gate electrodes. Undesired poly is removed by chemical or plasma (reactive gas) etching. An n-type dopant (phosphorus or arsenic) is introduced into the regions that will become the transistor source and drain. Either thermal diffusion or ion implantation may be used for this doping process. The thick field oxide and the poly gate are barriers to the dopant, but in this process, the poly becomes heavily n-type.

3. Another CVD process deposits an insulating layer, often SiO_2, over the entire wafer. The third masking step defines the areas in which contacts to the transistors are to be made. Chemical or plasma etching selectively exposes bare silicon or poly in the contact areas.

4. Aluminum (Al) is deposited over the entire wafer by evaporation from a hot crucible in a vacuum evaporator. The fourth masking step patterns the Al as desired for circuit connectins.

5. A protective passivating layer (often termed scratch protection or simply scratch) is deposited over the entire surface. A final masking step removes this insulating layer over the pads where contacts will be made. Circuits are tested using needle-like probes on the contact pads. Defective units are marked with a dot of ink and the wafer is then sawed into individual chips. Good chips are packaged and undergo a final test.

2.2 Process Monitoring

Once provided with proven designs, the process engineer is generally responsible for producing integrated circuits. In many cases, where technology is rapidly changing, this person is also responsible for changing the process to meet new design goals. These two demands require an intimate knowledge of how the processes are working. Process and device simulation, test chips, and instrumental methods are the three main tools used by the process engineer.

The tools used to test a process and the effort expended on process characterization and assurance will vary considerably depending on whether a new process is being developed or a mature one is being used.

2.2.1   Process and Device Simulation

Numerical simulation has emerged as an important aid to process and device development.

Process Simulation.   As VLSI technology moves towards finer line-widths, the topographical features and doping profiles of devices are becoming an increasing concern. Not only is greater line-width control required for high resolution, but it must be accomplished in a context where features in the third dimension are as large as the line-width itself. When process models can be established, simulation algorithms can often be used to explore process effects by simulating time evolution of the line-edge profile.

Physical models and algorithms to simulate lithography, etching, deposition, and thermal processes have been developed. For example, the SUPREM program, developed at Stanford, simulates thermal processes such as diffusion and oxidation, and the SAMPLE program, developed at Berkeley, permits the simulation of individual lithography, etching, and deposition processes (Neureuther, 1983).

Device Simulation.   The reason for modeling devices is twofold. The device designer and process engineer want to understand how a device operates, and the circuit designer seeks a quantitative description of the terminal behavior of the device. Many programs have been developed for device simulation (Engl *et al.*, 1983). For example, for the two-dimensional static analysis of MOS transistors, the TWIST program can be used (Liu, 1980). The detailed study of problems such as the weak-inversion and weak-injection punch-through phenomena in short-channel MOS devices is facilitated by such a program.

2.2.2   Test Chips

A test chip is a device that is manufactured on a silicon wafer alongside production integrated circuits. There are various test structures that make up a test chip and they are used to obtain information that would normally be very difficult, if not impossible, to get from the production chips. Test chips are intended to provide rapid analysis of the various fabrication process parameters. This analysis is made possible by the electrical measurements performed on the test chips.

Types of Test Structures.   There is a wide variety of uses for test structures and they range from checking line-width measurements to analyzing metal

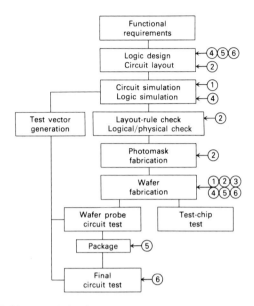

FIG. 2 Simplified integrated circuit production sequence illustrating where results from the six types of test structures are used. Test structures are used for (1) device parameter extraction, (2) layout-rule checking, (3) process parameter extraction, (4) random fault analysis, (5) reliability analysis, and (6) circuit parameter extraction.

step coverage to determining threshold voltages. There are six groups into which these usages fall:

1. Device parameter extraction
2. Layout-rule checking
3. Process parameter extraction
4. Random fault analysis
5. Reliability analysis
6. Circuit parameter extraction.

Figure 2 shows the production flow for an integrated circuit, and it shows where the test structure results are used in subsequent production runs. It should be obvious that one must make an initial run through the fabrication process before one has any test results that can lead to improvements. The uses of specific test structures are shown in Table I.

2.2.3 Instrumental Methods

This section summarizes instrumental methods found to be useful for solving problems that arise in VLSI technology development efforts and

TABLE I

RELATIONSHIP BETWEEN TEST STRUCTURES AS CIRCUIT ELEMENTS AND TEST CIRCUITS AND
THEIR USE IN DATA ACQUISITION

Test structure use	Resistor Discrete	Resistor Array	Capacitor large area	Diode discrete	Transistor Discrete	Transistor Array	Test circuit
Device parameter extraction	X		X	X	X		
Layout-rule checking		X					
Process parameter extraction	X		X	X	X		X
Random fault analysis		X	X			X	X
Reliability analysis		X	X		X		X
Circuit parameter extraction	X		X				X

explains their application to the problems. Some of these methods are most applicable to the analysis of VLSI circuit structures; others are more applicable to problems generated during experiments on the preparation of new materials for VLSI processing programs.

Morphology Determination. One of the first steps in most diagnostic efforts is examination of the shapes of relevant features: proximity between features, edge acuity of patterned lines, misalignment, and so on. These features are examined by optical microscopy, scanning electron microscopy, and transmission electron microscopy. The maximum useful magnification of these methods is approximately $1,000 \times$, $50,000 \times$, and $500,000 \times$, respectively. Since the magnification ranges overlap, few questions on morphology of device features can escape scrutiny. The newly developed laser scanning microscope has proved to be particularly useful for automating the inspection of the surfaces of patterned semiconductor wafers for particle contamination.

Chemical Analysis. Many different methods are required for the chemical analysis of materials used in VLSI technology. Spatial resolution requirements vary from atomic dimensions, as in the depth profiling of dopants, to essentially macroscopic dimensions, as in the bulk analysis of large area films or substrates. Vertical (depth) and lateral spatial resolution requirements for these studies are quite different. Sensitivity requirements range from 10^{11} atoms/cm^3 to 10^{21} atoms/cm^3. The chemicals usually sought in these studies are silicon dopants (arsenic, phosphorus, boron), oxygen, carbon, resist residue, various components of metallization, and metallic impurities. Thus, the chemicals run the gamut from light to heavy elements.

Auger electron spectroscopy, neutron activation analysis, Rutherford backscattering spectroscopy, scanning electron microscopy (by use of x-ray spectrometer attachments), electron probe, secondary ion mass spectroscopy, transmission electron microscopy (by use of an x-ray spectrometer attachment), x-ray emission spectroscopy, x-ray fluorescence, and x-ray photoelectron spectroscopy are among the techniques used for finding answers to the diverse questions of chemical analysis.

Crystallographic Structure and Mechanical Properties. An important aspect of device materials and process development programs is the analysis of crystallographic and mechanical properties of films and substrates. These analyses include the determination of substrate orientations and the determination of the degree of preferred orientation and crystallite size in grown and deposited films, the identification of phases and determination of unit cell parameters, the identification of amorphous regions and characterization of crystallographic defects, and the measurement of film stress.

Laser reflectance measurements of wafer curvature used to compute film stress, Rutherford backscattering spectroscopy, x-ray diffraction, transmission electron diffraction, and transmission electron microscopy are among the techniques used in the analysis of crystallographic and mechanical properties of films and substrates.

Electrical Mapping. In electrical mapping, an electron beam is used to locate regions in a device structure that differ in electrical activity, and in some cases, to measure the difference. Electrical mapping is of particular value in identifying the sites of device leakage and breakdown.

Two mapping methods are used. In one, the energy distribution of secondary electrons, produced when an electron beam strikes a device sample, is influenced by the local surface potential. The secondary electron flux reaching the detector reflects this potential. This phenomenon, essential to voltage contrast imaging, can be used to determine the potential of an element on a device surface.

In the other method, charges are generated in the device by the electron beam, and the charges are collected via a capacitor or junction. Local changes in morphology, material properties, and junction electric field cause corresponding local modulations of the collected current. This procedure is called electron beam induced current (EBIC) or charge collection microscopy.

Both types of electrical mapping can be performed with a scanning electron microscope; a transmission electron microscope can be used for EBIC studies.

2.3   IC Fabrication Yield

The presence of defects causes an integrated circuit to malfunction, mainly due to a number of unwanted open and short circuits. These are caused primarily by pinholes in gate oxides and excess reverse leakage currents in p-n junction diodes from which the transistors are formed. In addition, breaks in metallization tracks and defective contacts between conducting layers will also drastically impair circuit performance. The main origins of defects introduced at the wafer processing stage are:

1. Poor starting materials and contaminated chemicals and gases used in wafer fabrication. Of particular concern here are irregularities in the otherwise crystalline wafer that cause conducting "spikes" in p-n junctions. Contamination of furnaces by phosphorus can also adversely affect device parameters.

2. Poor processing of wafers. Defective contacts can be caused by incorrect etching, and misalignment of masks during processing can be responsible for a host of problems.

3. Poor environmental control of processing area. The performance of organic resists used to define device structures is dependent upon the humidity and temperature of the processing area, as are most fabrication steps.

Many factors contribute to the IC fabrication yield. Usually, 75% to 95% of all wafers have some operating chips. The percentage of functioning chips per wafer varies drastically depending on the complexity of the circuit. It varies from 5% for complex chips to 90% for simple logic circuits. It is important to note that in the early stages of developing a complex circuit, such as a microprocessor, the yield at wafer probe time may be very low. In particular, yields of 5% or even less may be common until the causes of such a low yield are well understood. On the other hand, for a highly optimized part that is in stable production, yields may be at a level of 50% or higher. Obtaining such a high yield, particularly for complex chips, is no easy task and is the result of a great deal of interaction between process engineers and chip designers.

Chip assembly (i.e., bonding and packaging) is also a source of yield reduction. Generally, 85% to 95% of the chips are successfully assembled. After assembly, the final package undergoes a final test (with or without burn-in). On the average, 60% to 95% of the packaged chips pass this testing stage.

To summarize, the main components of IC fabrication yield (Y) are wafer processing yield (Y_w), wafer probe yield (Y_p), assembly yield (Y_a), and final test yield (Y_t), Mathematically, this can be represented as $Y = (Y_w)(Y_p)(Y_a)(Y_t)$.

3. Design Validation Tools

It has become generally recognized that the computer is an essential tool for designing VLSI circuits. The key to the success of VLSI technology lies in the development of powerful design tools that help the designer produce an integrated-circuit chip. Excluding the tools dealing with systems or functional specifications, these tools can be broadly classified as design entry or logic capture systems, circuit layout tools (language based or graphics based), layout verification tools, simulation tools for functional and performance verification, and routing tools for interconnection and placement.

To shorten the design cycle and to decrease design costs, it is crucial to eliminate as many errors as possible before manufacturing an integrated circuit. There are several different kinds of verification tools: structural verification tools, simulation tools, performance verification tools, and logic verification tools.

Structural verification is the task of verifying that the structure of a design—the arragement of mask-layout shapes, the connections among those shapes or among the components of a design—satisfy a particular set of rules. For structural verification, the behavior of the components of the design is not considered, only their spatial relationships and connectivity.

Simulation is the principal debugging tool of the designer. It may also be used as an aid in engineering the circuit to achieve certain performance parameters, particularly speed and power dissipation. Also, ideally, a simulator is required at each interface in the hierarchy to verify that the detail created by designing the lower level from the higher level is a faithful representation and has not introduced any errors. The most common simulations are performed with software whose input is some form of machine-readable description of the design. These descriptions usually correspond to specifications of the system at different levels in the design hierarchy.

Performance verification techniques aim at the determination of the critical delays in a circuit, independent of the input patterns. Logic verification tools are also input pattern independent and verify that two design descriptions at the gate or structural level and at the functional level are formally equivalent.

Hardware accelerators or special-purpose engines have been used in computer-aided design applications for nearly 20 years. Many such machines have been built and tested specifically for such purposes as simulation, design rule checking, placement, and routing. Their uses are increasing and some of them are commercially available.

3.1   Structural Verification

Structural verification is subdivided into three areas: layout-rule checking (LRC), where mask geometries are verified to check if they satisfy a set of spacing, sizing, and enclosure rules; electrical-rule checking (ERC), where the circuit schematic is verified to find electrical errors due to wrong connections of the devices; and connectivity verification systems (CVS), where a netlist description extracted from the layout is compared against the netlist description extracted from an alternate description, such as the schematic diagram.

3.1.1 Layout-Rule Checking

Physical layout rules or design rules specify the legal or illegal relationships among the polygons used in the IC mask making and fabrication process. These rules account for necessary electrical separation of different components and signals, as well as for imperfections in the mask preparation and manufacturing processes.

Industrial rule sets can be very complex, especially when the shapes of geometries are not restricted. In addition, electrical considerations may add to the complexity of the rules. For example, capacitive coupling between lines requires that long, parallel lines be spaced more conservatively than short parallel runs. The electrical aspects of the rules are especially important in high performance circuits, where parasitic effects play a crucial role.

Layout-rule checkers have been developed by many companies. These programs can verify complex designs with complicated layout rules, and new layout rules can be added rather easily.

Over the past few years, several universities have developed layout-rule checkers that are based on the Mead-Conway simplified rules. Because the design styles used often require only Manhattan geometries and do not consider conditional rules, these programs are relatively simple and fast. A number of new approaches to LRC have emerged from this activity and have found application in industrial products as well. For example, the concepts of hierarchical and incremental LRC have been explored over the past few years and have been implemented in industrial systems.

Hierarchical LRC takes advantage of the fact that cells are often used more than once in a large design. Once the inside of a cell has been checked, the cell is marked as "done." Thereafter, for each instance of the cell, only its local context need be checked.

In incremental approaches, a background process checks the layout rules in the vicinity of each figure as it is added to the layout. Since manual layout is a slow process relative to the computing speed of a modern workstation, this is an effective way of using machine cycles that might otherwise have been wasted. It also permits errors to be corrected and rechecked in a tight, local loop so that the number of expensive, batch-mode checks can be reduced or even eliminated completely.

The techniques used by LRC systems can be classified into three categories: region operation based, raster based, and corner based. An example of the region operation based technique for LRC is the polygon or the rectangle method (Yamin, 1972). The input is a list of polygons each associated with a specific mask layer and a sequence of commands describing operations on all the objects of one or more layers. Commands include the merging of all intersecting polygons, intersection, union and difference of layers, etc. The design rules are expressed in terms of these commands. A typical way to spacing checks is to enlarge each polygon by half the minimum spacing and then to look for intersecting polygons. In the worst case, the number of comparisons needed to determine all polygon interactions is proportional to the square of the number of polygons.

The major advantage of the polygon method is that the algebra of polygons can easily be adapted to new design rules or processes. The major disadvantage is that the method is global and involves a time-consuming operation of polygon intersections that is proportional to the square of the number of polygons. The number of comparisons can be reduced by using algorithms that incorporate sorting and windowing schemes (Bentley and Ottmann, 1979).

In the raster based method of design-rule checking, the design layout is represented on a lambda grid. The term "pixel" is used to represent the smallest square unit of resolution. Each pixel contains a bit for each layer, indicating whether or not the layer is present at that point.

Baker's algorithm is an example of the raster-based method (Baker, 1980). It originated from the observation that layout-rule checks are local, in that they specify only minimum widths and spacings. In the Mead-Conway NMOS design rules, the largest minimum width or spacing is three lambda. Therefore, there should be sufficient information in a four-by-four window to determine whether any design rules are violated in that window. The LRC function is accomplished by passing this window over the design and checking to ensure that all four-by-four windows are error free.

A second raster scan LRC-algorithm is based on a simple model of the design rules in terms of a set of deterministic finite-state automata (DFA) that accepts the rasterized inputs and produces the error outputs (Eustace, 1981). The algorithm is flexible and technology-independent since the design rules are embedded in the form of transition tables of the DFAs. Changes in the design rules or even in the technology can be handled by simply redefining the transition tables without changing the algorithm.

The corner based approach to LRC takes a middle ground between the raster approach, which is based on local checks on bits, and the polygon method, which is global and manipulates larger entities such as polygons. It uses the fact that layout-rule violations of Manhattan geometry layouts can be detected by inspecting small regions around the corners on individual or derived mask layers (Arnold and Ousterhout, 1982).

3.1.2 Electrical-Rule Checking and Connectivity Verification

Once the mask patterns satisfy the physical layout rules, it is necessary to verify that they will actually implement a working circuit. The first step in this process is to recreate a netlist description of the circuit from the mask pattern data. This process is called extraction, which performs mask-level operations to recognize individual components such as transistors, capacitors, and nets. The extraction program also determines parameter values for simulation, such as the size of the transistors extracted as well as related parasitic capacitance values.

The extracted netlist provides the basis for a number of checks; in particular, electrical-rule checking and connectivity verification. An example of an electrical-rule check is to flag two or more threshold drops as a potential error. Using the length and width information, all of the pull-up/pull-down ratios are calculated and checked against a range of legal values (taking into account any threshold drops on the gates).

If a transistor-level netlist description of a circuit is available, either from manually generated simulator input data or from a schematic entry system, the pattern of interconnections among the components and the pattern of interconnections obtained from the extracted netlist can be compared. This process is called connectivity verification and is used to improve the probability of functionally correct silicon on the first fabrication run. In general, the comparison involves a one-to-one correspondence between the circuit elements, such as transistors, and the nets in the two circuits, not a functional equivalence.

For connectivity verification, each circuit is represented by a graph. The problem of determining that the two graphs are the same is then equivalent to the graph isomorphism problem. In most of the cases, good heuristics are available that can quickly detect if two graphs are isomorphic. If they are not isomorphic, the program can then isolate the subgraphs that differ in the two netlists. This information is then provided to the user who tries to locate and correct the error.

3.2   Simulation

Many different forms of simulation can be used for the verification of VLSI circuits at the various stages of the design process. They may be classified as behavioral simulators, register-transfer-level (RTL) simulators, gate-level logic simulators, switch-level simulators, circuit simulators, and timing simulators.

3.2.1   Behavioral and RTL Simulators

Behavioral simulators are used at the initial design phase to verify the algorithms of the digital system to be implemented. Not even a general structure of the design implementation is necessary at this stage.

Once the algorithms have been verified, a potential implementation structure is chosen. An RTL simulator can be used to verify the design at this level. Only crude timing models may be available, since the exact circuit parasitics and other implementation details are not yet known. Useful information relating to congestion and hardware/firmware trade-offs can be obtained from this level of analysis.

3.2.2   Gate-Level and Switch-Level Simulators

Depending on the design methodology and certain technology issues, a gate-level design may be undertaken where each of the RTL modules is further partitioned into low-level logic blocks or gates. A gate-level logic simulator may then be used to verify the design.

Recently, a new class of logic simulators has emerged specifically for the MOS designer. These switch-level simulators model an MOS system as a network of nodes connected by transistor "switches". This level of simulation can model the wide variety of logic structures used in MOS designs, including logic gates, pass-transistor logic, busses, and dynamic memory. Furthermore, such a simulator is fast enough to simulate entire VLSI systems because behavior is modeled at a logical level rather than at a detailed analog level.

3.2.3   Circuit and Timing Simulators

When accurate circuit models are available, circuit simulators provide precise electrical information (such as frequency response, time-domain waveforms, and sensitivity information) about the circuit under analysis. SPICE (Nagel, 1975) and ASTAP (Weeks *et al.*, 1973) are two popular circuit simulators. They are essentially based on the exact numerical solution of the network's differential equations. However, even with the increase in speed afforded by the waveform relaxation method (Lelarasmee *et al.*, 1982), exact numerical solutions are too slow for VLSI circuits.

Substantial speed improvements can be achieved if simulation algorithms are tailored to specific technologies or applications. Many components of digital MOS or I^2L circuits can be considered unilateral in nature. This characteristic—as well as the facts that these families are saturating, and hence accumulated voltage errors are lost at the extremes of signal swing, and that large digital circuits are relatively inactive at the gate level—are exploited in timing simulation. Timing simulators can improve simulation speed by up to two orders of magnitude while maintaining acceptable waveform accuracy. These savings are achieved by using node decoupling techniques in conjunction with simplified table look-up models for nonlinear devices.

3.3   Performance and Logic Verification

While simulation has been used successfully for the verification of large circuits, it cannot guarantee that certain timing specifications are met for all possible input combinations unless all such combinations are tried—an often impractical proposition. Performance verification techniques aim at the determination of the critical delays in a circuit, independent of the input patterns.

Logic verification tools are also input-pattern-independent and verify that two design descriptions at the gate or structural level and at the functional level are formally equivalent. At higher levels of the design process, verifying that a design implements the required function correctly is a serious bottleneck for complex IC designs and is an active research area.

4. Testing

The major techniques for achieving reliable operation can be classified into fault avoidance, fault detection, masking redundancy, and dynamic redundancy categories. Fault avoidance techniques try to improve reliability by lessening the possibility of failures. Better controls on quality and environment are among these types of techniques. Burn-in procedures also belong to this category.

Fault avoidance techniques attempt to decrease the possibility of failures. Fault detection and the remaining techniques deal with the inevitability of failures. Fault detection techniques can be further divided into the off-line testing and on-line testing categories. The purpose of off-line testing is to reveal permanent failures and manufacturing defects. Concurrent error detection (on-line testing) is most suitable for catching transient errors (due to intermittent failures, timing problems, noise, radiation, etc.).

Fault detection techniques supply warnings of faulty results. They may also provide diagnostic capabilities, with a resolution of some finite number of possible failure locations (such as a device or set of devices causing the fault). However, the use of fault detection techniques alone does not provide actual tolerance of faults. Fault masking, on the other hand, employs redundancy that provides fault tolerance by either isolating or correcting fault effects before they reach module outputs.

Fault masking is a "static" form of redundancy: the logical interconnection of the circuit elements remains fixed, and no intervention occurs from elements outside the module. Thus, when the masking redundancy is exhausted by faults in the module, any further faults will cause errors at the output. Therefore, regular testing is mandatory so that faulty elements are replaced in a timely manner.

Another approach to increased reliability utilizes redundancy in a "dynamic" way. Dynamic redundancy techniques involve the reconfiguration of system components in response to failures. The reconfiguration prevents failures from contributing their effects to the system operation. Reconfiguration is triggered either by internal detection of faults in the damaged subunit or by detection of errors in its output. Thus, fault detection techniques form the basis of dynamic redundancy.

In the rest of this section, we will mainly concentrate on test pattern generation for off-line testing. The basics of off-line testing are introduced in Section 4.1. In particular, the topics of fault modeling, fault equivalence, and fault simulation are discussed in some detail. Section 4.2 is on test generation techniques. Exhaustive, random, algebraic, structural, functional, and architectural approaches to test generation will be described. Testing regular circuits is the topic of Section 4.3, where test generation for programmable logic arrays (PLAs) is discussed as an example.

4.1 Off-Line Testing

In general, an off-line (explicit) testing process involves three steps:

1. Generating the test patterns. The goal of this step is to produce those input patterns that will exercise the circuit under test (CUT) under different modes of operation while trying to detect any existing fault.

2. Applying the test patterns to the CUT. There are two ways to accomplish this step. The first is external testing—the use of special test equipment to apply the test patterns externally. The second is internal testing—the application of test patterns internally by forcing the CUT to execute a self-testing procedure.

3. Evaluating the response obtained from the CUT. This step is designed with one of two goals in mind. The first is the detection of an erroneous response, which indicates the existence of one or more faults (go/no-go testing). The other is the isolation of the fault, if one exists (fault location). Our interest in this article will be go/no-go testing, since fault-location testing of VLSI circuits has only limited use.

4.1.1 The Test Generation Process

The test generation process represents the most important part of any explicit testing method. Its main goal is to generate those test patterns that, when applied to the CUT, sensitize existing faults and propagate a faulty response to an observable output of the CUT.

Rigorous test generation consists of three main activities:

1. Selecting a good descriptive model, at a suitable level, for the circuit under consideration.

2. Developing a fault model to define the types of faults that will be considered during test generation. The nature of the fault model is usually influenced by the model used to describe the circuit.

3. Generating tests to detect all the faults in the fault model. This part of test generation is the soul of the whole test process.

4.1.2   Failures and Fault Models

An important step in developing a testing strategy involves identifying the malfunctions to be tested for and deriving models for the logical effects of these faults. The underlying cause of a malfunction can be an improper design, erroneous use, or physical failure.

Physical failures can be either permanent or temporary. A permanent or hard failure is caused by a mechanical rupture or some wear-out phenomenon (e.g., metal migration). Usually, permanent failures are localized and can be minimized by careful processing and initial screening tests.

Temporary or soft failures occur at least ten times as often as permanent failures. They can be either transient or intermittent. A transient failure is caused by some externally induced signal perturbation. Careful attention to shielding and decoupling in the design of equipment is of value in reducing transient failures. An intermittent failure often occurs when a component is in the process of developing a permanent failure. The occurrence of intermittent failures is minimized in the same way that permanent failures are controlled.

Fault Models.   Fault models for physical failures in digital systems attempt to combine computational simplicity with an accurate modeling of real failures. They often represent compromises between the frequently conflicting objectives of tractability and accuracy. Only permanent faults are considered in the following discussion, in part because intermittent and transient faults are generally very difficult to model.

The single-stuck-line (SSL) fault model is the most common. An SSL fault is inserted into logic line x by conceptually cutting x and applying a constant signal d, which may be 0 or 1, to the output of x. Line x is now said to be stuck-at-d (s-a-d), and is unaffected by the normal logic signal applied to x by the remainder of the circuit. The SSL fault model allows only one line to be faulty at a time.

In a circuit containing n lines, $2n$ distinct SSL faults are possible. This number is modest compared to the corresponding number of bridging faults between pairs of lines $[n(n - 1)/2]$, or the number of multiple-stuck-line (MSL) faults $(3^n - 1)$.

A variation of the stuck-at fault model is the unidirectional fault, in which it is assumed that one or more stuck-at faults may be present, but all the stuck signals have the same logic value (all 0 or all 1). This is particularly appropriate for modeling some failure modes of storage media.

Although stuck-at faults have the convenient property that their effects are independent of the signals present in the circuit, there are failure modes that cannot be adequately modeled by such faults. For example, in order to develop tests for random access memories (RAMs), it is necessary to consider pattern-sensitivity faults in which the effect of the fault is dependent on the particular input applied to the device. For the newer, high density dynamic MOS circuits it may also be necessary to consider pattern-sensitivity faults (Abadir and Reghbati, 1983).

Open-circuit faults can affect the logical behavior of MOS circuits in ways that are very hard to model via conventional approaches. One such fault which is of special interest is the stuck-open fault occuring when a logic connection becomes improperly isolated from all sources of 0 and 1 signals. Stuck-open faults can cause complex and unexpected behavior in dynamic MOS and CMOS circuits by preventing capacitors from charging or discharging. An example of this is the parasitic flip-flop (PFF) fault, which can convert a combinational circuit to a sequential circuit. A PFF fault occurs when a line L becomes isolated from all signal sources except stray or parasitic capacitance that is capable of maintaining a previous value on L for a relatively long period of time.

The previous fault models all involve signals having incorrect values. A different class of faults (delay faults) occurs when a signal does not assume an incorrect value but instead fails to change value soon enough. More specifically, a delay fault occurs when a gate has a propagation delay exceeding the specified worst case.

Many situations occur in which a less detailed fault model is the most effective choice. For example, the most useful model for designing fault tolerant systems may be one in which it is assumed that any single module can fail in an arbitrary fashion. This is called a single module fault. The only restriction on the system is the assumption that at most one module will be faulty at any given time.

4.1.3 Fault Equivalence and Redundancy

The set of tests that detects a fault α is defined by the equation $T_\alpha = f \oplus f_\alpha$, where f and f_α are the functions realized by the normal and the faulty circuits, respectively. The set of tests that distinguishes between two faults α and β is defined by $f_\alpha \oplus f_\beta$. If such a test does not exist, i.e., $f_\alpha = f_\beta$, α and β are said to be equivalent. Equivalent faults can be grouped into an equivalence class and any test that detects one of them will detect all.

A fault α is said to dominate another fault β if T_β, the set of tests that detects β, is a subset of T_α. In other words, any test that detects β will also detect α. For fault detection, α can therefore be deleted from the initial list of faults to be considered. In general, for elementary gates of n inputs, only $n + 1$ SSL faults need to be on the initial fault list instead of the $2(n + 1)$ potential

SSL faults (Breuer and Friedman, 1976). The reduction of fault lists for multiple faults has also been addressed (Bossen and Hong, 1971).

If $T_\alpha = 0$, i.e., $f_\alpha = f$, the fault α is said to be undetectable and the circuit is said to be redundant with respect to α. Although a faulty circuit containing α would behave correctly, it is important that the existence of redundancy be determined and eliminated for the following reason. It is implicit in the SSL fault assumption that any fault will be detected before a second fault occurs. This may be impossible for a redundant circuit since the first fault may be undetectable. For such circuits, generation of tests for all detectable single faults is inadequate. Specifically, for a redundant circuit C and a set of tests $\{T\}$ that detects all detectable single faults in C, there may exist a sequence of faults α, β such that α is undetectable and the multiple fault (α, β) is detectable but is not detected by $\{T\}$.

4.1.4 Fault Simulation

Fault simulation determines the behavior of the circuit in the presence of each of the faults from a specified set. Due to the large number of potential faults in any large circuit and the complexity of simulation algorithms, it is usually assumed that only a single fault can be present in the circuit at any time. One of the uses of fault simulation is to determine the fault coverage of a given test sequence. The fault coverage is defined as the ratio of the number of detected faults to the total number of simulated faults. This measure of test quality can be used for improving the test sequence, if necessary. Fault simulation is also used for building dictionaries (in a data base) of the "signatures" of the different faults for the purpose of fault location. Actual faulty responses collected from the circuit under test are compared with the fault signatures in the data base to find the closest match and thereby identify the most probable failure.

4.2   Test Generation Techniques

Testing is done in order to discover defects in a digital system that could be caused during manufacture or because of wear-out in the field. The choice of test patterns is determined by factors such as the time available for test, the degree of access to internal circuitry, and the percentage of failures that are required to be detected. Different approaches to test pattern generation are discussed in this section.

4.2.1 Exhaustive and Random Testing

The concepts of generating test vectors for a digital circuit by some random process provides probably the simplest approach to the test generation problem. Moreover, operational experience and analysis have shown that, indeed, it can be an extremely effective means for fault detection (David and Thevenod-Fosse, 1981). A major problem with random testing is the determination of the relationship among test quality, length of random pattern tests (both pass/fail and diagnostic), and diagnostic resolution (Savir and Bardell, 1984).

A second conceptually simple approach to testing is the application of all 2^n input combinations to the (combinational) circuit under test. This is known as exhaustive testing and can require a prohibitively long test time for circuits with many inputs (McCluskey, 1984).

4.2.2 Algebraic Methods

Some investigators have considered the possibility of developing algebraic approaches to test generation by examining and manipulating the Boolean expressions that define the functions involved. With regard to the all-important sensitization problem, a question that repeatedly occurs is how can a given output be made sensitive to a given input? In other words, given an output function, $f(x_1, \ldots, x_n)$, and an input variable, x_i, at what values should we set $x_1, \ldots, x_{i-1}, x_{i+1}, \ldots, x_n$ so that f becomes sensitive to x_i (i.e., so that a change in x_i will cause a change in f)? The Boolean expression, denoted by f_i, that defines this situation is simply

$$f_i = df/dx_i$$
$$= f(x_1, \ldots, x_{i-1}, 0, x_{i+1}, \ldots, x_n) \oplus f(x_1, \ldots, x_{i-1}, 1, x_{i+1}, \ldots, x_n)$$

and f is sensitive to x_i if and only if $f_i = 1$.

This expression for f is known as the Boolean difference of f with respect to x_i (Akers, 1959). Thus, the set of all tests that detect the fault x_i s-a-0 is $\{x \mid x_i(df/dx_i) = 1\}$ and is defined by $x_i(df/dx_i)$. This expression implies that $x_i = 1$ and $(df/dx_i) = 1$. Since $x_i = 1$, then x_i applies the opposite value on the faulty input. The factor df/dx_i ensures that the excited fault affects the value of f. Similarly, the set of all tests that detect the fault x_i s-a-1 is defined by the Boolean expression $\bar{x}_i(df/dx_i)$.

Example 4.1 Consider the circuit of Figure 3 whose output is defined by the Boolean expression $f = (x_2 + x_3)x_1 + \bar{x}_1 x_4$. The set of all tests that detects the fault x_4 s-a-1 is defined by the Boolean expression

$$\bar{x}_4(df/dx_4) = \bar{x}_4[x_1(x_2 + x_3) \oplus (x_1(x_2 + x_3) + \bar{x}_1)]$$
$$= \bar{x}_1 \bar{x}_4. \qquad \blacksquare$$

In general, faults can exist not only on external or primary inputs but also on signal lines that are internal to the circuit. Consider a circuit C that realizes the

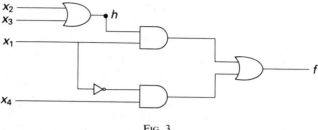

function $f(x)$ and let h be an internal signal of C. Then h can be expressed as a function of the inputs $h(x)$ and f can be expressed as a function f' of x and h (by considering h as an input). Then the set of all tests that detects the fault h s-a-0 is defined by the Boolean expression

$$h(x) \quad \frac{df'(x, h)}{dh}$$

and the set of all tests that detects the fault h s-a-1 is defined by the Boolean expression

$$\overline{h(x)} \quad \frac{df'(x, h)}{dh}$$

where $f'(x, h) = f(x)$.

Example 4.2   For the circuit of Figure 3, consider the fault h s-a-0. The output $f = (x_2 + x_3)x_1 + \bar{x}_1 x_4$ can be expressed as a function of h and x, $f' = hx_1 + \bar{x}_1 x_4$ and h can be expressed as a function of x, $h = x_2 + x_3$. Then

$$h(x) \quad \frac{df'(x_1, x_4, h)}{dh} = (x_2 + x_3)[f'(x_1, x_4, 0) \oplus f'(x_1, x_4, 1)]$$

$$= (x_2 + x_3)[\bar{x}_1 x_4 \oplus (x_1 + \bar{x}_1 x_4)]$$

$$= (x_2 + x_3)x_1. \qquad\blacksquare$$

The Boolean difference has many useful properties analogous to the classic derivative function of differential calculus. Many of the basic concepts and relationships of Boolean algebra are much more easily expressed and understood using this Boolean difference. The familiar Reed-Muller expansion, for example, turns out to be simply the Boolean version of the well-known Taylor series.

Once the potential usefulness of Boolean difference was recognized, researchers were quickly able to apply it to many aspects of the test generation process (Sellers *et al.*, 1968). Using such familiar notions as partial differences and chain rule manipulations, they were able to extend its use not only to

multiple stuck-at faults, using higher order differences, but also to asynchronous sequential circuits (Sellers *et al.*, 1968; Ku and Masson, 1975; Chiang
et al., 1972).

The primary importance of these and other algebraic methods (Armstrong,
1966; Bossen and Hong, 1971; Clegg, 1973; Kinoshita *et al.*, 1980) rests on the
fact that they permit concise descriptions of the many concepts involved in test
generation, and these in turn provide valuable insights into the underlying
processes and relationships. However, the practical application of the
algebraic techniques is severly limited by the number of variables involved.

4.2.3 *Structural Techniques*

Structural-level testing is usually based on the concept that if the structure
of the device under test conforms to that of the fault-free device, the device has
gone through an acceptable fabrication process. Single stuck-line is the most
commonly used fault model at this level of testing. D-algorithm (Roth *et al.*,
1967) and PODEM (Goel, 1981) are two of the most well-known techniques
in this category. Many of the test generation techniques reported in the
literature, are extensions and/or improvements to the D-algorithm (Jain and
Agrawal, 1983), or PODEM (Fujiwara and Shimono, 1983).

D-Algorithm. One of the classical fault-detection methods at the gate and
flip-flop level is the D-algorithm (Roth *et al.*, 1967) employing the path
sensitization technique (Breuer and Friedman, 1976). The basic principle
involved in path sensitization is relatively simple. In order for an input X to
detect a fault "line a is stuck-at-j, $j = 0, 1$," the input X must cause the signal a
in the normal (fault-free) circuit to take the value $\bar{j}$. This condition is necessary
but not sufficient to detect the fault. The error signal must be propagated along
some path, or parallel paths, from its site to an observable output.

Example 4.3   For the circuit in Figure 4 consider the fault line α stuck-
at-1. To excite the fault, we will generate a 0 at the fault site by selecting
$A = B = C = 1$. Two choices exist for propagating the fault either through

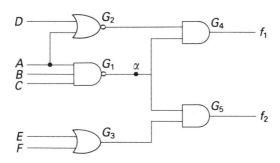

FIG. 4.

$G4$ or through $G5$. To propagate the fault through $G4$, the output of $G2$ must be 1 (to make the output of $G4$ sensitive to the value of α). This implies $A = D = 0$. But this contradicts the previous requirements. To propagate the fault through $G5$ requires the output of $G3$ to be 1, which could be justified by selecting either $E = 1$ or $F = 1$, leading to two tests $ABCE$, and $ABCF$. ∎

As shown in the above example, there may be several possible choices for error propagation and line justification. Also, in some cases there may be several initial choices to excite the fault. Some of these choices may lead to an inconsistency, and hence we backtrack and consider another alternative. If all the alternatives lead to an inconsistency, this implies that the fault cannot be detected.

To facilitate the path sensitization process, we introduce the symbol D to represent a signal that has the value 1 in the normal circuit and 0 in the faulty circuit, and $\bar{D}$ to represent a signal that has the value 0 in the normal circuit and 1 in the faulty circuit. For example, the outputs of 2-input AND and OR gates, each of whose inputs can take on the four composite values $\{0, 1, D, \bar{D}\}$ is defined by the tables of Figure 5a and 5b, respectively.

The path sensitization procedure can be formulated in terms of a cubical algebra (Breuer and Friedman, 1976) to enable automatic generation of tests. This also facilitates test generation for more complex fault models and for fault propagation through complex logic elements. We shall define three types of cubes (line values specified in positional notation).

1. For a circuit element E that realizes the combinational function f, the primitive cubes of f are a typical presentation of the prime implicants of f and $\bar{f}$. These cubes concisely represent the logical behavior of E.

Example 4.4   Consider a 3-input NAND gate with input lines 1, 2, 3 and output line 4. The primitive cubes describing the prime implicants of the output function $f(\beta_1)$ and $\bar{f}(\beta_0)$ are shown in Figure 6. ∎

AND

	0	1	D	$\bar{D}$
0	0	0	0	0
1	0	1	D	$\bar{D}$
D	0	D	D	0
$\bar{D}$	0	$\bar{D}$	0	$\bar{D}$

(a)

OR

	0	1	D	$\bar{D}$
0	0	1	D	$\bar{D}$
1	1	1	1	1
D	D	1	D	1
$\bar{D}$	$\bar{D}$	1	1	$\bar{D}$

(b)

FIG. 5.   Composite values for AND and OR gates.

1	2	3	4	
0	x	x	1	
x	0	x	1	β_1
x	x	0	1	
1	1	1	0	β_0

FIG. 6.   Primitive cubes of a 3-input NAND gate.

An important aspect in cubical algebra is the intersection of two cubes α and β. This process determines how the two circuit conditions specified by the two cubes α and β can be simultaneously satisfied. The intersection $\alpha \cap \beta$ is defined to be the value of the two cubes in each position in which they have identical values, and if one cube is unspecified (x) for some position, the intersection has the value of the other cube in that position. If the two cubes assign different values to the same line, then the intersection does not exist and the two cubes are said to be inconsistent.

Example 4.5   Let $\alpha = 0xx1$, $\beta = xx01$ and $\delta = 011x$, then $\alpha \cap \beta = 0x01$, and $\alpha \cap \delta = 0111$. Attempting to intersect β and δ leads to an inconsistency. ∎

2. A primitive D-cube of a fault in a logic element E specifies the minimal input conditions that must be applied to E in order to produce an error signal (D or $\bar{D}$) at the output of E. These input conditions can be determined from the primitive cubes of f, the normal function realized by E and f_α, the function realized by a faulty circuit. An input condition produces a faulty output $D(\bar{D})$ if it is contained in a prime implicant of $f(\bar{f})$ and also contained in a prime implicant of $\bar{f}_\alpha(f_\alpha)$. In other words, the input conditions that result in output $D(\bar{D})$ can be obtained by intersecting the inputs of each primitive cube of $f(\bar{f})$ with those for each cube of $\bar{f}_\alpha(f_\alpha)$.

Example 4.6   Consider the 3-input NAND gate described in Example 4.4 and the fault line 1 stuck-at-1. The primitive cubes of the faulty circuit are shown in Figure 7. The primitive D-cubes of the fault are derived by intersecting the inputs of each cube in $\beta_1(\beta_0)$ of Figure 6 with those for each cube in $\alpha_0(\alpha_1)$ of Figure 7. The only primitive D-cube for that fault is $\bar{D}11D$ derived by intersecting the first cube in β_1 with the cube in α_0. The primitive D-cubes of all stuck-at faults for the 3-input NAND gate are listed in Figure 8. ∎

3. The propagation D-cubes of a logic element E specify minimal input conditions to the logic element that are required to propagate an error signal on an input (or inputs) to the output of that element. Let the logical behavior of E be defined by two sets of primitive cubes β_0 and β_1 that result in 0 and 1 outputs from E, respectively. The propagation D-cube required to propagate an error on an input line r can be derived by intersecting cubes in β_0 with

1	2	3	4	
x	0	x	1	α_1
x	x	0	1	
x	1	1	0	α_0

FIG. 7.   Primitive cubes of a faulty 3-input NAND gate.

1	2	3	4	Fault
0	x	x	D	4 stuck-at-0
x	0	x	D	4 stuck-at-0
x	x	0	D	4 stuck-at-0
1	1	1	$\bar{D}$	4 stuck-at-1
D	1	1	$\bar{D}$	1 stuck-at-0
$\bar{D}$	1	1	D	1 stuck-at-1
1	D	1	$\bar{D}$	2 stuck-at-0
1	$\bar{D}$	1	D	2 stuck-at-1
1	1	D	$\bar{D}$	3 stuck-at-0
1	1	$\bar{D}$	D	3 stuck-at-1

FIG. 8.   Primitive D-cubes of single stuck-at faults for a 3-input NAND gate.

$r = 0(1)$ and with $r = 1(0)$. Propagation D-cubes for multiple input faults can be derived similarly as illustrated in the following example.

Example 4.7   Consider the propagation of the error signal D on one or more input lines of the 3-input NAND gate described in Example 4.4. The propagation D-cubes are shown in Figure 9. Note that the propagation D-cubes required for propagating a $\bar{D}$ on one or more input lines can be obtained by complementing the Ds and $\bar{D}$s in the cubes shown. ∎

Each element in the circuit under test can be described using the previously defined cubes. These cubes are then used by the D-algorithm to automatically

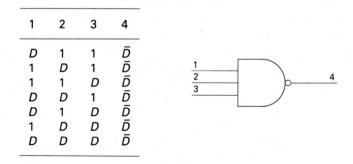

1	2	3	4
D	1	1	$\bar{D}$
1	D	1	$\bar{D}$
1	1	D	$\bar{D}$
D	D	1	$\bar{D}$
D	1	D	$\bar{D}$
1	D	D	$\bar{D}$
D	D	D	$\bar{D}$

FIG. 9.   Propagation D-cubes for a 3-input NAND gate.

generate a test for any stuck-at fault in the circuit, if such a test exists. The D-algorithm can be described as follows:

Procedure 4.1 (D-Algorithm)   To generate a test for a stuck-at fault in a combinational circuit:

Step 1. Fault excitation. Select a primitive D-cube of the fault under consideration. This generates the error signal D or $\bar{D}$ at the site of the fault. (Usually a choice exists in this step. The initial choice is arbitrary, but it may be necessary to backtrack and consider another possible choice).

Step 2. Implication. In Step 1, some of the gate inputs or outputs may be specified so as to uniquely imply values on other signals in the circuit. The implication procedure is performed both forwards and backwards through the circuit. Implication is performed as follows: Whenever a previously unspecified signal value becomes specified, all the elements associated with this signal are placed on a list B and processed one at a time (and removed). For each element processed, based upon the previously specified inputs and outputs, it is determined if new values of 0, 1, D, and $\bar{D}$ are implied. These implied line values are determined by intersecting the test cube (which specifies all the previously determined signal values of the circuit) with the primitive cubes of the element. If any line values are implied, they are specified in the test cube and the associated gates are placed on the list B.

An inconsistency occurs when a value is implied on a line that has been specified previously to a different value. If an inconsistency occurs, backtrack to the last point a choice existed, reset all lines to their values at this point and begin again with the next choice.

Step 3. D-Propagation. All the elements in the circuit whose output values are unspecified and whose input has some signal D or $\bar{D}$ are placed on a list called the D-frontier. In this step, select an element from the D-frontier and assign values to its unspecified inputs so as to propagate the D or $\bar{D}$ on its inputs to one of its outputs. This is accomplished by intersecting the current test cube describing the circuit signal values with a propagation D-cube of the selected element of the D-frontier, resulting in a new test cube. If such intersection is impossible, a new element in the D-frontier is selected. If intersection fails for all the elements in the D-frontier, backtrack to the last point at which a choice existed.

Step 4. Implication of D-propagation. Perform implication for the new test cube derived in Step 3.

Step 5. Repeat Steps 3 and 4 until the faulty signal has been propagated to an output of the circuit.

Step 6. Line justification. Execution of Steps 1 to 5 may result in specifying the output value of an element *E* but leaving some of the inputs to the element unspecified. The unspecified inputs of such an element are assigned values so as to produce the desired output value by intersecting the test cube with any primitive cube of the element which has no specified signal values that differ from those of the test cube.

Step 7. Implication of line justification. Perform implication on the new test cube derived in Step 6.

Step 8. Repeat Steps 6 and 7 until all specified element outputs have been justified. Backtracking may again be required.   ■

Example 4.8 For the circuit of Figure 10 and the fault G_2 stuck-at-1, the table in Figure 11 lists the primitive D-cubes of the fault and the primitive cubes of gates G_1, G_3, G_4, G_5, and G_6.

Assume we select the first primitive D-cube, implication will result in specifying lines 8 and 9 to have the value 1. At this stage the D-frontier list is empty and we cannot propagate the error signal. Thus, we must backtrack and select the second primitive D-cube of the fault. No signal values are implied by the new test cube. At this stage the D-frontier contains only gate G_4. The relevant propagation D-cube of G_4 is shown in Figure 12 (row 4), and row 5 of this table shows the test cube after the D-propagation through G_4.

Performing implication at this stage will not result in specifying any new lines. The D-frontier contains both G_5 and G_6. The relevant propagation D-cube of G_6 and the test cube after propagating the D through G_6 are shown

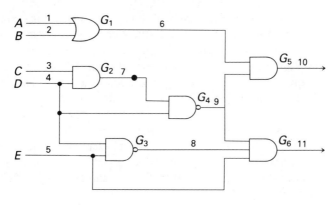

FIG. 10.

	1	2	3	4	5	6	7	8	9	10	11
Primitive D-cubes of the fault			X	0			$\bar{D}$				
			0	X			$\bar{D}$				
Primitive cubes of G_1	1	X					1				
	X	1					1				
	0	0					0				
Primitive cubes of G_3				0	X			1			
				X	0			1			
				1	1			0			
Primitive cubes of G_4				0			X	1			
				X			0	1			
				1			1	0			
Primitive cubes of G_5						0			X	0	
						X			0	0	
						1			1	1	
Primitive cubes of G_6				0				X	X		0
				X				0	X		0
				X				X	0		0
				1				1	1		1

FIG. 11. Cubical description of the circuit of Figure 10.

	1	2	3	4	5	6	7	8	9	10	11
Initial test cube			X	0			$\bar{D}$				
Implication			X	0			$\bar{D}$	1	1		
BACKTRACK											
Initial test cube			0	X			$\bar{D}$				
Propagation D-cube of G_4				1			$\bar{D}$		D		
Test cube after D-propagation			0	1			$\bar{D}$		D		
Propagation D-cube of G_6					1			1	D		D
Test cube after D-propagation			0	1	1		$\bar{D}$	1	D		D
BACKTRACK											
Propagation D-cube of G_5						1			D	D	
Test cube after D-propagation			0	1		1	$\bar{D}$		D	D	
Line justification	1		0	1		1	$\bar{D}$		D	D	

FIG. 12. Test generation trace.

in Figure 12, rows 6 and 7. The two inputs to the NAND gate G_3 are both
specified as 1. This implies that the output of G_3 should be 0, which leads to an
inconsistency as line 8 has already been specified to be 1. Thus, we will
backtrack to the last point a choice existed and consider the other element in
the D-frontier. The relevant propagation D-cube of G_5 and the test cube after
propagating the D through G_5 are shown in Figure 12, rows 8 and 9. At this
stage, the error signal has been propagated to an observable output (line 10).
Line justification of the 1 signal on line 6 results in specifying line 1 or 2 to
have the value 1.   ∎

The process of executing the D-algorithm can be represented as the process
of executing a sequence of subprocesses. Each one of these subprocesses
performs one of three basic operations on one element of the circuit under test.
These three basic operations are implication, D-propagation, and line
justification. Performing any of these three operations is very simply because
of the simple nature of the functions being considered (OR, AND, NAND,
etc.).

PODEM. A test generation algorithm called the PODEM (Path Oriented
Decision Making) algorithm was reported by Goel (1981) and shown to be
more efficient than the D-algorithm. This is particularly true for generating
tests for circuits in which the D-algorithm can become involved in a large
number of conflicts. An example of such a circuit is shown in Figure 13. For
the fault H s-a-0, the D-algorithm may go through the following steps: First,
the fault is excited by assigning $A = B = 1$ and $H = D$. To propagate the faulty
signal to the primary output R, D-drive operations are performed. This could
result in $N = 1$, $P = \bar{D}$, $Q = 1$, and $R = D$. Next, the D-algorithm begins to

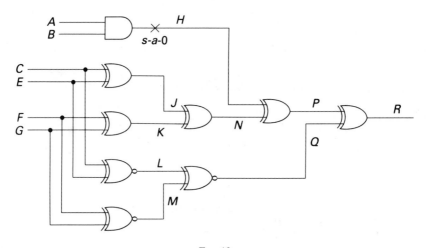

FIG. 13.

justify lines N and Q. However, since lines N and Q realize complementary functions, no justification is possible for the concurrent assignment $N = 1$ and $Q = 1$. Thus, the D-algorithm must enumerate input values exhaustively until the absence of the justification is confirmed. In this enumeration process, the D-algorithm backtracks tediously many times until it reaches the assignment $N = 1$ and $Q = 0$ (or $N = 0$ and $Q = 1$).

The PODEM algorithm attempts to address the problem of uncontrollably large numbers of remade decisions by working directly at the inputs to create a test for a fault. PODEM begins by assigning x's to all inputs. It then starts assigning arbitrary values to primary inputs. Implications of the assignments are propagated forward. If either of the following two propositions is true, the assignment is rejected:

1. The signal net for the stuck fault being tested has the same logic level as the stuck level.
2. There is no signal path from an internal signal net to a primary output such that the internal signal net has value D or $\bar{D}$ and all other nets on the signal path are at x.

Indeed, in both cases, the fault cannot be detected by the decisions made thus far; therefore, it is necessary to remake some decisions.

When PODEM makes assignments to primary inputs, it employs a "branch and bound" strategy. Here, the process of finding a test vector can be best described by considering a binary tree, wherein a node corresponds to an input line and the two branches correspond to assignments of a 0 or a 1 to that input line (see Fig. 14). The branching step is simply to go as deeply into the tree as

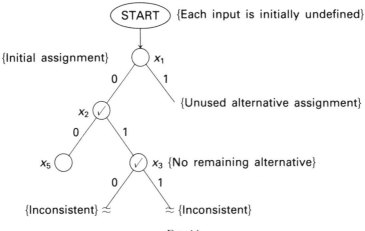

FIG. 14.

possible. The bounding step is going to the last node that has an untried brother.

The branch operation basically consists of making an intelligent choice on the next input line to be selected and the value to be assigned to it. This choice is made with the objective of bringing the test generation process closer to its goal of propagating a D or $\bar{D}$ to a primary output. The chosen input line and the value on that line are those that help towards meeting this objective. At the start, the objective is to excite the fault. Later, the objective is aimed at propagating a D or $\bar{D}$ one level closer to a primary output line. This is implemented by simply selecting that gate from the D-frontier that is closest to a primary output line.

Once the objective is determined in terms of which line inside the circuit should be assigned a specific value, the next step is to trace backwards in the logic diagram to determine an input line and the value on it that will help meet the objective. This backtrace operation is somewhat similar (but less complex) than the justification operation of the D-algorithm.

Consider the objective of setting a 0 (1) on the output line of an AND (OR) gate. In the backtrace operation, any input of the gate can be set to 0 (1) to achieve the objective. However, an intelligent choice is to choose that input which is most controllable among the inputs of that gate. Similarly, for the objective of setting a 1 (0) on the output line of an AND (OR) gate, all the input lines to that gate must be set to 1 (0). The least controllable input to the gate should be chosen. Thus, an early determination of the inability to set the chosen input will avoid time wasted attempting to set the remaining inputs of the gate. This process repeated iteratively will eventually lead to an input line and a binary value for it.

The PODEM algorithm can be implemented by using a LIFO stack. As an input (and its value) is selected, it is placed on the stack. A node is flagged if the initial assignment has been rejected and the alternative is being tried (see Fig. 14). If a node violates one of the two propositions and it is flagged, it is popped off the stack, hence bounding the branch-and-bound tree. Nodes continue to be popped off until an unflagged node is encountered. The process terminates when a test is found or the stack becomes empty (in which case no test exists). Since PODEM considers all input combinations if necessary, it is an algorithm; and therefore, if it does not find a test for a fault that fault is redundant.

Example 4.9   We will illustrate the PODEM algorithm by deriving a test for detecting the fault α s-a-0 in the circuit of Figure 15. The initial objective is to set the output of gate A to logic 1; i.e., the objective logic level is 1 on net 5. By going through the backtrace procedure, it can be determined that the next objective net is 1 (or 2) and the objective logic level is 0. Since net 1 is fed by

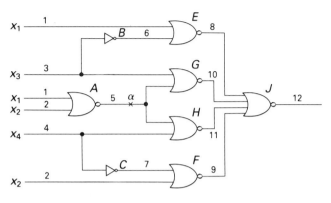

FIG. 15.

the primary input x_1, the current objective logic level (i.e., logic 0) is assigned
to the primary input x_1 as shown below:

1	2	3	4	5	6	7	8	9	10	11	12
0	X	X	X	X	X	X	X	X	X	X	X

Since $x_1x_2x_3x_4 = 0XXX$ is not a test for the fault, a second pass through the
algorithm results in the assignment of primary input x_2, which sets up D as the
output of gate A:

1	2	3	4	5	6	7	8	9	10	11	12
0	0	X	X	D	X	X	X	X	X	X	X

Since the output of gate A (i.e., net 5) is not X, it is necessary to find a gate
with D as its input, X as its output and closer to the primary output. Both gates
G and H satisfy the requirements. The selection of gate G and the subsequent
inital objective result in the assignment of primary input x_3:

1	2	3	4	5	6	7	8	9	10	11	12
0	0	0	X	D	1	X	0	X	$\bar{D}$	X	X

$x_1x_2x_3x_4 = 000X$ is not a test for the fault because the primary output is X.
Gate J and $\bar{D}$ on input net 10 and Xs on input nets 9 and 11. The initial
objective is to set the objective net 12 to logic 1. The selection of net 9 as the
next objective results in the assignment of primary input x_4:

1	2	3	4	5	6	7	8	9	10	11	12
0	0	0	0	D	1	1	0	0	$\bar{D}$	$\bar{D}$	D

Thus, the test for the fault α s-a-0 is $x_1 x_2 x_3 x_4 = 0000$. The same test could be found for the fault by applying the D-algorithm; however, the D-algorithm requires substantial trial and error before the test is found. This is because of the variety of propagation paths and the attendant consistency operations that are required. For example, α s-a-0 has to be simultaneously propagated to the output via the paths AGJ and AHJ; propagation along either path individually will lead to inconsistency.   ∎

Test Generation for Sequential Circuits.   While the D-algorithm and other test generation methods (e.g., PODEM) can handle purely combinational logic circuits, the testing of sequential circuits still remains as a major problem. This is mainly due to the fact that the bahavior of a sequential circuit depends not only on the present values of the inputs, but also on the set of past inputs. Therefore, in general, it takes an entire sequence of inputs to detect a fault in a sequential network.

Most of the techniques for testing sequential circuits can be classified into three categories:

1. A given sequential circuit is converted into a one-dimensional array of identical combinatorial circuits. Then most techniques for generating tests for combinational circuits are applicable (Breuer and Friedman, 1976; Muth, 1976).

2. The sequential circuit is tested by verifing whether or not it is operating in accordance with its state table (Kohavi, 1970). This is a functional approach to test generation.

3. Heuristic approaches are used (Marlett, 1986).

4.2.4 Functional Approaches

As the systems to be tested become larger, one approach taken to reduce the complexity of the test generation is to test a system by applying inputs that would verify its designed functions were indeed performed correctly. This is frequently called functional testing. An example of such an approach is the Abadir–Reghbati technique (Abadir and Reghbati, 1987).

Universal Test Sets.   Although circuit technologies are constantly changing, the basic circuit functions are still the same. The adders, multiplexers, registers, and counters in today's devices are functionally the same as those of 20 years ago. Therefore, the question that naturally arises is whether or not there exists a universal test set for a given function; i.e., a set of tests that will in some sense be good for testing any implementation of that function. Of course, the number of tests in such a test set should be small compared to the number required by exhaustive testing. Single stuck-at tests for certain standard arithmetic logic units (ALUs), for example, never seem to involve more than approximately 25 tests, regardless of the manufacturer's implementation. Might not a universal test set of say 50 tests exist that would be good for all such implementations?

Some modest but encouraging results have been reported in this regard, (Reddy, 1973; Akers, 1973; Betancourt, 1971). One familiar class of implementations for which universal test sets for stuck-at faults do exist are the so-called AND/OR implementations. These are implementations in which only AND and OR gates are used with all inversions occuring only at the inputs to the circuit. Figure 16 shows three such implementations for the function $f = (A + \bar{C})(\bar{A} + B + C)$, together with the universal test set that will detect not only single but also all multiple stuck-ats in any of these circuits.

It turns out that the size of the universal test set depends directly on the "non-unateness" of the function involved; i.e., on the number of input variables that appear both inverted and uninverted. A disappointing corollary is that if all input variables must appear both inverted and uninverted, then only the exhaustive test is guaranteed to work for all such circuits. On the other hand, when most of the variables are unate, surprisingly small universal test sets can often be found. The widely used "1 out of 16 multiplexer," which is unate in 16 of its 20 input variables, has a universal (AND/OR) test set of just 32 tests from a list of over one million possible choices.

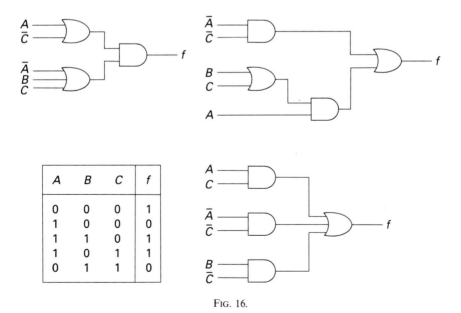

A	B	C	f
0	0	0	1
1	0	0	0
1	1	0	1
1	0	1	1
0	1	1	0

FIG. 16.

4.2.5   Architectural Methods

Among the most promising of recent test generation developments are the investigations that have attacked the test generation problem from essentially an "architectural" level. Most older test generation procedures ignore the functional identity of the various inputs, outputs, and signal paths involved in a given digital system, and simply try to generate the proper combinations of 0s and 1s to achieve certain designated goals. In contrast, these "macro-approaches" look directly at the architecture of the device involved to generate the test (Thatte and Abraham, 1980).

4.3   Test Generation for Regular Circuits

The preceding discussion has concentrated mostly on classical techniques of test generation for irregular combinational logic. The regularity of some circuits has resulted in some special techniques for their test generation. Programmable logic arrays (PLAs), memories, and iterative logic arrays are among such circuits. As an example, test generation for PLAs is discussed in the rest of this section.

4.3.1   Test Generation for PLAs

By virtue of its regular structure which simplifies the design of irregular combinational logic, the programmable logic array has found wide acceptance as an important LSI/VLSI logic component. For example, the BELLMAC-32A chip has eight PLAs, the largest of which has 50 inputs, 67 outputs, and 190 product terms.

For convenience in presentation, we assume that the inputs of the PLA are decoded by single-bit decoders, and that the PLA is implemented in NMOS technology, using a two-level NOR-NOR circuit. As shown in Figure 17, the PLA has n input lines, $2n$ bit lines, m product lines, p sum lines, and p output lines. The increasing popularity of PLAs has lead to a growing interest in the development of efficient fault-detection methods for these modules.

Fault Model for PLAs.   Bridging faults, crosspoint faults, and stuck-at faults are generally recognized to be the faults common in PLAs. Their definitions are given as follows:

1. Bridging faults. A short between 2 adjacent or crossing lines. Depending on the type of implementational circuitry, the result can be the ANDing or ORing of the logic values of the shorted lines. For example, in NMOS technology, an AND function between the shorted lines occurs.

2. Crosspoint faults. The absence (missing) or the unnecessary presence (extra) of a cross connection, or device, between a bit line and a product line, or between a product line and a sum line.

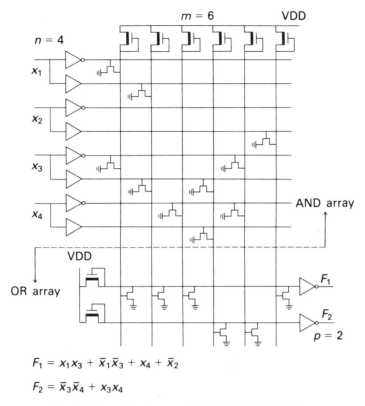

$$F_1 = x_1 x_3 + \bar{x}_1 \bar{x}_3 + x_4 + \bar{x}_2$$

$$F_2 = \bar{x}_3 \bar{x}_4 + x_3 x_4$$

FIG. 17.   Example of a normal PLA in NMOS technology.

3. Stuck-at faults. One of the lines stuck permanently to one of the 2 logic values, commonly caused by a short to ground or to power.

Note that the number of (single) crosspoint faults and crossline bridging faults is a function of the area of the PLA, while the number of the other (single) faults is linear in the number of input, output, and the product line.

Logical Manifestation of Faults.   The logical effects of crosspoint faults are the growth, shrinkage, appearance, and disappearance of product terms, defined as follows (Smith, 1979):

1. Growth. A missing device in the AND array causes an input variable to disappear from a product term resulting in the growth of the product term.
2. Shrinkage. The opposite of growth, caused by an extra device in the AND array.

3. Appearance. An extra device in the OR array causes the erroneous appearance of a product term in an output function.

4. Disappearance. The opposite of appearance, caused by a missing device in the OR array.

The above definitions are restricted because they neither cover the bridging or stuck-at faults nor fully describe the logical effect of some kinds of crosspoint faults. For example, a product line may be permanently deactivated if, due to a single extra device, both x and $\bar{x}$ are connected to this line. The result is most appropriately described as a disappearance of the product term from all the output functions containing it.

A broader classification of the logical effects that covers all three classes of faults is given as follows (Bose and Abraham, 1982):

1. Growth appearance. The growth of a product term or the appearance of a product term on an output line(s), leading a logical expansion of an output function(s).

2. Shrinkage disappearance. The shrinkage of a product term or the disappearance of a product term from an output line(s), resulting in a logical shrinkage or disappearance of an output function(s).

In has been shown that a single fault of any type can only produce a unidirectional error; i.e., it may cause a growth appearance or a shrinkage disappearance effect, but not both (Mak et al., 1982).

In the rest of this section, if not mentioned otherwise, the fault coverage is assumed to be for all single faults of predefined types, although the set of tests for single faults also covers many multiple faults (Agarwal, 1980).

Test Generation for PLAs. The common goal of test generation for normal PLAs (see Fig. 17) can be summarized as follows:

1. Generation of tests for all detectable faults;
2. Identification of all undetectable faults and the assessment of their effects on the PLA function.

From our earlier discussion, it is apparent that different single faults may have the same logical effect on the PLA function; therefore, the test for a group of faults also covers some faults of other types. As noted earlier, the crosspoint faults account for a significant proportion of the single faults. Since they are more localized in nature, potentially fewer tests for a single fault of this type exist than for a single stuck-at or bridging fault. The convention is to generate tests for all detectable crosspoint faults, remove from further consideration those faults of other types covered by the test set generated so far, and attempt to generate tests for the yet uncovered testable faults of the other types.

Path sensitization is the traditional method for fault detection. The fault is first activated by specifying a proper subset of the input lines. The excited fault is propagated, if possible, to an observable output through justification of the rest of the input lines as required. The approach has been employed by Smith (1979) for the generation of tests for all detectable single crosspoint faults. The set of all faults is derived from the structure of the PLA. Tests are then generated for the crosspoint faults in the AND array. As each test is generated, its coverage of other faults is also determined. The covered faults are removed from further consideration. After all detectable faults in the AND array have been covered, tests are generated for those crosspoint faults in the OR array that are not yet covered. The set of tests so generated is shown to cover all detectable stuck-type faults (Smith, 1979).

For the generation of a test for a single growth fault or missing device, consider the product line p_i that represents the product term $(x_1)(x_2)(x_3)$ in an 8-input PLA (Smith, 1979). A missing device between input line $\bar{x}_1$ and p_i would change p_i to $p'_i = (x_2)(x_3)$. The steps are as follows:

Step 1. The initial specification $S_i = 011xxxxx$ (where x stands for "don't care") will activate this fault.

Step 2. Any output line f_j that contains p_i can be chosen for fault propagation. All other product lines that also activate f_j must be set to 0 through justification of the rest of the input lines. The test pattern chosen must be one that is covered by the initial specification, S_i, but not by any of the other product terms contained in f_j. Let P_j be the set of product terms in f_j, then the test pattern must come from the set of cubes Q where

$$Q = S_i \,\#\, (P_j - p_i),$$

and $\#$ stands for the disjoint sharp operation. If Q is null, then another output line activated by p_i is chosen and Step 2 is repeated.

Since the $\#$ operation has the potential of creating many cubes, the above procedure can be quite costly. Research by Eichelberger and Lindbloom (1980) and Bose and Abraham (1982), both aimed at reducing the cost of test generation, are of particular interest.

Eichelberger and Lindbloom (1980) proposed a heuristic method that reduces the computation time for generating a test for a crosspoint fault. The initial specification step is identical to Step 1 of Smith's method (Smith, 1979) described above. Line justification of Step 2 to deactivate all other product terms in f_j is done by random assignment (this may require more than one try, or pass).

The PLA characteristic causing random test patterns to be ineffective (i.e., many used crosspoints per product term) is also the characteristic that renders the procedure of combining a random pattern with the initial specification step effective for sensitizing test paths. That is, if the u inputs to an AND gate are randomly assigned, then the probability of the output being 0 is $[(2^u - 1)/2^u]$. For k product lines, the probability p_0 of randomly generating an input specification which does not activate any of the k lines is:

$$p_0 = \prod_{i=1}^{k} \frac{2^{u_i} - 1}{2^{u_i}}.$$

If $p_0 = 0.5$, the probability of obtaining a test in 5 passes is better than 95%, if such a test exists. For 19 custom-made PLAs the reseachers managed to generate test sets that cover 99% of all detectable faults in 25 passes.

Rather than concentrating on the crosspoints, Bose and Abraham (1982) focused on the product terms. The initial test set was generated from the PLA specification. This test set was then reduced to a nonredundant set through logical operations.

Most of the test generation algorithms claim to cover a large percentage of all possible single faults. Furthermore, a majority of the undetectable single faults do not affect the normal function of the PLA (Smith, 1979); however, faults exist that are undetectable if the the circuit is redundant. Pradhan and Son (1980) demonstrated the existence of undetectable bridging faults that may invalidate the test set for other faults. They presented a design technique that eliminates all undetectable bridging faults.

5.   Design for Testability

Testing has become more difficult and more expensive with the development of increasing complex VLSI circuits. It has been shown that the test generation problem is in general NP-complete (Ibarra and Sahni, 1975).

Testability tends to be used somewhat imprecisely since there are various factors that contribute to test cost. Testing cost is determined mainly by the cost of test pattern generation and by the cost of test application. No attempt will be made to give a precise definition of testability. Instead, it will be assumed that testability is increased whenever the costs of test generation or of test application are decreased, or the fault coverage or fault diagnosability is increased. Of course, testability will be decreased by any increase in test cost or by any decrease in fault coverage or diagnosability.

Attempts to understand circuit attributes that influence testability have produced the two concepts of observability and controllability. Observability refers to the ease with which the state of internal signals can be determined at the circuit output leads. Controllability refers to the ease of producing a specific internal signal value by applying signals to the circuit input leads. Many of the design for testability (DFT) techniques are attempts to increase the observability or controllability of circuit design. The most direct way to do this is to introduce test points; i.e., additional circuit inputs and outputs to be used during testing. However, the cost of test points can be prohibitive because of IC pin limitations.

DFT techniques can be categorized into two classes: ad hoc and structured. Ad hoc techniques typically consist of a set of guidelines listing features that enhance or detract from testability. In contrast, structured DFT techniques involve the overall circuit structure and are implemented by general design rules.

A major difficulty with the ad hoc techniques is the requirement of adding extra control inputs or observation outputs. Testability measures help by allowing the use of only those additional external connections that are important for satisfying the testability requirements.

5.1   Scan Techniques

The structured techniques described in this section permit access to internal nodes of a circuit without requiring a separate external connection for each node accessed. This is made possible at the cost of additional internal logic circuitry used primarily for testing. Since there are more test points than external connections, the data must be transferred serially or scanned in and out of the circuit being tested.

Scan techniques have another important benefit in addition to increased accessibility: Because bistable elements can be accessed and tested directly, test pattern generation need only be done for combinational circuits.

A shift register or a multiplexer can be used to convert between parallel and serial data. The scan methods based on shift register techniques are often called scan path methods since during testing the system bistables are connected as a shift register or scan path. An example of a scan path approach is the LSSD technique developed at IBM. Fujitsu and Amdahl use the random access scan design technique that uses multiplexing and demultiplexing to implement the scan strategy for latch based systems.

5.2   Design of Testable Combinational Circuits

A number of design procedures have been proposed for the realization of easily testable combinational logic circuits. The prime objective of these design procedures is to minimize the number of fault-detection tests and/or simplify the generation of such tests. EOR embedding (Hayes, 1974) and syndrome-testable design (Savir, 1980) are two such techniques.

Hayes (1974) showed that any combinational logic circuit can be modified by embedding EOR gates so that the resulting circuit requires only five test patterns. This number of test patterns can be reduced to three by the "minimally testable design" approach (Saluja and Reddy, 1974). This number, three, is believed to be minimal under the general fault assumption. The "dual-mode logic" approach assumes a more stringent fault condition and arrives at a method of designing circuits that require two test patterns to detect those faults (DasGupta et al., 1980). All of these techniques achieve a very low cost of test application by minimizing the number of test patterns; however, all of them require significant amount of extra hardware, including gates and I/O pins and, therefore, have not gained much popularity. Syndrome-testable design minimizes the cost of test generation by simplifying the test generation process.

5.2.1   Syndrome-Testable Design

The syndrome of a Boolean function is defined as $S = K/2^n$, where K is the number of minterms realized by the function and n is the number of input lines. For example, the syndrome of a 3-input AND gate is $\frac{1}{8}$ and that of a 2-input OR gate is $\frac{3}{4}$. Since the syndrome is a functional property, various realizations of the same function have the same syndrome.

The input-output syndrome relation of a circuit having various intercon-nected blocks depends on whether the inputs to the blocks are disjoint or conjoint, as well as on the gate in which the blocks terminate. For a circuit having two blocks with unshared inputs, if S_1 and S_2 denote the syndromes of the functions realized by blocks 1 and 2, respectively, the input-output syndrome relation S for the circuit is:

Terminating gate	Syndrome relation S
OR	$S_1 + S_2 - S_1 \cdot S_2$
AND	$S_1 \cdot S_2$
EX-OR	$S_1 + S_2 - 2S_1 \cdot S_2$
NAND	$1 - S_1 \cdot S_2$
NOR	$1 - (S_1 + S_2 - S_1 \cdot S_2)$

If blocks 1 and 2 have shared inputs and realize the functions F and G, respectively, then the following relations hold:

Terminating gate	Syndrome relation S
OR	$S(F) + S(G) - S(FG)$
AND	$S(F) + S(G) + S(\bar{F}\bar{G}) - 1$
EX-OR	$S(F\bar{G}) + S(\bar{F}G)$

Example 5.1   Let us find the syndrome and the number of minterms realized by the circuit of Figure 18. We have

$$S_1 = \tfrac{3}{4}, S_2 = \tfrac{3}{4}, S_3 = 1 - S_1 S_2 = \tfrac{7}{16}, S_4 = \tfrac{1}{4}$$

Hence

$$S = 1 - (S_3 + S_4 - S_3 S_4) = \tfrac{27}{64}$$
$$K = S \cdot 2^n = (\tfrac{27}{64}) \cdot 2^6 = 27 \qquad \blacksquare$$

A fault in a logic circuit is said to be syndrome-testable if the syndrome of the circuit induced by the fault does not equal the syndrome of the fault-free circuit. Further, a logic circuit is said to be syndrome-testable with respect to a class of faults if any fault in the fault class is syndrome-testable. The class of faults considered here is the single stuck-at type. The testing scheme for syndrome-testable circuits is as follows: All 2^n possible input patterns are applied to the circuit under test exactly once, and its syndrome is recorded by counting the number of 1s appearing on the output of the circuit. If the actual syndrome equals the expected syndrome, the circuit is fault-free; otherwise, the circuit is faulty.

Savir (1980) presented a method for modifying the design of a general combinational circuit so that it will be syndrome-testable. However, he left open the question of whether one could always modify a circuit to achieve syndrome-testability. Markowsky (1981) showed that a combinational circuit can always be modified to be syndrome-testable for single stuck-at faults.

Savir (1981) proposed a method for syndrome testing circuits that are not syndrome-testable. The idea is to perform multiple constrained syndrome tests on various portions of the circuit in such a way that an overall full syndrome-test coverage will be achieved. Thus, with this method the extra pin-penalty associated with the testable design is traded off with the extra running time of the syndrome-test procedure.

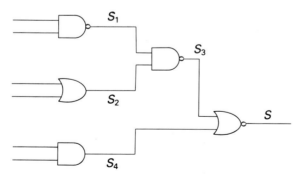

FIG. 18.

Barzilai *et al.* (1981) considered syndrome testing as a vehicle for self-testing VLSI circuits. They electronically partitioned the chip into macros in test mode. The macros were then syndrome tested in sequence. They also described a self-test architecture based on this concept.

Applicability of the syndrome-testable approach to the design of other types of circuits (Yamada, 1983), sometimes in the presence of other types of faults (Bhattacharya and Gupta, 1983), has been reported in the literature.

5.3   DFT for Regular Circuits

The regularity of some circuits has generated some special techniques to make them more easily testable. For example, easily testable bit-sliced designs have been reported by Sridhar and Hayes (1981). The rest of this section is devoted to a discussion of DFT techniques for PLAs.

5.3.1   Design of PLAs for Off-Line Testing

The problem of test generation for normal PLAs was discussed in Section 4.3.1. The complexity of this problem has given rise to the design of easily testable PLAs.

The key to the design of easily testable PLAs is the ability to control each bit line and each product line individually. Note that by changing the input pattern to the PLA, bit lines change in pairs, not individually. Similarly, in general, input patterns select more than one product line at a time, and hence, it is an involved process to trace the effect of bit line or product line faults on the output lines of the PLA.

One of the first designs of PLAs with product line and bit line selection capability was proposed by Fujiwara and Kinoshita (1981). An important feature of this design is that the test patterns are independent of the function implemented by the PLA. The main price paid for this function independence is the amount of added hardware—which includes two cascades of XOR gates, an extra product line, an extra sum line, a shift register, and augmented input decoders (see Fig. 19).

Control over the product lines and the bit lines is achieved through the shift register. Each product line P_i is ANDed by the complement of the contents of each S_i (Figure 20a). Thus, to disable all product lines except line i, one sets S_i to 0 and all other S_j's (from S_1 to S_{m+1}, except S_i) to 1. The extra product line P_{m+1} is arranged so that each row of the AND array has an odd number of devices. Similarly, the extra sum line S_{p+1} is arranged so that each column within the OR array has an odd number of devices.

The bit lines are controlled by the control array lines, C_1 and C_2 (Figure 20b). They disable all $\bar{X_i}$'s and X_i's, respectively. When both C_1 and C_2 are set

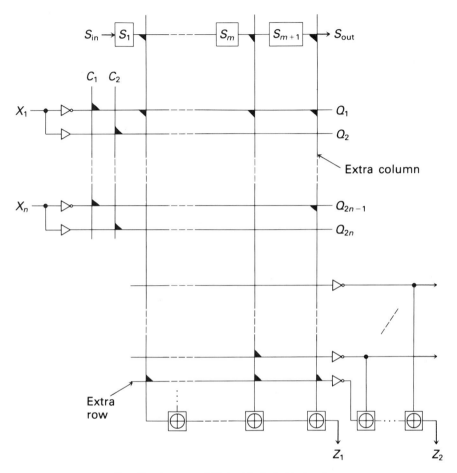

FIG. 19.   Augmented PLA with single-bit decoders.

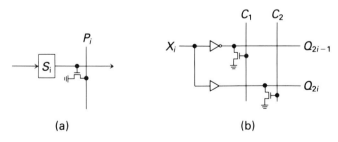

FIG. 20.   NMOS version of extra hardware.

to 0, the PLA is in its normal operation mode; when $C_1 = 1$, then all $\bar{X}$ rows in the AND array have the value 0; and when $C_2 = 1$, then all X rows are forced to 0.

The two cascades of XOR gates, located below and to the right of the OR array, are used as parity checkers to detect odd errors that propagate to them.

The testing scheme used on the augmented PLA is depicted in Table II, where $\epsilon_m = 0$ if m is even, $\epsilon_m = 1$ if m is odd, and x represents "don't care." It can be easily shown that this test set can detect all stuck-at faults in the shift register; single stuck-at faults on the lines of the control array, the AND array, and the OR array; single crosspoint faults in the AND and OR arrays; and multiple stuck-at fault on the lines of XOR gates (Fujiwara and Kinoshita, 1981).

Note that in the I^1 test, all the product lines are disabled. This simplifies testing for many stuck-at faults. In I^2 and I^3 tests, only the jth product line is enabled, and all the bit lines are disabled (set to 0). This simplifies the detection of crosspoint faults in the OR array. In the I^4 and I^5 tests, all the product lines are enabled, and only one of the bit lines is enabled (set to 1). This simplifies the detection of crosspoint faults in the AND array.

The test set depicted in Table II is termed universal because the test patterns, and the responses, are dependent only on the size of the PLA, not on its personality. The extra hardware in the augmented PLA can also be used to locate multiple crosspoint faults in the AND and/or OR arrays using a universal test sequence (Fujiwara and Kinoshita, 1981). This can be useful for PLA repair.

Note that the fault coverage of the scheme depicted in Table II is not complete; in general, multiple faults are not detected, and more importantly, bridging faults are not considered. These issues are addressed in later work (Fujiwara, 1984).

This design (Fujiwara and Kinoshita, 1981) has been criticized for the potentially long delay in the two cascades of XOR gates. This can be somewhat improved by connecting the gates in the form of parity trees. In

TABLE II

UNIVERSAL TEST SEQUENCE $A_{n,m+1}$

	$X_1 \ldots X_i \ldots X_n$	C_1	C_2	$S_1 \ldots S_j \ldots S_{m+1}$	Z_1	Z_2
I^1	$0 \ldots \ldots 0$	1	0	$1 \ldots \ldots 1$	0	0
$I_j^2 \ (j = 1,\ldots,m+1)$	$0 \ldots \ldots 0$	1	0	$1 \ldots 0 \ldots 1$	1	1
$I_j^3 \ (j = 1,\ldots,m+1)$	$1 \ldots \ldots 1$	0	1	$1 \ldots 0 \ldots 1$	1	1
$I_i^4 \ (i = 1,\ldots,n)$	$1 \ldots 0 \ldots 1$	0	1	$0 \ldots \ldots 0$	ϵ_m	x
$I_i^5 \ (i = 1,\ldots,n)$	$0 \ldots 1 \ldots 0$	1	0	$0 \ldots \ldots 0$	ϵ_m	x

most of the later PLA designs for testability, the delay issue has been one of the important design factors, and one or both of the XOR cascades have been eliminated.

One of the main advantages of the design for universal testability (Fujiwara and Kinoshita, 1981; Fujiwara, 1984) is that the test patterns, and the responses, are independent of the personality of the PLA. This property can be an advantage for built-in self-test (BIST) purposes. However, if universal testability is not a requirement, the amount of hardware overhead can be reduced considerably. An example is the scheme proposed by Khabaz (1983). As can be seen in Figure 23, the added hardware is a shift register, and an extra sum line. In particular, note that the control array for the inputs is non-existent.

The detection of AND array crosspoint faults, in Figure 21, is facilitated by the control array, which allows the selection of one bit line at a time. Such crosspoint faults are detected in Khabaz's scheme by the following procedure: For every product line P_i, the state $S(i)$ is assigned to the shift register and the input pattern $X(i)$ is applied (where $S(i)$ deselects all product lines except P_i, and $X(i)$ denotes an input vector that selects product line P_i). This should set

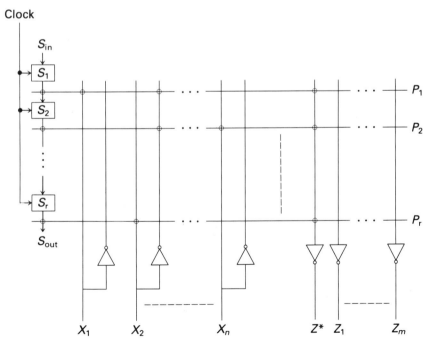

FIG. 21. Khabaz's design for testability scheme.

$Z*$ to 1 (Fig. 21). Next, bit lines are isolated by changing one input variable at a time in $X(i)$, while keeping the shift register state at $S(i)$.

Let $X(i - j)$ denote the input pattern that is identical to $X(i)$ in all bits except in the jth position. If the jth input variable is "don't care" for product line P_i, then this change from $X(i)$ to $X(i - j)$ should not change $Z*$; if it does, there is a fault. If, on the other hand, the jth input variable is "care" for product line P_i, then the change of input from $X(i)$ to $X(i - j)$ should change $Z*$ from 1 to 0; if it does not, there is a fault (Khabaz, 1983).

The crucial idea in enhancing PLA testability has been the provision of means to control individual product lines. As we have seen, most of the proposed methods achieved this key concept through the addition of a shift register to the PLA. However, the ability to select an individual product line can be implemented by adding to the AND array, instead of using a shift register. An example of such an approach is the technique described by Bozorgui–Nesbat and McCluskey (1984). In this scheme, extra inputs (and bit lines) are added such that the input pattern that selects a product line is at least a distance of 2 away from selecting any other product line. This serves two purposes. First, this inclusion of a shift register for product line selection is no longer required. Second, additional hardware for bit line selection is not required, since Khabaz's bit flipping method can be used to test for crosspoint faults in the AND array. It should be noted that during the normal operation of the PLA the extra bit lines have to be deactivated with additional circuitry (Bozorgui–Nesbat and McCluskey, 1984).

6. Built-In Self-Test

As chips and systems continued to increase in complexity, the effort required to generate their tests increased at an even more astonishing rate. Empirically, however, Goel (1980) showed that a test generator for combinational circuits, using some clever heuristics, consumes CPU time only at a rate approximating G^2, where G is the number of gates in the circuit. While this growth rate is much more tractable than exponential, it is still not very attractive. The cost of test generation process for very large structures could quite easily become intolerable.

There are other areas of concern in addition to test generation time and costs (Sedmak, 1979). It seems a natural extension of the design for testability idea to solve these concerns by building further aids to testing into the structure. The inclusion of on-chip circuitry to provide test vectors and to analyze output reponses is called built-in self-test (BIST). This is clearly different from concurrent checking (implicit testing) or system-level periodic testing. The terms built-in test (BIT) and self-test are sometimes used to refer to any of these schemes.

6.1   BIST for Regular Circuits

Regularity of some logic circuits has given rise to specific BIST designs for such circuits. Examples of such efforts are BIST for embedded RAMs (Sun and Wong, 1984) and for iterative arrays (Aboulhamid and Cerny, 1984). We will now look at the design of PLAs for built-in self-test.

6.1.1   Design of PLAs for Built-In Self-Test

The complexity or cost of testing can be classified into two categories: the complexity of test generation and the cost of test application. The optimum design for the first category is achieved by eliminating the expensive stage of test generation. Such a design can be accomplished by universal or function independent testing, such that the test patterns and the responses are predetermined independently of the function being realized (Fujiwara and Kinoshita, 1981). The cost of test application can be minimized by the BIST technique.

The BIST techniques for PLA design can be classified into two main categories. The techniques in the first class are an outgrowth, or extension, of the schemes for universal testability (Hua et al., 1984; Treuer et al., 1985). An example of this category is the design by Hua, Jou, and Abraham (1984), which laid out the Fujiwara and Kinoshita scheme (1981) in NMOS according to some interesting VLSI design concepts. In particular the augmented input decoders section of the PLA (Fujiwara and Kinoshita, 1981), was extended so that it can directly generate the universal test input sequence (Hua et al., 1984). As a second example, the BIST scheme of Treuer, Fujiwara, and Agarwal (1985), is an augmented and improved version of Fujiwara's recent design for universal testability technique (Fujiwara, 1984).

It should be obvious that not all designs for testability schemes are equally suitable for BIST extension purposes. For example, Khabaz's scheme (1983), discussed earlier, is not appropriate for built-in test.

The second class of BIST schemes are mainly based on signature analysis concepts. For example, in Hassan and McCluskey's approach (1983), linear feedback shift registers are used for pattern generation and output response evaluation. As shown in Figure 22, an n-bit linear feedback shift register (LFSR) generates pseudorandom test patterns. Three parallel input LFSRs compress the sequence of values that appear on the true bit lines, on the complementary bit lines, and on the output lines. The LFSR at the input lines is run through its maximum length of $2^n - 1$ to generate the three compressed signatures. This approach is particularly suited for PLAs that have a large number of product lines in comparison to the number of inputs.

Pseudorandom number sequences, which are attractive in many testing problems, are not very effective in PLA testing due to the high fan-in of PLAs.

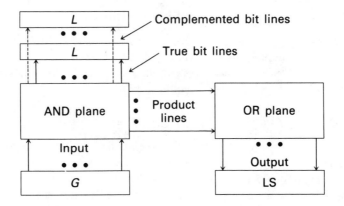

G: maximum length sequence generator using $P(x)$ as the
characteristic polynomial
L: parallel LFSR with $P(x)$ as the characteristic polynomial
LS: LFSR(s) used to compact the outputs

FIG. 22.   Hassan and McCluskey's BIST scheme.

For example, consider an n-input NOR gate. The stuck-at-1 fault on the first
input line of this gate can be detected only by the test pattern 000 . . . 0. Hence,
each pseudorandom pattern would have the probability $1/2^n$ of detecting this
fault. To test PLAs adequately and efficiently, a set of deterministic test
patterns might be required.

Daehn and Mucha (1981) presented an approach for designing nonrandom
test pattern generators by means of nonlinear feedback shift registers. As
shown in Figure 23, (modified) BILBOs are added to the NOR-NOR PLA
that are capable of generating the test patterns and decoding the test results.
Their scheme is based on the observation that all the stuck-at faults, crosspoint
faults, and bridging faults between adjacent lines, in a naked n-input NOR
array can be detected by applying the following $n + 1$ patterns:

$$0 \quad 0 \quad 0 \quad . \quad . \quad . \quad 0 \quad 0$$

$$1 \quad 0 \quad 0 \quad . \quad . \quad . \quad 0 \quad 0$$

$$0 \quad 1 \quad 0 \quad . \quad . \quad . \quad 0 \quad 0$$

$$. \quad . \quad . \quad . \quad . \quad . \quad .$$

$$0 \quad 0 \quad 0 \quad . \quad . \quad . \quad 0 \quad 1$$

which can be readily generated by means of a nonlinear feedback shift register
(see Fig. 23). By modifying the BILBO so that it has a mode of a nonlinear
feedback shift register, Daehn and Mucha were able to use the BILBO for both
nonrandom pattern generation and parallel signature analysis.

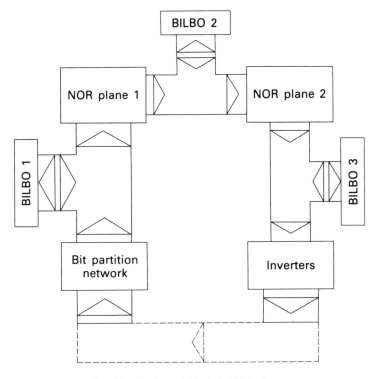

FIG. 23.   Daehn and Mucha's BIST scheme.

The Daehn and Mucha scheme tests the PLA in three steps. In the first step, test patterns are generated by BILBO 1 and the output response is compressed by BIBLO 2. The resulting signature is then shifted out for inspection. In the second step, BILBO 2 generates the test patterns and BILBO 3 compresses the output. The signature is shifted out again. Finally, testing of the output inverters and input decoders is performed by using BILBO 3 as a pattern generator and BILBO 1 as a parallel signature analyzer.

7.   Concluding Remark

We have described a few of the more significant concepts, problems, and techniques of design validation and testing of VLSI systems. With entire textbooks now being written on these topics and their many complications and generalizations, it would be naive to claim that we have done any more than highlight some of the main concepts (Reghbati, 1985; Pradhan, 1986; Miczo, 1986; Fujiwara, 1985). We hope that we have given the reader an awareness of the diversity and complexity of the problems involved in this increasingly important area.

Acknowledgments

This research is supported by the Natural Sciences and Engineering Research Council of Canada under Grant No. A0743.

References

Abadir, M. S., and Reghbati, H. K. (1983). Functional testing of semiconductor random access memories. *ACM Computing Surveys* **15** (3), 175–198.

Abadir, M. S., and Reghbati, H. K. (1987). Functional test generation using binary decision diagrams. *Int. J. Comp. & Math.* **13** (5), 413–430.

Aboulhamid, E. M., and Cerny, E. (1984). Built-in testing of one-dimensional unilateral interative arrays. *IEEE Trans. Comput.* **C-33** (6), 560–564.

Agarwal, V. K. (1980). Multiple fault detection in programmable logic arrays. *IEEE Trans. Comput.* **C-29** (6), 518–523.

Akers, S. B. (1959). On a theory of Boolean functions. *SIAM J. Comput.* **7** (4), 487–498.

Akers, S. B. (1973). Universal test sets for logic networks. *IEEE Trans. Comput.* **C-22** (9), 835–839.

Armstrong, D. B. (1966). On finding a nearly minimal set of fault detection tests for combinatorial nets. *IEEE Trans. Comput.* **C-15** (2), 63–73.

Arnold, M. H., and Ousterhout, J. K. (1982). Lyra: A new approach to geometric layout-rule checking. *Proc. 19th Design Automation Conf.*, pp. 530–535.

Baker, C. (1980). "Artwork Analysis Tools for VLSI Circuits." Tech. Report. MIT/LCS/TR-239. MIT, Cambridge, Massachusetts.

Barzilai, Z., Savir, J., Markowski, G., and Smith, M. G. (1981). The weighted syndrome sums approach to VLSI testing. *IEEE Trans. Comput.* **C-30** (12), 996–1000.

Bentley, J. L., and Ottmann, T. A. (1979). Algorithms for reporting and counting geometric intersections. *IEEE Trans. Comput.* **C-28** (9), 643–647.

Betancourt, R. (1971). Derivation of minimum test sets for unate logical circuits. *IEEE Trans. Comput.* **C-20** (11), 1264–1269.

Bhattacharya, B. B., and Gupta, B. (1983). Syndrome-testable design of combinational networks for detecting stuck-at and bridging faults. *Proc. IEEE ITC*, pp. 446–452.

Bose, B., and Abraham, J. A. (1982). Test generation of programmable logic arrays. *Proc. 19th Design Automation Conf.*, pp. 574–580.

Bossen, D. C., and Hong, S. J. (1971). Cause and effect analysis for multiple fault detection in combinational networks. *IEEE Trans. Comput.* **C-20** (11), 1252–1257.

Bozorgui-Nesbat, S., and McCluskey, E. J. (1984). Lower overhead design for testability of PLAs. *Proc. Int. Test Conf.*, pp. 856–865.

Breuer, M. A., and Friedman, A. D. (1976). "Diagnosis and Reliable Design of Digital Systems." Computer Science Press, Washington, D.C.

Chiang, A. C. L., Reed, I. S., and Benes,, A. V. (1972). Path sensitization, partial Boolean difference, and automated fault diagnosis. *IEEE Trans. Comput.* **C-21** (2), 189–194.

Clegg, F. W. (1973). Use of spoofs in the analysis of faulty logic networks. *IEEE Trans. Comput.* **C-22** (3), 229–234.

Daehn, W., and Mucha, J. (1981). A hardware approach to self-testing of large programmable logic arrays. *IEEE Trans. Comput.* **C-30** (11), 829–833.

DasGupta, S., Hartmann, C. R. P., and Rudolph, L. O. (1980). Dual-model logic for function independent fault testing. *IEEE Trans. Comput.* **C-29** (11), 1025–1029.

David, R., and Thevenod-Fosse, P. (1981). Random testing of integrated circuits. *IEEE Trans. Inst. Meas.* **IM-30** (3), 20–25.

Eichelberger, E. B., and Lindbloom, E. (1980). A heuristic test-pattern generator for programmable logic arrays. *IBM J. Res. Dev.* **24** (3), 15–22.

Engl, W. L., Dirks, H. K., and Meinerzhagen, B. (1983). Device modeling. *Proc. IEEE* **71** (1), 10–33.

Eustace, R. A. (1981). "A Deterministic Finite State Automata Approach to Design-Rule Checking for VLSI." M.S. Thesis, University of Central Florida, Orlando.

Fujiwara, H. (1984). A new PLA design for universal testability. *IEEE Trans. Comput.* **C-33** (8), 745–750.

Fujiwara, H. (1985). "Logic Testing and Design for Testability." MIT Press, Cambridge, Massachusetts.

Fujiwara, H., and Kinoshita, K. (1981). A design of programmable logic arrays with universal test. *IEEE Trans. Comput.* **C-30** (11), 823–828.

Fujiwara, H., and Shimono, T. (1983). On the acceleration of test generation algorithms. *IEEE Trans. Comput.* **C-32** (12), 1137–1144.

Goel, P. (1980). Test generation costs analysis and projections. *Proc. 17th ACM-IEEE DAC*, pp. 77–84.

Goel, P. (1981). An implicit enumeration algorithm to generate tests for combinational logic circuits. *IEEE Trans. Comput.* **C-30** (3), 215–222.

Hassan, S. Z., and McCluskey, E. J. (1983). Testing PLAs using multiple parallel signature analyzers. *Proc. 13th FTCS*, 422–425.

Hayes, J. P. (1974). On modifying logic networks to improve their diagnosability. *IEEE Trans. Comput.* **C-23** (1), 56–62.

Hua, K. A., Jou, J. Y., and Abraham, J. A. (1984). Built-in tests for VLSI finite state machines. *Proc. 14th FTCS*, pp. 292–297.

Ibarra, O. H., and Sahni, S. K. (1975). Polynomially complete fault detection problems. *IEEE Trans. Comput.* **C-24** (3), 242–249.

Jain, S. K., and Agrawal, V. D. (1983). Test generation for MOS circuits using D-algorithm. *Proc. 20th ACM-IEEE DAC*, pp. 64–70.

Khabaz, J. (1983). A testable PLA design with low overhead and high fault coverage. *Proc. 13th FTCS*, FTCS pp. 426–429.

Kinoshita, K., Takamatsu, Y., and Shibata, M. (1980). Test generation for combinational circuits by structure description functions. *Proc. 10th IEEE FTCS*, pp. 152–154.

Kohavi, Z. (1970). "Switching and Finite Automate theory." McGraw-Hill, New York.

Ku, C. T., and Masson, G. M. (1975). The Boolean difference and multiple fault analysis. *IEEE Trans. Comput.* **C-24** (1), 62–71.

Lelarasmee, E., Ruehli, A. E., and Sangiovanni-Vincentelli, A. L. (1982). The waveform relaxation method for time-domain analysis of large-scale integrated circuits. *IEEE Trans. CAD* **CAD-1** (3), 131–145.

Liu, S. (1980). Interactive two-dimensional design of barrier-controlled MOS transistors. *IEEE Trans. Elec. Dev.* **ED-27** (8), 1550–1558.

McCluskey, E. J. (1984). Verification testing. *IEEE Trans. Comput.* **C-33** (6), 541–546.

Mak, G. P., Abraham, J. A., and Davidson, E. S. (1982). The design of PLAs with concurrent error detection. *Proc. 12th FTCS, Symp. Fault-Tolerant Computing*, pp. 303–310.

Markowsky, G. (1981). Syndrome-testability can be achieved by circuit modification. *IEEE Trans. Comput.* **C-30** (5), 604–606.

Marlett, R. (1986). An effective test generation system for sequential circuits. *Proc. 23th ACM-IEEE DAC*, pp. 250–256.

Miczo, A. (1986). "Digital Logic Testing and Simulation." Harper & Row, New York.

Muth, P. (1976) A nine-valued circuit model for test generation. *IEEE Trans. Comput.* **C-25** (6), 630–636.

Nagel, L. W. (1975). "SPICE2: A Computer Program to Simulate Semiconductor Circuits." Memo ERL-M250, Elect. Res. Lab., University of California, Berkeley.

Neureuther, A. R. (1983). IC process modeling and topography design. *Proc. IEEE* **71** (1), 121–128.

Pradhan, D. (1986). "Fault-Tolerant Computing." Prentice-Hall, Englewood Cliffs, New Jersey.

Pradhan, D. K., and Son, K. (1980). The Effect of Undetectable Faults in PLA's and a Design for Testability. *Proc. IEEE ITC*, pp. 359–367.

Reddy, S. M. (1973). Complete test sets for logic functions. *IEEE Trans. Comput.* **C-22** (11), 1016–1020.

Reghbati, H. K. (1985) "VLSI Testing and Validation Techniques" IEEE Computer Society Press, Washington, D. C.

Roth, JP., Bouricius, W. G., and Schreider, P. R. (1967). Programmed algorithm to compute tests to detect and distinguish between failure in logic circuits. *IEEE Trans. Comput.* **C-16** (5), 567–580.

Saluja, K. K., and Reddy, and S. M. (1974). On minimally testable logic networks. *IEEE Trans. Comput.* **C-23** (1), 552–554.

Savir, J. (1980). Syndrome-testable design of combinational circuits. *IEEE Trans. Comput.* **C-29** (6), 442–451.

Savir, J. (1981). Syndrome testing of syndrome-untestabld combinational circuits. *IEEE Trans. Comput.* **C-30** (8), 606–608.

Savir, J., and Bardell, P. H. (1984). On random pattern test length. *IEEE Trans. Comput.* **C-33** (6), 467–474.

Sedmak, R. M. (1979). Design for self-verification: An approach for dealing with testability problems in VLSI-based designs. *Proc. IEEE ITC*, pp. 112–120.

Sellers, E. F., Hsiao, M. Y., and Bearnson, L. W. (1968). Analyzing errors with the Boolean difference. *IEEE Trans. Comput.* **C-17** (7), 676–683.

Smith, J. E. (1979) Detection of faults in programmable logic arrays. *IEEE Trans. Comput.* **C-28** (11), 845–853.

Sridhar, T., and Hayes, J. P. (1981). Design of easily testable bit-sliced systems. *IEEE Trans. Comput.* **C-30** (11), 842–854.

Sun, Z., and Wong, L. T. (1984) Self-testing of embedded RAMs. *Proc. IEEE ITC*, pp. 148–156.

Thatte, S. M., and Abraham, J. A. (1980). Test generation for microprocessors. *IEEE Trans. Comput.* **C-29** (6), 429–441.

Treuer, R., Fujiwara, H., and Agarwal, V. K. (1985). Implementing a built-in self-test PLA design. *IEEE Design and Test* **2** (2), 37–48.

Weeks, W. T., Jimenez, A. J., Mahoney, G. W., Mehta, D., Ouasemzadeh, H., and Scott, T. R. (1973). Algorithms for ASTAP–A network analysis program. *IEEE Trans. Cir. Theory* **CT-20** (11), 628–634.

Yamada, T. (1983). Syndrome-testable design of programmable logic arrays. *Proc. IEEE ITC*, pp. 453–458.

Yamin, M. (1972). XYTOLR: A computer program for integrated circuit mask design checkout. *Bell System Tech. J.* **51** (7), 1595–1610.

Software Testing and Verification

LEE J. WHITE

Department of Computing Science
The University of Alberta
Edmonton, Alberta, Canada

1. Introduction

Computer-program testing is currently a very active research field. There is the perception that formal program verification has a much more solid theoretical base, but is seldom utilized in practice. Testing is applied in virtually every software development project, yet the process is often not based

ADVANCES IN COMPUTERS, VOL. 26

upon a solid theoretical framework, even though it is expensive. This article will survey some of the basic concepts, approaches, and results in testing and will not necessarily be comprehensive or review all research methods. An excellent overview of software testing and validation techniques is provided in a tutorial format by Miller and Howden (1981). Texts on testing are available by Myers (1979) and by Beizer (1983).

Aside from the exact approach used for testing, there are two critical issues for the successful completion of a testing plan. A good software engineering methodology provides the required foundation for testing; this includes agreed-upon requirements, complete specifications, a systematic design methodology, walkthroughs and reviews, a structural code implementation, and a logical maintenance plan, which preserves the software structure, documentation, and test plan. The second critical issue is the necessity of articulating and agreeing upon the test plan early in the software life cycle. There should be agreement upon the test plan at the requirements stage, rather than frantically assembling this test plan as the software project approaches the implementation stage.

All of the software engineering methodology used provides a support and examination structure for the test plan, but no aspect is more important than the software specification. As this article will emphasize, the specification may be used to generate part of the test data, or may be used to decide whether or not the test data is correct. Thus the specification should be constructed with these or other testing functions in mind, since the software product is of questionable value if we cannot provide adequate confidence through testing.

In Section 2 we will consider the fact that no test strategy can be effective in detecting all errors in an arbitrary computer program. This does not preclude a test strategy being effective in detecting all errors for a specific program, but should provide an attitude of humility for both researcher and practitioner working with software verification. Any proposed testing methodology should be based upon scientifically sound principles, rather than an ad hoc approach, which is unfortunately the case far too often in contemporary practice. Thus it becomes important to involve the user with the test plan and testing process; if the objective of testing is to increase the confidence in the software quality, then it is imperative to describe the test plan to the user in simple terms. Too often the testing process only results in a large, incomprehensible file of test data.

Many software experts have argued that it is just as important to design software for easy maintenance and modification as it is to deliver that software with a minimum of errors. One of the reasons for this is the increased cost of maintenance and the extensive modifications many software systems will endure during this last but most important stage of the life cycle. The implications of this sort of extensive modifications of the software for testing are the following:

1. The specification of the software must also be modified. Any subsequent testing must be measured against this modified specification.
2. A modified test plan must also be constructed, to not only test the modified portions or modules of the software but also test interactions with other modules or portions of the software not directly affected by the changes.
3. The software must be entirely redesigned in order to incorporate the modifications. The reason for this is that the software characteristic of *structure* is designed by such modifications, and only through a redesign (not a "patch") can the integrity of structure be restored. Test plans and testing methodologies are in turn dependent upon this integrity of structure.
4. The additional testing should be carried out according to the modified test plan, added to a subset of the original test data on a test database with the same integrity and documentation as available when the software was first delivered.

Of course, it is precisely because precautions 1 through 4 are *not* observed in software maintenance that the process is so ineffective and costly. As is so true in other areas of endeavor, this level of investment at the beginning, whether it be in design or in maintenance, will pay dividends later through decreased cost at all stages of the software life cycle or during subsequent modifications.

This article will present a broad view of many important concepts needed for testing, either during design or under maintenance, together with an overview of a number of research results and approaches that will affect testing practice in the future. The object is to provide the practitioner with various models and methodologies that can be woven into a scientifically based test plan, rather than relying only upon an ad hoc approach.

1.1 Black Box Testing versus White Box Testing

One of the simplest ways to classify testing methods as "black box" or "white box" approaches. A *black box* testing approach will devise test data without any knowledge of the software under test or any aspect of its structure, whereas *white box* testing will explicitly use the program structure to develop test data.

1.1.1 Black Box Testing

Black box testing is often also known as *functional testing*, although in Section 5.3 we will describe an expanded version of functional testing, due to Howden (1985), which combines the black box and white box approaches.

One example of a strictly black box approach is to utilize the specifications to generate the test data. A concrete example of this approach is contained in Parnas (1972), where the objective of detailed specifications is to state the functional requirements completely and unambiguously, while leaving design decisions to the implementation. These specifications are then represented in the form of input–process–output, and can be conveniently used to generate test data. Another example of black box testing is *random test data generation*, where a random value is selected for each input variable of the program and each test data point then consists of these values collectively taken over all input variables. This is quite a simple and intuitively appealing approach, but it is unclear whether in general it will provide effective software error detection. Duran and Ntafos (1981) have reported experiments to show that random testing can be effective for at least some errors and classes of programs.

1.1.2   White Box Testing

A white box testing approach is based upon explicit knowledge of the software under test and its structure. For this reason, it is often also known as *structural testing*. Research has shown that there are inherent limitations to the use of white box testing alone, for test data based only upon the software code and structure will fail to detect the absence of certain features that might be missing in the software. Information and the associated test data must be derived from the software specifications, design documents, or from some other source. For example, a *missing path error* has been identified by Howden (1976), in which a required predicate does not appear in the given program to be tested. Especially if this missing predicate were an equality, it would be extremely difficult or impossible for a white box method to systematically determine that such a predicate should be present. We can only look to supplementary sources such as the software specification to provide information when such features might be missing within the given software.

Despite these disadvantages, a number of quite sophisticated and varied techniques have been developed and are presently used in both research and practice. One approach commonly used in practice involves *coverage measures*, including *statement coverage* and *branch coverage*. A detailed discussion of these techniques will be given in Section 4, but the basic idea is that a good test plan should certainly thoroughly exercise the various parts of the source code of the program. Thus, in statement coverage, each statement of the program should be executed for at least one input test point; in branch coverage each IF–THEN–ELSE predicate decision should have a true and a false outcome, and each of these should occur for at least one input test point. The simplicity of this approach is appealing, but it can be shown that many errors will not be detected by these coverage methods and the software must be instrumented to establish the extent of coverage for the set of test data.

Path-oriented testing methods also constitute a white box approach. Here the process of testing a computer program is treated as two operations:

1. selection of a path or set of paths along which testing is to be conducted,
2. selection of input data to serve as test cases, which will cause the chosen paths to be executed.

Thus in the research literature there have been proposed methods to select paths for testing, or proposed methods to select data along program paths, without necessarily specifying an associated approach for selecting those paths; in other cases, proposed methods have addressed both aspects. Section 6 will discuss a number of path-oriented testing methods.

Substantial research has been done and viable methods proposed based upon structural testing. Fewer systematic studies, methods, and results are available in the area of black box testing. Howden (1985) has argued persuasively for a systematic functional testing approach, which utilizes information and generates test data from specifications, the software source code, and other design documents. This process of amalgamating the best of several methodologies is a reasonable approach.

1.2 Module, Integration, and Acceptance Testing

There are various levels at which software testing occurs. The lowest level takes place with the software *module*, which is the smallest unit of software. Many debates have raged as to the optimum or maximum size of the module, but most software experts agree that a software module should be of a size and complexity so as to be easily understood and grasped by a programmer or analyst other than its author. The levels of testing can then be identified as:

1. *module test* (also known as a *unit test*), where each module is individually tested to ensure that its performance meets its stated specification;
2. *integration test* (also known as an *incremental test*), where a set of modules are tested together, ensuring that the combined specifications of these modules are met as the modules interact and communicate; this requires careful testing of the interfaces between the modules in this set as they communicate and exchange information; these module interfaces are a common source of errors, especially if the modules are written by different programmers;
3. *systems test* (also known as an *evaluation test*), where the entire software

system is tested against the system specification—that is, all of the modules operating together; it is usually understood that this test is conducted by the software developer and reported to the user;

4. *acceptance test*, where a designated team performs a series of system tests on the delivered software and usually makes the acceptance of the software (and subsequent payment) contingent upon the successful completion of these tests; this designated team is independent from those who developed the product, and may be the user or a third party hired by the user.

In the following discussion, material is drawn extensively from Myers (1979), copyright © 1979, John Wiley & Sons, Inc., and is reprinted by permission of the publisher.

In the application of module tests, and to a greater extent for integration tests, additional software must be developed by the test analyst. For each module, where input data comes from other modules or external sources, a *test-driver module* must be developed to model that relationship and to provide test cases in an appropriate format. For modules that receive data from the module (or modules) under test, a *stub module* must be developed to model this relationship; this is particularly important and complex in the event that there is a transfer of control or that the stub must return appropriate values in response to the data initially communicated from the module (or modules) under test.

A difficult philosophical decision must be made by the test analyst in terms of the order in which module and integration testing should be conducted. One approach is *top-down testing*, where a main module is tested first. This is followed by integration tests involving modules called by or receiving data from this module, and this process continues until all modules are involved in a system test. For example, in Figure 1, if we identify module A as the primary module (the calling program), it should first be tested, but note that it will require stubs corresponding to modules B, C, and D. Subsequently B, C, and D can be tested using module A, but again stubs will be required for modules E, F, and G.

An alternative philosophy is *bottom-up testing*, in which the terminal modules in the system are tested first, which will require driver modules. Next, modules are tested that connect to the terminal modules, until the main module is included, culminating in the system test. In Figure 1, bottom-up testing would suggest first testing modules E, F, C, and G, requiring drivers for B (for E and F), A (for C), and D (for G). There are trade-offs between the top-down and bottom-up approaches, and there also exist hybrids of the two. For example, one needs to trade off the cost of drivers and stubs. Tests are

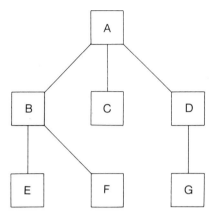

FIG. 1.   Top-down versus bottom-up testing. (From Myers, reprinted by permission of John Wiley & Sons, Inc., copyright © 1979).

generally easier to devise with bottom-up testing, but the main module is not involved until the end of the process, which could be a critical consideration. It is quite important to include these considerations in a test plan, for the costs of integration testing can become prohibitively high. A detailed discussion of these issues is given in Myers (1979).

1.3   Instrumenting and Monitoring Programs for Tests

In program testing, input test data is typically submitted to the program and then the corresponding outputs are examined for errors. There exist, however, more explicit techniques for studying the nature and behavior of a program, by observing the progress of its execution. These are known as *probes* or *monitors*, and are generally software sensors inserted into the source code. There must be methods or aids for capturing, organizing, and analyzing the probe output. For example, if one uses statement coverage as an approach to generate appropriate test data, the software must be instrumented with statement counters to determine the extent of statement coverage.

There are a number of different software probes that can be used:

1. documentation probes
    - counters, which count executions of branches, code blocks, or logical program breaks
    - traces of variable values

- traces of procedure invocation and timing
- sensors for evaluating min/max/first/last values for loop control variables or code blocks
2. probes inserted to check for "standard" errors
- division by zero
- out-of-bounds array references
- initialized variable references
- procedure argument or parameter mismatches

Leon Stucki (1977) developed an extensive instrumentation system for FORTRAN programs, called Program Evaluator and Test (or PET), which utilized these concepts. Several researchers have investigated the optimum placement of probes and monitor software; for example, see the work of J. C. Huang (1975) or C. V. Ramamoorthy and K. H. Kim (1975).

Another powerful tool for testing is the incorporation of *assertions*. At various points in the program, the programmer who originally designed and wrote the source code is aware that certain conditions must hold at that point. As a matter of fact, one can argue that this is the sort of documentation, including intuitive loop invariants, that is really needed from the program author, rather than the documentation usually provided. The tester can utilize these conditions or assert that alternative conditions are useful for testing. An example might be

$$\text{ASSERT } (A + B) < 12$$

The violations of this assertion can be pointed out, but they also can be used to control various software instrumentation. An example of the use of such a dynamic assertion checker is again provided by the PET system of Stucki (1977).

1.4 Categories of Errors

In discussing the subject of testing, we should note that three terms are identified that are sometimes used interchangeably, but represent quite different phenomena. A *failure* in a system is an observable event where the system violates its specifications. An *error* is an item of information (such as a variable value or a line of code) which, when processed by the system, may produce a failure. Not every error will produce a failure, since errors may not be observable, or error recovery procedures may be built into the program. A *fault* is a mechanical or algorithmic defect that will generate an error (i.e., a programming "bug"). Note that our tendency is to refer to both errors and faults as errors.

Another concept related to program errors is that of *coincidental correctness*. This occurs when a fault is tested, and yet coincidentally the test data results in correct output variables. If different test data had exercised that fault, the fault would have been detected by the generation of incorrect output variables. This indicates that redundant testing is always required, and that tests should be designed with coincidental correctness in mind.

Howden (1976) originally defined the classification of errors into *domain* and *computation errors*, and this classification has subsequently proven useful. Zeil (1983) has published a more detailed classification and characterization of these concepts. A program is said to exhibit a *domain error* when incorrect output is generated due to execution of the wrong path through a program. A *computation error* occurs when the correct path through the program is taken, but the output is incorrect because of faults in the computations along that path.

There are two types of domain errors, *path selection errors* and *missing path errors*. When a path is incorrectly selected and another path exists that would produce correct output, we identify this as a *path selection error*. Where the conditional statement and computations associated with part of the input data domain are missing entirely, it is called a *missing path error* (Howden, 1976).

The simplest case of a path selection error is the *predicate fault*, in which a fault in a predicate causes execution to follow the wrong path for some input data. Since the evaluation of a predicate may depend upon previous assignment statements, a fault in an assignment statement can also cause domain errors. This will be referred to as an *assignment fault*.

1.5   The Need for a Testing Oracle

One of the most expensive aspects of testing is the simple determination of whether or not the output corresponding to test data is correct. What often happens in practice is that the tester "eyeballs" the output to see if it is reasonable, as correct output is known for only a small subset of the total test cases examined. Clearly a *test oracle* is needed that can automatically check the correctness of test output. A number of researchers have argued that the specifications should be executable so as to aid in this determination. The concept of a test oracle was originally developed by Howden (1978b), and he indicated that test oracles may also assume the form of tables of values, algorithms for hand computation, or formulas in the predicate calculus.

In practice, the programmer (or user) must make this determination, and the time spent examining and analyzing these test cases is a major factor in the high cost of software development. From a theoretical or research standpoint, we must assume the existence of a test oracle in order to refer to test cases as correct or incorrect.

2. Mathematical Theory of Testing

In order to study concepts of program structure, digraphs are introduced as a potential model. A control flow graph is defined and utilized for a number of concepts needed in program testing, together with the technique of data flow analysis. The analysis of the structure and data flow in computer programs is probably one of the best-understood areas of software engineering; many of these basic concepts were originally given in Hecht (1977).

One of the reasons that a comprehensive theory of testing has been so difficult is that so many of the fundamental questions in this area are found to be undecidable, i.e., unsolvable. A number of these results are reviewed, including the observation that the problem of selecting a reliable test-data set is unsolvable, and that no general testing strategy can be devised that will be effective for all programs.

The papers of Goodenough and Gerhart (1975) and of Howden (1976) are then discussed, as it is the opinion of most researchers in the area of program testing that these two papers comprise the fundamental basis for a theory of testing. Many of the concepts and definitions from those two papers are now used throughout the literature in a fundamental way, so these papers will be surveyed in this review. Many of the notions in this section were previously developed in White (1981), copyright © 1981 North-Holland Publishing Co.

2.1   Graph Models

Computer-program structure can be captured at the appropriate abstract level through the use of a *directed graph* (*digraph*). A digraph consists of a set of *nodes* and *arcs*, where an arc is a directed line between two nodes. To apply this digraph model to computer programs, the digraph should contain exactly one *entry node*, which has no incoming arcs, and should also contain exactly one *terminal node*, which has no arcs leaving it. Moreover, for every node in the digraph, there should exist a sequence of arcs such that this sequence can be traversed in the direction of the arcs from the entry node to that specified node. This sequence of arcs is called a *directed path*. Similarly, for every node in the digraph, there should also exist a directed path from that node to the terminal node of the digraph. Any digraph with these properties has been called a *well-formed digraph* by some authors (see, for example, Paige, 1975). Figure 2 shows an example of a control flow graph, together with the corresponding flow

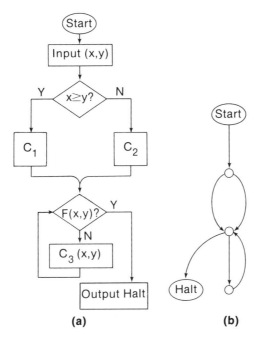

FIG. 2.   Flow chart (a) and corresponding control flow graph (b).

chart; note that most of the computational detail from the flow chart has been removed so that the emphasis is on the control flow. This control flow graph then appears as a digraph; we can determine whether or not it is well-formed.

2.1.1   Control Flow Graphs

In applying graph theory models of this type, the emphasis is placed on the decision points of a program, which determine the control flow, and there is less concern with the computational details and all the assignment statements of the program. For example, conditional transfers (such as the IF–THEN–ELSE construct) and the entry point of iteration loops (such as DO–WHILE or FOR loop constructs) constitute such decision points of a program where the flow of control may change depending upon the evaluation of a predicate expression. Although not recommended for use in well-designed programs ("structured programs"), another example of such a decision point is the occurrence of a GOTO construct.

We can now define a number of important concepts for program testing using this control flow graph model. A *control path* is defined to be a directed path from the entry node to the terminal node of the control flow graph. It should be noted that two directed paths that differ only in the number of times a particular iteration loop in the program is executed will be identified as distinct control paths. Thus the number of control paths in a program can be potentially infinite.

Every branch point of the program is associated with a general *predicate*. This predicate evaluates to true or false, and its value determines which outcome of the branch will be followed. A predicate is generated each time control reaches an IF or DO (or GOTO) statement in the given program. The *path condition* is the compound condition that must be satisfied by the input data point in order for the control path to be executed. The path condition consists of a set of constraints, one constraint for each predicate as it is encountered as the control path is traversed. The predicates are initially expressed in terms of program variables; since each of these program variables can be ultimately expressed in terms of the input variables using assignment statements along the control path, the predicates can be re-expressed as constraints in terms of only the input variables.

Not all the control paths that exist syntactically within the program are executable. If input data exist which satisfy the path condition, the control path is also an *execution path* and can be used in testing the program. If the path condition is not satisfied by any input value, the control path is said to be *infeasible* and is of no use in testing the program.

2.1.2   Static versus Dynamic Analysis

This brings to mind an important conceptual point when considering many issues in testing. *Static analysis* utilizes the computer program, examining this program for syntax errors and structural properties, but does not require execution of the program. *Dynamic analysis* requires execution of the program using input data. For example, one might be given a computer program in which the potential control flow is not well formed because no directed path from the entry node exists to reach some node of the program. This program defect can be detected by static analysis. Not every control path corresponds to an execution path, however, as some may prove to be infeasible, and this can only be detected by dynamic analysis. Another example of this distinction involves the concept of "reachable code." If there exists no control path by which to reach some specified set of code in a given program from the entry node (and thus the corresponding control flow graph is not well formed), this can be ascertained by static analysis. We say, however, that a statement (or a group of sequential statements) is *unreachable* if there exists no execution path that traverses that statement; again, this requires dynamic analysis to ascertain that this condition does or does not exist.

2.1.3   Symbolic Evaluation

Another approach used in testing is that of *symbolic evaluation*, which might also be thought of as another approach of static analysis, since the program is not actually executed with numerical data; an excellent survey of this area is provided by Clarke and Richardson (1981). The basic idea in symbolic evaluation is to allow the input variables to assume symbolic values and to express the output variables in terms of these symbols. These output variable expressions can then be examined to see if the program is computing the functions intended. One problem with this approach is that the computational functions, and thus the resultant symbolic output expressions, depend upon the path taken through the program. Thus, to effectively use symbolic evaluation, a specific control path must be selected, and the associated path condition obtained as a set of constraints to be satisfied must be expressed also in terms of the symbolic input variables. Then, for each control path, the computation can be explored by analyzing the symbolic output expression, and the feasibility of the path ascertained by determining that there exists at least one input point that satisfies the path condition. Many times the symbolic evaluation approach will show errors that might be difficult to determine using other methods. For this approach to be effective, the symbolic expressions should not be too complex; if they are too complex, their usefulness becomes limited.

2.2   Fundamental Problems of Decidability in Testing

One of the most important contributions of mathematics and computer science is the theory of decidability of computation. It has applications in many areas of computer science and is important in warning us not to attempt solutions to problems that can be proved unsolvable. In this section we will explore some of the decidability issues as applied to program testing, and it will become clear that many fundamental issues in testing are undecidable. This points out one more reason why the area of program testing is so difficult, and why approaches to testing have relied so heavily upon intuition, using heuristic and ad hoc techniques. Both the formal and informal aspects of the issues identified in this section are discussed by Brainerd and Landweber (1974).

A problem is said to be *undecidable* (or *unsolvable*) if it can be proved that no algorithm exists for its solution. One of the principal models for studying decidability issues is that of the *Turing machine*, which consists of a finite-state machine, together with an infinite-capacity external storage tape. A seminal result is that of the halting problem for the Turing machine, which is proved to be undecidable. The *halting problem* asks whether any given Turing machine will halt, given an arbitrary input.

If we are given another problem and wish to prove it undecidable, this may be accomplished by demonstrating that the decidability of the given problem implies the decidability of the halting problem (a contradiction). Almost all decidability proofs either directly or indirectly involve this method of reducing the halting problem to some other problem. It is almost immediate that it is undecidable whether a given computer program will halt, given an arbitrary input. In practical systems work, this problem is circumvented by carefully examining iteration loops to make sure they terminate under all conditions. The undecidability of this program halting problem means, however, that no computer system could be devised that will ascertain whether an arbitrary computer program will always terminate, given any input.

2.2.1 Computation of Equivalent Functions

A result with important implications for testing is that given two computer programs, the question as to whether they both compute the same function is undecidable (Brainerd and Landweber, 1974). If we identify one program as the "correct program" and consider the other program as the one we have before us which must be tested, this illustrates that even the availability of the "correct program" will not allow us in general to devise entirely reliable test data. For if we could prove the given program correct algorithmically by test data selection, the two programs would then be equivalent (compute the same function).

Another important application of this decidability result for testing involves control paths. If we ask in general whether two control paths from the same program, or from different programs, compute the same function, this question is again undecidable. When we must select test points, many times we need to know if different paths compute the same function. Yet this result shows that in general this cannot be effectively computed; intuitive and heuristic methods may have to be used. This also shows the essential difficulty with *symbolic evaluation*, since the problem of showing the equivalence of two symbolic expressions corresponding to two control paths is undecidable. Richardson and Clarke (1981) have devised a test strategy that compares symbolic expressions for control paths with symbolic expressions from program specifications; our basic result shows that again the question of whether the expressions are equivalent is undecidable. These authors report reasonable success with this task, however, as well as when expressions are from control paths from the same program. This illustrates an important point: Although a problem may in general be undecidable, techniques can be devised that are effective most of the time. Another approach is to identify special cases in which the problem may be decidable and an algorithmic approach would be appropriate.

2.2.2 Test Selection Problems

It has been proved that the test selection problem is so difficult that no general testing strategy can be constructed. From the observations we have made thus far, this result is not surprising. Howden (1976) has proved the test selection problem to be undecidable. He first makes an observation based upon a result reported by Goodenough and Gerhart (1975), that there exists a finite test set that reliably determines the correctness of a given program over its entire input domain. Howden then goes on to prove that the problem of constructing such a test set for an arbitrary program is undecidable. The essential issue is that, although we know that such a reliable test set exists for each program, no algorithmic method exists for constructing such a set for an arbitrary program. This pessimistic view of the difficulty of the test selection problem is entirely consistent with the observations we have made thus far.

2.2.3 Reachability Questions

Next consider the problem of determining the *feasibility* of a control path for a given program. We have already observed that data flow analysis will determine that a particular control path traverses the control flow graph from the entry node to the terminal node, and that all the variables encountered along that control path are properly defined—this is an example of static analysis. Yet this does not prove that there exists any input data point that will actually execute this control path. Recall that there is a path condition associated with each control path; Davis (1973) has shown that the problem of determining whether a solution exists to a system of inequalities is undecidable. Thus the path feasibility problem is undecidable, since an input point must be found to satisfy the associated path condition. It is interesting to note that, if the predicate constraints in the path condition can all be shown to be linear in the input variables, then the feasibility problem becomes decidable, since the technique of linear programming can be brought to bear on the solution of the linear constraints.

There are a number of testing issues whose decidability properties are quite unexpected. Consider the following problems, given an arbitrary program:

1. Will a given statement ever be exercised by any input data point?
2. Will a given branch ever be exercised by any input data point (where a *branch* corresponds to an arc of the control flow graph)?
3. Will a given control path ever be exercised by any input data point?

4. Will every statement in the program be exercised by some input data?
5. Will every branch in the program be exercised by some input data?
6. Will every control path in the program be exercised by some input data?

Weyuker (1979) has proved all of these problems to be undecidable. This is unexpected because, if we rephrase each question and ask about traversal of each construct from the entry node in the control flow graph, there is an efficient algorithmic solution to each question. Again, the requirement of the exercise of each construct by input data makes the problem undecidable. Weyuker indicates that problems 1 through 6 are extremely important, since the two commonly accepted criteria for adequate testing are that either every statement or every branch in the control flow graph should be executed at least once during the test-data set execution. Furthermore, if we can show that statements, branches, or control paths are never executed, not only can the testing procedures be simplified by recognizing this fact, but the unreachable ("dead") code can be eliminated, thus considerably simplifying the program. The problem is that these apparently static issues are really undecidable, because they must be viewed in a dynamic context as well.

Thus, as we observed earlier, data flow analysis methods can be applied to the control flow graph to identify parts of the control flow graph that cannot be reached by control paths, incomplete control paths can be found, and variables can be detected that are not properly initiated or defined. Yet only some cases of "dead code" can be identified in this way. Code may be unreachable, control paths infeasible, or branches never traversed, and the problems of detecting these situations are in general undecidable. One must keep these facts in mind when designing test data.

2.3 A Theoretical Foundation for Testing

Most researchers would acknowledge the pioneering paper of Goodenough and Gerhart (1975) as the first published paper to establish a sound theoretical basis for testing. Many definitions in testing that are commonly used today emerged from that analysis. Goodenough and Gerhart's "fundamental theorem of testing" has provided a model for other researchers to use as a goal in formalizing a testing concept. The paper on the reliability of path analysis strategies by Howden (1976) further elaborates on the Goodenough and Gerhart results, and many of the concepts in the Howden paper are now commonly used by the testing research community.

2.3.1 Test Selection Criteria

In the paper by Goodenough and Gerhart, the fundamental theorem of testing certainly establishes that there always exists a finite test set that reliably determines the correctness of a given program over its entire input domain. This theorem provides even further insight, however. Goodenough and Gerhart define a "test selection criterion," which specifies conditions that must be satisfied by a finite test set. For example, a criterion for a numerical program whose input domain is the integers might specify that each test should contain a positive integer, one negative integer, and zero; thus $\{-5, 0, 12\}$ and $\{-1, 0, 8\}$ are two of the test sets selected by this criterion.

A test set T is *successful* on program P if P is correct for every element of T. Suppose that T_1 and T_2 are two test sets that satisfy a test selection criterion S. If the criterion S is *consistent*, then T_1 is successful if T_2 is also successful. Suppose that P is incorrect for some input. Then a test selection criterion S is *complete* if there is an unsuccessful test T that satisfies the criterion S. From these definitions, the fundamental theorem of testing of Goodenough and Gerhart, as slightly modified by Howden (1976), follows:

> If there exists a consistent and complete selection criterion S for a program P, and if a test set T satisfying criterion S is successful, then P is correct.

The problem is that in selecting a test selection criterion there is a trade-off between the property of consistency and that of completeness. It is easy to define a test criterion with one property or the other, but it is difficult to achieve both properties. We will cite several examples from Weyuker and Ostrand (1980) that illustrate this point. Assume a program P that computes $X * X$, for X with integer values, while the output specification is $P(X) = X + X$. Since P is correct for $X = 0$ and $X = 2$, and incorrect for all other inputs, a criterion that selects as tests only subsets of $\{0, 2\}$ is consistent but not complete, as it does not indicate the error in P. A criterion that selects subsets of $\{0, 1, 2, 3, 4\}$ exposes the error in P, and is therefore complete but is not consistent, since $T_1 = \{0, 2\}$ is successful whereas $T_2 = \{0, 1\}$ is not. A slight change in the program, while retaining the same output specification, may completely change the completeness and consistency of this criterion. Suppose P' computes $(X + 2)$; then $X = 2$ becomes the only input for which a correct answer is produced. Now we find that subsets of $\{0, 2\}$ become complete but not a consistent criterion for P'. If P' computes $(X + 5)$, the criterion that selects subsets of $\{0, 1, 2, 3, 4\}$ now determines correctness for P'.

2.3.2   Construction of Finite Test Sets

Howden (1976) proves the problem of constructing a reliable finite test set for arbitrary programs to be undecidable. Thus, although we know that a reliable finite test exists, it is the problem of constructing such a set that is undecidable.

In the rest of his paper, Howden defines various types of errors we have already discussed in Section 1.4: computation errors, domain errors and missing path errors. These errors are analyzed by comparing the given program to a hypothetically correct program, which differs from the given program by the error under study. Although this model was quite restrictive, it yielded useful insight into the errors considered.

More recently a fundamental paper by Gourlay (1983) has formally explored the problem of testing when both the specifications and program must be continually modified. This has led to a characterization of the "neighborhood" of a correct program, explored by several other authors, including Howden (1976).

We have briefly examined the landmark papers of Goodenough and Gerhart and of Howden. Most researchers in program testing agree with Goodenough and Gerhart that what testing still lacks is a theoretically sound but practical definition of what constitutes an adequate test. Yet these two papers have certainly established a firm basis for the theory of testing.

3. Static Data Flow Analysis and Testing

Data flow analysis is concerned with program variables, classifying each variable occurrence as a *definition* or a *use*, as defined in Hecht (1977). These techniques are called *static* because they do not require actual execution of the software system, but only analyze the control flow characteristics of the program, together with the behavior of the program variables. The algorithms for data flow analysis are well known and are efficient, making this approach relatively inexpensive, and it can easily be incorporated into existing compilers. This provides an early detection of errors, and certain errors can be detected very reliably. Given the simplicity and economy of this approach, it makes sense that this is done as a preprocessing step, along with the detection of syntax errors, before any dynamic testing approaches are applied.

3.1 Variable Anomalies

In Section 2.1 we observed that a control flow graph is not well formed if there exists no control path by which to reach some specified set of code; this can be ascertained by static analysis. In the same manner, *variable anomalies* can be established by static algorithms; *variable anomalies* consist of undefined variable references, unused variables, or other misuses of program variables. A program variable reference must be preceded by a definition, and without any intervening undefinition (such as an exit from the procedure or scope of that variable). Similarly, a definition must be followed by a reference before another definition or undefinition of that variable. Violation of these rules for variable use does not imply that the program is necessarily incorrect, but it is a tipoff to poor design, and that execution of the program may produce incorrect results. A number of authors have studied these variable anomalies; for example, see Taylor and Osterweil (1980).

3.2   Data Flow Analysis

The notation for this section is drawn from Weyuker (1984) and reprinted by permission of North–Holland Publishing Co., copyright © 1984. A *definition* of variable x is provided either through a READ statement or when x occurs on the left side of an assignment statement. A *predicate use* (or P-*use*) of x occurs when x occurs in a control flow predicate. A *computation-use* (or C-*use*) of x occurs when x is used on the right side of an assignment statement or as an output variable. Of course, a C-use may indirectly affect the flow of control through the program as well.

Recall that in a control flow graph the nodes correspond to *blocks* of statements, always executed as a unit. Thus we can refer to a node containing a reference or a C-use of a particular variable. Similarly, if variables x_1, $x_2, \ldots, x_n$ occur in a predicate in node i, and the two successors of node i are nodes j and k, then we will say that arcs (i, j) and (i, k) contain P-uses of variables $x_1, x_2, \ldots, x_n$.

Recall that our objective here is to ascertain that a variable reference is preceded by a unique definition of that variable; we will trace the flow of control between nodes in a formal and careful way, again using the notation of Weyuker (1984).

Given a control graph and variable x, a path $(i, n_1, n_2, \ldots, n_m, j)$, $m > 0$, containing no definitions of x in nodes $n_1, \ldots, n_m$ is called a *DEF-clear path* with respect to x from node i to node j and from node i to arc (n_m, j). A node i has a *global definition* of a variable x if it has a definition of x and there is a DEF-clear path from node i to some node containing a C-use or arc containing a P-use of x.

There have been a number of systems described in the literature for the efficient determination of DEF-clear paths and global definitions of variables. These systems detect data flow anomalies and inform the user, who can then track down the corresponding program faults quite efficiently. DAVE was a system developed by Fosdick and Osterweil (1976), further described in Osterweil and Fosdick (1978), and with more recent analysis provided in articles such as Osterwell, *et al.* (1981). Frankl and Weyuker (1985) have described their system ASSET for this purpose, as well as for dynamic testing using criteria derived by data flow analysis; these will be described in Section 4.3.

3.3   Critique of Static Analysis

Static analysis can demonstrate that certain kinds of errors are absent from a given program, such as variable anomalies and control flow graphs that are not well formed, and this can be accomplished very efficiently and at low cost. Automatic systems are commonly available for this, which require no expensive programmer or tester interaction and no program execution. Very useful documentation can be generated at this stage, assuring both software developer and user of the reliability of the software to this extent.

Static testing cannot distinguish between execution paths and static control paths, as we have already observed. Static analysis cannot determine and analyze the functionality of a program, for this can only be demonstrated in a dynamic execution mode. Static testing can efficiently eliminate many types of errors, including those associated with variable anomalies, but cannot be effective against many errors only revealed by execution of the program.

4.   Coverage Measures

In Section 1.1.2 we gave several coverage measures as examples of white box testing. We want to expand on that discussion to show that, although coverage measures seem to be a systematic approach to testing, many errors will still escape detection.

4.1   Logic Coverage Measures

Sections 4.1.1 through 4.1.4 will present coverage measures referred to as "logic coverage" by Myers (1979), who provides an expanded discussion of this concept. The material in Section 4.1 is reprinted by permission of John Wiley & Sons, Inc., copyright ©1979. There is a certain ad hoc aspect to these measures, illustrated as we move from one coverage criterion to another in order to slightly strengthen it by including a test for an error condition missed in the previous criterion. Also in Section 2.2, we showed that it may not be possible to achieve one-hundred-percent coverage with any of these measures.

4.1.1   Statement Coverage

With *statement coverage*, every statement in the program is to be executed by the test set at least once. Unless one encounters reachability problems, this is certainly a requisite of a test plan. It is not nearly strong enough, however, for consider the example statement

$$\text{IF} \quad X > 0 \quad \text{THEN} \quad S;$$

In this case, we assume a null ELSE statement; thus with statement coverage, the ELSE condition might never be checked and yet contribute to a serious error.

4.1.2 Branch Testing (Decision Coverage)

We define *branch testing* (or *decision coverage*) if each predicate decision assumes a true and a false outcome at least once during the test set execution (or each possible outcome for a CASE statement). This coverage criterion clearly overcomes the problem with the null ELSE example previously given, but there are problems with decision coverage as well.

For example, consider a program with two successive IF–THEN–ELSE constructs; if tests are selected which execute the THEN–THEN alternative of these predicates, as well as the ELSE–ELSE alternative, then this criterion is satisfied. Yet the THEN–ELSE alternative is not adequately tested, and might well be in error.

4.1.3 Condition Coverage

Another weakness in branch testing is encountered with compound predicates such as

$$\text{IF}\quad (A > 0)\quad \text{AND}\quad (B < 5)$$

Branch testing will treat this compound predicate the same as a simple predicate, testing only for true and false outcomes and ignoring the fact that a false outcome could occur from two distinct Boolean clauses. For this reason, *condition coverage* will require that, during test set execution, each condition in a compound predicate assumes all possible outcomes at least once. Although it appears to strengthen decision coverage, there is still no requirement of a true predicate when both conditions are true.

4.1.4 Multiple Condition Coverage

As a result of this painful evolution of coverage measures, consider *multiple condition coverage*, which requires that during the test set execution all possible combinations of condition outcomes in each predicate are invoked at least once. It should be clear that this coverage measure implies (or is stronger than) decision coverage and condition coverage criteria. The reason for the term "possible" in the definition is that some combinations may be redundant. For example, for

$$(X \leq 5)\quad \text{AND}\quad (X < 10)$$

there are only three (not four) conditions generated, $X \leq 5$, $5 < X < 10$, and $X \geq 10$.

There are obvious deficiencies with any coverage measure of this type if used alone for test generation. These measures do not guarantee that every path is tested, nor are they based on a sufficient theoretical base to make clear which paths need not be tested. More to the point, these coverage measures do not take into account interaction between different predicates, which might occur along a common path. As a matter of fact, there have been proposals to take pairs of (or multiple) predicates at a time and generate more complex coverage measures. In the limit, as all possible combinations of predicates are considered, this is equivalent to considering all possible paths in test generation.

4.2   Iteration Loops

In the discussion of coverage measures we did not explicitly indicate how iteration loops would be treated as part of the coverage measure. One approach sometimes used is that an iteration loop is executed at least once or not at all as a portion of the coverage measure. Another approach is that coverage of the iteration loop will require execution exactly once (assuming this is possible), at least one execution multiple times, and no execution of the iteration loop as an adequate coverage for test generation. Clearly these ad hoc measures do not take adequate account of the structural information contained within the iteration loop, and are totally unsatisfactory. Fortunately there are some results by Zeil (1981) and by Wiszniewski (1985) that give some more helpful indications of the number of executions of an iteration loop for test generation, and these are based upon a more solid theoretical framework. These approaches will be discussed in Section 6.3.5.

4.3   Data Flow Testing

A number of authors have recommended the use of data flow analysis as the basis for dynamic testing; for example, see Woodward *et al.* (1980), Laski and Korel (1983), Rapps and Weyuker (1985), Weyuker (1984), and Ntafos (1984), with his description of "required element testing." These methods can be viewed as generalizations of the logic coverage measures, especially as developed in Weyuker (1984).

Following the development and notation from Weyuker (1984), with permission of North–Holland Publishing Co., copyright © 1984, and continuing definitions from Section 3.2, we can obtain a family of data-flow testing criteria, using $\mathscr{P}$ as a set of paths through the control flow graph:

1. $\mathscr{P}$ satisfies the *all-definitions* criterion if every global definition is used.

2. $\mathscr{P}$ satisfies the *all-uses* criterion if $\mathscr{P}$ includes a path from every global definition to each of its uses.
3. A *simple path* is one in which all nodes, except possibly the first and last, are distinct. A *loop-free path* is one in which all nodes are distinct. A path $(n_1,\ldots,n_j, n_k)$ is a *DU-path* with respect to a variable x if n_1 has a global definition of x and either (i) n_k has a C-use of x and $(n_1,\ldots,n_j,n_k)$ is a DEF-clear simple path with respect to x, or (ii) (n_j,n_k) has a P-use of x and $(n_1,\ldots,n_j)$ is a DEF-clear, loop-free path with respect to x.

Then $\mathscr{P}$ satisfies the *all-DU-paths* criterion if for every node i and every x that has a global definition in i, $\mathscr{P}$ includes every DU-path with respect to x. Note that if there are multiple DU-paths from a global definition to a given use, they must all be included in paths of $\mathscr{P}$.

Figure 3 shows a family of data-flow criteria from Weyuker (1984); similar hierarchies have been developed by Korel and Laski (1985) and Clarke *et al.* (1985). In Figure 3 the *all-nodes* criterion corresponds to statement coverage, and the *all-edges* criterion corresponds to branch coverage. The arrows in Figure 3 imply strict inclusion, indicating that the higher-level criterion implies a lower-level criterion.

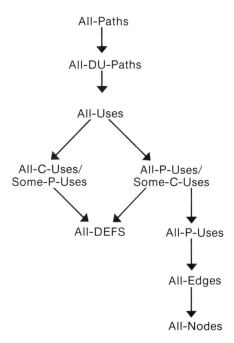

Fig. 3. Family of data-flow test-selection criteria. (From Weyuker, copyright © 1984, North–Holland Publishing Co.).

Moreover, Weyuker (1984) has also analyzed the complexity of these criteria. Consider a program with m variables, a assignments, b input statements, and c conditional transfers. If d represents the number of definitions in the program, it follows that

$$(a + b) < d < a + (b \cdot m)$$

since each input statement defines between one and m variables.

The all-nodes and all-edges criteria require at most $(c + 1)$ test cases. The all-DEFs criterion requires at most $(a + b \cdot m)$ test cases. All criteria indicating uses require at most

$$(1/4)(c^2 + 4c + 3)$$

test cases (see the derivation in Weyuker, 1984). The all-DU-paths criterion requires at most 2^c test cases, whereas it is well known that the all-paths criterion requires exponential effort. Weyuker argues that only extreme program configurations would require exponential test cases for all-DU-paths, and that it constitutes a reasonable criterion for most practical situations.

5.   Mutation Analysis and Functional Testing

In this section we review *mutation analysis* and a variant of this approach called *weak mutation testing*. As these techniques have developed, they now appear to be related to the classic black box approach, functional testing. Functional testing will also be examined, and related to mutation testing.

The primary objective of *mutation analysis* is to evaluate the degree to which a test set exercises a program, rather than the initial generation of that test. This approach was proposed by Budd *et al.* (1978), and a considerable literature exists on various developments and experiments using this approach; for example, a substantial development is given in DeMillo *et al.* (1978) and in Budd (1981). The area has been associated with a degree of controversy; this methodology is now well accepted as one systematic approach to testing, and it is especially valued in that a substantial amount of experimental work has been conducted and reported. Much of the material in Section 5.1 is drawn from Budd (1981), reprinted by permission of North–Holland Publishing Co., copyright ©1981.

Since the goal of testing is to increase our confidence in the program being tested, good test data should be associated with the form and function of the program. Mutation analysis develops a systematic approach by producing a large number of small incremental modifications in individual program statements. Thus the classes of faults in a program will be explicitly defined and associated with these modifications. Mutation analysis can be viewed as providing a measure of test data quality, and there have been a number of proposals to utilize this analysis in an iterative mode to improve the given test set.

A number of authors have suggested methods for functional testing, and there are also a substantial number of systems based on this approach. The fundamental idea is that functions be identified within the computer software or elsewhere, and in order to test the program, each of these functions must be tested over appropriately selected test cases. We shall see that the problem is to approach the generation of the functions and test cases systematically, and eventually automatically.

5.1   What is Mutation Analysis?

Mutation analysis is based on four assumptions; it is probably the defense of these assumptions that has provided a great deal of the controversy associated with this approach:

1. *The competent programmer hypothesis:* Experienced programmers write programs that are either correct or almost correct.
2. *The coupling effect:* Test data that detects small faults in a program (such as small changes in individual statements) is also likely to detect complex faults in that program.
3. *Mutant operators:* An adequate set of predefined incremental operators can be identified to capture nearly all simple faults in a given program; these operators will in general be different for each high-level programming language.
4. *Test oracle availability:* As usual, we must have some systematic way to ascertain the correctness of output for test data submitted to a given program.

Given a program P to be tested and a set of test cases T, T is first executed with P, and we assume this execution produces no errors. A number of alternative programs, called *mutants* of P, are then produced by small changes in P. Test set T is then executed on each of these mutants. Continuing this biological analogy, if at any point P and this mutant produce different output, we say this mutant has *died*; if identical output responses are obtained, we say the mutant *survives*.

If a large number of the mutants survive, then one conclusion that could be drawn is that the test set T is insufficient and additional test cases are needed. If the number of living mutants is small, and we are confident that the set of defined incremental operators, called *mutant operators*, is sufficient, then we can conclude that the test set has been relatively effective in eliminating mutants based on the incremental mutant operators. The test data must have been tied closely to the form and function of the program being tested. Also, the program has been carefully examined in generating the test data, and has been extensively exercised by that data. Budd (1981) has conducted empirical studies which support the assertion that if the set of test cases can eliminate a sizable percentage of mutants for a program *P*, then it is likely that *P* is correct.

The surviving mutants provide the tester with a new method of generating test data: to eliminate these mutants. This leads to an iterative testing process, terminating when nearly all the mutants have been eliminated.

5.1.1   Generation of Mutant Programs

Budd (1981) points out that in the generation of mutant programs it is not reasonable to construct the mutants in such a way that each corresponds to a possible fault the programmer might include in a given program. Rather, the mutant operators are chosen as indicators of whether the test data is sensitive to small changes in the program.

In practice, a number of mutation analysis systems have been developed and applied to FORTRAN, ALGOL, and COBOL languages, as well as a pilot system for an assembly language. Budd (1981) indicates that the system works best for languages in which small syntactic changes tend to produce only small semantic changes in the program; thus much higher-level languages such as APL or SETL would not be as appropriate for mutation analysis.

Mutant operators include such incremental changes to a program as changing a + operation to a − operation, adding one to an arithmetic expression, or interchanging two variables. The EXPER system (Budd, 1981) for FORTRAN programs contains twenty-two different types of such operators; in this description Budd shows how this mutation analysis implementation achieves the same testing effects as statement or branch coverage testing, data-flow analysis, predicate testing, and special values testing.

One of the serious problems with mutation analysis is the very large number of mutants that are generated and must be processed, even though many will quickly die off as the test set is applied. This growth has been characterized as $O(L^2)$, where L represents the number of lines in the program, yet the number of mutants may also depend upon the amount of data being processed. For example, Budd (1981) reports that two programs, each thirty-three statements in length, were analyzed by mutation analysis. The first was a text processing program, producing 859 mutants, whereas the second, a complex program for performing 3×3 matrix multiplication, had 2,382 mutants. Budd also argues that a more careful complexity analysis shows the number of mutants for an "average" program to vary with the product of the total number of data references (including constants) and the number of distinct data references. Even though this analysis is a bit more optimistic than $O(L^2)$, the number of mutants to consider grows very rapidly for even moderate-sized programs.

5.1.2 The Problem of Equivalent Mutants

A mutant program is said to be *equivalent* to the given program P if both have identical input–output responses. The set of equivalent mutants relative to program P then cannot be distinguished from P by any test sets, and will always survive any test set in mutation analysis. Budd (1981) indicates that between 4% and 10% of generated mutants are equivalent, with heavy clustering at 4%.

As indicated in Section 2.2, it is generally undecidable whether two programs are equivalent, so it will be difficult or impossible to tell whether during mutation analysis each surviving mutant is equivalent, or whether it could be removed by a suitably expanded test set. Researchers such as Budd (1981), working with mutation analysis, have indicated that in many instances simple techniques and intuition can be used to identify surviving equivalent mutants. Still, this remains as a serious theoretical and practical problem in the implementation of mutation analysis.

5.1.3 Summary of Mutation Analysis

Mutation analysis has emerged as providing a unifying approach to testing, both in test-set selection and in determination of the quality of the test set. A number of authors, such as Howden (1982), have referred to *mutation testing* when some of the techniques of mutation analysis are applied to test-set selection. Specifically this refers to the construction of tests designed to distinguish between mutant programs that differ by a single mutation transformation.

The underlying assumptions of mutation analysis are still quite controversial and contentious; the method can still be useful if used carefully and without requiring the validity of all the underlying assumptions. There are still serious problems in the implementation. Even a small number of mutation operators can lead to an enormous number of mutant programs. Another problem is the issue of equivalent mutants, and how surviving mutants can be identified as equivalent to the given program or not. The method requires substantial and complex software support, and there is not a systematic or automatic method for the generation of additional test data to eliminate surviving mutants.

5.2   Weak Mutation Testing—Another Approach

Howden (1982) has suggested a testing method which has many apparent similarities to mutation testing and hence has been called *weak mutation testing*. The description of this technique is drawn from that publication, reprinted by permission of IEEE, copyright © 1982. Test selection rules are obtained from arithmetic expressions and relations. Weak mutation testing differs philosophically from mutation testing in several ways:

1. In mutation testing, functions computed by the entire program are tested and compared to distinguish mutants. In weak mutation testing the focus is upon the testing of statement-level functions and expressions.

2. In mutation analysis, to obtain a comprehensive set of mutant programs the mutant operators must by necessity be quite dependent upon the specific programming language used. We shall see that, although weak mutation analysis concentrates on functions at the statement level, the defined mutations are not as dependent upon the specific programming language.

3. Howden (1985) points out that in mutation testing the classes of faults for which it is effective are explicitly defined; there is, however, no direct global way to obtain tests that will reveal these classes of faults. There is a trade-off here, in which the tests can be obtained only if the fault detection capability is *weakened*. This accounts for the motivation behind the term "weak mutation testing," where local test criteria can be obtained at the price of perceiving the effect of the weak mutation on the overall program behavior. Thus we shall see that we may have lost the ability to obtain global test sets that produce the required local test criteria to detect weak mutations.

5.2.1   Component Testing

Howden (1982) defines a *component* as an elementary computational structure in a program; examples of components are references to variables, arithmetic expressions and relations, and Boolean expressions. If P is a program containing a component C, then there is a mutation transformation that can be applied to C to produce C'; P' is then the mutant program corresponding to P and containing C'. In weak mutation testing it is required that a test t be constructed in which C is executed as t is applied to P, and that in at least one such execution of C, C produces a different value from C'. Notice that, even though C' produces a different value from C under test t, it is possible for programs P and P' to compute the same output under test t.

The component mutations then consist of the following:

1. *Variable reference:* This component mutation causes the component to reference a different variable. If v is a variable associated with a

component C, then in order for C to compute a value different from a possible mutation C' of C, it is necessary to execute C in an environment in which v has a value different from the values of all other variables in that environment.

2. *Variable assignment:* This component mutation causes the component to assign the value to a different variable. If v is a variable to which C assigns a value, then in order for C to return output different from a possible mutation C' of C, it is sufficient to execute C over data in which the value stored by C into v is different from the value currently stored in v.

These two types of component mutations are primitive and appear as parts of the other three kinds of components:

3. *Arithmetic expression:* This component mutation consists of arithmetic expressions that are off by an additive constant, off by a multiplicative constant, and have incorrect coefficients. The first two types of mutations can be easily distinguished from corresponding expressions, for if E' is an additive or multiplicative constant mutation of an arithmetic expression E, then it is sufficient to execute E over a single vector of values in order to distinguish E from E'. If E is an arithmetic expression in which one or more coefficients have been changed, then distinguishing mutation arithmetic expressions is more complex, and the size of test sets required to differentiate them may be quite large; Howden (1982) gives some ideas as to how these test sets can be chosen.

4. *Arithmetic relation:* This component mutation consists of arithmetic relations that contain incorrect relational operators and off-by-an-additive constants. An arithmetic relation R ($\exp_1 R \exp_2$) can be distinguished from a mutation R' in which the relation has been changed by executing R over data for which $\exp_1 < \exp_2$, $\exp_1 = \exp_2$, and $\exp_1 > \exp_2$. The off-by-a-constant mutation for an arithmetic relation can be detected by a suitably chosen single test point.

Howden (1982) indicates that his results for arithmetic relation mutations have been derived from work described by Foster (1980). Foster based his development on the assumption of integer variables, but the results can easily be generalized to real numbers. In his paper Foster has contributed several other ideas for testing techniques where no model is available for analysis:

5. *Boolean expression:* This component is a function of the form $B(E_1, E_2, \ldots, E_n)$, where E_i, $1 \leq i \leq n$, is an arithmetic expression or variable that evaluates to true or false, where the E_i are transformed by logical operators OR, AND, and NOT. A Boolean expression mutation can

then be viewed as one or more of the expressions E_i with a modified truth value. A test set can be constructed to distinguish B from all other Boolean expressions B' by constructing tests t so that all possible truth values for the E_i are generated. Again, this test set can grow exponentially, but Howden (1982) discusses some ways to control the growth of this set.

5.2.2 Comparison to Other Methods

Howden (1982) argues that weak mutation testing can be viewed as a refinement of branch testing. Weak mutation testing corresponds to a wider class of errors, and there are some subtle errors that require evaluation of branch functions over special kinds of test values, the sort of careful evaluation conducted in weak mutation testing but not in branch testing.

There are several advantages of weak mutation testing over mutation testing. The former is more efficient, as it is not necessary to carry out a separate program execution for each mutation; moreover, as we have seen by the various types of component mutations, only a few (or even one) tests may be required. A second advantage is that test data can be specified a priori, over which a component mutation must be executed in order that a different output value can be obtained. This means the user will have guidance as to what types of tests should be applied to the component. The disadvantage of weak mutation testing is that the overall program may act correctly over this same set of data and not indicate a different output behavior.

5.3 Functional Testing

A testing strategy that has been popular in industrial and commercial software applications has been known as "functional testing." This has traditionally been a black box approach in which the functional properties of the requirements or specifications are identified and test data selected to specifically test each of those functions.

There are two problems with this approach. First, although requirements and specifications provide many meaningful functions that can be the focus for functional testing, software may contain a much richer collection of functions than those put forth in specifications. Moreover, specifications are often inadequately described to provide the detailed information required for testing. A second problem has been the lack of any unifying and fundamental theoretical basis for such testing. Thus the commercial efforts using functional testing are both ad hoc and incomplete in scope.

Howden (1980; 1985) has developed an underlying theory for functional testing and has extended the concept to include functional components of the software as well. In this way, to a great extent he has overcome the two problems identified with the previous concept of functional testing. Howden's philosophy is that it is important to not only test the functions implemented by the program as a whole (which are best captured in requirements or specifications), but also to test the functions that constitute various parts of the program. There are many ways to decompose the program, each giving a different description of the functions that comprise that program. Howden's theory provides an insight into that decomposition, which at best should mirror the synthesis process by which the programmer has constructed the program, beginning with simple and primitive functions and routines, and evolving these into complex systems.

Howden provides two elements in his theory: functional synthesis and testability. Functional synthesis is a view of the way programs are written, and a summary of these ideas is given in the next section. Testability is a positive characteristic of this particular decomposition of the programming process, and is shown to be the essential ingredient for successful functional testing. Much of this material is drawn from Howden (1985), reprinted by permission of IEEE, copyright © 1985.

5.3.1   Functional Synthesis

Four types of functional synthesis are identified by Howden as at the appropriate level for functional testing:

1. *Algebraic synthesis*—The use of algebraic expressions in assignment statements and predicates provides an initial building block. As usual, these expressions are built from variables with either numerical or Boolean values.
2. *Conditional synthesis*—A more complex building block is the familiar IF–THEN–ELSE construction, but note that the predicate, the THEN, and the ELSE clause each constitute functions, where each is built up from algebraic expressions of various forms.
3. *Iterative synthesis*—Loop iteration is another fundamental construct, and the functional manifestation is most easily seen in the WHILE form, where the predicate function determines termination, whereas the body of the loop provides an additional function.
4. *Control synthesis*—The most complex building block of Howden is a high-level view of control using the familiar state transition model. This allows the description and modeling of many qualitative state concepts in programs which cannot be captured numerically; e.g., "user has failed to provide proper input data" or "end-of-file has been reached." The

programmer is expected to know the operation of the program sufficiently well to provide state transition diagrams as models of various important functional parts of that program.

5.3.2 Testability

Howden (1985) defines *testability* as the property that a finite set of tests can be specified that will determine if the program that implements a function contains one of a specified set of faults. More specifically, let f be a function implemented by all or part of a program, and let f' be the hypothetically correct but unknown function. Suppose a set of functions F is known to contain both f and f', and that it is possible to construct a finite set of tests T such that, for any function f' in F, if $f = f'$ over all tests in T, then $f = f'$ over all input data. Then f is said to be *testable* relative to F. The concept of *testability* is a further development of the notion of *completeness criteria*, identified earlier by Howden (1981; 1982).

As an example of a testable algebraic expression that might occur in algebraic synthesis, consider the form

$$f(x, y) = (ax + b)/(cy + d)$$

Assume that F contains f and all other functions that differ by only a single parameter from the set of four in this function. Then f is testable relative to F, for a single nonzero value of x and y for which the denominator is nonzero will suffice as set T.

At this point notice the similarity between testability and the test selection rules given in Section 5.2.1 for Howden's weak mutation testing. Howden (1982) developed the concept of testability and presented it along with the weak mutation testing approach. Although both are shown to be testable by Howden's criteria, they do represent different approaches to testing.

The concept of control synthesis differs substantially from the weak mutation components described in Section 5.2.1. Howden indicates that he was motivated to include control synthesis in functional testing as a result of an empirical study of errors in a large COBOL data processing system. This study showed that control synthesis faults had to be addressed using a different functional model.

In Section 1.5 we discussed the need for a test oracle, which is the type required for program parts for testing algebraic, conditional, and iterative synthesis. Howden (1982) requires a different type of oracle for control synthesis; the oracle (or programmer) must know what sequence of functions should be performed for a certain test case. Thus control synthesis can detect missing computational faults, as illustrated in Figure 4. Howden argues that, if the only kind of fault possible is a missing computation fault and we are

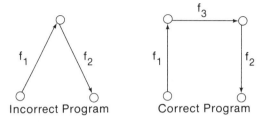

FIG. 4.   Missing computational fault. (From Howden, copyright © 1985, IEEE).

provided with a control synthesis oracle, then $f = f_1 f_2$ is testable for the missing computation fault f_3. When a systematic execution of the program is conducted, the required functional sequence will not be executed, thus revealing the missing computation fault.

5.3.3   Function Identification

Howden (1980) provides the sources of functions; they should be selected from

1. specifications—if informal, then verbs provide the functions; if formal, the functions can be obtained from formal assertions, tables, and formulas;
2. programs—select functions from elementary program statements, subroutines, and subpaths;
3. design information and design documents—these materials provide an additional source of functions; it is ideal if a mapping can be found from design functions to specific code fragments.

Howden emphasizes that the program should be well understood before functional testing is used. This advice certainly applies to other methods of testing as well.

5.3.4   Functional Test Coverage

Given the sources of functions identified in Section 5.3.3, various means must be found to select tests for these functions. Howden (1980) has identified the following methods of test coverage, and has found them to be useful for functional testing:

- tests to span domains of output variables or expressions, as well as input variables

- tests for both extreme values and interior values of synthesis functions
- tests for illegal values of variables or synthesis functions
- tests for various array or vector patterns; this may require partitioning arrays in various ways to provide the important test sets.

Howden (1980) performed experiments over a set of statistical and numerical analysis programs from the IMSL package (1978), and these programs contained eight distinct errors. He found that static analysis was most effective for 41 errors and dynamic testing for 42 of the errors. Functional testing was compared to a structural testing approach, consisting of a combination of branch testing and path testing. Functional testing was most effective in detecting 31 of the errors, whereas the structural testing approach was most effective in detecting ten of these errors. Howden (1980) has also applied the functional testing method to data processing programs in COBOL, with similar success.

5.3.5   Functional Testing and Coverage Measures

Howden (1980) observes that branch testing can be interpreted as an approximation to functional testing. It does not force combinations of branches, and does not construct testing over functionally important cases. We presented in Section 4.3 Weyuker's arguments that data flow coverage is a more powerful approach than branch testing. Howden indicates that if two program parts are related by data flow, then they may comprise the same function, and thus he argues that data flow methods can be viewed as functional testing.

5.3.6   Functional Testing and Mutation Testing

We have already observed the intimate relationship between functional testing and weak mutation testing. In mutation testing, entire mutant programs are considered as functions; whole programs are constructed using mutant operators. Thus there is no building up of intermediate synthesis, as is done in software design. Howden (1985) also observes that, as a result, mutation testing is not testable in the sense defined in Section 5.3.2.

6.   Path-Oriented Testing Models

Path-oriented testing is based on the use of the control flow of the program. In Section 1.1.2 we indicated that path-oriented testing requires that a set of paths be selected in some manner, and then subsequently a method must be found to select input test data that will cause those paths to be executed. In this section we will provide some examples of methods to accomplish both of these goals; as with many other aspects of testing we have discussed, both of these problems are difficult.

Despite the fact that we have identified the selection of paths and the selection of input data to execute those paths as separate operations, one of the conceptual advantages of path-oriented testing is the explicit association of the path and the input data that causes its execution.

Because of the presence of iteration loops, there is potentially an infinite number of distinct paths in a program. Even in a program without iteration loops, there is potentially an exponential number of distinct paths, as a function of the number of predicates in the program. Thus, for any nontrivial program it does not make sense to generate test data for all paths in that program.

In Section 2.1.1 a path was identified as infeasible if no input data exists that causes that path to be executed. We indicated that the problem of determining the feasibility of a path is undecidable; the problem of identifying infeasible paths is difficult at best in a practical situation. Infeasible paths are not indicative of improper program design and coding, but will occur in well-designed software. The tester must be aware of this problem.

We will consider how program paths can be used to guide the testing process, and some of the factors that must be accounted for to accommodate testing. The path selection process will be presented, including some metrics that are also available for this selection.

Three different path-oriented approaches will be presented: domain testing, perturbation testing, and partition testing. Another technique, called the sufficient paths criterion, will provide some insight into how paths might be selected; some experimental work conducted using this technique will be reported. An overview of domain testing and the sufficient paths criterion is given in White et al. (1981).

6.1   Path Testing Approaches

When paths are used for testing, this allows various graph-theoretic models to be used to assist in the path selection. For example, in order to achieve either statement coverage or branch coverage, a set of paths may be defined as a graph covering problem, where the paths cover either the vertices or the arcs, respectively, of the control flow graph for a given program. In order to present this approach more precisely, let us specifically consider branch coverage, which we know to be a stronger testing approach than statement coverage.

Huang (1979) defines a *minimal covering set* of paths and the associated path conditions such that if these path conditions are all satisfied, then every arc in the control flow graph will be traversed at least once (corresponding to branch coverage); moreover, this set should be minimal with respect to this property. A test set is then *minimally thorough* if every arc (or branch) in the control flow graph is traversed at least once during the execution of the test set; moreover, this test set should be minimal with respect to this property. From the discussion in Section 2.2, recall that if we find the minimal covering set of paths, this does not guarantee a minimally thorough test, as one or more of the paths in the minimal set may be infeasible. Ntafos and Hakimi (1979) have provided an efficient polynomial solution to the minimal covering path set problem; the complexity is $O(W^2)$, where W is the number of vertices of the control flow graph.

One would like to have a metric in order to guide path-oriented testing; for example, software managers are infamous in their desire for a single number to measure how testing is going—i.e., "test coverage." A study of metrics has been given by Woodward *et al.* (1980), including metrics for statement coverage, branch coverage, and some generalizations; the authors call these "test effectiveness ratios," measuring the percent coverage of the total number of required structures. In addition, Woodward *et al.* (1980) have provided some important experimentation on a collection of numerical software, in order to gain experience with these metrics. As a result of these experiments they have provided some further insights into path-oriented testing. They advocate testing as many of the shorter feasible paths as possible, since they are simpler and yet achieve good coverage. They further note that the presence of infeasible paths impedes the achievement of 100% coverage measures. They have provided a further study of how the number of infeasible paths can be reduced by utilizing a systematic methodology; this research is continuing. They also add a warning which we should make sure is communicated to software managers: An achievement of 100% coverage metric does not provide any guarantee of the absence of errors in the software. Other, more sophisticated metrics can be based on the data flow testing hierarchy of Weyuker (1984), which we discussed in Section 4.3 and presented as Figure 3. Experimentation with these metrics will be reported in the research literature over the next several years.

For the problem of the termination of path-oriented testing, another alternative to coverage metrics is to phrase the problem another way: In the selection of paths for testing, is there a point at which subsequent paths will give little or no information, and we can stop? This approach has led to the "sufficient paths criterion," which will be discussed in Section 6.3. This approach currently has a number of serious limitations, but does represent an interesting alternative to coverage metrics, especially in that this sufficient paths criterion can lead to the selection of improved paths for testing.

An excellent discussion of path-oriented testing and the selection of paths for this purpose is provided in the monograph *Software Testing Techniques* by Boris Beizer (1983). His approach is quite pragmatic, and he possesses a strong base of practical experience, which pervades his discussions. Beizer recommends the selection of simplest and functionally sensible paths to achieve the target coverage metric. He also suggests that additional paths should differ in small variations from previous paths selected; he argues that paths selected for testing represent an experiment, and in experimental design one attempts to change as few variables as possible in subsequent experiments. Beizer argues for paths that execute iteration loops once, more than once, and no times (if possible). He indicates that Huang (1979) has shown that some initialization problems can only be detected by two or more passes through the iteration loop, and this is his rationale for requiring multiple executions of an iteration loop within some selected path. Beizer has many other practical suggestions for the selection of test paths and should be consulted for other ideas.

Finally, one of the advantages of path-oriented testing is that these methods tend to be easier to automate than other approaches, such as functional testing. This can be very important, as testing requires extensive involvement and time of an experienced tester; a software producer becomes quite vulnerable if an experienced testing professional should leave his organization.

6.2 Domain Testing

The objective of domain testing is to demonstrate that it is possible to select test data for a restricted set of programs to detect a specified type of error, and yet to characterize the extent to which these errors could be detected for that program class. Much of the material in this section is drawn from White *et al.* (1981) and is reprinted by permission of North–Holland Publishing Co., copyright © 1981. In the following development, concepts of predicate interpretations and input space structure will be presented before the domain strategy is discussed.

6.2.1 Predicate Interpretation

A simple predicate is said to be *linear* in variables $V_1, V_2, \ldots, V_N$ if it is of the form

$$A_1 V_1 + A_2 V_2 + \cdots + A_N V_N \text{ ROP } K$$

where K and the A_i are constants and ROP represents one of the relational operations ($<, >, =, \leq, \geq, \neq$).

In general, predicates can be expressed in terms of both program variables and input variables. In generating input data to satisfy the path condition, however, we must work with constraints in terms of only input variables. If we replace each program variable appearing in the predicate by its symbolic value calculated in terms of input variables along that path, we get an equivalent constraint called the *predicate interpretation*. A single predicate can appear on many different execution paths. Since each of these paths will in general consist of a different sequence of assignment statements, a single predicate can have many different interpretations. The following program segment provides example predicates and interpretations:

```
READ A,B;
IF A > B
   THEN C = B + 1;
   ELSE C = B − 1;
D = 2 * A + B;
IF C ≤ 0
   THEN E = 0;
   ELSE
        DO I = 1,B;
             E = E + 2 * I;
        END
IF D = 2
   THEN F = E + A;
   ELSE F = E − A;
WRITE F;
```

In the first predicate, $A > B$, both A and B are input variables, so there is only one interpretation. The second predicate, $C \leq 0$, will have two interpretations, depending on which branch was taken in the first IF construct. For paths on which the THEN $C = B + 1$ clause is executed, the interpretation is $B + 1 \leq 0$, or equivalently, $B \leq -1$. When the ELSE $C = B - 1$ branch is taken, the interpretation is $B - 1 \leq 0$, or equivalently, $B \leq 1$. Within the second IF–THEN–ELSE clause, a nested DO loop appears. The DO loop is executed

$$\text{no times if } B < 1$$

$$\text{once if } 1 \leq B < 2$$

$$\text{twice if } 2 \leq B < 3$$

$$\text{etc.}$$

Thus the selection of a path will require a specification of the number of times that the DO loop is executed, and a corresponding predicate is applied to select the input points that will follow that particular path. Even though the third predicate, $D = 2$, appears on four different paths, it has only one interpretation, $2 * A + B = 2$, since D is assigned the value $2 * A + B$ in the same statement for each of the four paths.

6.2.2   Input Space Structure

An *input space domain* is defined as a set of input data points satisfying a path condition, consisting of a conjunction of predicates along the path. For simplicity in this discussion, each of these predicates is assumed to be simple. The input space is partitioned into a set of domains. Each domain corresponds to a particular execution path in the program and consists of the input data points that cause the path to be executed.

The boundary of each domain is determined by the predicates in the path condition and consists of *border segments*, where each border segment is the section of the boundary determined by a single simple predicate in the path condition. A "redundant" predicate is implied by some subset of the other predicates of the path condition; it can be removed, as no border segment will correspond to a redundant predicate. Each border segment can be open or closed, depending on the relational operator in the predicate. A *closed border segment* is actually part of the domain and is formed by predicates with $\leq$, $\geq$, or = operators. An *open border segment* forms part of the domain boundary but does not constitute part of the domain, and is formed by $<$, $>$, and $\neq$ predicates.

The general form of a simple linear predicate interpretation is

$$A_1 X_1 + A_2 X_2 + \cdots + A_N X_N \text{ ROP } K$$

where ROP is the relational operator, X_i are input variables, and A_i, K are constants. The border segment defined by any of these predicates is, however, a section of the surface defined by the equality

$$A_1 X_1 + A_2 X_2 + \cdots + A_N X_N = K$$

since this is the limiting condition for the points satisfying the predicate. In an N-dimensional space this linear equality defines a hyperplane, which is the N-dimensional generalization of a plane.

Consider a path condition composed of a conjunction of simple predicates. These predicates can be of three basic types: equalities (=), inequalities ($<$, $>$, $\leq$, $\geq$), and nonequalities ($\neq$). The use of each of the three types results in a markedly different effect on the domain boundary. Each equality constrains the domain to lie in a particular hyperplane, thus reducing the dimensionality of the domain by one. The set of inequality constraints defines a region within the lower-dimensional space specified by the equality predicates.

Equalities can arise from predicates that occur explicitly in the program, or that form from two or more inequalities that produce a coincidental equality. For example, if $X \leq A$ and $X \geq A$ are two inequalities that occur in a single path condition, then the result is a coincidental equality $X = A$.

6.2.3   Domain Testing Assumptions

The domain testing strategy is designed to detect errors and will be effective in detecting errors in any type of domain border under certain conditions. Test points are generated for each border segment, which, if processed correctly, determine that both the relational operator and the position of the border are correct. An error in the border operator occurs when an incorrect relational operator is used in the corresponding predicate, and an error in the position of the border occurs when one or more incorrect coefficients are computed for the particular predicate interpretation. The strategy is based on a geometrical analysis of the domain boundary and takes advantage of the fact that points on or near the border are most sensitive to domain errors. A number of authors have made this observation—e.g., Boyer *et al.* (1975) and Clarke (1976).

It should be emphasized that the domain strategy does not require that the correct program be given for the selection of test points, since only information obtained from the given program is needed. It will be convenient, however, to be able to refer to a "correct border," although it will not be necessary to have any knowledge about this border. Define the *given border* as that corresponding to the predicate interpretation for the given program being tested, and the *correct border* as the border that would be calculated in some correct program.

There are limitations inherent to any testing strategy, and these also constrain the domain strategy. Two such limitations were defined in Section 1.4 as coincidental correctness and missing path errors. As applied to domain testing, coincidental correctness can occur when a specific test point follows an incorrect path, and yet the output variables coincidentally are the same as if that test point were to follow the correct path. This test would then be of no assistance in the detection of the domain error that caused the control flow change. No path-oriented strategy can circumvent this problem.

The domain testing strategy will be developed and validated under a set of simplifying assumptions:

1. Coincidental correctness does not occur for any test case.
2. A missing-path error is not associated with the path being tested.
3. Each border is produced by a simple predicate.

4. The path corresponding to each adjacent domain computes a different function than the path being tested.
5. The given border is linear, and if it is incorrect, the correct border is also linear.
6. The input space is continuous rather than discrete.

Assumptions 1 and 2 have been shown to be inherent to the testing process, and cannot be entirely eliminated. Recognition of these potential problems, however, can lead to improved testing techniques. Assumptions 3 and 4 considerably simplify the testing strategy, for with them no more than one domain need be examined at one time to select test points. As for the linearity assumption, 5, the domain testing method has been shown to be applicable for nonlinear boundaries, but the number of required test points may become inordinate, and there are complex problems associated with processing nonlinear boundaries in higher dimensions. The continuous input space assumption, 6, is not really a limitation of the proposed testing method, but allows points to be chosen arbitrarily close to the border to be tested. An error analysis for discrete spaces is available (White *et al.*, 1978) and shows that pathological cases do exist in discrete spaces, for which the testing strategy cannot be used, but that these occur only when domain size is on the order of the resolution of the discrete space itself.

Any program that satisfies constraints 1 through 6 will be referred to as a *linearly domained program*.

6.2.4 Test Point Selection

The test points selected will be of two types, defined by their position with respect to the given border. An *ON* test point lies on the given border, while an *OFF* test point is a small distance ϵ from, and lies on the open side of the given border. Therefore we observe that, when testing a closed border, the ON test points are in the domain being tested and each OFF test point is in some adjacent domain.

Figure 5 shows the selection of three test points A, B, and C for a closed inequality border segment. If the OFF test point C is projected down on line segment AB, then the projected point must lie strictly between A and B on this line segment. Also, point C is selected a distance ϵ from the given border segment and will be chosen so that it satisfies all the inequalities defining the domain except for the inequality being tested.

The domain testing strategy for the two-dimensional case can be extended to the general N-dimensional case in a straightforward manner. Since an $(N - 1)$-dimensional hyperplane border segment is determined by N linearly

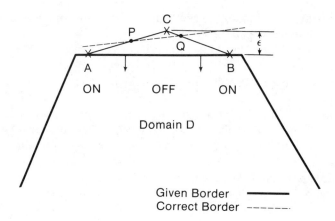

FIG. 5.   Test points for a two-dimensional linear border.

independent points, we have to identify N points on the correct border and these points must be guaranteed to be linearly independent. A single OFF test point is selected, whose projection on the given border is a convex combination of these N points. In addition, as in the two-dimensional case, the OFF point must also satisfy the inequality constraints corresponding to all adjacent borders.

The domain testing strategy requires at most $s(N + 3)$ test points per domain, where N is the dimensionality of the input space in which the domain is defined and s is the number of border segments in the boundary of the specific domain. Again, however, we can reduce this testing cost by using extreme points as ON test points and by sharing test points between adjacent domains. The following result from White and Cohen (1980) summarizes the results for domain testing: "For linearly domained programs, with each OFF point chosen a distance ϵ from the corresponding border, the domain testing strategy is guaranteed to detect all errors of magnitude greater than ϵ using no more than $s(N + 3)$ test points per domain, where N indicates the dimensionality of the input space and s is the number of predicates along the path to be tested."

6.2.5   Some Observations on Domain Testing

One of the major results of domain testing is that, subject to the assumption of a linearly domained program, reliable detection of domain errors requires a reasonable number of test points for a single path. This number of test points grows only linearly with the number of predicates along the path and the number of input variables. Specifically, for linearly domained programs, all domain errors can be detected using no more than $s(N + 3)$ test points per domain. However, the total cost is unacceptable for any practical program, as it will routinely contain an excessive number of paths, due to the presence of iteration loops.

A specific method by which to select the $N \times 1$ test paths for each border segment is given in Perera and White (1985). Clarke *et al.* (1982) have indicated that this $N \times 1$ test-selection strategy may result in inordinately large domain errors that remain undetected. They have suggested two improved selection techniques. The $N \times N$ selection strategy selects N ON points and N OFF points, each OFF point located at ϵ distance from the border segment. The $V \times V$ strategy selects an ON point at each vertex (or close to each vertex) on the border segment, with V OFF points, each located on a hyperplane ϵ from the border segment.

One way to view the results from domain testing is to observe that the number of test points required is a minimum for reliable detection of domain errors, and if coincidental correctness should occur, then even more test points would be required. In many places in the research testing literature, however, one finds reference to choosing only one test data point per path when a path-oriented strategy is utilized. This work shows clearly that in general this is inadequate for even a modest attempt at reliable testing.

Although we know that the problem of reliable test data generation is unsolvable, the domain testing research has shown that if attention is focused upon specific types of errors and a characterized subset of programs, reliable testing conditions can be obtained. Indeed, the problem here was to find the minimum set of conditions so that domain errors could be reliably detected.

Domain testing is an example of a structural approach, which uses only information from the program to be tested. Thus it is clear why only domain errors can be reliably detected, since they are intimately related to the structure of the given program. In order to detect computation errors or missing-path errors, we must obtain additional information, e.g., from the program specifications. This is precisely the approach of the research described in Section 6.4.

6.3   The Sufficient Paths Criterion

Although the number of required test points for each path in the domain strategy grows only linearly with the number of input variables and predicates along the path, the problem with this approach is that the number of paths grows in a highly combinatorial fashion and is potentially infinite. Moreover, many path-oriented strategies suffer from this basic problem.

In the definition of any automated path selection strategy, the questions that naturally arise are, "When does testing stop?" and "At what point is it possible to point to a particular program construct and say that it has been sufficiently tested, i.e., no errors remain undetected?" In general, we know that this problem has been proved undecidable, but a programmer's intuition suggests that such claims should be possible after the selection of a small number of test paths, especially if we possess a strategy in which we have specific confidence in terms of its ability to detect certain types of errors in some construct along that path for an appropriately restricted class of programs.

Zeil has developed a vector-space model for predicate errors (Zeil and White, 1981), for assignment errors (Zeil, 1983b), and for computation errors (Zeil, 1984), and this model has indicated substantive answers to these questions. It should be emphasized that this research and these results are essentially independent of the domain strategy and require only a path-oriented testing strategy that will reliably detect either domain errors or computation errors. Much of the material in this section has been drawn from White *et al.* (1981) and reprinted by permission of North–Holland Publishing Co., copyright © 1981.

6.3.1 Sufficient Testing Sets

In order to state these results more precisely, let us carefully define these questions and concepts. A set of paths is a *sufficient set* for a program construct if the failure to detect some error in that construct, using a reliable method of selecting data points along those paths, implies that this error would go undetected for any path through the program. We can then restate the questions more rigorously, as:

a) After a number of paths that pass through the construct have been tested, what is the marginal advantage of testing another path?
b) Is there a point (before nearly all paths have been tested) at which we may say that no more paths through some program construct need be chosen and tested, i.e., that this construct has been sufficiently tested?

6.3.2 Types of Testing Blindness

In order for us to characterize the minimal number of paths which must be tested, we first must clearly understand why multiple paths might be needed to detect an error in a construct (such as a predicate). The examples in Table I show three different reasons why a single path may not detect an erroneous predicate. These are termed *assignment blindness*, *equality blindness*, and *self-blindness*, and represent a seemingly pathological set of values for variables along the path, so that both the correct and the incorrect predicates evaluate to equal values.

TABLE I

A. ASSIGNMENT BLINDNESS

Correct	Incorrect
$A = 1$	$A = 1$
$\vdots$	$\vdots$
IF $B > 0$ THEN	IF $B + A > 1$ THEN
$\vdots$	$\vdots$

B. EQUALITY BLINDNESS

Correct	Incorrect
IF $D = 2$ THEN	IF $D = 2$ THEN
$\vdots$	$\vdots$
IF $C + D > 3$ THEN	IF $C > 1$ THEN
$\vdots$	$\vdots$

C. SELF-BLINDNESS

Correct	Incorrect
$X = A$	$X = A$
$\vdots$	$\vdots$
IF $X - 1 > 0$	IF $X + A - 2 > 0$
$\vdots$	$\vdots$

6.3.3 Results from the Vector Space Model

The vector space model has yielded an insight as to how multiple paths through a single construct can resolve the ambiguities due to various types of blindness. Results have been obtained for the effects of assignment errors in linearly domained programs and for the effects of predicate errors in more general vector spaces, for which Zeil (1983b) has characterized "vector-bounded programs." This has allowed the generalization of linear functions to polynomial or multinomial functions, for example. In his work on computation errors, Zeil (1984) also generalized his results to programs in which the computation assignment statements possessed errors that could be modeled as vector spaces.

To get a more specific and simpler intuition for his results, assume a linearly domained program; the vector space in question is then composed of

- one vector for each assigned program variable, for a total of M;
- one vector for each equality restriction on the path domain, at most N total, where N is the number of input variables.

The results of this research, which provides answers to questions (a) and (b) posed in Section 6.3.1 can be stated as follows for predicate errors and assignment errors:

> For any predicate in a linearly domained program, the smallest sufficient set of test paths will contain at most $(M + N + 1)$ paths; if a set of paths has been tested, which paths pass through the predicate of interest, a simple vector criterion, in Zeil and White (1981), will determine whether a proposed additional path is required to detect an error in that predicate.
>
> A minimal set of paths sufficient for testing a given sequential set of assignment statements in a linearly domained program will contain at most $M(M + N + 1)$ paths; if a set of paths has been tested, which paths pass through those assignment statements, a simple vector criterion, in Zeil (1981), will determine whether a proposed additional path is required to detect an error in those assignment statements.

Notice the substantially larger number of paths to detect assignment errors as opposed to predicate errors; both path measures are polynomial in M and N. Linearly domained programs have been assumed to achieve this result. Another serious problem, however, is that those vector criteria can only be applied post hoc to a selected path in conjunction with a set of previously selected paths. In the next section we will describe some experiments aimed at a solution to this problem.

6.3.4 Experiments Using the Sufficient-Paths Criterion

Experiments were conducted on linearly domained programs, by testing predicates using Zeil's sufficient-paths vector space criterion; these experiments are reported in White and Sahay (1985). Nine programs were used; they were linearly domained and tended either to be data-structuring programs (to perform sorting, searching, or set operations) or number-theoretic programs (such as Euclid's greatest common divisor or greatest common factor).

Zeil and White (1981) showed that each predicate to be tested is associated with an error space of maximum dimension $(M + N + 1)$, where N is the number of input variables and M the number of program variables. As each subsequent path through that predicate is chosen for testing, the resultant error space is reduced in dimension (or else that path is discarded and not tested). One of the primary reasons for these experiments was to develop heuristics for path selection to effect the most rapid reduction of predicate error spaces. Another reason for these experiments was to characterize the *irreducible error space* of a predicate, which cannot be reduced further by the selection of any other path through that predicate.

Zeil's sufficient-paths criterion indicates that an upper bound of $(M + N)$ on the number of paths required for testing a predicate and $p(M + N)$ paths would be required to test all p predicates in a program if each predicate were tested independently. Another objective of these experiments was to see how many paths were required for each of these cases.

Several heuristics emerged from these experiments, and they lead to improved path selection. In White and Sahay (1985), it is shown that the minimum sufficient set of paths required for testing a given predicate in a linearly domained program will contain at most $(M + Z + 1)$ paths, where Z is the number of independent equality restrictions encountered along the first path chosen for that predicate. Thus the first path should be selected through the given predicate with the fewest possible equality restrictions. In the experiments this was done, so $Z = 0$, and then $(M + 1)$ paths were typically chosen, showing this to be a tight bound. Subsequent paths for that predicate should be selected so as to eliminate vectors in the resulting error space.

In selecting predicates to test, those with the fewest paths leading to them should be chosen first; these tend to be predicates near the beginning of the program. Paths should be considered that are extensions of subpaths previously chosen for earlier predicates; these experiments have shown that this approach was quite successful, leading to a number of paths for testing all predicates which was at most only one more than the bound $(M + Z + 1)$ for a single predicate, far below the predicted bound of $p(M + N)$. It remains for further experimentation to see if these results will hold in general.

The irreducible error spaces in the experiments were found to contain unused variables, equality restrictions, and invariant expressions. One should be able to predict, a priori, the occurrence of the first two items; invariant expressions will require further study.

6.3.5 Loop Iteration Limits

Another result of Zeil's work on sufficient testing is to address the problem of iteration loop limits. Many testing researchers and practitioners have recommended that no more than k iterations of any loop be used for testing, but without any logical or theoretical justification. Zeil (1981) shows that if there is a path S with more than $(M + N)$ iterations of some single-entry, single-exit loop and a predicate error e detectable along S, then there exists another path S' with no more than $(M + N)$ iterations of that loop, such that, ignoring coincidental equalities, e is detectable along S'; N represents the number of input variables and M the number of program variables.

Zeil also makes a number of observations about this result, called the "Iteration Limit Theorem," which we should indicate here. This theorem guarantees only that a short path S' exists for which the error is detectable, but does not guarantee that the path S' is feasible or that the predicate interpretation involved is nonredundant. He also observes that, since the proof was independent of the surrounding program structure, the result holds regardless of the existence of nested iteration loops. The Iteration Limit Theorem applies, then, for the total number of iterations of an innermost loop in this nesting structure.

Another result in a similar vein and applying to domain testing has been presented by Wiszniewski (1985) and is called "iterated domains." In this paper he defines *elementary classes of paths*; an *elementary path* is a control path that does not execute any instruction more than once (i.e., it does not contain any iteration loops). Each elementary class of paths will then be composed of the elementary path and all paths that differ from that path only by the addition of an arbitrary number of loop iterations. This is the same notion as given by Howden (1981) some time ago and called "boundary-interior classes of paths."

Wiszniewski then goes on to prove that if the computations in a program *P* are primitive recursive, then only a finite number of paths from each elementary class need be tested. He argues that practical programs compute primitive recursive functions when the number of iterations of loops can be bounded.

Further research is needed to see whether this approach can be applied in practice. First one must be able to identify which paths to select to be tested. Next it must be mentioned that the number of elementary classes can grow exponentially even in small programs, an observation also made by Howden (1981). This result could certainly prove very useful in domain testing or in other testing methods where the number of control paths grows in an unacceptable combinatorial manner.

6.3.6 Perturbation Testing

Based upon the results of sufficient paths, Zeil has developed a new approach to testing called "perturbation testing." This has been applied to program assignment statements (Zeil, 1983b), computation errors (Zeil, 1984), and domain errors (Zeil, 1983a). In his previous results on sufficient paths, Zeil based the theory upon knowledge about the programs being tested (e.g., linearly domained, vector bounded, etc.). In practice we usually do not have this information. Perturbation testing only requires that the user make specific assumptions about the functional form of the error terms as perturbations. Thus one could begin by testing to eliminate all linear error terms and later expand this testing to cover higher-order error terms.

As an example, consider perturbation testing for computation errors (Zeil, 1984); Zeil compares this approach to *algebraic testing* as described by Howden (1978a). Zeil indicates that algebraic testing can be considered as a black box approach, where an a priori prescription is given to detect a computation error. For example, the class of multinomial functions on r variables with exponents less than q can be tested using q^r points arranged in a configuration called a "cascade set" (Howden, 1978a). With perturbation testing applied to the same multinomial functions, the output is observed with each test, a blindness error space computed, and test data subsequently selected that will substantially reduce that error space.

Zeil argues that algebraic testing is mathematically equivalent to this approach, but that perturbation testing offers more flexibility. He gives a multinomial example with three variables and maximum total exponent of three in one term; although this requires twenty-seven test points with algebraic testing, Zeil only needs nine test points. Of course, there is the additional computational work to construct and examine the blindness error space.

Until perturbation testing receives more use in practice, it remains to be seen whether practitioners can benefit from the insights provided by this highly structured testing approach.

6.4 Program Specification Testing and Partition Analysis

We have indicated that one of the primary limitations of structured testing methods, which include path-oriented techniques, is that they use only the program itself. A number of researchers are actively examining the possibility of generating test data from program specifications, especially to complement structural approaches such as path testing.

Gourlay (1983) has recently surveyed many aspects of the program testing problem and has included an area he calls "specification-dependent testing." He has pointed out that, due to the lack of one pervasive specification language, each research investigator utilizes his or her own specification language and thus various methods cannot be fairly compared. These specification languages range from very formal systems such as the predicate calculus to more procedural specification languages, which have been used to generate test data in addition to the computer programs themselves.

Cartwright (1981) has developed a very high-level language with which to express program specifications, and since it is procedural, this language allows him to generate test data from the specifications. Richardson and Clarke (1985) have also chosen to use a very high-level language for program specifications, and explicitly perform a path analysis of the specification to obtain a partition of the input space, which is used to further refine the path-testing partition from the original program. Gourlay (1981) has shown that specifications can be written using the flexibility and power of the predicate calculus, and yet test data can also be generated from specifications expressed in this more formal structure.

There are a number of executable functional specifications described in the literature. One example is provided by a system called DESCARTES, reported by Urban (1982). The specifications are developed using this system in a top-down modular approach. Partial specifications can be executed on the language processor through abstract execution. This has significant software development advantages, since the developer, with user approval, can proceed with software development convinced that the specification corresponds to what is required.

At the University of Maryland, Gannon, McMullin, and Hamlet (1981) have developed a compiler-based system, DAISTS (Data-Abstraction Implementation, Specification, and Testing System), that combines a data-abstraction implementation language with specification by algebraic axioms. This system was based on earlier conceptual work by Hamlet (1977a). In this system both verification and testing approaches are used. The verification is used to see if the axioms and implementation agree. Structural testing is applied to both code and axioms to evaluate the test data, and the axioms serve as the test oracle. The user writes specification axioms, the implementation, and test data; the system furnishes the test driver and evaluation of correctness. The authors indicate that the test data provides a severe exercise for the axioms or implementation or both.

This DAISTS system was applied to a practical example involving a record-oriented text editor, as documented in a paper by McMullin and Gannon (1983). The specification for this editor was written using algebraic axioms and serves as an oracle for judging the correctness of values returned by the functions of the implementation on the user inputs. This system should be even more impressive as it is applied to other implementation examples.

Each of these research efforts makes a contribution to specification testing. The system of Richardson and Clarke, together with the DAISTS and DESCARTES systems, provides the distinct advantage of a working system with which these researchers can conduct experiments to evaluate various approaches to specification and program testing. Richardson and Clarke (1981) best illustrate how to integrate both verification and testing, so we will focus on this integrated system for the remainder of this section, as an example of a specification testing technique. We will see the explicit use of many concepts and ideas previously studied.

6.4.1 Overview of Partition Analysis

The partition analysis system, first proposed by Richardson and Clarke (1981) and then later reported after extensive development and experimentation (Richardson and Clarke, 1985), obtains information from both the specification and the implementation. Much of the material in Section 6.4 is drawn from Richardson and Clarke (1985), and reprinted with permission of IEEE, copyright © 1985. Their method is applicable to various specification languages, both procedural and nonprocedural.

Partition analysis can be described in three steps:

1. Symbolic evaluation and other analysis techniques are used to determine the partition, obtaining the input points in each subdomain for both specification and implementation. The computation in each of these subdomains is obtained for both the specification and implementation.
2. Symbolic evaluation and other verification techniques are applied to the two computational descriptions, to determine equality over the specified subdomains. This will require additional redefinition of the subdomains, to reconcile any detected differences in the subdomains.
3. The subdomain and computational descriptions are used to derive test data. Additional test data may be developed for those subdomains where verification was not successful.

The first objective of partition analysis is to divide or partition the procedure domain into more manageable subdomains. The second objective is to partition the set of input data into subdomains so that the elements of each subdomain are accounted for uniformly by the specification and processed uniformly by the implementation.

The partition analysis system can handle both high-level formal specification languages based upon predicate calculus or state transformation methods, and low-level procedural languages. Richardson and Clarke (1985) have developed their own high-level language, called SPA, which is an extended PDL/ADA language (Kerner, 1983). The partition analysis approach seems not to work well with algebraic or axiomatic specifications.

6.4.2 Symbolic Evaluation and Verification

The authors use symbolic evaluation as a means to verify both that subdomains defined by the specification and the implementation are the same, and that computations for a subdomain are the same from those two sources. If the subdomains are not the same, then further partitioning may be necessary. If computations can be proved different, then the implementation differs from the specification and one or the other is in error. Richardson and Clarke possess considerable expertise with symbolic evaluation techniques; a symbolic execution system was developed by Clarke (1976) to generate test data, and a survey paper on the subject of symbolic evaluation was also provided (Clarke and Richardson, 1981).

These authors also use iteration loop analysis and symbolically represent iteration loops through a closed-form expression that captures the effect of that loop. This requires the derivation and solution of recurrence relations, which represent the changes to program variables made by iterations of the loop. For a discussion of these techniques see Cheatham *et al.* (1979) or Clarke and Richardson (1981).

It is not always possible to solve these recurrence relations or to prove that two computations or subdomain descriptions are the same. (It should be recognized that problems in the latter set are in general undecidable, from our discussion in Section 2.2.) At that point the verification has failed for these subdomains, and the issue is turned over to the testing phase of the system. Clarke and Richardson (1985) have observed that this occurs in surprisingly few cases for practical software systems.

6.4.3   Partition Testing

One could ask why partition testing would be necessary if the verification process were successful. We have already noted that verification is not always successful for all subdomains. In addition, a run-time environment is utilized for testing, rather than a conceptual environment as was used for verification. Another problem, however, is that it is unreasonable to assume that specifications are always correct or complete, and testing can bring this problem into focus.

Partition testing uses a combination of structural and functional methods to detect both computation errors and domain errors. Computation errors are detected by functional testing (Howden, 1980), including special value testing and extremal output value testing, as well as by a method proposed by Redwine (1983). Domain errors are detected by domain testing (White and Cohen, 1980), boundary value and condition coverage (Myers, 1979), and extremal input value testing (Howden, 1980). An objective is to unify these techniques so that these criteria can be automated. Notice that missing-path errors can also be detected, since specification information is provided.

6.4.4   Evaluation of Partition Analysis

Richardson and Clarke (1985) reports an extensive experimentation with the partition analysis system using thirty-four diverse programs. Documented errors in these programs were systematically detected by either symbolic evaluation or testing or both, including four missing-path errors. There were a number of instances where verification failed; in each of those cases the testing was able to discover any existing errors. Since most of these programs were either correct or had few errors, some method was sought to demonstrate the effectiveness of the test set. It is interesting that mutation analysis was applied, and for all thirty-four programs, the mutant programs were either killed by testing or were proved to be equivalent to the original program by the verification technique using symbolic evaluation.

7. Conclusions and Future Prospects

We have seen that, although many essential problems in program testing are undecidable, there has been notable progress with a number of testing approaches. This has been achieved by concentrating on certain classes of programs and also on the detection of certain types of errors. If we recall the approach to symbolic testing by Richardson and Clarke (1985), even though they were faced with potentially undecidable issues, they have succeeded through persistence and occasionally accepting less than total success in comparing two symbolic formulas. Their system is designed so as to not only recover from this failure, but to use it to positive advantage in a later testing phase.

We have identified as another question of major economic importance the need for a testing oracle to determine correctness. In practice this is one of the most difficult and costly problems, and it is not just a theoretical issue. Some progress has been made with executable specifications, but considerably more advancement is needed before we can claim to have automated this difficult aspect of testing.

There are many controversial issues in testing where both practitioners and researchers would not agree, but one area of common agreement by all knowledgeable software experts is that static testing should always be done prior to dynamic testing, for the advantages gained in the early detection of errors far outweighs its cost, which is low. Yet very few software projects perform systematic static testing.

Functional testing has been applied in practice without useful guidelines or a solid theoretical basis. This has to a large extent been provided by Howden in his work on functional testing (1980; 1985) and also by his research on weak mutation testing (Howden, 1982). These guidelines and research results should be implemented in software project test plans.

7.1 Future Prospects

Practical software projects have adopted the concepts of statement and branch coverage, best discussed by Myers (1979), as simple test plans for structural testing. There is considerable research activity in the area of data-flow testing, in which these simpler coverage measures are generalized to the more powerful data-flow coverage criteria. The most recent work has been reported by Frankl and Weyuker (1985) and Clarke *et al.* (1985). More experimental work is needed with these systems, and this improved testing technology needs to move out to practitioners and into current software project test plans.

We have seen the limitations of structural testing, yet this is one of the powerful testing tools available to the practitioner. The partition analysis system of Richardson and Clarke (1985) is one of the best examples of the unification of many techniques and approaches into a testing and verification system; they even utilized mutation testing to better evaluate the test set. There are still interesting research issues in structural testing, in the selection of the best paths, where the work on sufficient paths (Zeil, 1981) and on perturbation testing (Zeil, 1983b; 1984) needs to be extended to select best paths for any type of structural testing (including data-flow testing).

Another area of substantial research activity we have not mentioned is the application of logic programming to the problem of test-data generation. At one level this involves developing test-case specifications and implementing them in PROLOG (e.g., Ural and Probert, 1984). At a higher level, with more interesting consequences, logic programming can make a contribution to testing by deriving functional test data sets from a formal specification in PROLOG and a tool based on logic programming. A number of researchers are working in this area, including Gerhart (1985), Bouge (1985), Bouge *et al.* (1985), and on the industrial side, Pesch *et al.* (1985).

There is continuing research generally on formal specifications, and from the perspective of testing, the work on executable specifications is most needed. In Section 6.4 we identified the work of Gannon *et al.* (1981) as quite promising in this regard. Recently Day and Gannon (1985) reported on a test oracle based on formal specifications that was used in an introductory computer science course. Although the students in such a course are unfamiliar with testing methodology, they were required to state the specifications of their computer program assignments using the specification system developed, which utilized a BNF grammar. The authors report that most of the students were able to accomplish this task successfully.

This illustrates what we will expect of testing and verification in the next decade: Methodology now in the research phase will become embedded in software technology and will become pervasive, providing testing and verification tools that we can take for granted in terms of their efficiency and effectiveness.

REFERENCES

Beizer, B. (1983). "Software Testing Techniques." Van Nostrand Reinhold, New York.
Bouge, L. (1985). A contribution to the theory of program testing. *Theor. Comput. Sci.* **37** (2), 151–181.

Bouge, L., Choquet, N., Fribourg, L., and Gaudel, M. C. (1985). Application of PROLOG to test sets generation from algebraic specifications. *In* "Formal Methods and Software Development," Vol. 2 (H. Ehrig, C. Floyd, M. Nivat, and J. Thatcher, eds.), pp. 261–274. Springer Verlag, Berlin.

Boyer, R. S., Elspas, B., and Levitt, K. N. (1975). SELECT—A formal system for testing and debugging programs by symbolic execution. *Proc. Int. Conf. Reliable Software,* pp. 234–245.

Brainerd, W. S., and Landweber, L. H. (1974). "Theory of Computation." Wiley, New York.

Budd, T. A. (1981). Mutation analysis: Ideas, examples, problems and prospects. *In* "Computer Program Testing" (B. Chandrasekran and S. Radicchi, eds.), pp. 129–148. North–Holland, Amsterdam.

Budd, T. A., DeMillo, R., Lipton, R. J., and Sayward, F. G. (1978). The design of a prototype mutation system for program testing. *Proc. ACM Nat. Comput. Conf.,* pp. 623–627.

Cartwright, R. (1981). Formal program testing. *Proc. 8th Annu. ACM Symp. Principles Program. Lang.,* pp. 126–132.

Cheatham, T. E., Holloway, G. H., and Townley, J. A. (1979). Symbolic evaluation and the analysis of programs. *IEEE Trans. Software Eng.* **SE-5** (4), 402–417.

Clarke, L. A. (1976). A system to generate test data and symbolically execute programs. *IEEE Trans. Software Eng.* **SE-2** (3), 215–222.

Clarke, L. A., and Richardson, D. J. (1981). Symbolic evaluation methods—Implementations and applications. *In* "Computer Program Testing" (B. Chandrasekaran and S. Radicchi, eds.), pp. 65–102. North–Holland, Amsterdam.

Clarke, L. A., Hassell, J., and Richardson, D. J. (1982). A close look at domain testing. *IEEE Trans. Software Eng.* **SE-8** (4), 380–390.

Clarke, L. A., Podgurski, A., Richardson, D. J., and Zeil, S. J. (1985). A comparison of data flow path selection criteria. *Proc. 8th Int. Conf. Software Eng.,* pp. 244–251.

Davis, M. (1973). Hilbert's tenth problem is unsolvable. *Amer. Math. Mon.* **80**, 233–269.

Day, J. D., and Gannon, J. D. (1985). A test oracle based on formal specifications. *Proc. SoftFair II,* pp. 126–130.

DeMillo, R. A., Lipton, R. J., and Sayward, F. G. (1978). Hints on test data selection: Help for the practicing programmer. *Computer* **11** (4), 34–41.

Duran, J. W., and Ntafos, S. C. (1981). A report on random testing. *Proc. 5th Int. Conf. Software Eng.,* pp. 179–183.

Fosdick, L. D., and Osterweil, L. J. (1976). Data-flow analysis in software reliability. *ACM Comput. Surv.* **8** (3), 305–330.

Foster, K. A. (1980). Error sensitive test case analysis (ESTCA). *IEEE Trans. Software Eng.* **SE-6** (3), 258–264.

Frankl, P. G., and Weyuker, E. J. (1985). A data-flow testing tool. *Proc. SoftFair II,* pp. 46–53.

Gannon, J., McMullin, P., and Hamlet, R. (1981). Data-abstraction implementation, specification, and testing. *ACM Trans. Program. Lang. Syst.* **3** (3), 211–223.

Gerhart, S. (1985). Test data generation using PROLOG. Tech. Report No. 2, Wang Institute of Graduate Studies, Tyngsboro, Mass.

Goodenough, J. B., and Gerhart, S. L. (1975). Toward a theory of test data selection. *IEEE Trans. Software Eng.* **SE-1** (2), 156–173.

Gourlay, J. S. (1981). Theory of testing computer programs. Ph.D. dissertation, Department of Computer and Communication Sciences, The University of Michigan, Ann Arbor, Michigan.

Gourlay, J. S. (1983). A mathematical framework for the investigation of testing. *IEEE Trans. Software Eng.* **SE-9** (6), 686–709.

Hamlet, R. (1977a). Testing programs with finite sets of data. *Comput. J.* **20** (3), 232–237.

Hamlet, R. (1977b). Testing programs with the aid of a compiler. *IEEE Trans. Software Eng.* **SE-3** (4), 279–290.

Hecht, H. S. (1977). "Flow Analysis of Computer Programs." North–Holland, Amsterdam.
Howden, W. E. (1976). Reliability of the path analysis testing strategy. *IEEE Trans. Software Eng.* **SE-2** (3), 208–215.
Howden, W. E. (1978a). Algebraic program testing. *ACTA Inform* **10**, 53–66.
Howden, W. E. (1978b). A survey of dynamic analysis methods. *In* "Tutorial: Software Testing and Validation Techniques" (E. Miller and W. E. Howden, eds.), pp. 209–231. IEEE Computer Society, Washington, D. C.
Howden, W. E. (1980). Functional program testing. *IEEE Trans. Software Eng.* **SE-6** (2), 162–169.
Howden, W. F. (1981). Completeness criteria for testing elementary program functions. *Proc. 5th Int. Conf. Software Eng.,* pp. 235–243.
Howden, W. E. (1982). Weak mutation testing and completeness of program test sets. *IEEE Trans. Software Eng.* **SE-8** (4), 371–379.
Howden, W. E. (1985). The theory and practice of functional testing. *IEEE Software* **2** (5), 6–17.
Huang, J. C. (1975). An approach to program testing. *Comput. Surv.* **7**, 113–128.
Huang, J. C. (1979). Detection of data flow anomaly through program instrumentation. *IEEE Trans. Software Eng.* **SE-5** (3), 226–236.
"IMSL Library Reference Manual," Int. Math. and Statist. Libraries, Houston. 1978.
Kerner, J. S. (1983). Design methodology subcommittee chairperson's letter and matrix. *Ada Lett.* **2** (6), 110–115.
Korel, B., and Laski, J. (1985). A tool for data flow oriented program testing. *Proc. SoftFair II,* pp. 34–37.
Laski, J. W., and Korel, B. (1983). A data flow oriented program testing strategy. *IEEE Trans. Software Eng.* **SE-9** (3), 347–354.
McMullin, P. R., and Gannon, J. D. (1983). Combining testing with formal specifications: A case study. *IEEE Trans. Software Eng.* **SE-9** (3), 328–334.
Miller, E. F., and Howden, W. E. (1981). "Tutorial: Software Testing and Validation Techniques," second ed. IEEE Computer Society Press, Los Alamitos, CA.
Myers, G. J. (1979). "The Art of Software Testing." Wiley, New York.
Ntafos, S. (1984). On required element testing. *IEEE Trans. Software Eng.* **SE-10** (6), 795–803.
Ntafos, S. C., and Hakimi, S. L. (1979). On path cover problems in digraphs and applications to program testing. *IEEE Trans. Software Eng.* **SE-5** (5), 520–529.
Osterweil, L. J., and Fosdick, L. D. (1978). DAVE—A validation, error detection and documentation system for FORTRAN programs. *Software Pract. Experience.* **6**, 473–486.
Osterweil, L. J., Fosdick, L. D., and Taylor, R. N. (1981). Error and anomaly diagnosis through data flow analysis. *In* "Computer Program Testing" (B. Chandrasekaran and S. Radicchi, eds.), pp. 35–63. North–Holland, Amsterdam.
Paige, M. R. (1975). Program graphs, an algebra, and their implication for programming. *IEEE Trans. Software Eng.* **SE-1** (3), 286–291.
Parnas, D. L. (1972). A technique for software module specification with examples. *Commun. ACM* **15** (5), 330–336.
Perera, I. A., and White, L. J. (1985). Selecting test data for the domain testing strategy. Tech. Report TR-85-5, Department of Computing Science, University of Alberta, Edmonton, Alberta, Canada.
Pesch, H., Schnupp, P., Schaller, H., and Spirk, A. P. (1985). Test case generation using PROLOG. *Proc. 8th Int. Conf. Software Eng.,* pp. 252–258.
Ramamoorthy, C. V., and Kim, K. H. (1975). Optimal placement of software monitors aiding systematic testing. *IEEE Trans. Software Eng.* **SE-1** (4), 403–410.
Rapps, S., and Weyuker, E. J. (1985). Selecting software test data using data flow information. *IEEE Trans. Software Eng.* **SE-11** (4), 367–375.

Redwine, S. T. (1983). An engineering approach to test data design. *IEEE Trans. Software Eng.* **SE-9** (2), 191–200.

Richardson, D. J., and Clarke, L. A. (1981). A partition analysis method to increase program reliability. *Proc. 5th Int. Conf. Software Eng.*, pp. 244–253.

Richardson, D. J., and Clarke, L. A. (1985). Partition analysis: A method of combining testing and verification. *IEEE Trans. Software Eng.* **SE-11** (12), 1477–1490.

Stucki, L. G. (1977). New directions in automated tools for improving software quality. *In* "Current Trends in Programming Methodology, Vol. 2: Program Validation" (R. T. Yeh, ed.), pp. 80–111. Prentice Hall, Englewood Cliffs, New Jersey.

Taylor, R. N., and Osterweil, L. J. (1980). Anomaly detection in concurrent software by static data flow analysis. *IEEE Trans. Software Eng.* **SE-6** (3), 265–278.

Ural, H., and Probert, R. (1983). User-guided test sequence generation. *In* "Protocol Specification, Testing and Verification III" (C. Sunshine, ed.), pp. 421–436. North–Holland, Amsterdam.

Urban, J. E. (1982). Software development with executable function specifications. *Proc. 6th Int. Conf. Software Eng.*, pp. 418–419.

Weyuker, E. J. (1979). The applicability of program schema results to programs. *Int. J. Comput. Inf. Sci.* **8**, 387–403.

Weyuker, E. J. (1984). The complexity of data flow criteria for test data selection. *Inf. Process. Lett.* **19** (2), 103–109.

Weyuker, E. J., and Ostrand, T. J. (1980). Theories of program testing and the application of revealing subdomains. *IEEE Trans. Software Eng.* **SE-6** (3), 236–246.

White, L. J. (1981). Basic mathematical definitions and results in testing. *In* "Computer Program Testing" (B. Chandrasekaran and S. Radicci, eds.), pp. 13–24. North–Holland, Amsterdam.

White, L. J., and Cohen, E. I. (1980). A domain strategy for computer program testing. *IEEE Trans. Software Eng.* **SE-6** (3), 247–257.

White, L. J., and Sahay, P. N. (1985). Experiments determining best paths for testing computer program predicates. *Proc. 8th Int. Conf. Software Eng.*, pp. 238–243.

White, L. J., Teng, F. C., Kuo, H., and Coleman, D. (1978). An error analysis of the domain testing strategy. Tech. Report CISRC-TR-78-2, Ohio State University, Columbus, Ohio.

White, L. J., Cohen, E. I., and Zeil, S. J. (1981). A domain strategy for computer program testing. *In* "Computer Program Testing" (B. Chandrasekaran and S. Radicchi, eds.), pp. 103–113. North–Holland, Amsterdam.

Wiszniewski, B. W. (1985). Can domain testing overcome loop analysis? *Proc. 9th Comput. Software Appl. Conf.*, pp. 304–309.

Woodward, M. R., Hedley, D., and Hennell, M. A., (1980). Experience with path analysis and testing of programs. *IEEE Trans. Software Eng.* **SE-6** (3), 278–286.

Zeil, S. J. (1981). Selecting sufficient sets of test paths for program testing. Ph.D. dissertation, Ohio State University, Columbus, Ohio. Tech. Report OSU-CISRC-TR-81-10.

Zeil, S. J. (1983a). Perturbation testing for domain errors. Tech. Report 83-38, Univ. Mass., Amherst, Mass.

Zeil, S. J. (1983b). Testing for perturbations of program statements. *IEEE Trans. Software Eng.* **SE-9** (3), 335–346.

Zeil, S. J. (1984). Perturbation testing for computational errors. *Proc. 7th Int. Conf. Software Eng.*, pp. 257–265. Tech. Report 83-23 (1983), Univ. Mass., Amherst, Mass.

Zeil, S. J., and White, L. J. (1981). Sufficient test sets for path analysis testing strategies. *Proc. 5th IEEE Int. Conf. Software Eng.*, pp. 184–191.

Issues in the Development of Large, Distributed, and Reliable Software

C. V. RAMAMOORTHY
ATUL PRAKASH
VIJAY GARG
TSUNEO YAMAURA
ANUPAM BHIDE

Computer Science Division
University of California
Berkeley, California 94720

1. Introduction

Due to the increasing role of computers in our daily life, software companies are being challenged with bigger and more critical projects. Unfortunately, the ad hoc ways of developing programs do not succeed for large software systems. The problems that occur in large systems include fuzzy requirements,

ADVANCES IN COMPUTERS, VOL. 26

continual changes in requirements during development, difficulty in prediction of resource requirements, feasibility evaluation, testing, meeting nonfunctional goals such as performance and reliability, coordination of a large number of developers, and interaction of nontechnical factors like managerial policies with the technical factors. Automation, reusability, graphical aids, metrics, and knowledge-based systems would have to be supported in the future to alleviate these problems.

For tackling these problems, several models of software development life cycle have been proposed in the literature. These include the conventional waterfall model (Royce, 1970), rapid prototyping model, automatic programming model (Balzer, 1985), spiral model (Boehm, 1986), and reusability-driven development model (Ramamoorthy *et al.*, 1986b). There is considerable confusion as to which model is most appropriate in practice. In Section 2, we hope to shed more light on this issue by proposing a classification of software engineering techniques into phase-dependent and phase-independent parts and showing that almost all models use a subset of these techniques to define a new methodology for software development.

A major part of any large software development activity is understanding the requirements of the user. This activity may be done informally when writing code, as in ad hoc development, or through more formal methods, for instance, by using specification languages. This activity of requirement understanding turns out to be one of the most error-prone and expensive in large projects. It is complicated due to the fuzzy and incomplete nature of requirements specified by the user, lack of good specification tools, continuously changing requirements during the software life cycle, and the distributed nature of current software systems. In Section 3, we discuss these problems and what approaches can be taken to solve them.

Design is another major activity in software development, requiring much creativity and experience. There are two kinds of design activities, algorithm design and system design. Algorithm design is concerned with selection or development of the most appropriate algorithm for a particular task based on efficiency or simplicity concerns. System design is concerned with the overall organization of the system. We discuss the application of knowledge-based techniques to algorithm design and issues in system design in Section 4.

Quality assurance is a major concern for most software. Quality has to be assessed using appropriate software metrics. One of the most important quality factors is reliability. Software reliability has to be treated differently from hardware reliability theory for several reasons. In Section 5, we discuss the issues of software metrics and software reliability theory, with examples from existing software reliability models.

Software development of large projects involves several programmers, managers, and designers. A number of resources, for example program files, documents, and test cases, are produced during development. To avoid inconsistencies due to a high level of concurrency in the activities, and to keep track of the project, a resource and activity management system is needed. We discuss the features needed in a resource and activity manager in Section 6. We also discuss the advances required in data-base technology to support such a resource and activity manager.

Our major goal in this paper is to convey our thoughts on advances required in software engineering. If some of the techniques and tools discussed have been implemented, we attempt to give references to some of those systems. In other cases, the discussion is meant to generate ideas for active thinking and research.

2. The Software Life Cycle

Software systems go through many phases during their life cycle (i.e., the period from when someone gives the requirements for the system to the point when the system is used and finally "dies" after becoming obsolete). The phases basically characterize important steps or "milestones" during the life cycle. Broadly, the software life cycle can be divided into two parts—the *development phase* and the *operations and maintenance phase*. The development phase includes all the activities from the point the need for the product is identified to the point when the implemented product is tested and delivered for operation. The operations and maintenance phase includes all activities after delivery, such as fixing bugs discovered during operation and performance enhancements. During this phase, the system may also *evolve*, when major functionality is added to the system.

In order to get a better understanding of the software life cycle, various models have been proposed to describe the activities during the development phase. These models generally describe the phases a system *should* go through during its life cycle. The waterfall model (Royce, 1970), the most traditional one, divides the life cycle into requirements, design, coding, testing, and maintenance phases. The software goes from one phase to another sequentially. The rapid prototyping model advocates production in two main phases: prototype development and production quality software development. The first phase identifies the feasibility and ensures understanding between the customers and developers about the expected functionality of the system, while the second phase is concerned with the actual system development. The spiral model, proposed recently, believes in software development in many stages, where each stage is based on prototyping and risk analysis (Boehm, 1986). The automatic programming model advocates two primary stages in software development: specification development and then machine-assisted translation to code, with all maintenance changes being made to the specifications (Balzer, 1985).

There is considerable confusion in software engineering as to which model is most appropriate for software development. To illustrate the point, we show the phases of the conventional waterfall model in Figure 1 and that of reusability-driven model in Figure 2. The conventional waterfall model divides development activities into requirement specification, design, and coding phases. The reusability-driven methodology tries to "short-circuit" the long development cycle by recommending a search for reusable components, so that they do not have to be developed from scratch. Which one is more appropriate? The way we see it, the models are not really inconsistent with each other. They both advocate use of new software development techniques in place of ad hoc methods. The waterfall model says that requirement specification and design activities are very important, and therefore techniques must be developed to support these activities. Reusability-driven methodology says that reusability is a very important factor in software development, and therefore tools must be developed for making software reusable and storing reusable components in a library so that they can be retrieved for later reuse.

With this technique-based view of the software life cycle, we classify software engineering techniques into two broad categories: (1) *phase-dependent* and (2) *phase-independent* (Fig. 3). Phase-dependent techniques are

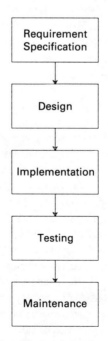

Fig. 1.   Waterfall model of software life cycle.

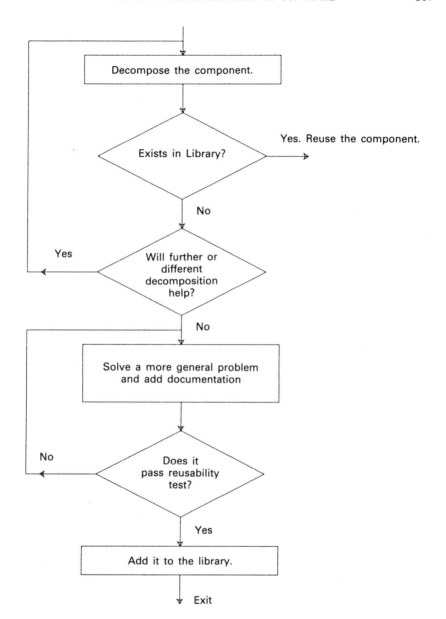

Fig. 2.   Reusability-driven software development methodology.

Techniques for Programming in the Large

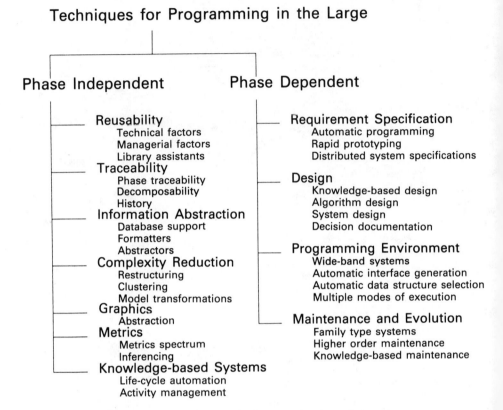

applicable primarily to a single phase of a software life cycle model. Techniques for requirement specification, prototyping, design, testing, and debugging are phase-dependent. Phase-independent techniques, on the other hand, are applicable to almost all the phases of the software life cycle. For example, the principle of reusability can be applied at any phase of the software life cycle. It is possible to reuse requirements, design, code, or even test cases. This reuse can lead to an increase in productivity and quality.

We consider it useful to classify software engineering techniques into phase-dependent and phase-independent parts because phase-independent factors, such as reusability, AI/expert system techniques, and metrics are generally given little attention in most life cycle models. For example, reusability considerations should guide the requirements development, decomposition, and other activities during software life cycle. Metrics should be applied at the requirements phase to predict cost, at the design phase to guide the decomposition process, and at the coding phase to estimate testing time required (Ramamoorthy *et al.*, 1985b). Use of these phase-independent techniques can cause substantial reductions in software cost. For instance, the recent spiral model (Boehm, 1986) incorporates use of risk analysis (which can be thought of as using quantitative metrics to determine risks involved in pursuing various strategies) in each of its phases. Almost all the life cycle models can be strengthened by incorporating some of these factors explicitly in their description.

No single development methodology may be appropriate for all development environments. The quality of supporting tools is an important factor in the effectiveness of a methodology. Reusability-driven methodology would not work if no tools are available to help develop or locate reusable resources. Other problems may be psychological or managerial. In the conventional model, a large amount of time might be spent developing specifications, thus delaying the writing of code. This may be psychologically discomforting, unless one learns to accept it, because seeing written code gives one an assurance that the project is progressing well. But this psychological problem may again be due to a lack of good tools for requirement specification; if programmers had good specification tools, they would probably start using them. An issue that remains is guidelines for selecting a methodology for specific environments. In the following section, we discuss the issues that must be resolved in the requirement specification area.

3. Requirement Specification

Requirements refer to the needs of the users. *Specification* is the description of what the system is supposed to do in order to meet its requirements. Requirement specification is becoming an important issue in software engineering because several studies show that 30% of the errors found during the testing and operation phase are due to poor understanding of requirements (Basili and Perricone, 1984). Also, these errors are found to be almost 10–100 times more expensive to correct than other kinds of errors during the operation phase (Boehm, 1981). To avoid these errors, one would like to remove any ambiguities, inconsistencies, or incompleteness in requirements as early as possible. Unfortunately, requirements expressed in natural language, though useful, are not amenable to automated analysis to test for ambiguities, inconsistencies, or incompleteness. Manual inspection can help but it is not foolproof because, for instance, the same document in natural language may be unambiguous and complete to one person and ambiguous and incomplete to another because of the inherent ambiguity of natural language. Several formal specification systems such as SREM (Software Requirements

Engineering Methodology) (Davis and Vick, 1977; Bell *et al.*, 1977; Alford, 1985), PSL/PSA (Problem Statement Language/Analyzer) (Teichroew and Hershey, 1977) and SADT (Structured Analysis and Design Technique) (Ross, 1977) have been developed to overcome these problems.

Our experience shows that several technical problems remain in the use of formal requirement specification techniques in real environments. We concentrate on five of the main problems:

1. Going from original requirements to requirement specifications.
2. Choosing a specification model.
3. Distributed systems modeling.
4. Specification of nonfunctional requirements.
5. Changing specifications.

3.1   Going from Original Requirements to Requirement Specifications

The requirement specification is derived from the user's original requirements. Going from user's requirements to a specification document is not as easy as it looks (in fact, it is probably the most difficult step in requirement specification). The first problem is that the user's requirements may have been stated in one or two sentences such as "I want to reduce the traffic jam by using a computer-aided system." On the other hand, the requirement specifications for this can be several hundred pages describing what computer-controlled traffic lights must do to prevent traffic jams. This requires a detailed analysis of user's requirements by experts in the area, and can be the most difficult task in requirement specification.

To avoid problems after implementation, at least three factors must be taken into account when users want to introduce a computer system. The first one, *problem purification*, is the analysis of the current situation to determine what are the *real* problems that have to be solved. The second one, the *future characteristics analysis*, is to examine and predict how these problems will change in the future. The last one, *safety analysis*, is to prevent the destruction and malfunction that can potentially be caused by the new system.

3.1.1   Problem Purification

It is very important to purify and specify the crucial problems that have to be solved by examining drawbacks and inconveniences of the present system. Sometimes the problems can be solved in a very simple way without developing a computerized system. The problem purification can be done by continuing to decompose the problems until they are reduced to the essential factors. Let us suppose the problem to be solved is to improve the traffic jam during commuting hours. Before attempting to computerize the traffic control, an analysis should be done to determine why traffic jams are created in the current system and what would be the resulting situation when the computer control is installed. The solution one would like to see may vary from user to user even if they have exactly the same problems.

For example, in the traffic jam problem, an analysis may show that the real problem is not the transit time lost due to the jams but the irritation caused to the drivers by waiting for a long time, thus leading them to act irrationally. This problem can be solved, even without using a computer system, by removing all the traffic signals on the intersections and not allowing drivers to go straight when they hit an intersection. No traffic will cross if all drivers must make either a left turn or a right turn (but not both) at the intersection because they do not have to stop and wait for a green signal, although they must take a zig-zag path to reach their destination.

If the real problem to be solved is the minimization of transit time, one solution is to minimize the number of cars, another is to increase traffic volume in a unit time. The first one can be done by prohibiting private cars during commuting hours and allowing only buses and commercial cars. If this solution is infeasible one-way traffic, synchronized signal switching, longer green signals, and left-turn-only signals can be used.

This kind of analysis gives a clear idea of the requirements of the system and avoids misunderstandings about the effect of the system. In other words, users can define what really needs to be improved in the present situation and declare what solutions would be acceptable before hand. Developers will specify the requirements and design and test according to these specifications. In the drivers' irritation problem, for example, users can say that they will be satisfied if the average waiting time for passing the intersection could be improved from 2 minutes to 45 seconds. Then developers do not have to worry about other fuzzy factors but only need to find out the special solution to meet this criterion. This will also provide a clear basis for testing the system when it is implemented.

3.1.2 Future Characteristics Analysis

Another important factor in understanding requirements is to analyze and predict how the problems will change in the future when the computer system is being used. In the traffic jam problem, how rapidly the number of cars is increasing year by year is one of the most important aspect for solving the problem. This factor will decide the valid period of life and the limitations for the system to be introduced.

3.1.3 Safety Analysis

Once the system is released to the public, it will play a very important role in the society. If bankers (users) asked developers to design banking system with automatic teller machines, security of the machines is going to be important. If the system is to control ICBMs, a more comprehensive safety analysis will be required to avoid a major accident.

There are two major approaches for coping with the safety problem. The first approach is to analyze what will be brought on by the malfunction of the system. If the system is closely related to the human life and environment, special consideration to multiple development/testing teams and fault-tolerant system design must be given.

The second approach is to provide alternative ways to cope with system malfunction. This means that the entire system should provide several different ways to control the same object and the computer-aided system should be just one of them. If the malfunction is detected, the control system should switch to a different form of control. In the traffic jam problem, if the computer-aided traffic signals do not work, option for other ways of controlling traffic flow (such as manual control by police officers) should be provided. The important thing is that the transfer from one system to another must proceed in a systematic and well-organized way. The consideration of the super-system (organization for controlling several lower systems) is critical for this purpose.

3.2 Choosing a Specification Model

As we have mentioned, it is not possible to generate specifications from informal requirements under program control, and it is also difficult to do it manually. Therefore, all the specification languages attempt to choose an underlying *model* that is thought to be similar to the way people think about program behavior. Most of the current languages assume either a control flow model or a data flow model. More research and data are needed to determine which model most facilitates transformation from the abstract ideas to a formal representation. Probably, the appropriate model depends a lot on the application. For example, a logic-intensive language might be appropriate for an application with highly coordinated parallel operations, such as robotics, but may not be so suitable for other applications, for example, those that are control-dominated. Table I shows the variety of models that have been used in specification languages. Readers should refer to Ramamoorthy and So (1978) and Addleman *et al.* (1985) for more details regarding these specification languages. We will illustrate the kind of issues that must be considered in selecting a model in the following section for distributed systems specification.

TABLE I

SOME REQUIREMENT SPECIFICATION SYSTEMS

System	Model emphasis
Data structured system design	Data flow oriented
Hierarchical development methodology	Algorithmic refinement
Structured analysis and design	Disciplined decomposition
Structured analysis/structured design	Decomposition
Software Cost Reduction (SCR)	Information hiding/Separation of concerns
SREM	Stimulus/Response
PSL/PSA	Data flow based
Vienna development method	Set theory
Jackson system development	Input conversion to output
User software engineering methodology	Interactive systems
PAISLey	Operational approach
System ARchitect's Apprentice (SARA)	Concurrent systems
GIST	Automatic programming

3.3 Distributed Systems Modeling

A major application area for requirement specification languages is distributed systems. Concurrency, timing-dependencies, process failures, unreliable communication media, and communication delays make it much harder to design distributed systems. Nevertheless, distributed systems are here to stay because of their numerous advantages. Because even small distributed systems can have subtle timing and concurrency errors, specification and analysis have been used much more often in distributed systems. Several models for specification of distributed systems have been proposed. Not all are equal in their modeling power. Generally, the more the modeling power of the system, the less the analytic power. Next we discuss the features that must be considered in the development of a model for distributed systems.

3.3.1 Synchronous vs. Asynchronous Communication

One design parameter in a specification language for distributed systems is whether the existence of bounded or unbounded channels is implicitly assumed between communicating processes. The coupled finite state machine (FSM) model (Zatiropulo et al., 1983; Bochmann, 1978) assumes that such channels exist. This implies that a sender of a message does not have to wait for the recipient to be ready for sending a message. In contrast, Hoare's Communicating Sequential Processes (CSP) (Hoare, 1978),

Selection/Resolution (S/R) model (Aqqarual, *et al.*, 1983), and Milner's Calculus of Communicating Systems (CCS) (Milner, 1980) assume that sender and recipient have to *rendezvous* in order to communicate. If one party is not ready to communicate, the other party just waits. At first sight, it may appear that models with an asynchronous mode of communication are more general, but that is not true. It is easy to simulate asynchronous communication with synchronous one by introducing extra processes for channels that buffer messages between sender and recipient (as in producer consumer problem). These channel processes can be made to simulate reliable or unreliable channels of any bounded length. Earlier models of distributed systems used message-based communication where messages were buffered in the channels. On send, therefore, a process does not have to wait assuming the channel to be unbounded. Verifying systems with asynchronous communication is harder because of the large number of states (infinite if channels are unbounded) associated with the complete system.

3.3.2   Shared Variable Based, Message Based, Multiparty

In general, we would like our specifications to be as abstract as possible, without unnecessary details that complicate their understanding. For this, the model of the specification language has to be close to the reality we want to model. Earlier languages for concurrent programming used to be shared variable based, with monitors or locks to control the sharing (Hansen, 1975; Schutz, 1979). This was appropriate because these languages were designed not so much for distributed programming as for concurrent programming in a single machine environment, e.g., for operating systems. But people began to realize that a shared memory model may not be appropriate for distributed systems where communication can only be through messages where messages can get lost, and communication is not instantaneous. All these factors force us to think of distributed systems in a different way from concurrent systems on a single machine. Researchers began to realize these problems and message-based systems, such as CSP (Hoare, 1978) and FSM (Bochmann, 1978) were proposed. One limitation of message-based systems is that they provide a two-party asymmetric communication, with one sender and one recipient. This makes the specification of multiparty communication hard. Recently, in Raddle (Forman, 1986), a multiparty symmetric communication facility, called *conversation* is provided. During a conversation, all parties can (1) read each other's local variables and (2) based on the read values, they can update their local variables. The values read in Step 1 are those just prior to the conversation to avoid any read-update problems. This operation is atomic, i.e., all the parties must rendezvous at the same time to complete the conversation.

The main difficulty with providing higher levels of communication and synchronization mechanisms is implementation. It is desirable to have to the specification language executable, for early discovery of errors, but it is more difficult to generate correct executable code for languages with more abstract communication mechanisms. Unless one is careful, deadlocks may arise in the executable code that were not there in the specification.

3.3.3   Analyzability of the Model

Debugging of specifications is necessary to avoid specification errors from propagating to the design and implementation phase. Manual inspections help, but automated analysis is needed for more thorough debugging. It has been observed that models with more expressive power are less analyzable. Simple models, like FSM, S/R and Petri Nets, can be automatically analyzed for deadlocks, livelocks, proper termination, etc. All these models rely on exhaustive reachability analysis, and therefore are limited in their expressive power to simple protocols where the number of possible states is finite (in Petri Nets though, protocols with infinite states can sometimes be handled with a trick to make the reachability graph finite). In contrast, language-based systems like CSP and Raddle are of much wider applicability to distributed system specification and programming, but they cannot be analyzed automatically. Several proof systems for CSP have been proposed but all of them are manual in nature, requiring human ingenuity to find the correct proof (Soundararajan, 1984; Schlichting and Schneider, 1984; Lamport and Schneider, 1984). The challenge in this area is to find the model with most expressive power that can also be analyzed automatically for interesting properties.

3.3.4   Decomposability of the Model

A specification model should be modular or hierarchical. One advantage of modularity is that it can make the writing and comprehension of specifications easier. Writing of specifications is easier because requirements usually have to be decomposed as more and more details are specified. With a modular specification model, requirements can first be stated in undecomposed form, and then decomposition of these specifications can be provided separately. Or, if one is going bottom-up, specifications of low-level modules can be specified first, and then higher level modules can be specified using these lower level modules.

Modularity can also aid in analysis by hiding unessential details from the higher layers; i.e., higher layers can be verified by using only the externally visible properties of lower layers and ignoring the details. The CCS and S/R models are examples of hierarchical systems. Petri Nets have some hierarchical properties in the sense that it is sometimes possible to reduce parts of a Petri Net to a single transition without changing its properties (Dong, 1983). But, in general, it is difficult to specify a protocol or a distributed system hierarchically using Petri Nets. Finite state machines suffer from the same disadvantage.

3.3.5 Service Specification vs. Implementation Specification

Not all specification languages specify exactly the same thing. We will illustrate the point by comparing temporal logic with the finite state machine model. Temporal logic is more suitable for *service* or *interface* specifications. It can be conveniently used to state that some of the properties are visible to an external observer over a possibly infinite amount of time. In contrast, the finite state machine model (as well as most other models) gives a procedural specification that has the desired properties. Properties are usually not given explicitly.

Both models have their advantages. If one was specifying alternating-bit protocol, specifications in temporal logic are hard to write and understand. On the other hand, finite state machine specifications are straightforward. But, if one wanted to state a property of the alternating-bit protocol (e.g., two messages sent are eventually delivered in the same order), temporal logic is more suitable.

Using more than one model for specification is one way to get the advantages of several models. For the above example, the working of the alternating-bit protocol may be specified in the finite-state machine model while temporal logic can be used for specifying its higher level properties. Several researchers have done that and even found ways to verify temporal logic specifications against finite state machine specifications (Karp, 1984; Manna and Wolper, 1984; Vardi and Wolper, 1986; Wolper, 1986).

3.3.6 Summary of Model Selection

It should be clear from the above discussion that a lot of research has to go into the selection of a model. A summary of some models specifically designed for distributed systems is presented in Table II. From the table, it is easy to see the trade-offs that must be made in choosing a model. The greater the expressive power, the more difficult it becomes to analyze or simulate specifications for errors. But, real problems have complicated requirements that cannot always be expressed in a simple model. The issue of the best model for distributed systems, or for other systems, is still far from resolved.

TABLE II

FEATURES OF SOME DISTRIBUTED PROGRAM SPECIFICATION SYSTEMS

Feature	FSM	PN	S/R	CSP	Raddle	CCS	Temporal logic
Automated analysis	y	y	y	n	n	n	n
Hierarchical	n	n	y	n	n	n	y
Structured	n	n	n	y	y	n	n
Synthesis tools	y	y	y	n	n	n	n
Reduction techniques	n	y	n	n	n	y	n
Service verification	y	n	y	n	n	y	n
Specification level	low	low	low	high	med	med	high
Communication	async	sync	sync	sync	sync	sync	none
Communication model	msgs	msgs	S/R	msgs	conversation	msgs	none
Applicability	lim	lim	lim	gen	gen	lim	lim

3.4 Specification of Nonfunctional Requirements

Nonfunctional requirements are as important as functional requirements in most cases. Nonfunctional requirements refer to constraints on such features as performance, reliability, and user-friendliness, as opposed to input-output functionality. Most specification languages tend to ignore the nonfunctional factors, assuming that performance is something that can be tuned after implementation. (The famous rule that almost 90% of the execution time is spent in 10% of the code seems to partly justify this.) Unfortunately, it is probably not appropriate to leave nonfunctional requirements to the implementation phase in large systems, especially those that are distributed; overall structure of the system can have a big impact on performance and reliability. Also, several distributed systems must contend with communication delays and must guarantee certain response time. It is too late to leave reliability and performance concerns to the implementation because there is only localized improvement that can be made at that phase (Ferrari, 1986). It seems that ways have to be found to deal with nonfunctional requirements very early in the life cycle.

Recently, performance issues have begun to receive attention in programming and specification languages. Such languages are usually designed by adding statements related to waiting for a certain time, to existing languages. One language for programming real-time systems is Illiad (Schutz, 1979). In Illiad, the system consists of concurrent processes. Data can be shared or local. If shared data is accessed, it must first be locked (in fact all the items needed must be locked together before access to avoid deadlocks). A *wait* construct is added to specify delays. In another system, RSL/REVS, timing constraints can be expressed and validated using the concept of validation paths (Davis and Vick, 1977). Accuracy is an issue that arises when trying to predict performance at specification level. The more abstract the level of the language, the more difficult it becomes to embed timing and performance constraints and the estimate of performance is less accurate. In the extreme case, that of logic-based, nonprocedural languages, it becomes almost impossible to deal with performance. The question as to at what level of abstraction is most appropriate for specifications is far from resolved.

3.5 Changing Specifications

Until now we were implicitly assuming in our discussion that once specifications are written, they could form a firm basis for design and implementation. Unfortunately, real life is more complicated. Large projects have the characteristics of fuzzy original requirements and long development periods. Experience has shown that requirements invariably change during the lifetime of the project as customers and developers become more clear about what they want from the system and also what they do not want. Also, it may be unreasonable to suspend design and implementation until specifications have stabilized completely because often the changes in specifications are a result of experience obtained from the design and implementation activities. What can be done to reduce the possibility of major repercussions from changing specifications on design and implementation? The question is still open to research but we discuss two promising techniques.

3.5.1 Rapid Prototyping

Rapid prototyping is a technique for determining the proper requirements of a system. A prototype of a subset of the system is developed with the intention of (1) making a *feasibility study*: test the principles of the new software to ensure that the system works and (2) *obtaining good user feedback*. The hope is that if the user can get hands-on experience with a prototype, early feedback will be obtained about the expected functionality from the final system. If the functionality demonstrated forms the core of the system, few changes would be expected in the design and implementation as a result of any other changes in requirements.

The prototyping approach has the disadvantage that it can lead to ad hoc code because there is often a tendency to patch the prototype to produce the final code. Psychologically, it is hard to throw away the prototyped code and start all over again for the final system (developing a prototype may also be expensive). A prototype developed with "speed" rather than with modifiability in mind can hardly be the right system to serve as the baseline for the final product. In addition, documentation of a prototyped system tends to be very inadequate. For these reasons, it can be expected that the prototyping approach, unless applied carefully, can lead to less reliable and modifiable code.

If the specifications in the specification language can be executed, or transformed to executable code, then the specification language can serve as the language for the prototype. The major difference between rapid proto-typing and executable specifications is that rapid prototyping is done by selecting functions to be prototyped depending on software development projects. In contrast, executable specification creates a system model from a formal specification language and simulates the model. In the future, executable specifications and rapid prototyping tools together with reusable program libraries are likely to be integrated to provide an automated software development/evolution support environment.

3.5.2   Steepest Gradient Approach

Solving the most important problems first helps in dealing with incomplete and fuzzy requirements. The user may not know exactly what he wants, but he may know what facilities are the most essential for the system to provide. For example, suppose a customer would like to have an extremely reliable telecommunication system that supports simultaneous voice, data, and video communication and provides a very flexible user interface. Also, suppose that the designers do not really understand how to achieve the requirements (this is the case for most large projects). This requirement may be difficult to achieve because it is not clear what user interface the user has in mind and how reliable the system should be. Designing the system to provide all the facilities may prove to be very expensive (or impossible) at first try, and eventually the user may change the requirements when it becomes clear that it is too costly to pay for all the features.

In the steepest gradient approach, the designers would determine the minimum, or most essential, facilities the user must have in order to use the system. These facilities are likely to be well defined and unlikely to change. In the telecommunication example, the facilities that are absolutely essential are voice communication; not providing it would make the system quite useless. This system should be designed to provide the minimum facility first. In the next revision of the system, other features can be added as the need for them is anticipated. Tom Gilb's evolutionary development methodology proposes the same ideas, but for different reason; his methodology was more concerned with how to achieve specified goals by the given deadlines. We are suggesting that the methodology also helps in dealing with fuzzy and incomplete requirements. The disadvantage of the methodology is that it does not say how to determine the relative importance of requirements. Also, if the system is first designed with only the most important requirements in mind, it may become difficult to modify the design later in order to incorporate other requirements.

It should be clear from the preceding discussion that requirement specification is still far from understood. A good requirement specification method must resolve all the above problems. In addition, it must provide a smooth transition to the design phase. In this paper, we are not making very clear distinction between requirement specification and design specification because it is usually hard to separate the two in practice (e.g., specification of an alternating-bit protocol can be treated as a requirement specification by one person and a design specification by another). We will just say that requirement specification should avoid specifying the design unless it is clear from experience that the specified design is most appropriate for the given task. In the following section, we discuss the issues related to the design of software.

4.   Software Design

It has been estimated that 30% of the time spent on software development goes into design. Since this is the stage where the most important decisions are taken, it also makes this stage very error prone. In most cases, these decisions cannot be made mechanically. Not much headway has been made in automation or formalization of this stage but some recent attempts are noteworthy.

4.1   Knowledge-Based Design

The crucial importance of design to software quality has motivated researchers to attempt to automate the design process by looking into the ways humans design algorithms and decompose requirements. It has been observed that the way a solution is designed depends on the expertise of the developer and his exposure to similar problems. The processes designers go through are understanding the problem, planning a solution, executing their solution, noticing difficulties, refining the solution, verifying its correctness, and finally evaluating the solution for its efficiency. Human designers use some rules while going through these processes. Some of the examples of the rules as given in Kant (1985) are:

1. If a component needs to be refined and its output is a subset of its inputs, refine the component to an element-by-element, generate-and-test algorithm.

2. If an algorithm looks at part of the inputs to do the same kind of tests, try saving information rather than recomputing; for example, with dynamic programming.
3. If an exponential algorithm is created, try to improve it or find an alternative unless it can be shown that the problem itself is exponential.

If these rules can be stated formally and applied in a knowledge-based system, the design problems will be alleviated to some extent. DESIGNER (Kant, 1985) is one of the examples of recent attempts.

Program design languages supporting symbolic processing can also be useful during design. Problems in an algorithm are often discovered by a mental execution on a sample problem. This mental execution is usually done at an abstract level where all the steps need not be stated precisely. In computer terms, this translates to symbolic execution at a very high level. Symbolic execution has a long history of research and it remains an issue how the future systems will use this capability to understand problems and formulate solutions for them.

4.2   System Design

Most of the preceding discussion was pertinent to *algorithm design* rather than *system design*. System design primarily involves decomposition of the system into modules. From the software engineering point of view, the decomposition problem is more important than the algorithm design problem. Many design methodologies have been discussed in the literature, the most popular ones being *functional decomposition* (Parnas, 1972; Dijkstra, 1976), *data flow design* (Stevens *et al.*, 1974; Myers, 1978), and *data structure design* (Warnier, 1974; Jackson, 1975).

Functional decomposition simply tell us to divide the given function into subfunctions step-by-step. This method has been advocated by a large number of authors (Parnas, 1972; Dijkstra, 1976; Linger *et al.*, 1979; Wirth, 1973). It is primarily useful for application to well understood and stable requirements. The advantage of this approach is that it usually leads to good hierarchical design if carefully applied. However, since it does not give comprehensive criteria to decompose the given function, there could be innumerable decompositions to the same problem. This makes application of the technique more of an art than a science. For example, we can decompose functions with respect to time, shared data, data flow, and flowchart. It also requires that the task of problem modeling and program construction be addressed simultaneously.

Data flow design methodology decomposes the program by finding input modules, transformation modules, and output modules. It is primarily suited for design problems where a well-defined data flow can be derived from the problem specifications. Two criteria have been proposed to evaluate the design: *coupling* and *cohesion* (Stevens *et al.*, 1974; Myers, 1978). Coupling is the measure of the strength of association established by a connection from one module to another. Cohesiveness is the measure of strength among procedure elements in the same module. Good design is considered to have a low degree of coupling and a high degree of cohesiveness (Stevens *et al.*, 1974; Myers, 1978). The advantage of this technique is that since it decomposes the given function according to data flow, the resulting modules usually will have very high cohesion. Furthermore, if we treat the data flow diagram as concurrent asynchronous processes that pass messages, the design is useful in distributed and parallel systems as well. One problem of this method is that sometimes it may be difficult to identify transformations on data. Furthermore, partitioning of a program into input and output branches can be artificial in many designs.

The *data structure design* method was proposed by Jackson and is thus called Jackson Methodology (Jackson, 1975). It is primarily useful for business and other systems with well-understood data structures. It obtains a program structure by first designing input/output data structures. Decomposition is based on the hierarchical nature of these data structures. Partitioning is done by creating the program component corresponding to the components of these data structures. If the data structures for a problem specification are reasonably well defined and the problem mirrors the data structures, most of the people using this method will come up with remarkably similar program structures. Although this is a very desirable property of this method, this method is not easily applicable to highly concurrent programs with interprocess communication.

There are other design methodologies, such as logical construction of programs proposed by Warnier (1974), programming calculus proposed by Dijkstra (1976), structural analysis and design technique (Ross, 1977), and Higher Order Software (HOS) (Hamilton and Zeldin, 1976). Warnier's method is fairly similar to Jackson's methodology. A more thorough discussion of these methodologies can be found in Bergland (1981) and Vosbury (1984).

Basically, all these methodologies are derived from experience. Design steps are performed manually, and very few computer-assisted tools have been developed. Methodologies look simple and easy on paper, but they are sometimes difficult to apply in real design activities (Bergland, 1981). Most of them are oriented to business applications. The features of such applications include simple and well-known transformations as well as emphasis on the input-output data structures. These methodologies do not address control dominant applications; e.g., real time application. None of them consider performance, fault-tolerance, and security, which are becoming more important in many applications. Applications are becoming more complex, critical, microprocessor based, distributed, and message oriented. Current methodologies do not address these issues very well, necessitating the need for new design methodologies.

It would be very desirable to have tools with which, given a formal requirement specification, one could generate an implementation in an automated environment. The key issues in achieving this would include developing design specification languages and their support environments as well as program generators. We are already beginning to see tools such as SSL (Buckles, 1977), PDS (Davis and Vick, 1977), HOS (Hamilton and Zeldin, 1976), and designer/verifier assistant (Moriconi, 1979), which help in automating some parts of the design process.

A limitation of current systems is that they do not facilitate documentation of *reasons* for taking certain decisions during design. Understanding the reasons for previous decisions can be very crucial if a need is felt later for revising the design. A good design methodology should encourage designers to document the alternative decisions considered at each step and the reasons for choosing a particular one.

Once a high-level design is completed, it must usually be verified by implementation and testing. We do not address the issues related to implementation because it is a fairly well-understood area. The major advances we see in the implementation area are development of sophisticated programming environments with support for interactive debugging incremental compilation, and graphical support. Readers should refer to Ramamoorthy *et al.* (1986a) for a more detail discussion of the issues in this area. The issue we will address now is that of software quality assurance.

5.   Software Quality Assurance

Software quality assurance aims to guarantee that software products possess a certain acceptable level of quality before being released. Due to our society's increased dependence on computers, software engineers become responsible for the quality of software, analogous to that of other industrial products. Software quality is defined as the totality of features and characteristics of a product or service that bears on its ability to satisfy given needs. Quality is made up of many factors, including reliability, reusability, and efficiency. In this section, first we will introduce various metrics that are useful for quality assurance as well as for project control. We then focus on one of the most important quality factors, reliability, and discuss the issues in modeling of software reliability. Finally, we discuss testing and other techniques to improve software reliability.

5.1   Software Metrics

Metrics are the measures of properties of systems. Software metrics are used to measure the quality of software systems and to control the productivity of software projects. Software metrics should have several important properties:

1. *Automatable:* In order to get rid of ambiguity and subjectiveness that might result from the manual measuring process, the metrics must be processed automatically. High speed and accuracy will be obtained by computer-aided metrics system.

2. *Feasible:* The primary goal of engineering is to find ways to realize the system with low cost and time. If it is not feasible to collect evaluation metrics within reasonable cost, the metrics are not going to be used in practice.

3. *Understandable:* What is measured by a metric should be clear. The metrics must have theoretical and scientific foundation as well as empirical ones. If a formula is introduced, clear and meaningful explanation for its use should be given.

4. *Sensitive:* The metrics should be sensitive to all the factors that affect the quality to be estimated. It should not be sensitive to unrelated factors. Almost all of existing metrics lack this characteristic.

5. *Applicable:* The metrics should be widely applicable to a large class of systems. They should not be limited to a particular programming language, programming environment, a life-cycle phase, or the size of the system. In particular, applicability of metrics to earlier stages of life cycle, such as requirement and design, is important for early control of the software development process.

6. *Useful:* The purpose of metrics should not be to measure values. They must be used as a feedback mechanism for the software development activity. In Ramamoorthy *et al.* (1985b), the authors proposed *metrics-guided methodology*, where each software development activity is guided by metrics.

7. *Flexible:* Software quality or complexity cannot be estimated using one number. Different people have different perceptions of relative importance of factors used for estimating software properties. For example, data complexity may be the most important factor to one user and control complexity to another. Several kinds of metrics should be shown to the users so that they can get a good idea of the properties of the system.

After designing the metrics, it is necessary to validate their usefulness. The metrics would have to be validated against real software projects to determine their effectiveness. Unfortunately, experimental validation is usually difficult to carry out. As software development is a rather complex task, there are many factors involved, including software development environments, the quality and number of personnel, the availability and quality of various tools, the programming language in which the software is written software methodologies used. Most current work on the validation of metrics is done for Halstead's software science (1977) and McCabe's metrics (1976). More work is needed for validating other metrics.

5.2   Software Reliability Modeling

Software reliability has been defined as the probability that a *software fault*, which causes *deviation* from required output by more than *specified tolerances* in a *specified environment*, does not occur during a *specified exposure period* (Yeh *et al.*, 1984). Thus, we could formarlly define reliability as

$$R(i) = P \text{ [no failure in } i \text{ runs]}$$

or

$$R(t) = P \text{ [no failure in interval } (0, t)]$$

Assuming that inputs are selected independently according to some probability distribution function, we have

$$R(i) = [R(1)]^i = (R)^i$$

where $R = R(1)$. We can define the reliability R as follows:

$$R = 1 - \lim \frac{n_f}{n}$$

where

$$n = \text{number of runs,}$$

$$n_f = \text{number of failures in } n \text{ runs.}$$

This is the operational definition of software reliability.

Software reliability is a function of many factors. More specifically, it is dependent on the software development methodology. If good development methodology is used, the programs are likely to contain less bugs. Software reliability is also dependent on the validation methods. A software will be more reliable if a comprehensive set of testing strategies have been applied to validate it. Software reliability is also dependent on the language in which the program is written. The higher the level of the programming language, the easier it is to detect errors.

5.2.1   Development of a Software Reliability Model

Software reliability modeling is different from that of hardware. Unlike hardware, software does not deteriorate. It is more difficult to ensure that software will not receive invalid inputs (e.g., user mistyping a command). In hardware, all components of the system are generally used at all times; therefore, it is possible to estimate system reliability from the reliability of individual components and their connectivity information. In contrast, software reliability can only be measured by simulating the real environment in which the software is intended to be used. The portion of the code that is executed most has to be the most reliable.

In view of these differences between hardware reliability and software reliability, the theory needs to be treated differently. Software reliability models must take the following properties of software errors into account:

1. The same program can have different reliability in different environments depending on which portion of the code gets executed more often.
2. There is no physical deterioration of software.
3. Software errors are usually correlated. In other words, software errors do not usually occur independently. For example, an error committed during the requirement specification can cause correlated errors during design and implementation since they are developed according to the same requirement specification.
4. New errors can be introduced during the correction of a previous error.
5. Software reliability is dependent on the experience and educational level of the developer. For instance, if a developer does not understand some tools, such as compilers and operating systems, he or she is likely to make the same mistakes over and over again during software development.

At present, almost all the software reliability models make simplifying assumptions that may not hold in practice. It is, therefore, important to check the validity of assumptions made by the models before applying them in practice.

5.2.2 Evaluation Criteria for Software Reliability Models

A set of desirable features for a software reliability model was developed by Bastani (1980). These features are summarized as follows:

1. *Language independent:* The language in which the algorithm is expressed should have no bearing on the application of the reliability model. In other words, the reliability model should give the same result for two equivalent programs in different programming languages, such as Fortran and machine language.
2. *Methodology independent:* It is easier and simpler to assume that reliability models are methodology independent, even though a program developed using a top-down, structured programming technique, is likely to be more reliable than an unstructured program. It is difficult to quantify the effect of

methodology used because software development is a very complex task involving many human factors that make the software quality rather unpredictable. It is, therefore, safer to assume that software is developed using the worst kind of methodology.

3. *Test selection criteria:* If it was possible to do exhaustive testing, software could be made perfectly reliable. Since that is not possible either theoretically or practically, one has to accept limited testing. The objective is then to maximize the software reliability with a minimum amount of testing. This can be achieved by using testing strategies, such as boundary-value testing, range testing, and path testing (Myers, 1979), that attempt to exercise error-prone constructs. Almost all software reliability models assume that the test environment is identical to the operational environment. This limits the applicability of these models in cases that require a high confidence in the reliability estimate.

4. *Correction errors:* It is very desirable for the model to include errors that are committed during an error correction; remember that it is possible to introduce new errors when correcting old ones.

5. *Representativeness:* The models should indicate how well the program has been tested. Specifically, they should indicate whether the input domains have been adequately covered (Bologna and Ehrenberger, 1978), whether the test cases accurately simulate the operating environment (Brown and Lipow, 1975), and whether the test cases are adequate to detect all likely errors (Demillo *et al.*, 1978). Models that assume the test cases have the same distribution as the operational environment indirectly assume representativeness (Bastani, 1980).

6. *Input distribution:* The kind of input distribution assumed by the models is important since the reliability estimate depends heavily on the input distribution. As an example of an extreme case, if input distribution is constant (i.e., only one input is used), the program will either fail or succeed — giving a reliability of 0 or 1 respectively.

7. *Program complexity:* Complex software is likely to require more testing than a simpler one for estimating reliability. Unfortunately, most software reliability models do not treat this aspect seriously. Most models either completely ignore this aspect or treat only one complexity measure (Bastani, 1980).

8. *Model validation:* It is extremely important to adequately validate a proposed model. Unfortunately, it is particularly difficult to validate software reliability models due to the lack of availability of sufficient data. Validation is complicated by the fact that most software evolve constantly during the entire life cycle leading to corresponding changes in reliability.

9. *Time:* The *exposure period* should be independent of extraneous factors such as machine execution time. Thus, the basic unit of exposure period

should be the number of runs. However, for some programs (e.g., an operating system) it is difficult to determine what constitutes a "run." In such cases, the unit of time may be the CPU time (Musa, 1975). This will also be necessary when the software reliability measure is to be integrated with the hardware reliability measure for a particular system environment.

10. *Ease of data collection:* The data needed for the software reliability should be easy to collect; otherwise its applicability would be limited.

5.3 Assumptions in Various Reliability Models

None of the existing software reliability models meet all the above criteria. Modeling becomes very difficult as an attempt is made to satisfy all these properties. We illustrate the kind of assumptions models make by using examples from reliability growth models and validation phase reliability models.

5.3.1 Reliability Growth Models

Reliability growth models are used at testing and debugging phases of software development. Since errors that are detected are assumed to be corrected, the reliability of a program increases with testing and analysis. The major assumption of all software reliability growth models is: *inputs are selected randomly and independently from the input domain according to the operational distribution.*

This is a very strong assumption and will not hold in general, especially so in the case of process control software where successive inputs are correlated with time during system operation. The assumption is necessary in order to keep the analysis simple. Some relaxations of this strong assumption have been proposed in Ramamoorthy and Bastani (1982). There are two types of reliability growth models: *error-counting* and *nonerror-counting* models.

Error-Counting Models. The error-counting models estimate both the number of errors remaining in the program as well as its reliability. Deterministic, Bayesian, and Markov error-counting models have been proposed. The Musa model (1975) is the first model to insist on execution time. Littlewood developed a model where the failure rate of successive errors is stochastically decreasing, unlike the previous models which assume that all errors have the same failure rate. We will now discuss briefly the General Poisson Model (GPM) (Zvegintzov *et al.*, 1980), which is a generalization of many previous models.

GPM is a simple and clear model. Reliability is expressed as a function of time and number of errors. It assumes:

1. Consecutive inputs have the same disjoint failure probabilities.

2. All errors have the same disjoint failure rates.
3. No new errors are introduced upon error correction.

Unfortunately, many facts in practice invalidate its assumptions. In practice, (1) failure rates are not independent, as earlier errors usually have larger failure rates since they are easier to detect, (2) detection of errors depends on the testing strategy used, and (3) new errors are introduced in general by imperfect correction.

Nonerror-Counting Models. The nonerror-counting models do not consider the number of errors remaining in a program. Instead, they consider the effects of the remaining errors. This permits a simple modeling of the possibility that new errors are introduced while correcting an error. Among many nonerror-counting models, we will briefly discuss the Goel and Okumoto's imperfect debugging model (1979) and the input domain-based stochastic model developed at Berkeley (Bastani, 1980).

Unlike almost all the other models, the Goel and Okumoto imperfect debugging model does not assume that faults are removed with certainty when detected. In this model, the number of faults is treated as a Markov process, and the transition probabilities are controlled by the probabilities of imperfect debugging. These features make this model one of the most promising models of software reliability. However, it still assumes that:

1. Time between failures are independent.
2. The probability of the exposure of each fault is the same.
3. No new faults are introduced when correction faults.

This model is recommended for estimating software reliability during integration testing of software development where debugging is not perfectly carried out (Goel, 1985).

In the input domain-based stochastic model:

1. Successive inputs have independent failure probability.
2. An assumption is made regarding the distribution of the change in the residual error size after each correction.
3. An assumption is made regrading the initial error size.
4. The testing process is assumed to be identical to the operational environment.

The drawback of the model is that some of the parameters are difficult to estimate. This model has been successfully used for the EPRI (Electrical Power Research Institute) project (Ramamoorthy et al., 1981).

5.3.2   Validation Phase Reliability Models

In the validation phase, errors are found but not corrected. The Nelson model (1978) is based on the *operational definition* of software reliability mentioned earlier. Test cases are selected randomly according to the operational distribution. Then,

$$R(1) = 1 - \frac{n_f}{n}$$

where

n = total number of test cases

n_f = number of failure out of these n runs

The Nelson model is one of the few models whose theoretical foundations are sound. However, it suffers from a number of practical drawbacks:

1. In order to have a high confidence in the reliability estimate, a large number of test cases must be used.
2. It does not take into account the continuity factor in the input domain. For example, if the program is correct for a test case, then it is likely that it is correct for all test cases executing the same sequence of statements.
3. It assumes random sampling of the input domain. Thus, it cannot take advantage of the testing strategies that have a higher probability of detecting errors (e.g., boundary value testing). Furthermore, for most real-time control systems the successive inputs are correlated if the inputs are sensor readings of physical quantities, like temperature, which cannot change rapidly. In these cases, we cannot perform random testing.
4. It does not consider any complexity measure of the program.

5.3.3   Correctness Measures for Reliability

Software for critical applications must have a reliability estimate of 1. In these cases, the confidence in the estimate is very important. Correctness measures tell how accurate the reliability estimate is. The methods for improving the confidence in reliability estimates include the error seeding and program mutation approaches, the software science approach (Halstead, 1977), the statistical approach (Yeh *et al.*, 1984; Bologna and Ehrenberger, 1978), and the input domain-based approach (Bastani, 1980). In this subsection, we discuss the error seeding and mutation approaches because of their importance. The method of *error seeding* was suggested by Mills (1972) as a quantitative method for estimating reliability. This method assumes that the reliability of a program is related to the number of errors removed from it. Error seeding involves inserting a known number and type of artificial errors in the program. This seeding is done by someone other than the testers. Then, during testing, when both real and seeded errors are found, the number of remaining real errors can be simply computed from the number of remaining seeded errors using

$$\frac{\text{remaining number of real errors}}{\text{remaining number of seeded errors}} = \frac{\text{number of real errors found}}{\text{number of seeded errors found}}$$

The proportion of errors not discovered will indicate the quality of the testing process and, thus, the quality of the reliability estimate is used to estimate program reliability.

The idea is similar in *mutation* (Demillo *et al.*, 1978). The program is changed by some simple mutations, usually syntactic in nature. Then, testing should detect all mutations that change the meaning of the program. This can be used to estimate how effective the testing is in removing errors.

Error seeding and mutation require extra effort during testing to detect and correct artificial errors in addition to the real ones. Therefore, these schemes are not always practical. In such cases, other approaches mentioned earlier may have to be used.

5.4   Test Strategies for Reliability

Software testing is the process of systematic execution of a program under controlled circumstances to verify its quality. The basic steps involved are requirement analysis, program analysis, test data selection, formulation of testing strategy, actual execution of the program, and checking whether results are as expected, and if not, locating the errors and correcting them. These errors may have been made during the requirement understanding phase, specification phase, design phase, implementation phase, or while trying to fix another error during testing. As Dijkstra noted, testing shows the presence of errors, but *not* their absence (Dahl *et al.*, 1972).

One way of ensuring that a program is error-free is by *program proving*— formally proving that the program is correct. It was observed that program proving was extremely difficult for large programs. One problem is that the proofs, generated manually, tend to be much larger and more complex than the program itself, leading one to wonder whether the proof was error-free. In view of this, testing has to be carried out to assure that the software meets the informal requirements of the user. Program proving is mainly applied to critical parts of the software, such as the security kernel of an operating system where presence of even a single bug could lead to compromise of the whole system.

Exhaustive testing is not possible because there are potentially infinite number of inputs to be tested for (including both valid and invalid inputs).

Therefore, test cases have to be designed judiciously so that one obtains desired confidence in the quality of the software with a minimum amount of effort and money spent in testing. This problem of test case design is discussed next.

5.4.1 Test Case Design

There are two basic approaches one could take in designing test cases: the *black box* approach and the *white box* approach (Myers, 1979). In the black box approach, the test cases are derived from the external specifications and requirements of the system. The internal structure of the software is largely ignored. Thus, the black box approach does not care *how* the system is implemented. It merely verifies the end results but does not ensure that all the statements in the program are executed. The black box approach is good for acceptance testing because test cases are derived from external environment in which the system is supposed to operate.

In the white box approach, the test cases are derived from the internal structure of the program. Thus, an attempt might be made to execute all the statements or all the branches in the program. Thus, white box testing takes into account how the system is implemented.

Usually, white box testing is carried out at the module level and black box testing at the system level. Some methods of white box testing are statement coverage, branch coverage, and path coverage which are basically methods to improve test coverage (discussed in next section). Methods for black box testing include random testing (Thayer *et al.*, 1978), testing at boundary values (Myers, 1979), and error guessing where a list of error-prone situations is created, based on intuition and experience, and test cases are based on that list.

5.4.2 Test Coverage

Since exhaustive testing, which includes testing for all the valid as well as invalid inputs, is not feasible, some appropriate selection of test cases has to be made so that *test coverage* is large (i.e., a large portion of the program is tested). Since extensive testing does not guarantee complete absence of errors, an important issue arises about when to stop testing. Normally, the answer depends on the application for which the software is intended. More testing is required if the software is intended for a critical application, such as a nuclear reactor or a space shuttle. Usually, some probabilistic models might be used to estimate the quality of the software, which we have discussed earlier.

5.4.3 Testing at Specification and Design Level

Currently, most of the testing is carried out only after the coding has been done. Statistics show that a large proportion of the errors occur during the specification and design phase. Also, it is much more difficult to correct specification errors and design errors, as compared to coding errors, in an implemented system. Therefore, it seems logical to do testing after specification and design phases. The idea is to discover the errors in the phase in which they occur, so that they can be corrected easily. Formalization of requirement and design specifications, and usage of executable specifications, might help in this process.

5.4.4 Automatic Tools for Testing

Although many techniques have been developed for testing, the testing process is still largely labor intensive (and hence expensive!). The programmer still has to enter the test data, verify the results, and locate the bugs manually, although there may be some guidelines and tools for doing each step. However, the situation is beginning to change. Many tools have been developed during the past few years to automate test data generation, locate potential errors, and verify of results. Some of the functions of these tools include static analysis, dynamic analysis, symbolic execution, and intermodule interface analysis.

In *static analysis*, structural flaws such as unreachable code and potential errors such as unused variables are reported. In *dynamic analysis*, facilities for executing the program, studying its behavior, and verifying any assertions during execution are generally present.

Symbolic execution can be used to generate test data to exercise a particular path (Howden, 1978). The idea behind symbolic execution is to execute the path using symbolic data objects instead of the real ones. The conditions that have to be satisfied during symbolic execution are then analyzed to give the desired inputs. *Intermodule interface analysis* basically involves checking that a module assumes the correct interfaces for other modules. Some examples of automatic tools that help in testing include the *lint* program in UNIX (trademark of Bell Laboratories) for discovering potential bugs in C programs, Fortran Automatic Code Evaluation System (FACES) (Ramamoorthy and Ho, 1975) developed at Berkeley for NASA, and DAVE (Osterweil and Fosdick, 1976) developed at the University of Colorado for analyzing Fortran programs using symbolic execution.

5.4.5 Untestable Requirements

It may not be possible to test for all the requirements of the system. Things that cannot be tested include parts of real-time critical systems, and defense systems. The main problem is that the actual inputs may not be available. For example, if a defense system is supposed to work in case of a nuclear attack, it would not be possible to test it under actual conditions for verification. Other things that cannot be tested include certain attributes, constraints, and nonfunctional requirements such as flexibility, evolvability, and several aspects of concurrent and distributed systems.

One way of overcoming the problem of untestable requirements is to do *dual development and testing*. In this method, two implementations are developed using independent designs for the same requirements. Then these independent implementations are tested for the same inputs. Any inconsistency between the results indicates an error in one of them, or both. This approach was experimented with in the EPRI project (Ramamoorthy *et al.*, 1981) which involved development of pilot software for nuclear power plant safety operation. The main characteristic of this software was that the timing dependencies made it almost impossible to determine correct outputs for a set of inputs. Dual development and testing eliminated the need for determining the correct outputs a priori, because it would be very unlikely for two independent implementations to have identical errors (Ramamoorthy *et al.*, 1981). Of course, dual development might be more expensive, but testing is considerably simplified and cheaper.

Another approach is to develop a testbed that simulates the expected environment as closely as possible. Simulation studies can be carried out on this testbed to catch as many bugs as possible. None of these approaches is foolproof and only a good software development methodology can give us any confidence in the software.

5.4.6   An Algorithm for Reliability Assessment

This section briefly describes a systematic method to assess and control the reliability from the available failure data. More detailed descriptions are found in Goel (1984). The algorithm consists of the following steps:

1. Study the failure data so as to gain an insight into the nature of the process being modeled.
2. Choose a reliability model based on an understanding of the testing process and the assumptions of the various models.
3. Obtain estimates of parameters of the model using a method such as the least-squares or maximum-likelihood method.
4. Obtain the fitted model by substituting the estimated values of the parameters in the chosen model.
5. Perform goodness-of-fit tests, and if the model fits, proceed to the next step. Otherwise, collect additional data or go to Step 2 to find a more appropriate model.
6. Compute confidence regions for the parameters of the model in order to assess the uncertainty associated with their estimation.

7. Obtain performance measures together with their confidence bounds such as (a) detected faults by distribution, (b) undetected faults vs. time distribution, (c) software reliability after s failures, (d) time to next failure distribution, and (e) time to kth failure distribution.
8. Make some decisions whether to release the system or continue testing.

We describe below how each of the above steps can be implemented in a software reliability assessment environment (SRAE):

1. The failure data should be automatically collected by utilizing a test coverage monitor and a test history monitor. The test coverage monitor checks the thoroughness of the test to a program based on some coverage measure such as paths. It is possible to enhance the program so as to provide success/failure records for each path. The failure data can be applied to the input domain model. The test history monitor simply records the execution time of a program and failure date and time by a certain distribution of the input. The data is useful for most of the reliability models. Some of the models assume the representativeness; however, it is difficult to obtain test data to meet this assumption.
2. This phase must find appropriate reliability models for a program and available data. SRAE must store knowledge of each reliability model such as (a) assumptions for the model, (b) required data, (c) applicability and limitation of the model, (d) applicable life-cycle phase, and (e) past experience of the model. SRAE must provide a mechanism to locate the candidate models for a given program at a certain life-cycle phase. Since there is no universally applicable reliability model, we need to apply several models in sequence, each of which is most appropriate to a certain development phase.
3. to 7. These features are provided by well-known statistics calculation packages such as maximum-likelihood estimation. Therefore, SRAE is required to invoke these packages using available data and utilize the results.
8. The decision must be made by managers and software engineers. SRAE must provide objective information to help in the decision-making process. At this phase, SRAE must provide this information in a user-friendly manner. Also, it would be helpful if SRAE provides past experiences of the application of the model.

In summary, a sophisticated system is a requirement for reliability assessment. None of the existing software reliability models meet all the desirable criteria for software models. Only experimental validation can show how well they model the actual situation. There is a scope of considerable theoretical and experimental research in this area. Another open issue is how hardware and software reliability theories interact. We know that different assumptions need to be made in hardware and software reliability theories, but it is still not clear how one would estimate the overall reliability of a system that consists of both hardware and software.

6. Software Management

Proper management of resources becomes a critical problem during a large software project. This problem can be solved partially by using data-base technology. Most current programming environments, such as UNIX, are not based on data bases. The management of software production also involves adoption of a methodology and a discipline during the software development process. Knowledge bases, based on rules, can help in imposing this discipline on software developers. Thus, there are two aspects of software management: data base (DB) support and knowledge base (KB) support. There are two components corresponding to these two aspects: resource manager and activity manager. Section 6.1 describes resource management and Section 6.2 deals with activity management. Then Section 6.3 discusses some of the issues that DB/KB technology has to address for supporting software management.

6.1   Resource Management

Resources are defined as objects such as personnel, managers, programs, documentation, and programming tools that are used in the software development process. Current information must be available on each of these resources and one must be able to trace from one resource to others. A major weakness of most current programming systems is the weak hierarchical model of resources and lack of emphasis on relations among resources. For example, in most conventional programming environments the users deals with *files* that act as *resources*. These files are independent of each other and are organized in a tree form (in directories). This model, we believe, is too weak to support good software engineering principles because the files are treated as discrete entities having no relationships among each other.

Another limitation in most programming environments is that it is difficult to associate attributes with files or resources; therefore, conventional programming environments are ignorant of type of the information inside the files and treat them alike. Thus, facilities for retrieving a resource are primitive. For example, UNIX has the *ls* and *file* commands to retrieve resources. These commands result in displaying too much redundant data, thus hampering productivity. The software designer has to do all the bookkeeping alone, and has to resort to making artificial directories to keep the resources organized.

Relocation of resources, maintaining backups, and removing the resources also has to be done manually by the designer. The problem becomes more intense when one has to deal with a big project using hundreds of files spread in a maze of directories. Decomposition of a program into smaller modules also results in a larger number of files discouraging the user to modularize the program. UNIX alleviates the problem by providing many options with *ls* command, but the problem is still essentially unsolved.

Various projects have attempted to tackle these problems. We will describe the approach we took at Berkeley in the GENESIS project. The first task we tackled was to provide a more powerful model to represent resources and provide more sophisticated retrievability based on this model.

In search of a more powerful model, we abstracted out the concept of objects, the links between them and their attributes. With this abstraction, the entity relation attribute (ERA) model (Chen, 1983a) was the closest to our requirements. ERA models information as consisting of entities. Entities are similar to nouns in English, and have attributes that correspond to adjectives in English. They are also related to each other; these relations correspond to verbs in English. Out of the many ERA models proposed (Chen, 1983b), we used the model with following restrictions:

1. Only entities have attributes; i.e., relations do not have any attributes.
2. We allow only binary relations between entities, although relations could be many-to-many.
3. Relations are directional; relations in one direction are referred to as *primary* while in opposite directions as *complementary*.

As shown by Chen (1983a, 1983b), these restrictions do not decrease the expressive power of the model. They make the retrieval efficient and the user model more simple and elegant. This model lets us attach attributes to entities and define relationships between two entities.

There was one other serious contender for our choice of the model—the relational model. We chose to provide the entity relational model instead of the relational model because entity relational model is closer to the natural language. There is a straightforward one-to-one correspondence between underlying concepts of English and the entity relational model. This makes the user interface very simple to learn and use. The relational model, on the other hand, forces software personnel to think of everything in terms of tuples, which is unnatural to their thought process.

6.1.1 Concepts Supported by the Model

With ERA as the basic model, many important software engineering concepts can be supported. Various entities, relations, and attributes that are needed in a software engineering environment are described next. The subsequent discussion also points out important underlying concepts that GENESIS supports for promoting reusability.

Entities.   Although developers can add their own entity types to make the system more suitable to their project, there are three primary entity types in an environment:

1. *Software resources:* These entities correspond to various resources that are used in a software development project. In conventional programming environments, all these resources are treated as files and are managed by programmers themselves. Examples of such entities are requirements specification for a project, design of a layer, design of a module, source of a module, test cases for a module, and documentation of a module.

2. *Software tools:* These entities correspond to the tools that manipulate software resources. They have certain attributes and relations with other entities. Examples of such tools are editors, compilers and profile generator.

3. *Software personnel:* These entities correspond to the personnel who use software tools to manipulate software resources. Modeling of personnel lets GENESIS distinguish between their responsibilities and hence enforce protection on other entities.

These entities are input to the system using the Entity Specification Language, to be described later. As more tools are developed, they are added to the data base, making the system evolvable. The user is also free to define his or her own resource types.

Attributes.   An attribute describes functional and nonfunctional aspects of a particular software entity. It consists of two parts: attribute name and attribute value. The user can access software resources using queries qualified with these attributes. Some of the attributes that are predefined in GENESIS are as follows:

1. *Classification:* This attribute is valid only for software resources and describes the nature of a resource. The value of this attribute could be requirement, design, source, test case, document, library or object code. Each entity gets a label according to its function.

2. *Hierarchy:* This attribute classifies the entity into one of the hierarchies as shown in Figure 4. This hierarchy consists of family, member, layer, module, and procedure. With this attribute, we support software family concept and layering.

Software family concept is important because it captures the notion of *evolution* of a system. Various releases of a system can be considered part of a

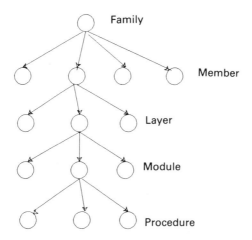

Fɪɢ. 4.   Hierarchy classification of resources.

same family. *Layering* has been accepted as a standard software development technique (Dijkstra, 1968; Parnas, 1979). With the layered structure, the development simplifies because of information hiding. It also results in greater modifiability of the system because a layer can be replaced by another without worrying about other layers. This way new *members* can be generated for a family.

3. *Other attributes:* Functional and nonfunctional keywords can be attached to resources to help in retrieval of resources from software libraries. Usage of functional keywords and the abstraction of resources also encourage reusability of other entities besides source code. For example, often when the source code is too machine dependent, requirements and design can be reused.

Nonfunctional attributes are provided to help retrieval from libraries. Example of these attributes are reliability, memory requirements, and performance. In addition to these nonfunctional attributes, metrics about the quality and complexity of each resource can also be stored. Most of the work in complexity metrics is done at the source level (Special issue, 1983). GENESIS intends to apply metrics at requirements and design level. These metrics can be used to help decide whether something should be reused or not, based on complexity, as well as to guide the design process itself (Ramamoorthy *et al.*, 1985b).

Relations.   Only binary relations are allowed in GENESIS. Relation is the primary mechanism to provide traceability. Traceability among requirements, design, and source code is important for both software managers and programmers. It provides means to verify that all requirements are provided and tested. It also helps in software evolution as the impact of a *modification request* (Rowland and Welsch, 1983) can be traced down to the modules affected.

⟨*Classification*⟩_to_⟨*Classification*⟩ *Relation*

This set of relations are used for tracing from one class of entities to the other. For example, a requirement entity is related to one or more design entities. With this specification, all designs that correspond to a specific set of requirements can be traced.

⟨*Hierarchy*⟩_to_⟨*Hierarchy*⟩ *Relation*

This set of relations lets GENESIS trace from one level in the hierarchy to its children in the lower hierarchy. For example all procedures can be traced from a module.

Other Relations

Refers is used for tracing resources depending on their reference. Contains is used to implement libraries. Similarly, Inputs, Outputs, and Affects provide other forms of traceability.

In order to make use of the above concepts, we need a language to enter information about entities in a data base. Also, we need another mechanism for retrieving resources satisfying the given criteria from the data base. We have provided in GENESIS two mechanisms for defining and accessing and extracting resources: Entity Specification Language (ESL) and (2) Resource Extractor (REX). These are integral parts of the GENESIS Programming environment. Entity Specification Language lets the programmer specify software resources. The translator transforms it into internal representation that is stored in a data base. Resource Extractor retrieves information from the data base, and, thus, provides traceability among software resources. All software resources, such as source, design, documents, and personnel are connected to each other by some relation.

The ERA model thus formed improves traceability, which is lacking in the UNIX programming environment. In this manner, ESL and REX attempt to remove deficiencies of the UNIX programming environment in handling big projects that employ hundreds of programmers (Ramamoorthy et al., 1985a; Aho et al., 1984).

6.1.2   Entity Specification Language (ESL)

Entity Specification Language lets the software personnel insert, modify, or delete information about various entities in the system. GENESIS uses a data base to store all this information (Stonebraker et al., 1976). ESL lets the user define, modify, or delete entities in the system. An example of interaction with ESL is as follows:

```
Personnel: John Smith /* a software entity */
Type: programmer      /* an attribute */
Responsible_for: IO_Interface, Error_Reporter
```

Here, Responsible_for is a relation that relates software modules with software personnel. The simplified BNF grammar of ESL is given in as follows:

```
<entity_command>::=<command> entity_name
                {<relation_modify>
                |<attribute_modify>}
<command>::=edit|delete|purge|rename|retype
<relation_modify>::={Remove} relation_name
                            entity_name
<attribute_modify>::={Remove} attribute_name
                            attribute_value
```

6.1.3   Resource Extractor (REX)

Resource Extractor lets programmers extract resources with attribute or relation qualification. It uses the concept of *sets* to retrieve entities. A set consists of one or more entities. Some sets are predefined for the user corresponding to each of the entity types. For example, all the software documents will be members of set documents. The programmer can retrieve a subset by making an attribute or relation qualification or can also take the union, intersection, and difference of various sets. To illustrate the usefulness of the model we present some of the example queries of users of such a model. The syntax of an REX query is as follows:

```
SET <set-name1>=<set-name2>
                {<attribute-qualification>
                |<relation-qualification>}
SET <set-name1>=<set-name2>
                <set-operators><set-name3>
<set-operators>::=AND|OR|DIFF
```

The above query retrieves all those members from <set-name2> which satisfy attribute and relative qualifications and puts it in set-name1.

```
LIST <set-name>{<attribute-qualification>
                |<relation-qualification>}
```

This query lists all the elements from <set-name> that satisfy attribute and relation qualifications. Some examples of REX queries are as follows.

```
/* List all the source code affected by
   a change in file: Getcommand c */
LIST Software_Resource affected
   by Getcommand and
            (classification=source_code)

/* Give me all requirements having
   high performance
but the corresponding sources having
   low performances */
/* step 1-get all requirements with
   high performance */
SET High_Req=Software_Resources
           Classification=Requirements
           Performance=High

   /* step 2-get corresponding Source_code with
   low performance */
   LIST Software_Resource with
       Classification=Source_Code
       Relation req_to_source set High_Req
       Performance=Low

   /* Give me all test cases relevant for the
   source check_for_err */
   LIST Software_Resource with
     Classification=Test_Cases
     Relation source_to_test check_for_err
```

Multiple Hierarchies. In UNIX, there is only one kind of hierarchy that corresponds to relation contains. Since ESL provides many other useful relations like `affects`, `layer_to_module`, and `req_to_design`, more than one hierarchy is available to the programmer.

The real use of hierarchy in UNIX is the organization of files to avoid overcrowding at just one directory. Some of the standard UNIX commands like `1s -R` and `cp -r` use the `contains` relation between directories and files to recursively trace down the hierarchical structure of the file system. But these commands do not provide much traceability. In ESL REX, multiple hierarchies provide different kinds of traceability. For example,

```
SET module_to_trace= All with status INCOMPLETE
LIST Software_Resource
   affected_by
   module_to_trace
```

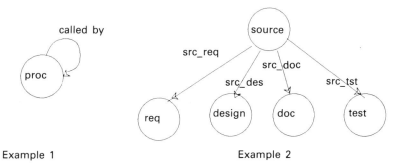

Fig. 5. Examples of Graphical Trace.

This query will list only those modules that are affected directly by the module under consideration. We can choose to focus on any one of these modules and then apply the same query to trace further down the hierarchy.

Graphical Tracing.   REX also provides a graphical trace. As explained above, the information is in the form of relations and sets. This information can also be seen from a graph-theoretic point of view. REX lets the user define a graph and then make queries based on that graph. Each node of this graph is a set of elements. Each edge stands for a relation and is directed. One of the nodes is defined by the user as a *root* node. Graphical closure of a set is defined as a set of all those elements that can be reached from the root node through relations. For example, suppose that the graph the user defines is as shown in Example 1 of Figure 5. Now if the user asks for graphical trace of a particular procedure, a set of all procedures that call that procedure directly or indirectly will result. Thus, self-loops are very useful for getting information from multiple levels of a hierarchy. Other such examples would be the a f f e c t relation with in source files.

To consider another class of applications, examine the graph in Example 2 of Figure 5. If the root node is a source node, then the user can retrieve all those software entities that are related to a particular source with relations in interest. Thus, after defining the graph, the user can make graphical trace on l e x c. This will retrieve him all requirements, design, documents, and test cases related to l e x c. Similarly, graph trace can be applied in different ways to improve retrievability. Currently users specify the graph by enumerating all edges, but we plan to provide general interface for graph specification.

6.1.4 Dynamic View of Files

One problem that hierarchy poses in the UNIX programming environment is how to deal with different files in different directories. While working on a project, a software engineer has to remember unimportant directory names that contain some relevant files. Since the retrieval ability in UNIX is poor, the programmer has to switch the current working directory to the location where the files are, and then use his or her recognition ability to get the needed files. The very concept of current working directory makes the user's view of the overall file system limited.

We use the concept of focus in addition to working directory. *Focus* is defined as a set of files satisfying a particular criterion independent of their locations in the file system. For example, if a programmer wants to work on the files whose group_owner is GENESIS and whose classification is set to unclassified, then the focus can be set to the result obtained by the corresponding query. Now in the current session, the programmer can work on the files in this focus without having to worry about switching back and forth among directories and checking their time stamps and other attributes.

```
SET FOCUS=ALL WITH
        GROUP_OWNER GENESIS
        CLASSIFICATION UNCLASSIFIED
```

As another example, consider the case when a programmer wants to focus on modules whose test coverage is low. The focus could be set by the following command:

```
SET FOCUS=All Modules with Test_coverage=low
```

6.2   Activity Management

A project can be viewed as a sequence of activities. Each *activity* is defined as an invocation of a software tool to manipulate a software resource. Examples of activities include reading a file, updating a resource, executing code, renaming a file, testing a module, and writing design. Activity management is important because every time an activity takes place, there is a potential of introducing errors and getting outdated or erroneous information.

In GENESIS (Ramamoorthy *et al.*, 1985a), an expert system called *Activity Manager* is proposed for doing activity management. The aim of Activity Manager is to keep a check over the sequence of activities by a rule-based protection mechanism. Its functions include pointing out potential inconsistencies, automating certain activities for the user, ensuring protection, and defining the software development methodology. Some of the rules used by Activity Manager are given in Figure 6.

One use of Activity Manager is in managing multiple personnel on a system. Multiplicity of personnel raises issues of coordination, establishing protection

1. Only manager can change requirements.
2. Only manager can change a resource after the resource has been classified as tested.
3. If source code is changed after the module has been certified as implemented, then there could be inconsistency between documentation and the source code.
4. If a module is changed by someone else, the programmer may be unaware of the change.
5. If a bug is discovered by a programmer, the developer of the module may be unaware of it and should be sent a message.
6. Users of the system are not allowed to make any changes to any part of the system.
7. If a person wants to update a module which is already being updated or used by someone else, then there are chances of inconsistency.
8. If source code has been modified, but not compiled, and the programmer is executing the old object code, then there are chances of inconsistency.
9. If a programmer is debugging a module that uses other untested modules, then he or she could be looking for the bug at the wrong place.
10. If the source code is changed, then a bug could have been introduced. This could be checked by running previous test cases and comparing outputs.
11. If a file has not been touched for one year, then it could be put in backup.
12. If during debugging, a program works correctly on one test case but does not work when modified, then the error is probably located in the modules that were recently modified.

FIG. 6. Examples of rules for Activity Manager.

domains, and detection of problems that might arise due to lack of flow of information between them. With appropriate knowledge of the project personnel, and software and hardware entities, the management can be automated partially. Rules 1, 2, 4, 5, and 7 on Figure 6 address the task of managing multiple personnel in the system.

Another example of activity management is keeping track of information about the files used in a project. The directory and file structure is very dynamic in big projects because lots of files are created, deleted, and modified in short intervals. If a group member modifies a file and fails to inform other group members, then there is no way of determining who modified the file last time. Similarly, if a programmer modifies a particular module and forgets to inform others, then another person who is using that module might in vain try to determine the cause of anomalous behavior in his module. Rules 3, 4, 7, 8, and 10 address these issues.

6.3 Issues in Use of DB/KB for Software Engineering

In building an integrated software engineering environment, one of the most important decisions that must be considered is the level of data-base support to be provided. It has become apparent from experience that adding data-base capabilities to a software engineering environment multiplies its powers. Until now, this has been a neglected area in many traditional software environments. Software engineering environments have data-base requirements very different from those for traditional data-base applications. They are much closer to the requirements of engineering design data bases (or CAD data bases). In the area of CAD data bases, only recently have researchers realized, after spending a lot of effort trying to tailor conventional data bases to their needs, that this will not work and that they need special data bases designed for their needs. CAD data bases designed on top of conventional data bases seem ad hoc systems and have terrible performance. We strongly suspect that software engineering environments built around conventional data bases would run into similar performance problems. We propose that it is best to develop a *special-purpose*, fully integrated data base as the core of a software engineering environment.

To our knowledge, no work has been done in developing data bases specifically for software engineering environments. However, some work has been done in developing data bases for engineering design applications. Therefore, we will review those concepts that have evolved in the CAD system community which seem applicable to software engineering data bases.

6.3.1 CAD Data-Base Concepts

The three main areas where engineering design data bases have different requirements from ordinary commercial data bases are data models, access methods, and the concept of transactions. Engineering data is usually spatially related. Therefore, data structures for ordinary data organization like B-Trees do not work very well. Since the data for software engineering data bases does not have this special characteristic, we will not discuss the data access methods that have been developed by the CAD community.

The CAD Data Model. It has been suggested that the relational model is not powerful enough to capture the specialized needs of design data. A consensus seems to be emerging within the CAD community on a semantic data model for design data.

A data model for design data must manipulate *objects* rather than *records*, and hence the model is also called the *object model*. Records or relations are entities at too low a level to be really useful.

Two essential features in a data model for storing design data for any complex system are *configuration management* and *version management*. A good construct for configuration management is a "part-of" hierarchy. For example, a single register is "part-of" a register file, which in turn is "part-of" an ALU. This hierarchy provides a directed acyclic graph structure for constructing complex systems. A special case of this structure, which might occur in practice, is the tree structure where every part belongs to only one structure. In the case of software design, the objects for which configuration management would be useful are modules/packages and procedures. A collection of logically related procedures along with their data structures would form a module. These modules can themselves be part of bigger modules that perform well-defined global functions.

It has been proposed in the object-oriented data model world that procedures should be associated with each type of object. These procedures can be used in manipulating objects of that type. Examples of such object-oriented programming environments are Smalltalk and Loops. One can envisage object-oriented software engineering environments, which have requirement specifications, design modules, source code modules, system prototypes, test case files, and documentation modules as the objects. With each object, procedures are associated for manipulating that object. Such software engineering environments can be ideally supported on top of object-oriented data bases.

In a design environment, an update to an object, e.g., a register, should not destroy the old version of the register design. This is in contrast to the conventional data-base model where old values of data do not have to be stored but can be discarded right away. There are a number of reasons why old data needs to be stored in design data bases; for example, they might describe an object that is still supported in the field. The history of design changes might also help provide new insights into the design process. A design might progress as follows (Katz and Lehman, 1984): Initially, a design is *in-progress*. Designers modify the in-progress version until it is ready for release. They can create *alternatives*, which are hypothetical variants of an in-progress version. These permit designers to explore experimental design solutions without making changes to the in-progress version. Several alternatives can be merged into the in-progress version. When a design is ready for release, it is first made *effective* for testing and internal distribution. Effective versions cannot be updated without once again becoming in-progress. Effective versions become *released* when the designed object is sent into the field. Released versions can be *archived* and later *restored* when immediate access is necessary.

Design data bases differ radically from conventional data bases regarding the method for storing versions. An attempt to implement versions on top of conventional data bases is likely to be very inefficient since low-level support from the data base does not exist. Each separate version is likely to be implemented as a named collection of files. This is very inefficient from the viewpoint of storage. Some of the approaches suggested for maintaining versions for CAD data bases are (1) file-level versions (described above), which are inefficient from the storage viewpoint, (2) shadow pages (page level versions), (3) differential files (a form of record level versions), and (4) negative differential files (Katz and Lehman, 1984). It is important to note that the efficient methods (the last three methods) all require low-level access to the data in the data base and thus must be implemented as an integral part of the data base. Current work on versions has mainly concentrated on versions for integrated circuits. It is an interesting open problem to devise efficient methods of maintaining versions for software modules.

An interesting data model that combines version management and configuration management treats the design as an AND-OR graph where the AND nodes are the configurations and the OR nodes are the versions/ alternatives (Katz, 1985). This gives an integrated treatment of versions and configurations.

Another concept that has been proposed for CAD data bases is that of *interface descriptions*. Interface descriptions describe abstract behavior of objects. This is similar to package interface in modern programming languages such as Ada.

Transactions in the CAD Environment. Big software projects are completed by large teams of programmers working simultaneously but independently on different parts of the overall program. One of the primary aims of a software engineering environment is to provide controlled access to software project resources (requirements, design, and code) to the programmers working independently and to ensure that they do not interfere with each other.

The data base community has long been successful in developing sophisticated mechanisms to support transactions in conventional transaction processing environments, such as airline reservation systems and electronic fund transfer systems. The main concepts that characterize transactions in conventional data bases are consistency, automaticity, and durability. Transactions must leave the data base in a consistent state and be automatic. This means that either all the updates that were part of a transaction must take place or none should take place. Durability means that the data base must survive soft and hard system crashes.

Design transactions differ considerably from conventional transactions. An important difference is that the notion of consistency in design transactions is considerably more complex than in conventional transactions. For example, an airplane design is consistent only if the plane can still fly with its redesigned wing. A modification to a program is consistent only if it leaves the source code still in agreement with the specifications. Such consistency in general can only be checked by invoking complicated checking programs such as simulation tools.

Katz (1985) points out the following differences between design and conventional transactions:

1. Design transactions are of long duration. Designers interact with their data for long periods of time; i.e., for days and weeks as opposed to minutes, at the most, in the case of conventional transactions. Thus, mechanisms that arbitrate access to shared data by forcing transactions to wait when their data is not available are not suitable in the design environment because suspended transactions would have to wait too long. Real-time access is critical in most transaction processing environments, but designers are willing to try again later if the data they need to access is not presently available.

2. Design transactions touch large volumes of design data. A transaction in a software engineering environment may consist of implementing an entire module and making sure that it is consistent with the specifications. This can involve writing large amounts of code and changing parts of other modules. Therefore, design data bases can best be used as shared repositories from where data is extracted when needed.

3. Design transactions demand more than serial consistency. (This has already been discussed.)

4. Design transactions and conventional transactions differ in respect of recovery from a crash. In the case of conventional data bases, only committed transactions are recovered. In the case of design transactions, it is useful to recover as much work as possible after a crash. This work, however, may not be permanently reflected in the data base.

5. Design transactions are not ad hoc. Designers known in advance what portions of the design they will be working on and hence all the required resources can be acquired at the beginning of a transaction. Deadlock and abortion of transactions in this case is intolerable because these transactions are long running and hence a lot of work might have to be thrown away.

Katz (1985) proposes that a more appropriate paradigm for acquiring design data is to view the design data base as a library. In the case of software engineering environments, this would mean that software resources are checked out to designers who return them when they are done. A librarian process traverses and manipulates the hierarchical design structure on behalf of a programmer. It would know (1) which software resources have already been checked out, (2) who has them, and (3) when they will be returned. A reservation system can be implemented so that programmers could reserve certain groups of resources just like books from the library.

In summary, resource and activity management is very important in large software projects. Currently, much of the management is done without computer support. Appropriate use of data bases can vastly improve this management. But conventional data-base technology, is unsuitable for the task. There are several similarities between CAD and software development. Research in CAD data bases is likely to have a major impact on data bases for software engineering environments.

7. Conclusion

Software engineering deals with techniques for the development of the most challenging kind of software. This software is developed by multiple teams of people working concurrently and using imprecise requirements. The software must be highly reliable and meet its functional and nonfunctional specifications. There have been significant contributions of ideas regarding specification, design, resource management, and software reliability. But, still more research is required before these ideas can be put to practice. Traditional techniques of distributed systems, data bases, and programming languages, are not sufficient to provide support for the development of large systems. In this paper, we have given our views on major problems that remain in software engineering and how they might be tackled in the future.

Acknowledgements

We thank members of the GENESIS group at Berkeley for many stimulating discussions on the topics discussed in this paper. We would especially like to thank C. Davis, M. Evangelist, C. Fritsch, M. Kim, D. Perry, and R. Yacobellis for giving comments on the ideas presented in this paper.

References

Addleman, D. R., Davis, M. J., and Presson, P. E. (1985). "Specification Technology Guidebook." Boeing Technical Report, CDRL A003.

Aggarwal, S., Kursan, R. P., and Sabani, K. (1983). A Calculus for protocol specification and validation. "Protocol Specification, Testing, and Verification III." (H. Rudin and C. H. West, eds.). North Holland.

Aho, A. V., Kernighan, B. W., and Weinberger, P. J. (1984). Awk—A pattern scanning and processing language. *Unix Programmer's Manual*, Vol. 2.

Alford, M. W. (1985). SREM at the age of eight; The distributed computing design system. *IEEE Computer* 36–46.

Balzer, R. (1985). A 15-year perspective on automatic programming. *IEEE Trans. on Software Eng.* SE-11 no (11), 1257–1268.

Basili, V. R., and Perricone, B. T. (1984). Software errors and complexity: An empirical investigation. *Commun. ACM* **27** (1), 42–52.

Bastani, F. B. (1980) "An Input Domain-Based Theory of Software Reliability and Its Application." Ph.D. Dissertation, Computer Science Division, University of California, Berkeley, California.

Bell, T. E., Bixler, D. C., and Dyer, M. E. (1977). An extendable approach to computer-aided software requirements. *IEEE Trans. Software Eng.* **SE-3** (1), 6–15.

Bergland, G. D. (1981). A guided tour of program design methodologies. *IEEE Computer* **14**(10), 13–37.

Bochmann, G. V. (1978). Finite state description of communication protocols. *Computer Networks* **2**, 361–371.

Boehm, B. W. (1981). "Software Engineering Economics." Prentice-Hall Inc., Englewood Cliffs, New Jersey.

Boehm, B. W. (1986). "A spiral model of software development and enhancement. *Proc. IEEE 2d. Software Process Workshop.*

Bologna, S., and Ehrenberger, W. (1978). "Applicability of Statistical Models for reactor Safety Software Verification." Unpublished report.

Brown, J. R., and Lipow, M. (1975). Testing for software reliability. *Proc. Internat'l Conf. on Reliable Software*, pp. 518–527.

Buckles, B. P. (1977). Formal module specifications. *Proc. 1977 Annual Conf. ACM.*

Chen, P. S. (1983a). "The Entity-Relationship Approach to Software Engineering." Elsevier Science, New York.

Chen, P. S. (1983b). "The Entity-Relationship Approach to Information Modeling and Analysis." North-Holland Publ., Amsterdam.

Dahl, O.-J., Dijkstra, E. W., and Hoare, C. A. R. (1972). "Structured Programming." Academic Press, New York.

Davis, C. G., and Vick, C. R. (1977). The software development system. *IEEE Trans. Software Eng.* **SE-3** (1), 69–84.

Demillo, R. A., Lipton, R. J., and Sayward, F. G. (1978). Hints on test data selection: Help for the practicing programmer. *IEEE Computer* **11** (4), 34–41.

Dijkstra, E. W. (1968). The structure of "THE"—Multiprogramming system. *Commun. ACM* **11** (5), 341–346.

Dijkstra, E. W. (1976). "A Discipline of Programming." Prentice-Hall, Englewood Cliffs, New Jersey.

Dong, S. T. (1983). "The Modeling, Analysis, and Synthesis of Communication Protocols." Ph.D. Dissertation, Department of EECS, University of California, Berkeley, California.

Ferrari, D. (1986). Considerations on the insularity of performance evaluation. *IEEE Trans. Software Eng.* **SE-12** (6), 678–683.

Forman, I. R. (1986). "Raddle: An Informal Introduction." MCC Technical Report STP-182-85.

Goel, A. L. (1985). "Software reliability models: assumptions, limitations, and applicability," *IEEE Trans. Software Eng.* **SE-11** (12), 1411–1423.

Goel, A. L., and Okumoto, K. (1979). A time-dependent error detection rate model for software reliability and other performance measures. *IEEE Trans. Reliability* **R-28** (3), 206–211.

Halstead, M. H. (1977). "Elements of Software Sciences." Elsevier Science, New York.

Hamilton, M., and Zeldin, S. (1976). Higher order software—A methodology for defining software. *IEEE Trans. Software Eng.* **SE-2** (1), 9–32.

Hansen, P. B. (1975). The programming language concurrent pascal. *IEEE Trans. Software Eng.* **SE-1** (2), 199–207.

Hoare, C. A. R. (1978). Communicating sequential processes. *Commun. ACM* **21** (8), 666–677.

Howden, W. E. (1978). DISSECT–A symbolic evaluation and program testing system. *IEEE Trans. Software Eng.* **SE-4** (1), 70–73.

Jackson, M. A. (1975). "Principles of Program Design." Academic Press, New York.

Kant, E. (1985). Understanding and automating algorithm design. *IEEE Trans. Software Eng.* **SE-11** (11), 1361–1374.

Karp, R. A. (1984). Proving failure-free properties of concurrent programs using temporal logic. *ACM Trans. Program. Lang. Syst.* **6** (2), 239–253.

Katz, R. H., and Lehman, T. J. (1984). "Database Support for Versions and Alternatives of large Design Files," *IEEE Trans. Software Eng.* **SE-10** (2), 191–200.

Katz, R. (1985). "Information Management for Engineering Design." Springer-Verlag, Berlin.

Lamport, L., and Schneider, F. B. (1984). The "Hoare Logic" of CSP, and all that. *ACM Trans. Program. Lang. Syst.* **6** (2), 281–296.

Linger, R. C., Hevner, A. R., and Mills, H. D. (1979). "Structured Programming: Theory and Practice." Addison-Wesley, Reading, Massachusetts.

McCabe, J. (1976). A complexity measure. *IEEE Trans. Software Eng.* **SE-2** (4), 308–320.

Manna, Z., and Wolper, P. (1984). Synthesis of communicating processes from temporal logic specifications. *ACM Trans. Program. Lang. Syst.* **6** (1), 68–93.

Mills, H. D. (1972). "On Statistical Validation of Computer Programs." IBM Rep. FSC72-6015. Federal Systems Division, IBM, Gaithersburg, Maryland.

Milner, R. (1980). A calculus of communicating systems. *Lecture Notes on Computer Science* **92,** Springer-Verlag, Berlin.

Moriconi, M. (1979). "A designer/verifier's assistant. *IEEE Trans. Software Eng.* **SE-5** (4), 387–401.

Musa, J. D. (1975). A theory of software reliability and its applications. *IEEE Trans. Software Eng.* **SE-1** (3), 312–327.

Myers, G. J. (1978). "Composite/Structured Design." Van Nostrand Reinhold, New York.

Myers, G. J. (1979). "The Art of Software Testing." John Wiley and Sons, New York.

Nelson, E. (1978). Estimating software reliability from test data. "Microelectronics and Reliability" **17** (1) 67–74.

Osterweil, L. J., and Fosdick, L. D. (1976). DAVE—A validation error detection and documentation system for FORTRAN programs. *Software Practice and Experience,* **6** (4), 473–486.

Parnas, D. L. (1972). On the criteria to be used in decomposing systems into modules. *Commum. of ACM* **15** (12), 1053–1058.

Parnas, D. L. (1979). Designing software for ease of extension and contraction. *IEEE Trans. Software Eng.* **SE-5** (2), 128–138.

Ramamoorthy, C. V., and Bastani, F. B. (1982). Software reliability—Status and perspectives. *IEEE Trans. Software Eng.* **SE-8** (4), 354–371.

Ramamoorthy, C. V., and Ho, S. F. (1975). Testing large software with automated software evaluation systems. *IEEE Trans. Software Eng.* **SE-1** (1), 46–58.

Ramamoorthy, C. V., and So, H.H. (1978). "Software Requirements and Specifications: Status and Perspectives." Technical Report UCB/ERL M78/44, Electronics Research Laboratory, Dept. of EECS, University of California, Berkeley, California.

Ramamoorthy, C. V., Mok, Y. R., Bastani, F. B., Chin, G. H., and Suzuki, K. (1981). Application of a methodology for the development and validation of reliable process control software, *IEEE Trans. Software Eng.* **SE-7** (11), 537–555.

Ramamoorthy, C. V., Garg, V., and Aggarwal, R. (1985a). Environment modeling and activity management in GENESIS. *SoftFairII: Secon Conference on Software Development Tools, Techniques and Alternatives.*

Ramamoorthy, C. V., Tsai, W.-T., Bhide, A., and Yamaura, T. (1985b). Metrics guided methodology. *COMPSAC* pp. 111–120.

Ramamoorthy, C. V., Garg, V. K., and Prakash, A. (1986a). Programming in the large. *IEEE Trans. Software Eng.* **SE-12** (7), 769–783.

Ramamoorthy, C. V., Garg, V. K., and Prakash, A. (1986b). Reusability support in GENESIS. *COMPSAC*, 299–305.

Ross, D. T. (1977). Structured analysis (SA): A language for communicating ideas. *IEEE Trans. Software Eng.* **SE-3** (1), 16–34.

Rowland, B. R., and Welsch, R. J. (1983). The 3B20D Processor & DMERT Operating System: Software Development System, *Bell System Tech. J.* **12** (1), 275–289.

Royce, W. W. (1970). Managing development of large software systems: Concepts and techniques. *Proc. of WESCON*, **14,** 1–9 in section A/1.

Schlichting R. D., and Schneider, F. B. (1984). "Using message passing for distributed programming: Proof rules and disciplines. *ACM Trans. Program. Lang. Syst.* **6** (3), 402–431.

Schutz, H. A. (1974). On the design of language for programming real-time concurrent processes. *IEEE Trans. Software Eng.* **SE-5** (3), 248–255.

Soundararajan, N. (1984). Axiomatic semantics of communicating sequential processes. *ACM Trans. Program. Lang. Syst.* **6** (4), 647–662.

Special issue on software metrics. (1983). *IEEE Trans. Software Eng.* **SE-9** (11).

Stevens, W. P., Myers, G. J., and Constantine, L. L. (1974) Structured design. *IBM Systems Journal.* **13** (2), 115–139.

Stonebraker, M., Wong, E., Kreps, P., and Held, G. (1976). The design and implementation of INGRES. *ACM Trans. Database Syst.* **1** (3), 189–222.

Teichroew, D., and Hershey, E. A. (1977). PSL/PSA: A computer-aided technique for structured documentation and analysis of information processing systems. *IEEE Trans. Software Eng.* **SE-3** (1), 41–48.

Thayer, R. A., Lipow, M., and Nelson, E. C. (1978). "Software Reliability." North-Holland, Amsterdam.

Vardi, M. Y., and Wolper, P. (1986). "An automata-theoretic approach to automatic program verification. *Proc. 1st Symp. on Logic in Computer Science.*

Vosbury, N. A. (1984). Process design. "Handbook of Software Engineering" (C. R. Vick and C. V. Ramamoorthy, eds.). Van Nostrand Reinhold, New York.

Warnier, J. D. (1974). "Logical Construction of Programs." Van Norstrand Reinhold, New York.

Wirth, N. (1973). "Systematic Programming." Prentice-Hall, Englewood Cliffs, New Jersey.

Wolper, P. (1986). Expressing interesting properties of programs in propositional temporal logic. *Proc. 14th ACM Symposium on Principles of Programming Languages*, pp. 184–193.

Yeh, R. T., Mittermeir, R., Roussopoulos, N., and Reed, J. (1984). A programming environment framework based on reusability. *Proc. COMPDEC*, pp. 277–280. TRW Defense and Space Systems Group, Redondo Beach, California.

Zafiropulo, P., West, C. H., Rudin, H., Cowan, D. D., and Brand, D. (1983). Towards analyzing and synthesizing protocols. *IEEE Trans. Commun.* 235–240.

Zvegintzov, N., Angus, J. E., Schafer, R. E., and Sukert, A. (1980). Software reliability model validation. *Proc. Annual Reliability and Maintainability Symposium*, pp. 191–199.

AUTHOR INDEX

SUBJECT INDEX

C

Contents of Previous Volumes